JOHN CALVIN

Steward *of* God's Covenant

VINTAGE SPIRITUAL CLASSICS

General Editors
John F. Thornton
Susan B. Varenne

ALSO AVAILABLE

JOHN CALVIN

Steward

of

God's Covenant

SELECTED WRITINGS

EDITED BY

John F. Thornton and *Susan B. Varenne*

PREFACE BY

Marilynne Robinson

VINTAGE SPIRITUAL CLASSICS

VINTAGE BOOKS
A DIVISION OF RANDOM HOUSE, INC.
NEW YORK

A VINTAGE SPIRITUAL CLASSICS ORIGINAL, FEBRUARY 2006
FIRST EDITION

Library of Congress Cataloging-in-Publication Data
Calvin, Jean, 1509–1564.
Steward of God's covenant : selected writings of John Calvin / edited by John F. Thornton
and Susan B. Varenne ; preface by Marilynne Robinson.—1st ed.
p.   cm.—(Vintage Spiritual Classics)
Includes bibliographical references (p.).
1. Bible—Commentaries.   2. Christian life—Reformed authors.   I. Thornton,
John F., 1942–   II. Varenne, Susan B.   III. Title.   IV. Series.
BX9420.A32 T46 2005
230'.42—dc22
2005053842

Vintage ISBN-10: 1-4000-9648-0
Vintage ISBN-13: 978-1-4000-9648-0

Book design by Fritz Metsch

www.vintagebooks.com

146119709

CONTENTS

by John F. Thornton and Susan B. Varenne, General Editors

A turn or shift of sorts is becoming evident in the reflections of men and women today on their life experiences. Not quite as adamantly secular and, perhaps, a little less insistent on material satisfactions, the reading public has recently developed a certain attraction to testimonies that human life is leavened by a Presence that blesses and sanctifies. Recovery, whether from addictions or personal traumas, illness, or even painful misalignments in human affairs, is evolving from the standard therapeutic goal of enhanced self-esteem. Many now seek a deeper healing that embraces the whole person, including the soul. Contemporary books provide accounts of the invisible assistance of angels. The laying on of hands in prayer has made an appearance at the hospital bedside. Guides for the spiritually perplexed have risen to the tops of bestseller lists. The darkest shadows of skepticism and unbelief, which have eclipsed the presence of the Divine in our materialistic age, are beginning to lighten and part.

If the power and presence of God are real and effective, what do they mean for human experience? What does He offer to men and women, and what does He ask in return? How do we recognize Him? Know Him? Respond to Him? God has a reputation for being both benevolent and wrathful. Which will He be for me and when? Can these aspects of the Divine somehow be reconciled? Where is God when I suffer? Can I lose Him? Is God truthful, and are His promises to be trusted?

Are we really as precious to God as we are to ourselves and our loved ones? Do His providence and amazing grace guide our faltering steps toward Him, even in spite of ourselves? Will God abandon us if the sin is serious enough, or if we have episodes of resistance and forgetfulness? These are fundamental questions any person might address to God during a lifetime. They are pressing and difficult, often becoming wounds in the soul of the person who yearns for the power and courage of hope, especially in stressful times.

The Vintage Spiritual Classics present the testimony of writers across the centuries who have considered all these difficulties and who have pondered the mysterious ways, unfathomable mercies and deep consolations afforded by God to those who call upon Him from out of the depths of their lives. These writers, then, are our companions, even our champions, in a common effort to discern the meaning of God in personal experience. For God is personal to us. To whom does He speak if not to us, provided we have the desire to hear Him deep within our hearts?

Each volume opens with a specially commissioned essay by a well-known contemporary writer that offers the reader an appreciation of its intrinsic value. A chronology of the general historical context of each author and his work is provided, as are suggestions for further reading.

*   *   *

We offer a final word about the act of reading these spiritual classics. From the very earliest accounts of monastic practice—dating back to the fourth century—it is evident that a form of reading called *lectio divina* ("divine" or "spiritual reading") was essential to any deliberate spiritual life. This kind of reading is quite different from that of scanning a text for useful facts and bits of information, or advancing along an exciting plot line to a climax in the action. It is, rather, a meditative approach by which the reader seeks to savor and taste the beauty and truth of every phrase and passage. This process of contemplative reading has the effect of enkindling in the reader compunction for past behavior that has been less than beautiful and true. At the same time, it increases the desire to seek a realm where all that is lovely and unspoiled may be found. There are four steps in *lectio divina*: first to read, next to meditate, then to rest in the sense of God's nearness, and, ultimately, to resolve to govern one's actions in the light of new understanding. This kind of reading is itself an act of prayer. And, indeed, it is in prayer that God manifests His Presence to us.

by Marilynne Robinson

John Calvin entered prominently into the theater of Renaissance religious controversy in 1536 as a defender of those then suffering extreme persecution on religious grounds in France. His expressed intention in writing the first version of his *Institutes of the Christian Religion*, as stated in the Prefatory Address to Francis I, was to set before the king an account of the beliefs of the persecuted which should make plain to him that they were not heretics, that it was indeed their persecutors who had strayed from the true faith. He says that his original intention had been "solely to transmit certain rudiments by which those who are touched with any zeal for religion might be shaped to true godliness," but that he felt the work must be offered to the king because "the fury of certain wicked persons has prevailed so far in your realm that there is no place in it for sound doctrine." Since it was the role of the prince to protect orthodoxy in his realm—no doubt exactly what Francis intended with his persecutions—the reversal of perspective here is ironic. The persecutions, Calvin says, are destroying "sound doctrine." That an account of the beliefs of those being burned as heretics in the streets of Paris, on the king's authority, should be offered as identical with an account of the most elementary truths of Christianity is a very bold stroke, rhetorically speaking, and one that establishes from its first two paragraphs the terms of Calvin's argument, which are also anticipated in the very title he has given his treatise. There is nothing unfamiliar, in the Bible or in the narratives of Christian origins, about the idea that the true faith might survive only among an oppressed remnant.

Calvin uses the examples of Noah, of Elijah, of Christ himself to assert with perfect confidence the authority of the beliefs of the condemned, against the doctors of the Sorbonne, against the consensus of the Church, and against the power of the State.

In 1535 Calvin's cousin Pierre Robert, called Olivetan, had published a translation of the Bible from the Hebrew and Greek, to which Calvin contributed two prefaces, one in Latin and one in French. Of greater interest here is Olivetan's own preface. It anticipates Calvin's address both in its identification of the true Church with the persecuted and in its satire on the dedication as a convention. In it he mocks the custom among writers of dedicating their work to powerful figures, so that they "wear the livery of some very illustrious, very excellent, very high, very puissant, very magnificent, very redoubtable, very triumphant, very sacred, most blessed, beatified and holy name." He dedicates the book instead to the "poor church" to whom it has always belonged. "For did not Christ give himself to such abject, small, and humble people; and did not he familiarly declare to them the great secrets of the kingdom he said would belong to them?" And Olivetan lists the titles of nobility that will be "glorious and magnificent in the Kingdom of Heaven": *Injuries, Blames, Chasses, Decries, Desavoues, Abandonnes, Excommunies, Anathematises, Confisques, Emprisonnes, Gehennes, Bannis, Eschelles, Mitres, Decraches, Chaffaudes, Exoreilles, Tenaielles, Fletris, Tires, Traines, Grilles, Rotis, Lapides, Brules, Noyes, Decapites, Demembres.* Some of these terms are plain in their meaning and others are rather technical. Rabelais would publish a similar list in the *Fourth Book of Pantagruel* (1552). Here Olivetan, in noting the forms persecution took in those days, makes less delicately the very assertion Calvin would make in his address to the king, that persecution itself can be the mark of the true church. Olivetan says, "He [Christ] desires those who have been as he was in this world." His translation was commissioned by the Waldensians, who allied themselves with the Reformation in 1530. The Waldensians, or Vaudois, were a sect that arose in the twelfth century or earlier, had been denounced as heretics and had suffered severe and continuous persecution, and managed nevertheless to survive in significant numbers, finding refuge in the valleys of the Alps. Their religious practice depended on the use of the Scriptures in French, and when they approached Olivetan, they had only two surviving manuscript translations. They were experiencing extraordinary persecution in France while Calvin wrote his first version of the *Institutes*.

The crucial thing to note, if Calvin is to be taken at his word, is that he understood his *Institutes* to be the articulation of a highly developed religious understanding held by others before him. Certainly the consistency of his theology over his lifetime and the high degree of integration of the elements of doctrine support this. The rapid spread of his influence and the stability of Reformed tradition over time, including its resistance to assimilation by Lutheranism, suggest that it was neither original with him nor essentially dependent on him. Europe had had a very long history of dissent before the Reformation, dissent which was punished as heresy and therefore driven underground, its presence erased, insofar as possible, by the burning of books and the proscription of ideas. That such measures were thought necessary and were practiced systematically from the thirteenth century onward is evidence of the persistence and the vigor of dissent. There are anticipations of Calvin in the writings of John Wycliffe, the sermons of Meister Eckehart, and the work of Jan Hus. The use of vernacular languages in preference to Latin practiced by them all was intended to make Scripture and teaching available to the common people, but the leaders of these movements were clerics and university professors, as was Luther. In other words, the phenomenon of dissident movements that were popular and at the same time intellectually grounded was recurrent after the twelfth century, despite the suppression of these movements as heresy. Mere circumstance would have created points of similarity among them that differentiated them from the Church, for instance a definition of ministry and sacraments that would allow them independence from a priesthood ordained by the Church. The degree to which these movements anticipated the Reformation in any particular of doctrine may be disputed, but the fact of their persistence, unsheltered from the worst the powers of England and Europe could do to them, provided an example for those who did not submit themselves to religious conformity within the secular state, those in whose defense Calvin wrote. This is not to say Calvin merely recorded a preexisting theology. His own brilliance and his powerful engagement with every aspect of his subject make the whole body of his work entirely distinctive. It is to say, however, that his posture from the outset was one of deepest sympathy with those undergoing persecution—sympathy in the sense of identification. He made himself the voice of faith that had endured every coercion and that could only anticipate further assaults as the situation in Europe became more volatile. And he joined his fate with these faithful in the fact of defending them.

The Augsburg Treaty of 1555 would be designed to resolve conflict between Catholics and Lutherans through the principle of *cuius regio, eius religio*—the religion of a ruler determines the religion of his subjects. This was not a change in the state of things that had prevailed in Europe to that point, except as an acknowledgment that there was now a second religion able to claim the loyalty of secular rulers. Luther had found powerful support among German princes, and of course there were loyal Catholic princes throughout Europe. So the pattern of state protection for one or the other of these churches was established in fact long before it was established by treaty. But there were, as well, the sects who were neither Catholic nor Lutheran.

The degree to which Calvin might have wished and hoped to see a reformed and unified Church as something practically attainable depends on whether he saw himself as part of a new movement of reformation which could negotiate its differences with the Catholic Church or as the voice and champion of much older movements and beliefs, long and vehemently rejected by the Church. He says little on any point of doctrine, from the role of the papacy to the number and nature of the sacraments, that could suggest he was seeking middle ground. And as much as he explores a theology he explores also a state of consciousness, the experience of a radical individuality, which he takes to be, granting a fallen world, the definitive state of all human consciousness, and therefore the appropriate basis for the knowledge of man and of God. He does not distinguish the workings of conscience that made the persecuted loyal to their belief from belief itself. The felt experiences of individual knowing and perceiving are the basis of his anthropology and of his metaphysics. Nothing in Calvin's thought is more striking than his evocation of perception, which has the potency and the splendor of a true apprehension of God. He quotes with approval the words of Virgil, "that all things are full of joy," accounting thus for the pagan poet's insight: "Yea, when Virgil meant to praise the power of God, by error he put in a wrong name."

Calvin has long been treated as an apostle of gloom dominating a gloomy city. And indeed, waking as he and they did for thousands of mornings to the fact that the city had a hostile army encamped outside its walls would very probably have dampened anyone's spirits in some degree. The specifics of the historical situation tend to be forgotten, and this presumed melancholy ascribed to the baleful influence of Calvin's temperament and his theology. The polemic against Calvin over the centuries has been virulent, and very effective. He himself has been associated with repression and persecution so insistently that to read his theology as based in exploration of the consciousness of the persecuted may surprise some readers. Calvin did indeed approve the execution by the governors of Geneva of Michael Servetus, a Spanish physician and theologian who had been sentenced to death by the Inquisition in France and had escaped to Geneva. Also, even in his address to the king he is careful to distinguish those he defends— otherwise unspecified—from the Anabaptists (here he calls them Catabaptists) and "other monstrous rascals" who were also suffering persecution. While these things are to be regretted, they are not comparable to the religious suppression and violence then customary in England and Europe, and certainly they provide no justification for the harshness of Calvin's historical reputation. Ferocious polemic was the style of the period. Calvin was not so remarkable for it as Martin Luther or Thomas More.

Since he must necessarily make his apologia by expounding his theology, he defines it over against other theologies—Catholicism on one hand, and on the other, doctrines of what is called the radical Reformation. It was not his purpose to create a haven or an apologia for dissenters of every stripe—Servetus had called the Trinity a Cerberus—and it was dangerous to his cause to be perceived as doing so. He meant to give a foothold to an embattled worldview he deeply espoused. He did this in the first place through his writing, which provided a virtual catechism for the use and instruction of those who were of one mind with him, and then by helping to stabilize the revolution and Reformation in Geneva while producing a virtual literature of sermons and textual interpretation. In light of its great historical importance, it is difficult to remember that his Geneva was a small town, a republic of about ten thousand inhabitants that grew to a population of about fifteen thousand with the arrival of refugees. That is to say, at its largest it just exceeded the present population of Mitchell, South Dakota. It was under siege for many years, crowded and often short of food. Religious lines were battle lines in those days, which is not stranger than our own recent obsession with contending economic models. All this gave religious loyalties and alliances great significance for the survival of the community. It is regrettable but not surprising that religious tolerance was rare in those circumstances, and by no means only in cities that were fragile and isolated.

There is a singular gravity in Calvin's theology which disturbs modern readers, much as the prophetic writings of the Old Testament do also. It is no coincidence that Calvin gave thousands of pages of lectures on Jeremiah, preached scores of sermons on the book of Job, and wrote at great length on the Psalms. Those of us who live our lives in relative security have difficulty understanding how overpowering assertions of faith will arise from precisely those extremes of trial and grief we might assume would instead raise questions about the goodness of God, or about his very existence. We must assume that our experience, fortunate as we are in it, nevertheless limits our understanding of most human experience. It certainly does not become us to dismiss these voices crying from the depths, even when they bespeak a far more passionate vision than we can imagine sharing.

When he wrote his address to the king, John Calvin was a most improbable defender of anyone. Having no resources but the courage of youth and, in an extraordinary degree, virtuosity in the intellectual accomplishments Europe in the Renaissance valued, he was already assuming the role, the burden, that would be his for almost the whole of his life. Because he was indeed recognized as a spokesman for the non-Lutheran Reformation, for what historians would call the Reformed tradition, he was able to give the movement focus and coherency, the weight of scrupulous scholarship, a respected voice in controversy, and a theology fully as grand in its scale as the theology of Thomas Aquinas. Because he succeeded over the years, by restraint and diplomacy, in forestalling most attacks on the always vulnerable populations for whom he spoke, he was burdened by responsibility for their safety. He had little to work with besides Geneva, a crowded and turbulent mountain town with a good many printing presses in it and imposing walls around it. He had the sympathy of certain French nobles whose martial impulses were among his major problems, and he had a truly astonishing capacity for work. What he achieved while he lived can be measured not only by the continuing influence of his thought, but also by the violence that engulfed Europe after his death, and came near destroying the Protestant people of France, those he had first defended. His life might be seen as a great tragedy, were it not for the strength of his work, which has had incalculable impact on the thought and culture of the West and the whole Christian world.

*   *   *

Calvin worked with an undeviating discipline that suggests urgency. It suggests also a visionary intensity. He was a classic Renaissance humanist by education, a great stylist in Latin, a sensitive interpreter of Hebrew and Greek, and one of the creators of French as a language of thought. His humanism is expressed precisely in his understanding of the teaching of Genesis, that humankind is made in the image of God, the likeness being "that glory of God which peculiarly shines forth in human nature, where the mind, the will, and all the senses, represent the Divine order." Here he interprets verse 27 of the first chapter of Genesis in terms that explicitly include woman as sharer in God's image. More to the present point, he places this incandescent divinity—it is the glory of God that "shines forth" from human nature—at the very center of individual experience and presence. And this sacredness is an attribute not of saints only, nor of Christians only, but is inherent and also manifest in all human beings as such. Two great poles of Calvin's thought, of his ethics and his aesthetics, are a true perception of others, and a true perception of oneself. Perception is at the center of his theology, both because it is the felt and active potential for experiencing the sacred, and also because it is the image, the great gift, "a remarkable instance of the Divine goodness which can never be sufficiently proclaimed." This is the Calvin who is infamous for speaking in radically disparaging terms of this same human nature—over against the God whom, in its unfallen state, it would faithfully mirror.

Here we have a paradox, one that can remind us, perhaps, of how little we challenge our own language. For example, we feel we know certain things about the physical universe. It is inconceivably vast, it is expanding, and its rate of expansion is accelerating. How do we compare the energy that drives the universe to the energy expended in the striking of a match? There is no way to state any proportion between them, in scale or duration. The second term could only be vanishingly small, set against the first, and assuming that the greater energy could by any means be quantified. That the striking of a match amounts to virtually nothing in the roar of the universe, comparatively speaking, does not in any way lessen its reality or change its nature. And in fact the energy the match stores and releases, like the mind that contrived it and the hand that holds it, all express that cosmic energy, though how and why we cannot say. We do not bother ourselves with these problems of incommensurability, or relationship, though we routinely assume that such imponderables surround us on every side. It is as if the world of daily life existed without reference to those seas of space/time which we know in fact contain it altogether. Only the grandest religious thought has even attempted to create a wholly integrated model of reality, typically employing the language of myth or epic to assert human meaning in the context of a dauntingly nonhuman universe. We moderns have abandoned the effort, and for us that seems to serve as an equivalent to solving the problem.

But for Calvin, a conceptual problem of just this kind lies at the center of all meaning. The Creator is, by his reckoning, utterly greater than any conception we can form of his creation, and at the same time free, present, just, loving, and intimately attentive to fallen humankind, collectively and one by one. It is as if we were to find a tender solicitude toward us in the fact that the great energy that rips galaxies apart also animates our slightest thoughts. It is as if we were to propose that that great energy only exists to make possible our miraculously delicate participation in it. The first assertion of Calvin's theology, both in order and in centrality, is the continuous, unmediated character of the relationship between God and any human soul. So Calvin's problem, the challenge to his language, is to render, and to explore, the singular, defining likeness that exists within an inexpressible unlikeness.

In the Europe of Calvin's time, misery and death were common under the best circumstances and were compounded by the brutality of a civilization in which, for example, judicial torture was routine. This was also the Europe of the Renaissance, where humanism was expressed in the highest intellectual and cultural achievement. So the hyperbolic extremes of Calvin's exaltation of human nature on the one hand, and his sense of its utter fallenness on the other, might have presented a paradox his earlier readers would not have seen as a contradiction. Indeed, a theology that did not address the problem of evil as radically present in human life could hardly be taken as serious enough to deserve attention, especially among those who bore the brunt of persecution that, as with the Waldensians, could take the form of massacre.

Calvin's famous doctrine of "total depravity" is remarkable in this context because, notoriously, it makes meaningless, in cosmic terms, moral distinctions of better and worse. The temptation to draw sharp lines of good and evil must have been powerful in the circumstances in which he wrote, so it is important to note that this is an impulse the doctrine precisely forbids. And he applies it specifically to matters of religion. He says, "Though experience testifies that a seed of religion is divinely sown in all, scarcely one in a hundred is found who cherishes it in his heart, and not one in whom it grows to maturity so far is it from yielding fruit in its season." In other words, the inability to value and nurture a universally shared intuition is also universal, an aspect of human nature more flagrant in some than in others, but true of us all. Yet this doctrine serves as well as a counterweight to Calvin's rapturous humanism, which is as remote from us as the notion of total depravity is unwelcome to us. Calvin calls humankind "the loftiest proof of divine wisdom." He says, "[Humankind] have within themselves a workshop graced with God's unnumbered works, and at the same time, a storehouse overflowing with inestimable riches. . . . They feel in many wonderful ways that God works in them; they are also taught, by the very use of these things, what a great variety of gifts they possess from his liberality. They are compelled to know—whether they will or not—that these are the signs of divinity; yet they conceal them within. Indeed, there is no need to go outside themselves, provided they do not, by claiming for themselves what has been given them from heaven, bury in the earth that which enlightens their minds to see God clearly." The "signs of divinity" intrinsic to any human being again make relative all other judgments—the human being simply as such should compel awe. Our failure to acknowledge what ought to be obvious in ourselves and others—indisputably a potent factor in history—is "foul ungratefulness." Neither aspect of Calvin's thought—human sublimity nor abject human failure—can be understood in the absence of the other. Now that we are not only content with normality as a standard but seriously anxious when we think we may not be entirely able to satisfy it, and now that we are persuaded that an alloy of minor goodness and minor badness (the second being as essential as the first) is the limit of normal aspiration, our joy in our powers needs no countervailing doctrine of universal fallibility.

Likewise, the insistence of Calvin on viewing the evils of the world as a chastisement and instruction with which God favors the pious as freely as he does the reprobate has the surprising effect of sanctifying the persecutor, and transforming into evidence of divine care the suffering that might otherwise be interpreted as divine hostility or abandonment. Whether these doctrines had such importance for Calvin because they could hearten the persecuted and rescue them from descending into mere hatred, or whether in his formulations of these doctrines he was exploring assumptions that had allowed the persecuted to endure, is something we will never know. It can be said, however, that the posture of his faith and the theology that sustained it may not be distinguished, one from the other.

*　　　*　　　*

All major Christian theology seems to have arisen in polemical contexts. There is no particular irony in this—Jesus himself disputed with the religious scholars of his time, and there was even dispute between Peter and Paul. Nevertheless the fact of polemical context complicates interpretation. It raises the question of whether in any instance the controverted position is fairly represented. Polemic grounds theology to an important degree in the moment of its writing. Would a theologically informed Pelagian have been satisfied by Augustine's account of Pelagianism? The passage of time and the brilliance of Augustine's attack have made the question moot. Certainly it is rare to see an adequate account of one's own beliefs made by someone who does not share them, and this is particularly true if he feels these beliefs merit attack. Add to this the passions of those convinced that ultimate truth is at issue, passions compounded by the drastic means used through most of Christian history to suppress or end controversy, and it is obviously unrealistic to assume objectivity on any side. When, let us say, Luther made his critique of the Church of his time, he was addressing a cultural and intellectual state of things immediate to him and lost to us. He would not have addressed the best possible understanding of Peter Lombard or Thomas Aquinas, however that might be determined, but the understanding he took to be prevalent and authoritative among his contemporaries. In the circumstances that create major theology, no controversialist will speak over the heads of practice and consensus. It would not be relevant to the argument if he were to address himself to an ideal version of the body of thought on which his adversaries' position rests, rather than on his adversaries' own version of it.

This is only to say that the controversial method and tone of so much major theology should be thought of not as substance but as accident, to use the old language. Was Karl Barth unfair to von Harnack and Schleiermacher? The brilliance of the theology he created in rejecting theirs makes the question trivial. If in fact their theology was being understood in the early twentieth century as removing ethical barriers to war, then of course it would be in those terms that he took exception to it and very much to his credit that he did so. But great theology can only be great for its substance, whatever its occasion. Regrettably, the tone of indignation or emergency is often alienating to readers who do not see past the passions of its moment to the conceptual grandeur of the vision proposed by it.

Yet it is true that any theology is written as a challenge to prevalent theologies. For instance, Calvin, in launching into his argument with the statement that the beginning of everything must be the knowledge of God and of oneself, is asserting that one may know God in ways or by means that are not only analogous to self-knowledge but are in fact a reflex of it. This is a remarkable assertion, one which, if offered as a thesis or a proposition, would raise doubts in any mind. Indeed, it is a conceptualization of the radical individualism which has always come under attack by the critics of the Reformation. But Calvin was not dealing here in theses or propositions. He did not set out to refute or prove but to enlist. Think what a wonderful creature you are—"such agile motions of the soul, such excellent faculties, such rare gifts, especially bear upon the face of them a divinity that does not allow itself readily to be hidden." And think what a terrible creature you are, how inclined to indolence and selfishness, dishonesty, pride and error, cruelty. Everything about you that is wonderful points to God, because it is his much marred but still perceptible image. Everything that is terrible about you points to God, because in confronting it you feel the vastness of the difference between yourself and any conception you can form of him. "To this extent we are prompted by our own ills to contemplate the good things of God; and we cannot seriously aspire to him before we begin to become displeased with ourselves." This paradox, which is typically Calvinist, enlarges and complicates the meaning of self and self-knowledge by placing them in the moment of the grandest, indeed the most metaphysical, experience of the wonder of being.

It is to be noted that Calvin treats humankind not as a species but as a universal individual, a brilliant and passionate individual. If Thomists assumed the human capacity for knowledge and understanding, then here is human consciousness in the moment of true knowing and understanding. To say that man in the abstract can acquire the capacity for reason and knowledge is one thing, and to say that human consciousness by its very nature dwells on the frontier of the profoundest knowledge is another. To say that the order of nature reveals divine intent is one thing, and to say that the beauty that floods our senses has the meaning of vision and revelation is another. Calvin never pauses to dignify the question of the existence of God. To him God is simply manifest—"Men cannot open their eyes without being compelled to see him." And so is the intentional presence of God, as guide and teacher: "Although the Lord does not want for testimony [in nature] while he sweetly attracts men to the knowledge of himself with many and varied kindnesses, they do not cease on this account to follow their own ways, that is, their fatal errors." Calvin's implicit reply to those who denounced the subjectivism of the beliefs he defended is that God himself chooses to engage human consciousness thus intimately, that to do so is his being toward us, and that to feel the presence and the meaning of his attention is our being toward him. It is important to note that this is a metaphysics consistently explored and developed throughout Calvin's writing. And it is an epistemology.

To assume that objectivity can be looked for in matters of religion, as critics of the Reformers often do, when it is not naive, is a pure statement of faith. Tradition is simply the accumulated subjectivities of individuals—Paul, Augustine, Francis of Assisi. That these are authoritative figures only underscores the fact that subjectivity is in itself nothing to be dismissed out of hand. If tradition sets these men apart on the grounds that God, so to speak, acted upon them directly, those who revere Luther and Calvin feel that they also were instruments of God. The Reformers' *sola Scriptura* is often treated as literalism or bibliomancy, in either case as an evasion of discipline and reason. But such a view is by no means consistent with the acute critical attention both of them, but Calvin especially, brought to bear on the text. As a scholar of Hebrew and Greek, he continually reminds the reader of the difficulties of translating Scripture and the need to bring an awareness of exegetical standards to bear on it. And he makes the case for his own interpretation of any difficult passage, often explaining on what grounds a reader might choose to interpret it otherwise. That is to say, he neither offers his reading as if it were the product of unique inspiration, nor encourages the reader to interpret Scripture without also taking account of issues of language and context. Insofar as the standard is attainable, it is precisely objectivity that governs his approach to the reading of the Bible. Again, though, the old opposition of objectivity and subjectivity describes a distinction that tends to disappear under scrutiny, and is not even apparently appropriate when applied to religious thought. Calvin's own preoccupations are clearly inscribed throughout the whole body of his work.

The question of the structure of the solar system, already raised by Copernicus, is an instance of a characteristic use by Calvin of subjective perception in the interpretation of the Bible. Although in his commentary on Joshua he accepts without remark the miracle at Jericho as described in the text—the sun was halted in its course—in his commentary on Genesis, also written in 1563, he is specifically respectful of astronomy. He says, "Astronomy is not only pleasant, but also very useful to be known; it cannot be denied that this art unfolds the admirable wisdom of God. Wherefore, as ingenious men are to be honored who have expended useful labour on this subject, so they who have leisure and capacity ought not to neglect this kind of exercise." He says, "Moses makes two great luminaries [the sun and the moon]; but astronomers prove, by conclusive reasons, that the star of Saturn, which, on account of its great distance, appears the least of all, is greater than the moon. Here lies the difference; Moses wrote in a popular style things which, without instruction, all ordinary persons are able to understand; but astronomers investigate with great labour whatever the sagacity of the human mind can comprehend. Nevertheless, this study is not to be reprobated, nor this science to be condemned, because some frantic persons are wont boldly to reject whatever is unknown to them. . . . Since the Spirit of God here opens a common school for all, it is not surprising that he should chiefly choose those subjects which would be intelligible to all. . . . For since the Lord stretches forth, as it were, his hand to us in causing us to enjoy the brightness of the sun and moon, how great would be our ingratitude were we to close our eyes to our own experience? . . . Let the astronomers possess their more exalted knowledge; but, in the meantime, they who perceive by the moon the splendour of night, are convicted by its use of perverse ingratitude unless they acknowledge the beneficence of God."

Calvin preserves the literal meaning of the text by making it a record of perception rather than an account of the physical structure of the solar system. In doing so, he does not at all imply that this is the only way in which nature is to be understood—God's "admirable wisdom" is revealed by the methods of science also. These two constructions of reality, though utterly different, are not opposed. Neither excludes the other. And Calvin is never more French than in his insistence on the aesthetic character of perception. The beauty of what we see is burdened with truth. It signifies the power of God and his constant grace toward the human creature. It signifies the address of God to the individual human consciousness. Icons were defended by the Church from criticism by the Reformers as the books of the unlettered, the means by which the common people could be instructed in the faith. For Calvin, there is great, continuous instruction in perception itself.

In the *Institutes*, Calvin uses the fact of astronomy as an argument for the existence and immortality of the soul. "The powers of the soul are far from being confined to functions that serve the body. Of what concern is it to the body that you measure the heavens, gather the number of the stars, determine the magnitude of each, know what space lies between them, with what swiftness or slowness they complete their courses, how many degrees this way or that they decline? . . . here is an activity of the soul distinct from the body. I have put forth one example, from which it will be easy for my readers to derive the rest. Manifold indeed is the nimbleness of the soul with which it surveys heaven and earth, joins past to future, retains in memory something heard long before, nay, pictures to itself whatever it pleases. Manifold also is the skill with which it devises things incredible, and which is the mother of so many marvelous devices. These are unfailing signs of divinity in man." Calvin sees the creative freedom and ingenuity of human beings in the world as yet another manifestation of the divine. This is neither the Calvin nor the Calvinism of folklore, but the language is unambiguous.

The Reformers did not concede either orthodoxy or the authority of tradition to those with whom they disputed. They were sons of the Church, remarkable for nothing more than for the depth of their learning in all that pertained to it. Calvin especially made extensive use of the writings of the early Christian fathers and of the saints of the Church to buttress his positions on questions of doctrine and to challenge the teachings and practice of the Church of his day. These claims and counterclaims can never be made decisively, but from the point of view of the Reformers, that fact is sufficient in itself to counter the argument that tradition weighed against them. Continuity with tradition is as difficult to assess as objectivity and as open to tendentious interpretation. Peter Abelard had pointed out centuries earlier that there were contradictions among the fathers and saints themselves. And the step from Aquinas to Luther was arguably not longer than the step from Augustine to Aquinas. If Luther in fact intended a return to Augustine, like Aquinas a doctor of the Church, then the question of continuity with tradition becomes more complicated still.

*   *   *

Calvin died in 1564, the year Michelangelo died, the year Shakespeare was born. He was a contemporary and perhaps an acquaintance of Rabelais, whose friend and publisher, the poet Étienne Dolet, was accused of heresy and finally burned for it and, among other things, for publishing Calvinist books and having in his possession books printed in Geneva. Calvin's *Institutes of the Christian Religion* was translated into English in 1561 by Thomas Norton, author with Thomas Sackville of *Gorboduc*, the earliest English tragedy, first performed in 1561. A number of Calvin's sermons and commentaries were translated by Arthur Golding, whose most famous work was a 1567 translation of Ovid's *Metamorphoses* used by Shakespeare. Golding also translated *Abraham's Sacrifice (Abraham Sacrifiant)*, the first drama in the French language, written in blank verse by Calvin's friend and associate Théodore de Bèze in 1552. Calvin and those he influenced were very central to the great literary project of the Renaissance, the appropriation of the vernacular languages of Europe for the lofty uses formerly reserved to Latin.

The early translations of Calvin's work convey some sense of the beautiful prose, Latin or French, for which he was famous. Other translations vary widely, but in general their language frequently falls short of lucidity, not to say refinement. Their stodginess is an obstacle to an understanding of this quintessentially Renaissance figure. His breadth of reference and fluency of allusion, a virtuosic summoning of the powers of the mind and memory and interpretive skill which to him bespoke the soul itself, can be made to feel rather wooden. The patience of his exegetical approach can obscure the movement of his interpretation of Scripture, and the distinctiveness of his approach to the text can be difficult to perceive simply because his influence has been so great that his methods are by now familiar. Yet there are things to be noted in his manner of interpretation that are deeply rooted in his theology and will not have their proper power if this is not borne in mind. For example, he is perfectly at ease with the human authorship of the Bible. He points out features of Luke's narrative method, he notes the elegance of phrasing of the author of Hebrews. This is consistent with his very exalted notion of human beings and human brilliance, fallibility notwithstanding. For example, in his commentary on Psalm 8, Calvin translates a famous phrase as "thou hast made him [man] a little lower than God," preferring this understanding of the Hebrew *Elohim*, which can mean both "God" and "angels." He acknowledges that the Septuagint and the Epistle to the Hebrews both make the more familiar, and less exuberant, interpretation of the word. He says he does not disapprove of their choice, since it means "that the condition of men is nothing less than a divine and celestial state. But," he says, "as the other translation seems more natural, and as it is almost universally adopted by the Jewish interpreters, I have preferred following it." He is not dissuaded by the example of the Epistle, "for we know what freedoms the apostles took in quoting texts of Scripture." So far from being a literalist himself, he does not think the apostles were literalists. His translation clearly supports his sense of the place of humankind in the cosmic order—nothing intervenes between it and God, either ontologically or in terms of sacredness. We are, says Calvin, "not far removed from the divine majesty." Then, being Calvin, he immediately turns to the other side of the human paradox. In the Fall, "from a state of the highest excellence, we were reduced to a condition of wretched and shameful destitution." But our restoration is effected in Christ: "His excellence and heavenly dignity . . . are extended to us also, seeing it is for our sake he is enriched with them."

The crucial role of perception in Calvin, who bases so much of his definition of the divine in humanity on the brilliance of the human capacity for perception, is evident in the consistency with which he associates "election" with the radical understanding of the presence of God, and of his nature as manifest in Christ. He says in a sermon on Isaiah 53, "Faith is not given to all, but is a singular gift that God keeps as a treasure for those he has chosen; and let us know that it is our duty to cleave to him, knowing the while that none of us gains faith by his own effort, but God has enlightened us and given us eyes by his Holy Spirit, and in doing so has declared his power." He is speaking here specifically of response to Scripture—"Let us note carefully, therefore, that when the Gospel is preached it will be mere useless sound until our Lord shows that it is he who speaks: for he does not bestow that blessing upon all." ("The elect" and "election" are terms used twenty-three times in the New Testament, seven times by Jesus, and are therefore significant in all classical theology, though folklore attributes the notion to Calvin and blames him for it.)

In any case, it may seem paradoxical that Calvin worked to the end—even on his deathbed—to elucidate the Scriptures for the purposes of teaching and preaching. But paradox is entirely characteristic of his thought. The great focus of his labors was to make the Bible accessible through the methods of humanist scholarship and criticism and through patient explication of its historical context and its unforced meaning. Clearly then he did not believe that election implied passivity on the part of anyone, though this is commonly thought to be implied by it. Calvin assumes it is the will of God that the Scriptures should be available in the common language, and that they should be taught and preached with care and great reverence. Indeed, this primacy of Scripture is the basis of the worship and polity of the church he helped to establish.

Calvin's reader and hearer are always that implied second person, the universal individual so near divinity, that soul he addresses in his appeals to the sense of God any human being can find within himself or herself. As with the wonders of the mind and body, and as with the splendors of the heavens and the earth, so with the sacred texts and the Gospel itself. Again and again he invokes the authority of their beauty.

Calvin's influence is so widespread as to elude description in this small space, but nowhere is it more evident than in the thought and writing of the early New Englanders, who were, through historical accident, the products of a substantially Calvinist culture. They struggled with their religious heritage as New England moved from its status as a self-protective refugee population to a people more at ease with the world. Yet there remains in all their work the ravishment, or the shock, of revelatory perception, whether of the sea, or of a slant of light, or of the floods of humanity crossing on the Brooklyn ferry. Henry David Thoreau said, "I stand in awe of my body, this matter to which I am bound has become so strange to me. I fear not spirits, ghosts, of which I am one—that my body might—but I fear bodies, I tremble to meet them. What is this Titan that has possession of me? Talk of mysteries! Think of our life in nature, daily to be shown matter, to come in contact with it—rocks, trees, wind on our cheeks! the *solid* earth! the *actual* world! the *common sense*! *Contact! Contact! Who* are we? *Where* are we?" Behind the aesthetics and the metaphysics of classical American literature, again and again we find the Calvinist soul, universal in its singularity, and full of Calvinist wonder.

Background to the Reform

1506 Johann Tetzel (1465–1519), a Dominican monk, begins selling indulgences in Germany. Pope Julius II is seeking to finance the rebuilding of St. Peter's in Rome.

1510 Martin Luther (1483–1546), a fervent Augustinian monk and professor of biblical theology at the University of Wittenberg, is sent to Rome to represent his religious order with respect to the observant controversy. The dispute is focused on the question of whether strict withdrawal from the world should be the ideal of monasticism, or whether orders should be directed outward in the service of preaching and ministering to the laity. The controversy is not settled. Luther, who expects to find Rome a holy site, is shocked by the self-indulgence and cupidity he sees among the clergy there and in the pontifical court itself. Luther returns home, and for the next six years he will keep the rule of his order in the strictest manner, while lecturing on the Bible.

1512 Luther receives his doctorate in theology and assumes the chair of biblical theology at Wittenberg.

On a personal level, Luther is tormented spiritually by the question of how to be sure of his personal salvation by God. He has followed diligently the rules of religious life, kept the vigils, said his prayers, and submitted himself to corporal discipline—as if he could earn his salvation by his own proper actions. He is filled with doubt and fear and cannot find peace. He tries everything he can to create a proper disposition to receive God's grace in himself.

He searches for insight into how he can reconcile his sense of the tragedy of sin and his exalted notion of a just God.

1516 Luther is convinced that the true justice of God is revealed in the Gospel. In his thinking, he comes to reverse the notion, commonly held in the Middle Ages, that we must make amends to God for our sins through personal acts of atonement and, instead, comes to understand that the love of God first envelops the sinner, who is then justified by his or her faith in God's love. On reading Romans 1:17, one day in the spring of the year, Luther finds, through these words, a way to have absolute confidence in his redemption: "For I see no reason to be ashamed of the gospel; it is God's power for the salvation of everyone who has faith—Jews first, but Greeks as well—for in it is revealed the saving justice of God: a justice based on faith and addressed to faith. As it says in scripture: *Anyone who is upright through faith will live.*" Grace, Faith, Scripture. For Luther these are the essentials for salvation.

Luther observes with disgust the current customs of the Roman Church, especially the sale of indulgences, which he despises as an abhorrent form of spiritual fraud. By this practice the faithful are led to believe that their donation of money will guarantee them or their departed loved ones a place in heaven and will even free a soul from purgatory. He sees, as well, the poor spiritual quality of the priests hearing confession, with the disastrous results of a superficial piety reigning among Christians who are far removed from the true sources of salvation. In a standoff with the official Church, Luther affirms that people must put their faith in Jesus Christ alone and not in their own prayers, their own merits, or their own good works. Among the young monks who become his fervent disciples is Martin Bucer, who will later become spiritual leader of the city of Strasbourg when John Calvin takes up residence there.

Desiderius Erasmus of Rotterdam, the greatest of the Renaissance humanists, publishes his Greek New Testament, which will influence Luther's German translation and John Calvin's own studies and commentaries. It prepares the way not only for challenges to the normative Latin Vulgate version of the Bible but for a fresh tradition of vernacular translation.

1517 On October 31, Luther posts his Ninety-five Theses at the castle church of Wittenberg. He is protesting the indulgence that has been issued as a result of the arrangement between Pope Leo X, Archbishop Albert of the nearby duchy of Brandenburg, and the banking house of Fugger. Johann Tetzel is actively promoting the sale. Luther's main point is to stress that the consequences of sin can only be removed by faith in the Gospel. No amount of money charitably donated can relieve one of this personal responsibility.

1519 In July at Leipzig, Luther debates his Ninety-five Theses with Roman Church officials. At the heart of the debate is Luther's contention about the legitimate extent of papal authority. In the heat of the argument, Luther goes so far as to say that the Church does not need an earthly head, since Christ himself is its head. According to Luther, the Church does not rest on the rock of the papacy but on faith in Christ. He goes even further to claim, with evidence, that past church councils could very well be in error and that the only legitimate authority for Christians must be the Bible.

1520 On June 15, Luther is excommunicated. In August Luther publishes an appeal to all German Christians. He attacks Rome on three points: the priesthood, the right of clergy to be the sole interpreters of the Bible, and the reservation of the right by the pope alone to convene councils. To these Luther opposes three principles: all Christians are priests by virtue of their baptism; Scripture is intelligible and directly accessible to whoever reads it with faith; and all the faithful are responsible for the work formerly undertaken by church councils in matters of doctrine and belief. Luther casts the pope as the Antichrist, the ruler of Babylon.

Luther recasts the structure of the Church by reducing the number of sacraments from seven to three, retaining baptism, the Eucharist, and a modified form of confession. He redefines the Mass, rejecting the Scholastic doctrine of transubstantiation (by which the Church teaches that the bread and wine are physically changed in substance into the body and blood of Christ). He nonetheless continues to believe that Jesus is present in the

Eucharist. He also rejects the notion of the Eucharist as a priestly sacrifice. He thus undercuts the dependence of the laity on the priesthood. Instead he proposes that the Mass is a promise of the remission of sins and that only faith in that promise makes the sacrament fruitful.

Luther's treatise *On Monastic Vows* rejects monasticism as a misguided attempt to please God and earn merit before him with man's own works. Many monks and nuns on reading it feel justified in leaving the religious life. Luther himself will eventually marry Katharina von Bora (1499–1552), an ex-nun, in 1525. They will have six children.

1521 On January 3, the papal pronouncement *Decet romanum pontificem* declares Luther and his followers anathema. Half of Western Christianity will choose to side with Luther.

The defense of the Reform occupies Luther until his death. His vast body of work marks the evolution of his own thinking and the progress of the Reform. His translation of the Bible into German remains one of the crowning works of that language. His commentaries and his writings are received with great enthusiasm by many Christians. His struggles with the Church and with his personal fears nourish his teaching. He understands, as did his favorite church father, Augustine, human nature to be under an interminable assault by concupiscence. The only hope one can have for salvation is absolute faith in the redemptive work of Christ and personal union with him. Thus interiorized, Christianity for Luther is no longer a matter of the Church hierarchy determining the means of salvation while benefiting, not least fiscally, from the practices of piety.

John Calvin

1509 Born July 10 in Noyon, France, Jean Cauvin is the second of four sons of Gerard Cauvin. The family name later becomes latinized to Calvinus, and John prefers Calvin as a young man. His family are devout Roman Catholics, with his father, a lawyer, working as secretary for the local bishop and as procurator for the province of Picardy. His mother, Jeanne Le Franc, inculcates

Catholic piety in her children and takes them to Catholic shrines. Gerard and Jeanne wish all their sons to become clerics.

1521 Young Calvin is educated at the local College des Capettes in Noyon with his brothers and the sons of other aristocratic and influential families. This year he receives prospectively a benefice and chaplaincy in the Cathedral of Noyon through his father's influence.

1523 In August John leaves Noyon for Paris to enter the College de la Marche at the University of Paris to study theology in preparation for the priesthood. After several months he transfers to the College Montaigu, a bastion of resistance to the new evangelical ideas. He proves to be an excellent student of Latin. Here he participates in religious discussions at the house of George Cop, physician to the French king Francis I, where the "New Learning" of humanism is working as a leaven for reform in the Church. The ferment of ideas includes a certain sentiment of individual freedom and critical thinking, which inform efforts to translate the Bible into the vernacular, with corresponding commentary and interpretation, thus putting Scripture into the hands of the laity. These movements are seen to undermine the traditional control of the Church by giving impetus to independent thought and action.

By now the heresies of Martin Luther are finding readers everywhere, not least among the professors at the Sorbonne. The inviolability of the human conscience, salvation by faith alone, the corruption of the Roman Church through the selling of indulgences, questioning the necessity of an intermediary priesthood between each person and God, and encouraging the individual to read and meditate on the books of Scripture for him- or herself—all these stir the fires of revolt against the spiritual and temporal power of the Roman Church.

The Augustinian monk, Jean Vallière, arrives in Paris. Suspected of heresy, he is arrested immediately and put to death.

1527 Calvin is given the title Curé of Saint-Martin de Marteville in the Vermandois in northern France, and the parish funds help support his student life. By the end of the year his schooling is complete in grammar, rhetoric, logic, arithmetic, geometry, astronomy, and music. Calvin is friendly with people who are influenced by Luther and other reform-minded individuals, but he remains tied to the Roman Church.

1528 Calvin's father, who has fallen out with the chapter of Noyon over accounting matters, now advises his son to study law. Calvin inscribes himself as a student at Orléans, which has a celebrated faculty of law. His mind is naturally suited to the logic and clarity required by legal studies. This inclination for precision will be evident in his later theological works.

1529 Calvin goes to Bourges to continue his studies there, where the Italian Andrea Alciati has just been installed to teach Roman law.

1531 Calvin's father dies. He had been excommunicated from the Catholic Church for allegedly not being responsible about the episcopal accounts. Calvin's brother Charles is infuriated by the charge against his father and follows his inclinations to sympathize with Reformist ideas. Soon he will deny the Catholic dogma of the Eucharist and die outside the Church. Calvin is now free to continue his religious studies and Reformist activities. Like Luther in Saxony, he has become very critical of the abuses in the French Catholic Church. He comes to consider himself as one chosen by God to work for the spiritual regeneration of the world.

After a year in Bourges, where Calvin has begun preaching Reformist ideas in private, he returns to Paris. He has earned his doctor of law degree and is master of both Greek and Hebrew. He publishes his first book, a commentary on the treatise *De Clementia* ("Concerning Mercy") by Seneca, a Roman philosopher. Martin Luther's concept of salvation by faith alone is circulating in the city as are his pleas for church reform, all of which are compelling to Calvin.

1533 Calvin's friend, Nicholas Cop, becomes rector of the University of Paris. Calvin helps Cop compose a speech on Christian philosophy for the inauguration of the academic year. The discourse is a sort of sermon on the Beatitudes and is inspired by

Lutheran ideas on the Reform, especially salvation by faith alone. This is too much for Francis I, who sends his royal inquisitors after Cop and his associates. They are forced to flee the city. Calvin goes to stay in Angoulême with his friend Louis de Tillet, curé of Claix. It is thought that Calvin, who seldom speaks personally about himself, about this time decides to put himself definitively to the work of the Reform.

1534 Calvin experiences a conversion that he describes in the preface to his "Commentary on the Psalms." He is gripped by the fundamentals of the Reform and tells how "God subdued my soul to docility by a sudden conversion." In May he gives up his benefice in Noyon, where there is an effort to put him in prison. He escapes to Nérac in the Béarn region of southwestern France. Here he meets Le Fevre, whose translation of the Bible into French has been condemned by the Sorbonne to be burned. When Calvin next returns to Paris, there is in process a campaign by the Lutherans against the Mass, and it has turned violent. Several heretics are burned at the stake. Now known to be a sympathizer of the Reform, Calvin must flee. He escapes to Metz and then to Strasbourg.

1535 Calvin has now totally rejected Roman Catholicism, and he joins the war being waged against Rome by the Reformers. He writes a letter to Francis I, dated August 1, in which he argues for abandoning Catholicism altogether in favor of the "new gospel" of the Reformers. This letter will serve as a prologue to the *Institutes*.

1536 The first edition of the *Institutes of the Christian Religion*, written in Latin and published in Basle, appears. It is John Calvin's theology of the majesty of God and the corrupt helplessness of his creature, man, who is predestined by God's intention to either eternal glory or eternal damnation, about which he can do nothing. It is an immediate bestseller. Calvin will continue to revise and develop the ideas expressed in the *Institutes* until his death. The first edition comprises six chapters; the final one of 1559 has eighty. The *Institutes* will be regarded as the central work of Reformation theology.

In July Calvin finds himself in Geneva. Originally headed

for Strasbourg, the spread of the Habsburg-Valois Wars between Holy Roman Emperor Charles V and Francis I causes him to detour instead. Calvin has settled his family affairs and has influenced two brothers and his sisters to share his views on the Reform. The Swiss Protestant preacher Guillaume Farel (1489–1565) convinces Calvin to remain in the city to teach theology.

Geneva, a city of fifteen thousand people and French-speaking, is torn by grave dissensions. Some partisans of the Reform have been banished. The Catholic bishop is struggling to retain power. The followers of William Farel oppose the new pastors nominated by the city magistrate. Calvin uses his influence to moderate affairs with the result that the new elections favor Farel. The city adopts religious reforms. The bishop is forced to flee, monasteries are dissolved, Mass is abolished, and papal authority is denounced. Priests are imprisoned, altars desecrated, and citizens fined for not attending Protestant sermons. Conflict continues with some wanting general reform while others, like Calvin and Farel, seek radical reform. Opposed to Calvin are the Libertines, who advocate having magistrates in control of the clergy. Calvin wants a theocracy, that is, a city controlled by the clergy. The Libertines embrace a philosophy of the sovereignty of desires and refuse to submit their hedonistic tendencies to either spiritual or temporal powers. Calvin detests these notions.

The same laws condemning the practice of Catholicism are established at Zurich, Basle, and Bern.

1537 Legislation for a new government in Geneva, heavily influenced by Calvin, is introduced. Such measures as mandating communion four times a year, exercising moral censorship, and dictating excommunication for the disobedient are voted on. The city is now divided into the "jurants" and "nonjurors," or those who do accept or do not accept this legislation. Calvin is unable to surmount the widespread disorder in the city.

1538 The Council of Geneva exiles Farel and Calvin. Calvin leaves for Strasbourg, where he devotes himself to teaching the New Testament to French refugees. Cardinal Jacopo Sadoleto (1477–1547), bishop of Carpentras, writes an open letter to the

Genevans charging that schism is a crime. Calvin responds with a letter of his own detailing the corruption of the Roman Church.

While in Strasbourg Calvin profits from his association with Martin Bucer (1491–1551), a German Protestant Reformer and close associate of Martin Luther, who has many ideas about ecclesiastical organization. Bucer advocates the creation of small professing communities of faith that can work to reactivate the larger church.

Although he is both ill and poor from his ascetic practices, Calvin marries Idelette de Bure. She is the widow of an Anabaptist he had converted. They will have one son who will die very young.

1540 Calvin attends Catholic/Protestant conferences in Hagenau, Worms, and Ratisbon, where he is applauded for his keen debating powers.

1541 The Libertines fall from power, and Geneva sends for Calvin, who is persuaded to return. He arrives on September 13. Calvin's intention is to stay only long enough to sort out the problems facing the city and then return to Strasbourg. He will, however, remain in Geneva for the next twenty-three years until his death.

The magistrate of Geneva now holds supreme power, with a consistory exercising secular power and with ministers governing religious practices. Calvin begins to oppose the city councils by aligning the preachers behind him. The clergy succeed. Calvin draws up his Ecclesiastical Ordinances, which govern, rather despotically, every detail of a citizen's life. The medieval church structure is abandoned and a new structure created that takes for its model something closer to apostolic times. Though Gospel liberty is preached, the conduct of all citizens is rigidly disciplined.

Calvin works diligently to establish his own versions of liturgy, doctrine, church organization, and norms of ethical behavior. The sermon is central to religious services, and every element in worship must come from the Scriptures. His doctrine is centered on the majesty of God and on man, who is helpless in the face of God's will. God alone knows who is predestined to be saved and who is not. The law of the Christian state is the Bible. The clergy are to teach the law, and the state has the duty to enforce it. Gambling, drunkenness, dancing, profane songs, all forms of theater, and immodest dress are prohibited. Even the colors of clothing and hair styles are regulated. Censorship lays a heavy hand on the press, and it is a criminal offense to criticize Calvin or members of the clergy. Calvin will remain the town's virtual dictator until his death.

Calvin's humanitarian efforts to improve Geneva result in hospitals, care for the poor, a good educational system, a sewage system, and new industries. He fixes the statutes for the Academy founded in 1536 by Farel. It is dedicated essentially to the interpretation of Scripture. Due to the quality of the professors it attracts, the Academy of Geneva will come to know considerable success.

The French edition of the *Institutes* is published.

1547 The force of the state-issued dogmatic decrees in Geneva is evidenced by the execution in June of a young man, Jacques Gouet, who is accused of impiety. He is first severely tortured and then beheaded as punishment for abusing regulations governing every citizen's life. In the next five years there will be fifty-eight people sentenced to death and seventy-six to exile, with numerous citizens given prison terms in order that morals and discipline be preserved.

1549 Calvin's wife dies. He does not remarry.

1553 Michael Servetus (b. 1511), a Spanish Unitarian who had disputed with Calvin in the past over points of doctrine, is burned at the stake on October 27. Servetus had criticized Calvin's *Institutes* and had come to Geneva to dispute Calvin face-to-face. On the day of the execution, Calvin disputes with Servetus and then sees him burn. The Libertines, Calvin's political enemies in Geneva, had played a role in instigating the confrontation between Servetus and Calvin.

1555 A revolt against Calvin's rule of Geneva is led by Ami Perrin, a commissioner for Geneva who had persuaded Calvin to return in 1541. The Libertines are behind the revolt, which is immediately suppressed. The leaders are executed, and Calvin's hold is now reinforced. French refugees in Geneva surge to his support.

The first Huguenot (as French Calvinists are called) congregation to have a permanent minister is established in Paris.

1559 The Academy established in Geneva is now a school for missionaries of the Reform. It will become the University of Geneva. The school opens with 162 students, mostly French Huguenots. By 1664 there will be over 1,500 students in the French-speaking university. Théodore de Bèze (1519–1605) is the first director of the new university. After Calvin's death, he will become head of the Reform Church in Geneva. Missionaries from the university will take the doctrines of the Reform to the Netherlands, Germanic countries, England, Scotland, Poland, and Hungary. Calvinism will find its way to the New World as well, where its predominant trait of social humanism perdures. The members of the people of God exist in solidarity with one another, and they owe one another mutual assistance.

The first synod, or national council, of the Huguenots is held in Paris. There are now seventy-two local congregations, each represented by elders. Most Huguenots live near the port city of La Rochelle and in the Béarn region of southwestern France.

A final edition of Calvin's *Institutes* is published.

Henry II determines to rid France of the Reformers. Persecution, arrests, and executions take place. In spite of the repression, new churches of the Reform continue to constitute themselves.

1560 John Knox (1513–72) founds the Church of Scotland, based on Calvinist reforms. The celebration of Mass is forbidden, the jurisdiction of the pope abolished, and the Scottish Confession of Faith is approved.

1561 There are now 2,150 Huguenot churches in France, with a million members.

1562 At the massacre of Vassy on March 1, twelve hundred French Huguenots are killed by the forces of the Catholic Duke of Guise. The first War of Religion begins. The subsequent massacre on St. Bartholomew's Day (August 24, 1572, in Paris) results in the murder of two thousand French Calvinists. There will be eight French civil wars involving the Catholics and the Huguenots. The religious freedom achieved by the Edict of Nantes in 1598 will be destroyed by Cardinal Richelieu in 1629 with the terms of the Peace of Alais. The civil and political rights of the Huguenots are revoked at this time, and many flee to seek sanctuary in other countries.

1563 The Council of Trent closes after setting the stage for the reform of Catholicism. The *Catechism of the Council of Trent* (1566) is very effective in disseminating Catholic doctrine as clarified by the Council. However, the gulf between Catholics and Reformers is not bridged. This breach continues in Western Christendom to the present day.

1564 Worn out by unceasing labor and after a long illness and much physical suffering, John Calvin dies on May 27. He has preached sermons daily, even when ill, all the while writing exegetical works on Scripture. He leaves only 225 French crowns in his estate. Ten are designated for the university, ten for the poor, and the rest to his nephews and nieces. He is buried without much ceremony in the Cimetière des Rois. The tombstone carries only the initials "J.C." At least 4,271 of his letters remain, along with the *Institutes*, hundreds of sermons, and his vast collection of commentaries on the books of the Bible (see Suggestions for Further Reading). Four and a half centuries later, Calvinism itself is a legacy that continues to leaven spiritual life in America and around the globe.

JOHN CALVIN

Steward *of* God's Covenant

A NOTE ON THE TEXTS

To anyone lacking Latin or Renaissance French, much of the writings of John Calvin must remain inaccessible. While his major works—the *Institutes of the Christian Religion* being the prime example—are available in English in both book and electronic form, many of his characteristic expressions—his sermons, letters, tracts, polemics, writings on liturgy and church regulations—are not.

The present volume has been designed to offer the reader a look at the spirituality of Calvin, which has necessitated excluding a good deal of his other work (see "Works of John Calvin," in Suggestions for Further Reading, p. 415). However, included are, among others, selections from the *Institutes*; from his extensive commentaries, often line by line and even word by word, on books of the Hebrew Bible as well as on the Gospels and the Epistles of the New Testament; and from his prayers and sermons.

Most of the texts have been adapted from a series of translations of Calvin's works made in the nineteenth century by the Calvin Society of Edinburgh. An attempt has been made to render these older translations reader-friendly for contemporary users by employing, for the most part, modern punctuation and spelling. Scriptural references—again, for the most part—are Calvin's own. He had a remarkable memory but sometimes it was not exact, so the reader can always double-check any given quotation against his favorite edition of the Bible. Footnotes have intentionally been kept to a bare minimum to avoid the tendency to fussy excess so characteristic of scholarly editions of classic texts.

From
The Necessity of
Reforming the Church
(1543)

In 1544 Holy Roman Emperor Charles V presided over an imperial diet at Spires that would try to deal with the religious divisions besetting his domains. Théodore de Bèze (1519–1605), a Geneva colleague, defender, and early biographer of John Calvin, described the events that preceded the diet:

> *The year before, Charles V having, in the view of turning all his strength against the French, promised the Germans that for a short period, until a General Council were held, which he engaged to see done, neither party should suffer prejudice on account of religious differences, but both enjoy equal laws, the Roman Pontiff, Paul III, was exceedingly offended and addressed a very severe expostulation to the Emperor, because, forsooth, he had put heretics on a footing with Catholics, and, as it were, put his sickle into another man's corn. Caesar gave what answer seemed proper, but Calvin, because the truth of the gospel, and the innocence of the godly, was deeply injured by that letter, repressed the audacity of the Pontiff. A diet of the empire was at this time held at Spires, and Calvin, availing himself of the occasion, published a short treatise on the Necessity of Reforming the Church. I know not if any writing on the subject, more nervous or solid, has been published in our age.* *

*Théodore de Bèze, *The Life of John Calvin,* trans. Henry Beveridge (Philadelphia: Westminster Press, 1909), pp. 38–39.

THE NECESSITY OF
REFORMING THE CHURCH

A Humble Exhortation
to the most invincible Emperor Charles V
and the most illustrious Princes and other Orders,
now holding a Diet of the Empire at Spires
that they seriously undertake the task
of restoring the Church
presented in the name of all those who wish Christ to reign

BY DR. JOHN CALVIN

August Emperor,
This Diet is summoned by you in order at last to deliberate and
decide, along with the Most Illustrious Princes and other Orders
of the Empire, upon the means of ameliorating the present condition of the Church, which we all see to be very miserable and
almost desperate. Now, therefore, while you sit for this consulta-
tion, I humbly beg and implore, first of your Imperial Majesty,
and at the same time of you also, Most Illustrious Princes and distinguished gentlemen, that you will not decline to read and diligently consider what I have to lay before you. The magnitude and
weight of the cause may well incite you to an eagerness to listen. I
shall set the matter so plainly in front of you that you can have no
difficulty in determining what part you must play. Whoever I am,
I here profess to plead in defense both of sound doctrine and of the
Church. In this character I seem at all events entitled to expect that
you will not deny me audience, until such time as it may appear
whether I falsely usurp the character, or whether I faithfully perform its duties and make good what I profess. But though I feel
that I am by no means equal to so great a task, yet I am not at all
afraid that, after you have heard the nature of my office, I shall be
accused either of folly or presumption in having ventured thus to
bring this matter before you. There are two things by which men
are wont to recommend, or at least to justify, their conduct. If a

thing is done honestly and from pious zeal, we deem it worthy of praise; if it is done under the pressure of public necessity, we at least deem it not unworthy of excuse. Since both of these apply here, I am confident, such is your equity, that I shall easily approve my design in your eyes. For where can I exert myself to better purpose or more honestly, where, too, in a matter at this time more necessary, than in attempting, according to my ability, to aid the Church of Christ, whose claims it is lawful in no instance to deny, and which is now in grievous distress and in extreme danger? But there is no occasion for a long preface concerning myself. Receive what I say as if it were the united voice of all who either have already taken care to restore the Church or desire that it should be restored to true order. On my side are several exalted Princes and not a few distinguished communities. For all these I speak though an individual, so that it is more truly they who at the same time and with one mouth speak through me. To these add the countless multitude of pious men, scattered over the various regions of the Christian world, who yet unanimously concur with me in this pleading. In short, regard this as the common address of all who so earnestly deplore the present corruption of the Church that they are unable to bear it any longer and are determined not to rest till they see some amendment. I know with what odious names we are marked down for disgrace; but meanwhile, whatever be the name by which it is thought proper to call us, hear our cause, and after that judge what place we are entitled to hold.

First, then, the question is not whether the Church suffers from many and grievous diseases, for this is admitted even by all moderate judges; but whether the diseases are of a kind whose cure admits of no longer delay, so that it is neither useful nor proper to wait upon too slow remedies. We are accused of rash and impious innovation, for having ventured to propose any change at all in the former state of the Church. What? Even if it has been done with good cause and not imperfectly? I hear there are persons who, even in this case, do not hesitate to condemn us; they think us right indeed in desiring amendment, but not right in attempting it. From them, all I would ask at present is that for a little they suspend judgment until I shall have shown from the facts that we have not been prematurely hasty, have attempted nothing rashly, nothing alien to our duty, and have in short done nothing until compelled by the highest necessity. To enable me to prove this, it is necessary to attend to the matters in dispute.

We maintain to start with that when God raised up Luther and others who held forth a torch to light us into the way of salvation and on whose ministry our churches are founded and built, those heads of doctrine in which the truth of our religion, those in which the pure and legitimate worship of God, and those in which the salvation of men are comprehended, were in a great measure obsolete. We maintain that the use of the sacraments was in many ways vitiated and polluted. And we maintain that the government of the Church was converted into a species of horrible and insufferable tyranny. But perhaps these statements have not force enough to move certain individuals until they are better explained. This, therefore, I will do, not as the subject demands, but as far as my ability will permit. Here, however, I have no intention to review and discuss all our controversies; that would require a long discourse, and this is not the place for it. I wish only to demonstrate how just and necessary the causes were which forced us to the changes for which we are blamed.

To accomplish this, I must show that the particular remedies which the Reformers employed were apt and salutary; not here intending to describe the manner in which we proceeded (for this will afterward be seen), but only to make it manifest that we have had no other end in view than to ameliorate in some degree the very miserable condition of the Church. Our doctrine has been, and is every day, assailed by many cruel calumnies. Some declaim loudly against it in sermons; others attack and ridicule it in their writings. Both rake together everything by which they hope to bring it into disrepute among the ignorant. But there is in men's hands the Confession of our Faith, which we presented to your Imperial Majesty. It clearly testifies how undeservedly we are harassed by so many odious accusations. We have always been ready in times past, as we are at the present day, to render an account of our doctrine. In a word, there is no doctrine preached in our churches but that which we openly profess. As to contested points, they are clearly and honestly explained in our Confession, while everything relating to them has been copiously treated and diligently expounded by our writers. Hence judges who are not unjust must be satisfied how far we are from every kind of impi-

ety. This much certainly must be clear alike to just and unjust, that
the Reformers have done no small service to the Church in stirring
up the world as from the deep darkness of ignorance to read the
Scriptures, in laboring diligently to make them better understood,
and in happily throwing light on certain points of doctrine of
the highest practical importance. In sermons little else used to
be heard than old wives' fables and fictions equally frivolous. The
schools resounded with brawling questions, but Scripture was seldom mentioned. Those who held the government of the Church
had this one concern, to prevent any diminution of their gains.
Accordingly, they readily tolerated whatever brought grist to their
mill. Even the most prejudiced admit that our people have in some
degree reformed these evils, however much they may impugn our
doctrine at other points.

But I do not wish that all the profit the Church has derived
from our labor should avail to mitigate our fault, if in any other
respect we have injured her. Therefore let there be an examination
of our whole doctrine, of our form of administering the sacraments, and our method of governing the Church; and in none of
these three things will it be found that we have made any change
in the old form, without attempting to restore it to the exact standard of the Word of God.

All our controversies concerning doctrine relate either to the
legitimate worship of God or to the ground of salvation. As to
the former, certainly we exhort men to worship God in neither a
frigid nor a careless manner; and while we point out the way, we
neither lose sight of the end, nor omit anything which is relevant
to the matter. We proclaim the glory of God in terms far loftier
than it was wont to be proclaimed before, and we earnestly labor
to make the perfections in which his glory shines better and better
known. His benefits toward ourselves we extol as eloquently as we
can. Thus men are incited to reverence his majesty, render due
homage to his greatness, feel due gratitude for his mercies, and
unite in showing forth his praise. In this way there is infused into
their hearts that solid confidence which afterward gives birth to
prayer. In this way too each one is trained to genuine self-denial,
so that his will being brought into obedience to God, he bids
farewell to his own desires. In short, as God requires us to worship

him in a spiritual manner, so we with all zeal urge men to all the spiritual sacrifices which he commends.

Even our enemies cannot deny our assiduity in these exhortations, that men look for the good which they desire from none but God, that they confide in his power, trust in his goodness, depend on his truth, and turn to him with the whole heart, rest on him with full hope, and resort to him in necessity, that is, at every moment, and ascribe to him every good thing enjoyed, and testify to this by expressions of praise. That none may be deterred by difficulty of access, we proclaim that a fountain of all blessings is offered us in Christ, from which we may draw everything needful. Our writings are witnesses, and our sermons also, how frequent and sedulous we are in recommending true repentance, urging men to renounce their reason, their carnal desires, and themselves entirely, that they may be brought into obedience to God alone, and live no longer to themselves but to him. Nor indeed do we overlook external duties and works of charity, which follow on such renewal. This, I say, is the sure and unerring form of divine worship, which we know that he approves, because it is the form which his Word prescribes. These are the only sacrifices of the Christian Church which have attestation from him.

Since, therefore, in our churches, God alone is adored in pure form without superstition, since his goodness, wisdom, power, truth, and other perfections are there preached more fully than anywhere else, since he is invoked with true faith in the name of Christ, his mercies celebrated with both heart and tongue, and men constantly urged to a simple and sincere obedience; since in short nothing is heard but what tends to promote the sanctification of his name, what cause have those who call themselves Christians to take us up so ill? First, since they love darkness rather than light, they cannot tolerate the sharpness with which we, as in duty bound, rebuke the gross idolatry which is apparent everywhere in the world. When God is worshipped in images, when fictitious worship is instituted in his name, when supplication is made to the images of saints, and divine honors paid to dead men's bones and other similar things, we call them abominations as they are. For this cause, those who hate our doctrine inveigh against us and represent us as heretics who dare to abolish the worship of God as approved of old by the Church. Concerning this name of *Church*, which they are ever and anon holding up before them as a kind of shield, we will shortly speak. Meanwhile how perverse, when these infamous corruptions are manifest, not only to defend them, but to dissemble and represent them as the genuine worship of God!

Both sides confess that in the sight of God idolatry is an execrable crime. But when we attack the worship of images, our adversaries immediately take the opposite side and lend support to the crime which they had with us verbally condemned. Indeed, as is more ridiculous, while they agree with us as to the term in Greek, it is no sooner turned into Latin than their opposition begins. For they strenuously defend the veneration of images, though they condemn idolatry. But these ingenious men deny that the honor which they pay to images is worship, as if, when compared with ancient idolatry, it were possible to see any difference. Idolaters pretended that they worshipped the celestial gods, though under corporeal figures which represented them. What else do our adversaries pretend? But is God satisfied with such excuses? Did the prophets on this account cease to rebuke the madness of the Egyptians, when, out of the secret mysteries of their theology, they drew subtle distinctions under which to screen themselves? What too do we suppose the brazen serpent which the Jews worshipped to have been, but something which they honored as a representation of God? "The Gentiles," says Ambrose (in Ps. 118), "worship wood, because they think it an image of God, whereas the invisible image of God is not in that which is seen, but precisely in that which is not seen." But what is done today? Do they not prostrate themselves before images, as if God were present in them? Unless they supposed the power and grace of God to be attached to pictures and statues, would they flee to them when they desired to pray?

I have not yet adverted to the grosser superstitions, though these cannot be confined to the ignorant, since they are approved by public consent. They adorn their idols now with flowers and chaplets, now with robes, vests, girdles, purses, and frivolities of every kind. They light tapers and burn incense before them, and carry them on their shoulders in solemn state. They assemble from long distances to one statue, though they have similar things at home. Likewise, though in one shrine there may be several images of the Virgin Mary or someone else, they pass these by, and one is frequented as if it were more divine. When they pray to the image of Christopher or Barbara, they mutter the Lord's Prayer and the angel's salutation. The fairer or dingier the images are, the greater is their excellence supposed to be. They find new commendation in fabulous miracles. Some they pretend to have spoken, others to have extinguished a fire in the church by trampling on it, others to have moved of their own accord to a new abode, others to have dropped from heaven. While the whole world teems with these and similar delusions, and the fact is perfectly notorious, we who have brought back the worship of the one God to the rule of his Word, who are blameless in this matter, and have purged our churches, not only of idolatry but of superstition also, are accused of violating the worship of God, because we have discarded the worship of images, that is, as we call it, *idolatry*, but as our adversaries will have it, *idolodulia*.

But besides the clear testimonies which occur everywhere in Scripture, we are also supported by the authority of the ancient Church. All the writers of a purer age describe the abuse of images among the Gentiles as not differing from what is seen in the world in the present day; and their observations on the subject are not less applicable to our age than to the persons whom they then censured. As to the charge they bring against us, of discarding images as well as the bones and relics of saints, it is easily answered. For none of these things ought to be assessed at more than the brazen serpent, and the reasons for removing them were not less valid than those of Hezekiah for breaking it. It is certain that the *idolomania* with which the minds of men are now fascinated cannot be cured otherwise than by removing the material cause of the infatuation. We have too much experience of the absolute truth of Augustine's sentiment (*Epistolae* 49): "No man prays or worships looking on an image without being impressed with the idea that it is listening to him." Similarly (in Ps. 115:4): "Images are more likely to mislead an unhappy soul having a mouth, eyes, ears, and feet than to correct it, because they neither speak, nor see, nor hear, nor walk." Again: "The effect as it were extorted by the external shape is that the soul living in a body thinks a body which it sees so very like its own must be percipient." As to the matter of relics, it is almost incredible how impudently the world has been cheated. I can mention three relics of our Savior's circumcision; likewise fourteen nails which are exhibited for the three by which he was fixed to the cross; three robes for that seamless one on which the soldiers cast lots; two inscriptions that were placed over the cross; three blades of the spear by which our Savior's side was pierced, and about five sets of linen clothes which wrapped his body in the tomb. Besides they show all the articles used at the institution of the Lord's Supper, and endless absurdities of this kind. There is no saint of any celebrity of whom two or three bodies are not in existence. I can name the place where a piece of pumice-stone was long held in high veneration as the skull of Peter. Decency will not permit me to mention fouler exhibitions. It is therefore undeservedly that we are blamed for having studied to purify the Church of God from such impurities.

In regard to the worship of God, our adversaries next accuse us, because, in omitting trivialities not only foolish but also tending to hypocrisy, we worship God more simply. That we have in no respect detracted from the spiritual worship of God is attested by fact. Indeed, when it had in a great measure sunk into a desuetude, we have reinstated it in its former rights. Let us now see whether they are justly angry with us. In regard to doctrine, I maintain that we make common cause with the prophets. For, next to idolatry, there is nothing for which they rebuke the people more sharply than for falsely imagining that the worship of God consisted in external show. For what is the sum of their declarations? That God neither cares for nor values ceremonies considered only in themselves; that he looks to the faith and truth of the heart; and that the only end for which he commanded and for which he approves ceremonies is that they may be pure exercises of faith, and prayer, and praise. The writings of all the prophets are full of evidence to this effect. Nor, as I have observed, was there anything for which they labored more. Now it cannot without effrontery be denied that when the Reformers appeared the world was more than ever afflicted with this blindness. It was therefore absolutely necessary to urge men with these prophetic rebukes and divert them, as by force, from that infatuation, lest they might any longer imagine that God was satisfied with bare ceremonies, as children are with shows. There was a like necessity for urging the doctrine of the spiritual worship of God—a doctrine which had vanished from the minds of men. That both of these things have been and still are being faithfully performed by us, both our writings and our sermons clearly prove.

In inveighing against ceremonies themselves, and also in abrogating a greater part of them, we confess that there is indeed some difference between us and the prophets. They inveighed against their countrymen for confining the worship of God to external ceremonies, which, however, God himself had instituted; we complain that the same honor is paid to frivolities of man's devising. They condemned superstition, but left untouched a multitude of ceremonies which God had enjoined, and which were useful and appropriate to an age of tutelage; our business has been to correct numerous rites which had either crept in through oversight or been turned to abuse, and which, moreover, by no means accorded with the time. For if we are not to throw everything into confusion, we must always bear in mind the distinction between the old and the new dispensations, and the fact that ceremonies, whose observance was useful under the law, are now not only superfluous but absurd and wicked. When Christ was absent and not yet manifested, ceremonies by shadowing him forth nourished the hope of his advent in the breasts of believers; but now they only obscure his present and conspicuous glory. We see what God himself has done. For those ceremonies which he had commanded for a time he has now abrogated forever. Paul explains the reason: first, that since the body has been manifested in Christ, the types had to be withdrawn; and second, that God is now pleased to instruct his Church in a different manner (Gal. 4:3ff.; Col. 2:8, 16, 17). Since then God has freed his Church from the bondage which he himself had imposed upon it, what perversity, I ask, is this that demands from men a new bondage in place of the old? Since God has prescribed a certain economy, how presumptuous to set up one contrary to it and openly repudiated by him! But the worst of all is that though God has so often and strictly banned from worship all fabrications made by men, the only worship paid to him consisted of human inventions. What ground, then, have our enemies to clamor that in this matter we have dissipated religion to the winds? First, we have not laid even a finger on anything which Christ does not discount as worthless when he declares that it is vain to worship God with human traditions. The thing might perhaps have been more tolerable if the only effect had been that men's labor was lost by an unavailing worship. But since, as I have observed, God in many passages forbids any new worship unsanctioned by his Word, declares that he is gravely offended by such audacity, and threatens it with severe punishment, it is clear that the reformation which we have introduced was demanded by a strong necessity.

I am not unaware how difficult it is to persuade the world that God rejects and even abominates everything devised for worship by human reason. The grounds for this error are numerous. "Everyone thinks highly of his own," as the old proverb expresses it. Hence the offspring of our own brain delights us more; and besides, as Paul admits (Col. 2:23), this fictitious worship often presents some show of wisdom. Besides, as it has for the most part an external splendor which pleases the eye, it is more agreeable to our carnal nature than that which alone God requires and approves, but which is less ostentatious. But there is nothing which so blinds the minds of men, so that they judge wrongly in this matter, as hypocrisy. For while it is incumbent on true worshippers to give heart and mind, men always want to invent a mode of serving God quite different from this, their object being to perform for him certain bodily observances and keep the mind to themselves. Moreover, they imagine that when they thrust external pomps upon him, they have by this artifice evaded the necessity of giving themselves. This is the reason why they submit to innumerable observances which without measure and without end miserably exhaust them, and why they choose to wander in a perpetual labyrinth, rather than worship God simply in spirit and in truth.

It is, then, impudent calumny in our enemies to accuse us of alluring men by compliance and indulgence. For were the option given, there is nothing which the carnal man would not prefer to do, rather than consent to worship God as prescribed by our doctrine. It is easy to use the words faith and repentance, but the things are most difficult to perform. Whoever therefore makes the worship of God consist in these by no means loosens the reins of discipline, but compels men to the course which they are most afraid to take. Of this we have most trustworthy proof from fact.

Men will allow themselves to be constrained by numerous severe laws, to be tied to numerous laborious observances, and to bear a severe and heavy yoke; in short, there is no annoyance to which they will not submit, provided there be no mention of the heart. Hence, it appears that there is nothing to which the human mind is more averse than to that spiritual truth which is the constant theme of our sermons, and nothing with which it is more engrossed than that splendid show on which our adversaries so strongly insist. The very majesty of God extorts this much from us, that we are unable to withdraw entirely from his service. Therefore, as we cannot evade the necessity of worshipping him, it remains for us to seek out indirect substitutes, lest we be obliged to come directly into his presence; or rather, by means of external ceremonies like specious masks we hide the inward malice of the heart and interpose bodily observances like a wall of partition lest we be compelled to come to him with the heart. It is with the greatest reluctance that the world allows itself to be driven from such subterfuges as these; and hence the outcry against us for having dragged them from the lurking places, where they safely played with God, into the light of day.

In prayer we have corrected three things. Discarding the intercession of saints, we have brought men back to Christ, that they might learn both to invoke the Father in his name and trust in him as Mediator; and we have taught them to pray first with firm and solid confidence, and second with understanding also, instead of muttering over confused prayers in an unknown tongue as they did before. Here we are assailed with bitter reproaches for being offensive to the saints, and also for depriving believers of an immense privilege. Both charges we deny. It is no injury to saints not to permit the office of Christ to be attributed to them. There is no honor of which we deprive them, except one improperly and rashly bestowed upon them by human error. I shall mention nothing which may not be expressly pointed out. First, when men are about to pray, they imagine God to be at a great distance, and that they cannot have access to him unless conducted by some patron. Nor is this false opinion current among the rude and unlearned only, but even those who would be thought leaders of the blind entertain it. Then in looking for patrons, everyone follows his own fancy. One selects Mary, another Michael, another Peter. Christ they very seldom honor with a place in the list. Indeed, there is scarcely one in a hundred who would not be amazed, as at some new prodigy, were he to hear Christ named as an intercessor. Therefore, passing Christ by, they all trust to the patronage of saints. Then superstition creeps in further and further, till they invoke the saints promiscuously, just as they do God. I admit, indeed, that when they desire to speak more definitely, all they ask of the saints is to assist them before God with their prayers. But more frequently they lose this distinction, and address and implore at one time God, and at another the saints, just according to the impulse of the moment. Indeed each saint has a peculiar province allotted to him. One gives rain, another fair weather; one delivers from fever, another from shipwreck. But, to say nothing of these profane heathen delusions which everywhere prevail in churches, this one impiety may suffice for all: that, in inviting intercessors from this quarter and from that, the whole world neglects Christ, whom alone God has set forth, and confides more in the patronage of the saints than in the protection of God.

But our critics, even those of them who have rather more regard to equity, blame us for excess in having discarded entirely from our prayers the mention of dead saints. But I should like to know from them how they conceive those to sin, who faithfully observe the rule laid down by Christ, the Supreme Teacher, and by the prophets and apostles, and do not omit anything which either the Holy Spirit has taught in Scripture or the servants of God have practiced from the beginning of the world to the age of the apostles? There is scarcely any subject on which the Holy Spirit more carefully prescribes than on the proper method of prayer. But there is not a syllable which teaches us to have recourse to the assistance of dead saints. Many of the prayers offered up by believers are extant. In none of them is there even a single example of such a thing. Sometimes, indeed, the Israelites entreated God to remember Abraham, Isaac, and Jacob, and David similarly. But all they meant by such expressions was that he should be mindful of the covenant which he had made with them, and bless their posterity according to his promise. For the covenant of grace, which was ultimately to be ratified in Christ, those holy patriarchs had received in their own name and that of their posterity. Wherefore the faithful of the Israelite Church do not, by such mention of the patriarchs, seek intercession from the dead, but simply appeal to the promise which had been deposited with them until it should be fully ratified in the mind of Christ. What a mad infatuation, then, to abandon the form of prayer which the Lord has commended, and without injunction or example to introduce into prayer the intercession of saints! But briefly to conclude this point, I take my stand on the declaration of Paul, that no prayer is genuine which does not spring from faith, and that faith cometh by the Word of God (Rom. 10:17). In these words, he has, if I am not mistaken, distinctly declared that the Word of God is the only sure foundation for prayer. And while he elsewhere says that every action of our lives should be preceded by faith, that is by assurance of conscience, he shows that this is specially requisite in prayer, more so indeed than in any other matter. It is, however, still more relevant to the present point, when he declares that prayer depends on the Word of God. For it is just as if he had prohibited all men from opening their mouths until such time as God put words into them. This is our wall of brass, which all the powers of hell will in vain attempt to break down. Since, then, there exists a clear command to invoke God only; since again one Mediator is offered, whose intercession must support our prayers; since a promise has, moreover, been added, that whatever we ask in the name of Christ we shall obtain, men must pardon us if we follow the certain truth of God rather than their frivolous fictions.

It is surely incumbent on those who in their prayers introduce the intercession of the dead, that they may be thereby assisted more easily to obtain what they ask, to prove one of two things: either that they are so taught by the Word of God, or that men have license to pray as they please. But in regard to the former, it is plain that they are destitute of both scriptural testimony and approved example of the saints. As to the latter, Paul declares that none can invoke God save those who have been taught by his Word to pray. On this depends the confidence with which it is fitting that pious minds be supplied and instructed when they engage in prayer. The world supplicates God, dubious meanwhile of success. For it relies on no promise, nor does it perceive the force of what is meant by having a Mediator through whom it will assuredly obtain what it asks. Moreover God enjoins us to come free from doubt (Matt. 21:22). Accordingly prayer proceeding from true faith obtains favor with God whereas prayer accompanied with distrust of this kind rather alienates him from us. For this is the proper mark which discriminates between genuine invocation of the one God and the profane wandering prayers of the heathen. Indeed, this lacking, prayer ceases to be divine worship. It is to this James refers when he says: *If any man lack wisdom, let him ask of God; but let him ask in faith, doubting nothing. For he that doubteth is like a wave of the sea, driven with the winds, and tossed* (James 1:6). It is not surprising that without Christ as true Mediator, he thus wavers in uncertainty and distrust. For, as Paul declares (Rom. 5:2; Eph. 2:18), it is through Christ only that we have boldness and access with confidence to the Father. We have, therefore, taught men when brought to Christ no longer to doubt and vacillate in their prayers, as they were wont to do; we bid them rest secure in the Word of the Lord, which, when once it penetrates the soul, drives far from it all the doubt that is repugnant to faith.

It remains to point out the third fault in prayer which I said that we have corrected. Whereas men generally prayed in an unknown tongue, we have taught them to pray with understanding. Every man accordingly is taught by our doctrine to pray in private so that he understands what he asks of God. So also the public prayers in our churches are framed so as to be understood by all. Natural reason prescribes that it should be so, even if God had given no precept on the subject. For the design of prayer is to make God the witness and confidant of our necessities, and as it were to pour out our hearts before him. But nothing is more at variance with this than to move the tongue without thought and intelligence. Yet to such a degree of absurdity had it come, that to pray in the vulgar tongue was almost turned into an offense against religion. I can name an archbishop who threatened with incarceration and the severer penalties anyone who should repeat the Lord's Prayer aloud in any language but Latin. The general belief, however, was that it did not matter in what language a man prayed at home, provided he had what was called a final intention in praying. But in churches it was held to belong to the dignity of the service that Latin should be the only language in which prayers were couched.

There seems, as I have just said, something monstrous in wishing to hold converse with God in empty sounds of the tongue.

Even if God did not declare his displeasure, nature herself with-out any teacher rejects it. Besides it is easy to infer from the whole tenor of the Scripture how deeply God abominates such an inven-tion. As to the public prayers of the Church, the words of Paul are clear: the unlearned cannot say Amen if the benediction be pro-nounced in an unknown tongue (1 Cor. 14:16). This makes it the more strange that those who first introduced this perverse practice ultimately had the effrontery to maintain that the very thing, which Paul regards as ineffably absurd, was conclusive of the majesty of prayer. Our adversaries may ridicule, if they will, the method by which in our churches all pray together in the popular tongue, and men and women without distinction sing the Psalms; if only the Holy Spirit bears testimony to us from heaven, while he repudiates the confused, unmeaning sounds which are uttered elsewhere, we are content.

In the second principal branch of doctrine, namely that which relates to the grounds of salvation and the method of obtain-ing it, many questions are involved. For when we tell a man to seek righteousness and life outside himself, that is in Christ only, because he has nothing in himself but sin and death, controversy immediately arises about the freedom of the will and its powers. For if man has any ability of his own to serve God, he does not obtain salvation entirely by the grace of Christ, but in part bestows it on himself. On the other hand, if the whole of salvation is attrib-uted to the grace of Christ nothing is left over for man by which, that is by some virtue of his own, he can assist himself to procure salvation. Now our opponents concede that man is assisted by the Holy Spirit in good living, but in such a way that they nevertheless claim for him a share in the operation. This they do, because they do not perceive how deep the wound is which was inflicted on our nature by the fall of our first parents. No doubt, they agree with us in holding the doctrine of original sin; but they afterward modify its effects, maintaining that the powers of man are only weakened, not wholly depraved. Their view then is that man, being tainted with original corruption, is in consequence of the weakening of his powers unable to act aright; but that, being aided by the grace of God, he has something of his own and from himself which he may contribute. Again though we do not deny that man acts spon-taneously and of free will when he is guided by the Holy Spirit, we maintain that his whole nature is so imbued with depravity that of himself he possesses no ability whatever to act aright. Thus far, therefore, we dissent from those who oppose our doctrine, that they neither humble man sufficiently, nor duly estimate the blessing of regeneration, while we so prostrate him that he is reduced to nothing so far as spiritual righteousness is concerned, and must learn to seek it, not partially, but wholly from God. To some not very equitable judges, we seem, perhaps, to carry the matter too far. But there is nothing absurd in our doctrine, and nothing at variance either with Scripture or with the general consent of the ancient Church. Indeed we are able without difficulty to confirm our doctrine to the very letter out of the mouth of Augustine. Accordingly several of those who are otherwise ill disposed to our cause, but somewhat sounder in their judgments, do not venture to contradict us on this head. It is certain, as I have observed, that we differ from others only in this, that by convincing man of his poverty and powerlessness we train him better in true humility, so that renouncing all self-confidence, he throws himself entirely upon God; and similarly in gratitude, so that he ascribes, as in truth he ought, every good thing which he possesses to the kindness of God. They, on the other hand, intoxicating him with a perverse opinion of his own virtue, precipitate his ruin, and fill him up with impudent arrogance against God, so as to ascribe to himself no less than to God the glory of his justification. To these errors they add a third: that in all their discussions concerning the corruption of human nature, they usually stop short with the grosser carnal desires, without touching the deeper-seated diseases which are much more cardinal. Hence it is that those who are trained in their school easily forgive themselves the most shocking sins as no sins at all, if only they are hid.

The next question relates to the merit and value of works. Now we give good works their due praise, nor do we deny that a reward is reserved for them with God. But we make three reservations, on which the whole of our remaining controversy concerning the work of salvation hinges.

First, we maintain that of whatever kind a man's works may be, he is regarded as righteous before God simply on the ground of gratuitous mercy, because God, without any respect to works, freely adopts him in Christ, by imputing the righteousness of

Christ to him as if it were his own. This we call the righteousness of faith, that is when a man, empty and drained of all confidence in works, feels convinced that the only ground of his acceptance with God is a righteousness which is wanting to himself, and is borrowed from Christ. The point on which the world always goes astray (for this error has prevailed in almost every age), is in imagining that man, however partially defective he may be, still in some degree merits the favor of God by works. But Scripture declares: *Cursed is everyone that continueth not in all things that are written in the book of the law to do them* (Gal. 3:10). Under this curse must necessarily lie all who are judged by works, none being exempted except those who entirely renounce all confidence in works and put on Christ, that they may be justified in him by the gratuitous acceptance of God. The ground of our justification, therefore, is that God reconciles us to himself, from regard not to our works but to Christ alone, and by gratuitous adoption makes us his own children instead of children of wrath. So long as God regards our works, he finds no reason why he ought to love us. Wherefore it is necessary that he should bury our sins, impute to us the obedience of Christ which alone can stand his scrutiny, and adopt us as righteous through his merits. This is the clear and uniform doctrine of Scripture, *witnessed*, as Paul says, *by the law and the prophets* (Rom. 3:21), and so explained by the Gospel that a clearer law cannot be desired. Paul contrasts the righteousness of the law with the righteousness of the Gospel, placing the former in works, and the latter in the grace of Christ (Rom. 10:5, etc.). That we are judged righteous in the sight of God he does not divide in two between works and Christ, but ascribes it to Christ entirely.

There are here two questions: first whether the glory of our salvation is to be divided between ourselves and God; and second whether as in the sight of God our conscience can with safety put any confidence in works. On the former question, Paul's decision is: let every mouth *be stopped, and the whole world become guilty before God. All have sinned, and come short of the glory of God, being justified freely by his grace, through the redemption that is in Christ Jesus;* and this *to declare his righteousness, that he might be just, and the justifier of him which believeth in Jesus* (Rom. 3:19, etc.). Hence he declares all glorying in the flesh to be excluded. We simply follow this definition, while our opponents maintain that man is not justified by the grace of God, in any sense which does not reserve part of the praise for his own works.

On the second question, Paul reasons thus: *If they which are of the law be heirs, faith is made void, and the promise made of none effect.* Thence he concludes: *it is of faith, . . . to the end the promise might be sure to all thy seed* (Rom. 4:14, 16). And again: *Being justified by faith, we have peace with God* (Rom. 5:1), and no longer dread his presence. But he realizes that everyone feels in his own experience that our consciences cannot but be vexed and disquieted with perpetual unrest so long as we look for protection from works, and that we enjoy serene and placid tranquillity only when we have resort to Christ as the one haven of true confidence. We add nothing to Paul's doctrine; but that restless dubiety of conscience, which he regards as absurd, is placed by our opponents among the primary axioms of their faith.

The second reservation which we make relates to the remission of sins. Our opponents, not being able to deny that men during their whole life walk haltingly and often even fall, are obliged to confess, whether they will or not, that all need pardon in order to supply their want of righteousness. But then they invent satisfactions, with which those who have sinned may purchase back the favor of God. In this class they place first contrition, and next works which they call works of supererogation and the penalties which God inflicts on sinners. But as they are still sensible that these compensations fall far short of the just measure required, they call in the aid of a new species of satisfaction from another quarter, namely from the benefit of the keys. They say that by the keys the treasury of the Church is unlocked, so that what is wanting to ourselves is supplied out of the merits of Christ and the saints. We, on the contrary, maintain that the sins of men are forgiven freely, and we acknowledge no other satisfaction than that which Christ accomplished, when, by the sacrifice of his death, he expiated our sins. Therefore we preach that it is by the benefit of Christ alone that we are reconciled to God, and that no compensations are taken into account, because our heavenly Father, content with the sole expiation of Christ, requires none from us. In the Scriptures we have clear proof of this doctrine of ours, which indeed ought to be called not ours, but rather that of the Church Catholic. For the only method of regaining the divine favor is set forth by the apostle, that *he hath made him to be sin for us who knew no sin, that we might be made the righteousness of God in him* (2 Cor. 5:21). And in another passage, where he is speaking of the remission of sins, he declares that through it righteousness without works is imputed to us (Rom. 4:5). We therefore strenuously denounce for the execrable blasphemy it in fact is, the idea of our adversaries, of meriting reconciliation with God by satisfaction, and buying off the penalties due to his justice, for it destroys the doctrine which Isaiah delivers concerning Christ, that *the chastisement of our peace was upon him* (Isa. 53:5).

The absurd fiction concerning works of supererogation we discard for many reasons, but two are of more than sufficient weight: one, that it is impossible to tolerate the idea of man being able to perform to God more than he ought; and the other, that as by the term supererogation they for the most part understand voluntary acts of worship which their own brain has devised, and which they obtrude upon God, it is lost labor and pains, so far are such acts from being expiations appeasing the divine anger. Moreover, this mixing up of the blood of Christ with the blood of martyrs and forming out of them a heterogeneous mass of merits or satisfactions to buy off the punishments due to sin is something we neither tolerate nor ought to tolerate. For, as Augustine says (in *Joann. Ev. Tract.* 84): "No martyr's blood has been shed for the remission of sins. This was the work of Christ alone, and in this work he has bestowed something not to be imitated but to be gratefully received." With Augustine, Leo admirably agrees, when he thus writes (*Ep.* 81 and 97): "Though precious in the sight of God has been the death of his many saints, yet no innocent man's slaughter was the propitiation of the world; the just received crowns, did not give them, and the constancy of the faithful has furnished examples of patience, not gifts of righteousness."

Our third and last reservation relates to the recompense of works. We maintain that it depends not on their own value or merit, but rather on the mere benignity of God. Indeed our opponents themselves admit that there is no proportion between the merit of the work and its reward. But they do not attend to what is of primary moment in the matter, that the good works of believers are never so pure as to be able to please without pardon. They do not consider, I say, that they are always sprinkled with some spots or blemishes, because they never proceed from that pure and perfect love of God which is demanded by the law. We therefore teach that the good works of believers always lack the spotless purity which can stand the inspection of God; indeed, that when they are tried by the strict rule of justice, they are to a certain extent impure. But when once God has graciously adopted believers, he not only accepts and loves their persons, but their works also, to dignify them with a reward. In a word, as we said of man, so we may say of works: they are justified not by their own desert, but by the merits of Christ alone, the faults by which they would otherwise displease being covered by the sacrifice of Christ. This consideration is of very great practical importance, both in retaining men in the fear of God, that they may not arrogate to their works what proceeds from his fatherly kindness, and also in inspiring them with the best consolation, lest they despond when they reflect on the imperfection or impurity of their works, by reminding them that God, of his paternal indulgence, is pleased to pardon it.

We come now to the sacraments, in which we have not made any correction which we are unable to defend by the sure and approved authority of God. Whereas seven sacraments were supposed to have been instituted by Christ, we have discarded five of this number and have demonstrated them to be ceremonies of man's devising, with the exception of marriage, which we acknowledge to have been indeed commanded by God, but not in order that it might be a sacrament. Nor is it a dispute about nothing when we separate rites thus superadded on the part of men, even if in other respects they should be neither wicked nor useless, from those symbols which Christ with his own lips commended to us, and was pleased to make the attestation of spiritual gifts—gifts to which, as they are not in the power of man, men are quite unable to testify. It is assuredly no vulgar matter to seal upon our hearts the sacred favor of God, to offer Christ, and represent the blessings we enjoy in him. This being the office of the sacraments of Christ, failure to discriminate between them and the rites originating with man is to confound heaven with earth. Here, indeed, a twofold error had prevailed. Making no distinction between things human and divine, they seriously derogated from the sacred Word of God, on which the whole power of the sacraments depend; and they also falsely imagined Christ to be the author of rites which had no higher than a human origin.

From baptism similarly we have cut away many additions which were partly useless, and partly, from their superstitious tendency, harmful. We know the form of baptism which the apostles received from Christ, which they observed during their lifetime, and which they finally left to posterity. But the simplicity which had been approved by the authority of Christ, and the practice of the apostles, did not satisfy succeeding ages. I am not at present discussing whether those people were influenced by sound reasons, who afterward added chrism, salt, spittle, and tapers. I only say what everyone must know that to such a height had superstition or folly risen that more value was set on these additions than on the genuineness of baptism itself. We have studied also to banish the preposterous confidence which stopped short at the external act and paid not the least regard to Christ. For in the schools as well as in sermons, they so extolled the efficacy of signs that instead of directing men to Christ, they taught them to confide in the visible elements. Last, we have recalled the ancient custom that the administration of the sacraments at the same time be accompanied by doctrine, expounding with all diligence and fidelity both their advantages and their legitimate use, so that in this respect even our opponents cannot find anything to criticize. But nothing is more alien to the nature of a sacrament than to set before the people an empty spectacle, unaccompanied with explanation of the mystery. There is a well-known passage, quoted by Gratian from Augustine: "If the word is wanting, the water is nothing but an element." What he means by *word* he immediately explains when he says: "That is, the word of faith, which we preach." Our opponents therefore ought not to think it a novelty when we disapprove of the exhibition of the sign, separated from an understanding of the mystery. For this is a sacrilegious divorce, which reverses the order instituted by Christ. Another additional fault in the mode of administration commonly used elsewhere is that the thing which they consider as a religious act is not understood, just as is the case in magical incantations.

I have already observed that the other sacrament of the Christian Church, the Holy Supper of our Lord, was not only corrupted but nearly abolished. Wherefore it was the more necessary for us to labor in restoring its purity. First, it was necessary to eradicate from the minds of men that impious fiction of a sacrifice, the source of many absurdities. For, besides the introduction of a rite of oblation in opposition to the express institution of Christ, there had been added a most pestilential opinion that this act of oblation was an expiation for sin. Thus the dignity of the priesthood, which belonged exclusively to Christ, had been transferred to mortal men, and the virtue of his death to their own act. Thus also its application had availed for the living and the dead. We have, therefore, abrogated that fictitious immolation and restored communion, which had been in large measure rendered obsolete. For provided men went once a year to the Lord's Table, they thought it enough for all the remainder of that period to be spectators of what was done by the priest, under the pretext, indeed, of administering the Lord's Supper, but without any vestige of the Supper in it. For what are the words of the Lord? Take, he says, and distribute among yourselves. But in the Mass, instead of taking, there is a pretense of offering, while there is no distribution, and even no invitation. The priest, like a member cut off from the rest of the body, prepares it for himself alone and alone consumes it. How immense the difference between the things! We have besides restored to the people the use of the cup, which though it was not only permitted but committed to them by our Lord, was taken from them, it could only be at the suggestion of Satan. Of ceremonies, there are many which we have discarded, partly because they had multiplied beyond measure, partly because some savored too much of Judaism, and others, being the inventions of ignorant men, ill accorded with the seriousness of so high a mystery. But, granted that there was no other evil in them than that they had crept in through oversight, was it not a sufficient ground for their abolition that we saw the vulgar gazing upon them in stupid amazement?

In condemning the fiction of transubstantiation, and likewise the custom of keeping and carrying about the bread, we were impelled by a stronger necessity. First, it is repugnant to the plain words of Christ; and second, it is abhorrent to the very nature of a sacrament. For there is no sacrament when there is no visible symbol to correspond to the spiritual truth which it represents. And with regard to the Supper, what Paul says is clear: *We being many are one bread, and one body: for we are all partakers of that one bread* (1 Cor. 10:17). Where is the anthology or similitude of a visible sign in the Supper to correspond to the body and blood of our Lord, if there is neither bread to eat, nor wine to drink, but only some empty phantom to mock the eye? Add that to this fiction a worse superstition perpetually adheres, that, as we have seen, men cling to the bread as if to God, and worship it as God. While the sacrament ought to have been a means of elevating pious minds to heaven, the sacred symbols of the Supper were abused for an entirely different purpose, and men, content with gazing upon them and worshipping them, never once raised their mind to Christ.

The carrying about of the bread in solemn state, or setting it on an elevated spot to be adored, are corruptions quite alien to the institution of Christ. For in the Supper the Lord sets before us his body and blood, but it is in order that we may eat, and drink. Accordingly, in the first place he gives the command, by which he bids us take, eat, and drink; and then in the next place he adds and annexes the promise, in which he testifies that what we eat is his body, and what we drink is his blood. Therefore those who keep the bread set apart or carry it about to be worshipped, seeing they separate the promise from the command, in other words sever an indissoluble tie, imagine indeed that they have the body of Christ, whereas in fact they have nothing but an idol which they have devised for themselves. For this promise of Christ, by which he offers his own body and blood under the symbols of bread and wine, belongs to those only who receive them at his hand, to celebrate the mystery in the manner which he enjoins. But those who pervert them at their own will to a different purpose, and so have not the promise, retain only a fiction of their own devising.

Last, we have revived the practice of explaining the doctrine and unfolding the mystery to the people whereas formerly the priest not only used a strange tongue, but muttered in a whisper the words by which he pretended to consecrate the bread and wine. Here our critics have nothing to grumble at, unless it be that we have simply followed the command of Christ. For he did not by a silent exorcism command the bread to become his body, but with a clear voice declared to his apostles that he gave them his body.

At the same time, as in the case of baptism, so also in the case of the Lord's Supper, we explain to the people faithfully and as carefully as we can its end, efficacy, advantages, and use. First, we exhort all to come with faith, that by means of it they may inwardly discern the thing which is visibly represented, that is the spiritual food by which alone their souls are nourished unto life eternal. We hold that in this ordinance the Lord does not promise, or set forth by signs, anything which he does not exhibit in reality. We therefore preach that the body and blood of Christ are both offered to us by the Lord in the Supper and received by us. Nor do we thus teach that the bread and wine are symbols, without immediately adding that the truth they represent is conjoined with them. We are not silent about the nature and excellence of the fruit that comes to us from this source, and how noble the pledge of life and salvation which our consciences therein receive. Nor indeed will anyone with candor deny that with us this solemn ordinance is much more clearly explained, and its dignity more fully extolled, than is the rule elsewhere.

In the government of the Church, we do not differ from others in anything for which we cannot give a most sufficient reason. The pastoral office we have restored, both according to the apostolic rule and the practice of the primitive Church, by insisting that everyone who rules in the Church shall also teach. We hold that none are to be continued in the office but those who are diligent in performing its duties. In selecting them our advice has been that this is a matter where greater and more religious care should be exercised, and we have ourselves studied so to act. It is well known what kind of examination bishops conduct by means of their suffragans or vicars. We might even be able to conjecture what its nature is from the fruit which it produces. It is needless to observe how many lazy and good-for-nothing persons they everywhere promote to the honorable rank of the priesthood. Among us, even if some ministers be found of no great learning, none is admitted who is not at least tolerably fit to teach. That all are not more perfect is to be imputed more to the calamity of the times than to us. This, however, is and always will be our just boast, that the ministers of our Church cannot seem to have been carelessly chosen if they be compared with others. But while we are superior in a considerable degree in the matter of trial and election, in this we particularly excel, that no man holds the pastoral office among us without executing its duties. Accordingly none of our churches is seen without the ordinary preaching of the Word of God.

As it would shame our adversaries to deny these facts (for in a matter so clear, what would they gain by denial?), they quarrel with us, first concerning the right and power of ordination, and second concerning its form. They quote ancient canons, which give the superintendence of this matter to the bishops and clergy. They allege a constant succession by which this right has been handed down to them, even from the apostles themselves. They deny that it can be lawfully transferred elsewhere. I wish they had by their merit retained a title to this boasted possession. But if we consider first the order in which for several ages bishops have been advanced to this dignity, next the manner in which they conduct themselves in it, and last the kind of persons whom they are accustomed to ordain and to whom they commit the government of ' churches, we shall see that this succession on which they pride themselves was long ago interrupted. The ancient canons require that he who is to be admitted to the office of bishop or presbyter shall previously undergo a strict examination, both as to life and doctrine. Clear evidence of this is extant among the acts of the fourth African Council. Moreover, the magistracy and people had a discretionary power of approving or refusing the individual who was nominated by the clergy, in order that no man might be intruded on those unwilling or not consenting. "Let him who is to preside over all," says Leo (*Ep.* 90), "be elected by all; for he who is appointed, while unknown and unexamined, must of necessity be violently intruded." Again (*Ep.* 87): "Let regard be had to the attestation of honorable men, the approval of the clergy, and the consent of the magistracy and people. Reason permits no other mode of procedure." Cyprian also contends for the very same thing, and indeed in stronger terms, affirming it as sanctioned by divine authority that the priest, the people being present, be elected before the eyes of all, that he may be approved as fit and worthy by the testimony of all. While this rule was in force, the Church was in a state of good order, for the letters of Gregory are full of passages which show that it was carefully observed in his day.

As the Holy Spirit in Scripture imposes on all bishops the necessity of teaching, so in the ancient Church it would have been thought monstrous to nominate a bishop who would not by teaching demonstrate that he was a pastor also. Nor were they admitted to the office on any other condition. The same rule prevailed in regard to presbyters, each being set apart to a particular parish. Hence those decrees: "Let them not involve themselves in secular affairs, let them not make distant excursions from their churches, let them not be long absent." Then it was enjoined by synodal decrees that at the ordination of a bishop all the other bishops of the provinces should assemble, or if this could not be conveniently done, at least three should be present. The object of this was that no man might force an entrance by tumult, or creep in by stealth, or insinuate himself by surreptitious artifices. To the ordination of a presbyter, each bishop admitted a council of his own presbyters. These things, which could be narrated more fully and confirmed more accurately in a set discourse, I mention here only in passing because they afford an easy means of judging how much consideration is due to this smoke of succession which our bishops emit to blind us.

They maintain that Christ left as a heritage to the apostles the sole right of appointing to churches whomever they pleased; and they complain that, in exercising the ministry without their authority, we have invaded their province with impious audacity. How do they prove it? Because they have succeeded the apostles in an unbroken series. But is this enough, when all other things are different? It would be ridiculous to say so: they do, however, say it. In their elections, no account is taken either of life or doctrine. The right of voting is wrested from the people. Indeed, even the rest of the clergy have been excluded and the dignitaries have attracted all the power to themselves. The Roman pontiff, again, wresting it from the provincial bishop, arrogates it to himself alone. Then, as if they had been appointed to secular dominion, there is nothing of which they think less than episcopal duty. In short, while they seem to have entered into a conspiracy to have no kind of resemblance either to the apostles or to the holy Fathers of the Church, they merely cover themselves with the pretense that they are descended from them in an unbroken succession—as if Christ had ever enacted it into a law, that whatever might be the conduct of those who presided over the Church, they should be recognized as holding the place of the apostles; or as if the office were some hereditary possession, which passes alike to the worthy and the unworthy. Moreover, as is said of the Milesians, they have taken precautions not to admit a single worthy person into their society; or if perhaps by error they have admitted him, they do not permit him to remain. It is of the majority I speak, for I do not deny that there are a few good men among them. But they are either silent through fear, or given no hearing. Here are persons who persecute the doctrine of Christ with fire and sword, who permit no man with impunity to speak sincerely of Christ, who in every possible way impede the course of truth, who strenuously resist our attempt to raise the Church from the distressed condition into which they have brought her, who suspect all those who take a deep and pious interest in the welfare of the Church, and either keep them out of the ministry, or, if they have been admitted, thrust them out—such persons might indeed be expected with their own hands to install into the office faithful ministers to instruct the people in pure religion!

But since the view of Gregory has passed into a common proverb, that "those who abuse privilege deserve to lose privilege," they must either become entirely different from what they are, and select a different sort to govern the Church, and adopt a different method of election, or they must cease to complain that they are improperly and injuriously despoiled of what in justice belonged to them. Or, if they want greater frankness, let them obtain their bishoprics by different means from those by which they have obtained them, ordain others to the office in a different method and manner, and, if they wish to be recognized as bishops, fulfill their duty by feeding the people. If they would retain the power of nominating and ordaining, let them restore that just and serious examination of life and doctrine, which has for many centuries been obsolete among them. But this one reason ought to be as good as a thousand, that any man, who by his conduct shows he is an enemy of sound doctrine, whatever title he may meanwhile boast, has lost all title to authority in the Church. We know what injunctions ancient councils gave concerning the heretic, and what power they leave him. Certainly they expressly forbid any man to apply to him for ordination. No one, therefore, can lay claim to the right of ordaining, who does not by purity of doctrine preserve the unity of the Church. We maintain that those who in the present day in the name of bishops preside over churches are such unfaithful ministers and guardians of sound doctrine that they are rather its bitterest enemies. We maintain that their sole aim is to banish Christ and the truth of his Gospel, and sanction idolatry and impiety, the most pernicious and deadly errors. We maintain that they not only in word pertinaciously attack the true doctrine of godliness, but are infuriated against all who would rescue it from obscurity. Against the many impediments which they throw in the way, we studiously expend our labor on behalf of the Church. For so doing, they expostulate with us that we make an illegal incursion into their province.

As to the form or ceremony of ordination, this is indeed a mighty matter about which to worry us. Because with us the hands of priests are not anointed, because we do not breathe into their faces, because we do not clothe them in white and garments of this kind, they think our ordination is not duly performed. But we read of no other ceremony in ancient times than the laying on of hands. Those other forms are recent, and have nothing to recommend them but the exceeding scrupulousness with which they are now generally observed. But how much is this to the point? In matters so important, a higher than human authority is required. Hence, as often as the circumstances of the times demand, we are at liberty to change such rites as men have invented without express sanction, while those of less antiquity are of much less importance. They put a chalice and paten into the hands of those whom they ordain to be priests. Why? That they may empower them to sacrifice. But by what command? Christ never conferred this function on the apostles, nor did he ever wish it to be undertaken by their successors. It is absurd, therefore, to trouble us about the form of ordination, in which we differ neither from the rule of Christ, nor from the practice of the apostles, nor from the custom of the ancient Church, whereas that form of theirs, which they accuse us of neglecting, they are unable to defend by the Word of God, by sound reason, or by the pretext of antiquity.

On the subject of ecclesiastical rule, there are laws out of which we readily adopt those that are not snares for the conscience, or that contribute to the preservation of common order; but those which had either been tyrannically imposed to hold consciences in bondage, or contributed rather to superstition than to edification, we were forced to abrogate. Here our enemies first charge us with fastidiousness and undue haste, and second accuse us of seeking carnal indulgence, by shaking off the yoke of discipline in order that we may act the wanton as we please. But, as I have already observed, we are by no means averse to the reverent observance of whatever rules are fitted to ensure that all things be done decently and in order; nor, in regard to every single observance which we have abrogated, do we refuse to show cause why we were required to do so. Assuredly there is no difficulty in proving that the Church labored grievously under a load of human traditions, and that it was necessary in her interest that this load should be lessened. There is a well-known complaint by Augustine, in which he deplores it as the calamity of his time that the Church, which God in his mercy wished to be free, was even then so overburdened that the condition of the Jews was more tolerable *(Ep. secunda ad Januarium)*. It is probable that since that period the number has increased almost tenfold. Even more has the rigorous exaction of them increased. What then if that holy man were now to rise and behold the countless multitude of laws under which miserable consciences groan oppressed? What if, on the other hand, he were to see the strictness with which the observance of them is enforced? Those who censure us will perhaps object that we might with Augustine have lamented over anything which displeased us, but that we ought not to have put our hand to the work of correction. This objection is easily refuted. For this pernicious error of supposing that human laws are necessarily observed had to be corrected. As I have said, we do not deny that laws enacted with a view to external policy ought to be carefully obeyed, but for ruling conscience, we hold that there is no legislator but God. To him alone then let this authority be reserved, which he claims for himself in many passages of Scripture. In this matter, first the honor of God was subverted, from which it is impious to derogate in any degree, and then also genuine liberty of conscience, which as Paul strenuously insists, must not be subjected to the will of men. As it was, therefore, our duty to deliver the consciences of the faithful from the undue bondage in which they were held, so we have taught that they are free and unfettered by human laws. This freedom, purchased by the blood of Christ, may not be prostituted. If anyone thinks we are blamable in this, he must attribute the same blame to Christ and his apostles. I do not yet enumerate the other evils which compelled us to set our face against human traditions. I shall mention only two, and I am confident that, after I have mentioned them, all impartial readers will be satisfied. The one is that as some of these traditions demanded things which it was impossible to perform, their only effect was to lead men to hypocrisy, or plunge them into despair; and the other, that all of them practiced what our Savior rebuked in the Pharisees: they had made the commandments of God of none effect.

I will here adduce examples by which this will be made more clear. There are three things, in particular, for which they are offended with us: first, that we have given liberty to eat flesh on any day; second, that we have permitted marriage to priests; and third, that we have rejected the secret confession which was made in a priest's ear.

Let our opponents answer honestly. Is not the man who may have tasted flesh on Friday punished more severely than the man who may have spent the whole year in a constant course of licentiousness? Is it not deemed a more capital offense in a priest to marry than to be caught a hundred times in adultery? Do they not pardon the man who has scorned many of the divine precepts on easier terms than the man who may have neglected once a year to confess his sins into the ear of a priest? Is it not monstrous, I ask, that it should seem a slight and venial offense to violate the holy law of God, and that it should be judged an inexpiable crime to transgress the decrees of men? The case, I admit, is not without precedent. For, as I have already observed, the wickedness with which Christ charges the Pharisees is: *Thus have ye made the commandment of God of none effect through your tradition* (Matt. 15:6). Moreover, the arrogance of Antichrist of which Paul speaks is *that he as God sitteth in the temple of God, showing himself that he is God* (2 Thess. 2:4). For where is the incomparable majesty of God, after mortal man has been exalted to such a height that his laws take precedence of God's eternal decrees? I omit that an apostle describes the prohibition of meats and of marriage as a doctrine of devils (1 Tim. 4:1–3). That is surely bad enough, but the crowning impiety is to set man in a higher rank than God. If they deny the truth of my statement, I appeal to fact.

As to those two laws of celibacy and auricular confession, what are they but dire murderers of souls? As all the ministers of their churches vow perpetual chastity, it becomes unlawful for them, the vow being made, ever to take wives. What, then, if one has not received the gift of continence? "There must be no exception here," is the answer. But experience shows how much better it would have been never to have imposed this yoke upon priests than to shut them up in a furnace of lust, to burn with a perpetual flame. Our adversaries recount the praises of virginity; they recount also the advantages of celibacy, in order to prove that priests have not been rashly interdicted from marrying. They even represent it as decent and honorable. But will they by all these things prove that it is lawful to fetter consciences which Christ not only left free and unfettered, but whose freedom he has vindicated by his own authority, and at the price of his own blood? Paul does not presume to do so (1 Cor. 7:36). Whence then this new license? Again, though virginity be extolled to the skies, what has this to do with the celibacy of priests, with whose impurity the whole world is tainted? If the chastity which they profess in word they also exhibited in deed, then perhaps I might allow them to say that it is rightly done. But when every man knows that the prohibition of marriage is only a license to priests to commit gross sin, with what face, I ask, dare they make any mention of propriety? As to those whose infamy is not notorious, to avoid the necessity of discussing the matter with them at length, I leave them to the tribunal of God, that they may talk there of their chastity.

It will be said that this law is imposed on none but those who vow spontaneously. But what greater necessity can be imagined than that by which they are forced to vow? The condition announced to all is that none shall be admitted to the priesthood who has not previously bound himself by vows to perpetual celibacy, that he who has vowed must be forced, even against his will, to perform what he has once undertaken, and that no excuse to the contrary can be entertained. They maintain that a celibacy so exacted is voluntary. Rhetoricians are welcome to detail the disadvantages of marriage and the advantages of celibacy, in order to improve their style by declaiming on such topics in the schools. However much truth they may speak, it will hardly prove the propriety of leading miserable consciences into a deadly

snare, in which they must perpetually writhe till they are stran-
gled. And the ridiculous part is that in all this indecent infamy
even hypocrisy finds a place. For, whatever their conduct may be,
they deem themselves better than others, for the simple reason
that they have no wives.

The case is the same with confession. For they enumerate the
advantages which follow from it. We on the contrary are equally
prepared to point out not a few dangers which are justly to
be feared, and to refer to numerous most grievous evils which
have actually flowed from it. These, I say, are the kind of arguments which both parties may employ. But the perpetual rule of
Christ, which cannot be changed or deflected in this direction or
in that, which cannot without impiety be controverted, is that conscience should not be brought into bondage. Besides, the law on
which our opponents insist is one which can only torture souls and
ultimately destroy them. For it requires every individual to confess all his sins once a year to his own priest; if this be not done, it
leaves him no hope of obtaining pardon. Those who have made a
serious attempt, that is in the true fear of God, have found it
impossible thus to do even a hundredth part of this. Being unable
to extricate themselves by any remedy, they were driven to despair.
Those, again, who desired to satisfy God in a more careless manner, found this confession a most suitable cloak for hypocrisy. For,
thinking that they obtained an acquittal at the bar of God as soon
as they had disgorged their sins into the ear of a priest, they were
bold to sin more freely, since they were disburdened in such an
expeditious way. Then, having in their minds a fixed persuasion
that they fulfilled what the law enjoined, they thought that any
kind of enumeration would comprehend all their sins, though in
point of fact it did not include a thousandth part. See then on what
ground our adversaries clamor that we have destroyed the discipline of the Church: simply because we have studied to succor
miserable consciences lest they perish under the pressure of a most
cruel tyranny, and have dragged hypocrites out of their hiding
places into open day, that they might both examine themselves
more closely and begin to have a better idea of the divine judgment which they formerly evaded.

But someone will say that however numerous the abuses and
however deserving of correction, laws in other respects sacred and

useful and as it were consecrated by antiquity ought not to have been thus abolished instantly and completely.

In regard to the eating of flesh, my simple answer is that the doctrine we hold accords with that of the ancient Church, in which we know there was freedom to eat flesh at all times, or to abstain from it.

The prohibition of the marriage of priests I admit to be ancient, as is also the vow of perpetual continence taken by nuns and monks. But if we concede that the declared will of God outweighs human custom, why, when perfectly aware that the will of God is with us and clearly supports our view, do they seek to quarrel with us about antiquity? The doctrine is clear: *Marriage is honorable in all* (Heb. 13:4). Paul expressly speaks of bishops as husbands (1 Tim. 3:2; Titus 1:6). As a general rule, he enjoins marriage on all of a particular temperament, and declares the interdiction of marriage to be a *doctrine of devils* (1 Tim. 4:3). What does it avail to set human custom in opposition to the clear declarations of the Holy Spirit, unless men are to be preferred to God? Further it is of importance to observe how unfair those judges are, who in this matter allege against us the practice of the ancient Church. Is there any antiquity of the Church, either earlier or of higher authority, than the days of the apostles? But our opponents will not deny that at that time permission to marry was granted to all ministers of the Church, and used by them. If the apostles thought it expedient that priests be restrained from marrying, why did they defraud the Church of so great a boon? Yet after them about two hundred and fifty years elapsed until at the Council of Nicaea, as Sozomen relates, the question of enjoining celibacy on ministers was raised, but by the interference of Paphnutius, the whole affair was passed over. For it is related that after he, being himself a bachelor, had declared that a law of celibacy was not to be tolerated, the whole council readily assented to this opinion. But, superstition gradually increasing, the law, which was then repudiated, was at length enacted. Among those canons, which, because of their antiquity as well as the uncertainty of their author, are called apostolical, there is one which does not permit any clerical persons, except singers and readers, to marry after they have been admitted to office. But by a previous canon, priests and deacons are prohibited from putting away their wives under the pretext of religion. And in the fourth canon of the Council of Gangra, anathema is pronounced against those who distinguish a married from an unmarried presbyter, so as to absent themselves when he officiated. Hence it appears that there was still in those times considerably more equity than a subsequent age manifested.

Here, however, it was not my intention to discuss this subject fully. I only thought it proper to indicate in passing that the primitive and purer Church is not in this matter so adverse to us as our enemies pretend. But grant that it is, why do they accuse us so fiercely, as if we were confusing things sacred and profane, or as if we could not easily retort against them that we agree far better with the ancient Church than they do? Marriage, which the ancients denied to priests, we allow. What do they say to the licentiousness which has everywhere obtained among them? They will deny that they approve it. But if they were desirous to obey the ancient canons, it would be proper to punish it more severely. The punishment which the Council of Neo-Caesarea inflicted on a presbyter who married was deposition; while one guilty of adultery or fornication, it punished far more severely, adding to deposition excommunication also. In the present day, the marriage of a priest is deemed a capital crime, while for his hundred acts of libertinism he is fined a small sum of money. Doubtless, if those who first passed the law of celibacy were now alive, instructed by present experience, they would be the first to abrogate it. However, as I have already said, it would be the height of injustice to condemn us on the authority of men, in a matter in which we are plainly acquitted by the voice of God.

With regard to confession, we have a briefer and readier defense. Our opponents cannot show that the necessity of confessing was imposed earlier than Innocent III. For twelve hundred years this tyranny, for which they contend with us so keenly, was unknown to the Christian world. But there is a decree of the Lateran Council. True; but of the same description as many others. Those who have any tolerable knowledge of history are aware of both the ignorance and the ferocity of those times. This indeed is in accordance with the common observation that the most ignorant governors are always the most imperious. But all pious souls will bear me witness, in what a maze those must be entangled who think themselves bound by that law. To this cruel torturing of consciences has been added the blasphemous presumption of making it essential to the remission of sin. For they pretend that none obtain pardon from God but those who are disposed to confess. What is this, I ask, but for men to prescribe by their own hand the mode in which a sinner is reconciled to God, and to withhold the pardon, which God offers simply, until a condition which they have added shall have been fulfilled? On the other hand, the people were possessed with this most pernicious superstition: that as soon as they had disburdened themselves of their sins, by pouring them into the ear of a priest, they were completely freed from guilt. This opinion many abused by a more unrestrained indulgence in sin, while even those who were more influenced by the fear of God paid greater regard to the priest than to Christ. The public and solemn acknowledgment (exomologesis, as Cyprian calls it), which penitents were in ancient days obliged to make when they were to be reconciled to the Church, no sane man does not commend and willingly adopt, provided it be not diverted to some other end than that for which it was instituted. In short, we have no controversy in this matter with the ancient Church; we only wish, as we ought, to loose a modern tyranny of recent date from the necks of believers. Besides, when any person, in order to obtain consolation and counsel, visits his minister in private, and familiarly confides to him the causes of his anxiety, we by no means deny it to be useful, provided it be done freely and not of constraint. Let every man, I say, be left at liberty to do in this matter what he feels to be expedient for himself; let no man's conscience be obliged by fixed laws.

I hope your Imperial Majesty, and you, Most Illustrious Princes, will be satisfied with this apology. It is certainly just.

From

The Institutes of

the Christian Religion

OF THE KNOWLEDGE
OF GOD THE CREATOR
BOOK 1

Chapter 1

THE KNOWLEDGE OF GOD AND OF OURSELVES
MUTUALLY CONNECTED. NATURE OF THE CONNECTION.

Sections

1. The sum of true wisdom—namely, the knowledge of God and of ourselves. Effects of the latter.
2. Effects of the knowledge of God, in humbling our pride, unveiling our hypocrisy, demonstrating the absolute perfections of God, and our own utter helplessness.
3. Effects of the knowledge of God illustrated by the examples, 1. of holy patriarchs; 2. of holy angels; 3. of the sun and moon.

1. Our wisdom, insofar as it ought to be deemed true and solid wisdom, consists almost entirely of two parts: the knowledge of God and of ourselves. But as these are connected together by many ties, it is not easy to determine which of the two precedes and gives birth to the other. For, in the first place, no man can survey himself without forthwith turning his thoughts toward the God in whom he lives and moves, because it is perfectly obvious that the endowments which we possess cannot possibly be from ourselves; nay, that our very being is nothing else than subsistence in God alone. In the second place, those blessings which unceasingly distill to us from heaven are like streams conducting us to the fountain. Here, again, the infinitude of good which resides in God becomes more apparent from our poverty. In particular, the miserable ruin into which the revolt of the first man has plunged us compels us to turn our eyes upward; not only that while hungry and famishing we may thence ask what we want, but being aroused by fear may learn humility. For as there exists in man something like a world of misery, and ever since we were stripped of the divine attire, our

naked shame discloses an immense series of disgraceful properties, every man being stung by the consciousness of his own unhappiness in this way necessarily obtains at least some knowledge of God. Thus, our feeling of ignorance, vanity, want, weakness, in short, depravity and corruption, reminds us that in the Lord, and none but he, dwell the true light of wisdom, solid virtue, exuberant goodness. We are accordingly urged by our own evil things to consider the good things of God; and, indeed, we cannot aspire to him in earnest until we have begun to be displeased with ourselves. For what man is not disposed to rest in himself? Who, in fact, does not thus rest, so long as he is unknown to himself; that is, so long as he is contented with his own endowments and unconscious or unmindful of his misery? Every person, therefore, on coming to the knowledge of himself is not only urged to seek God, but is also led as by the hand to find him.

2. On the other hand, it is evident that man never attains to a true self-knowledge until he has previously contemplated the face of God and come down after such contemplation to look into himself. For (such is our innate pride) we always seem to ourselves just, and upright, and wise, and holy, until we are convinced, by clear evidence, of our injustice, vileness, folly, and impurity. Convinced, however, we are not, if we look to ourselves only, and not to the Lord also, he being the only standard by the application of which this conviction can be produced. For, since we are all naturally prone to hypocrisy, any empty semblance of righteousness is quite enough to satisfy us instead of righteousness itself. And since nothing appears within us or around us that is not tainted with very great impurity, so long as we keep our mind within the confines of human pollution, anything which is in some small degree less defiled delights us as if it were most pure, just as an eye to which nothing but black had been previously presented deems an object of a whitish, or even of a brownish hue, to be perfectly white. Nay, the bodily sense may furnish a still stronger illustration of the extent to which we are deluded in estimating the powers of the mind. If at midday we either look down to the ground or on the surrounding objects which lie open to our view, we think ourselves endued with a very strong and piercing eyesight, but when we look up to the sun and gaze at it unveiled, the sight which did excellently well for the earth is instantly so dazzled and

confounded by the refulgence as to oblige us to confess that our acuteness in discerning terrestrial objects is mere dimness when applied to the sun. Thus, too, it happens in estimating our spiritual qualities. So long as we do not look beyond the earth, we are quite pleased with our own righteousness, wisdom, and virtue; we address ourselves in the most flattering terms, and seem only less than demigods. But should we once begin to raise our thoughts to God, and reflect what kind of Being he is, and how absolute the perfection of that righteousness, and wisdom, and virtue, to which, as a standard, we are bound to be conformed, what formerly delighted us by its false show of righteousness will become polluted with the greatest iniquity; what strangely imposed upon us under the name of wisdom will disgust by its extreme folly; and what presented the appearance of virtuous energy will be condemned as the most miserable impotence. So far are those qualities in us, which seem most perfect, from corresponding to the divine purity.

3. Hence that dread and amazement with which as Scripture uniformly relates, holy men were struck and overwhelmed whenever they beheld the presence of God. When we see those who previously stood firm and secure so quaking with terror that the fear of death takes hold of them, nay, they are, in a manner, swallowed up and annihilated, the inference to be drawn is that men are never duly touched and impressed with a conviction of their insignificance until they have contrasted themselves with the majesty of God. Frequent examples of this consternation occur both in the book of Judges and the Prophetical Writings; so much so that it was a common expression among the people of God, *We shall die, for we have seen the Lord.* Hence the book of Job, also, in humbling men under a conviction of their folly, feebleness, and pollution, always derives its chief argument from descriptions of the divine wisdom, virtue, and purity. Nor without cause: for we see Abraham the readier to acknowledge himself but dust and ashes the nearer he approaches to behold the glory of the Lord, and Elijah unable to wait with unveiled face for his approach, so dreadful is the sight. And what can man do, man who is but rottenness and a worm, when even the cherubim themselves must veil their faces in very terror? To this, undoubtedly, the Prophet Isaiah refers, when he says (Isa. 24:23), *The moon shall be con-*

founded, and the sun ashamed, when the Lord of Hosts shall reign; that is, when he shall exhibit his refulgence, and give a nearer view of it, the brightest objects will, in comparison, be covered with darkness.

But though the knowledge of God and the knowledge of ourselves are bound together by a mutual tie, due arrangement requires that we treat of the former in the first place, and then descend to the latter.

Chapter 2

WHAT IT IS TO KNOW GOD.
TENDENCY OF THIS KNOWLEDGE.

Sections

1. The knowledge of God the Creator defined. The substance of this knowledge and the use to be made of it.
2. Further illustration of the use, together with a necessary reproof of vain curiosity, and refutation of the Epicureans. The character of God as it appears to the pious mind, contrasted with the absurd views of the Epicureans. Religion defined.

1. By the knowledge of God, I understand that by which we not only conceive that there is some God, but also apprehend what it is for our interest, and conducive to his glory, what, in short, it is befitting to know concerning him. For, properly speaking, we cannot say that God is known where there is no religion or piety. I am not now referring to that species of knowledge by which men, in themselves lost and under curse, apprehend God as a Redeemer in Christ the Mediator. I speak only of that simple and primitive knowledge to which the mere course of nature would have conducted us had Adam stood upright. For although no man will now, in the present ruin of the human race, perceive God to be either a father, or the author of salvation, or propitious in any respect, until Christ interpose to make our peace; still it is one thing to perceive that God our Maker supports us by his power, rules us by his Providence, fosters us by his goodness, and visits us with all kinds of blessings, and another thing to embrace the grace

of reconciliation offered to us in Christ. Since, then, the Lord first appears, as well in the creation of the world as in the general doctrine of Scripture, simply as a Creator, and afterward as a Redeemer in Christ, a twofold knowledge of him hence arises: of these the former is now to be considered; the latter will afterward follow in its order. But although our mind cannot conceive of God without rendering some worship to him, it will not, however, be sufficient simply to hold that he is the only being whom all ought to worship and adore, unless we are also persuaded that he is the fountain of all goodness, and that we must seek everything in him, and in none but him. My meaning is: we must be persuaded not only that as he once formed the world, so he sustains it by his boundless power, governs it by his wisdom, preserves it by his goodness, in particular, rules the human race with justice and judgment, bears with them in mercy, shields them by his protection; but also that not a particle of light, or wisdom, or justice, or power, or rectitude, or genuine truth, will anywhere be found, which does not flow from him, and of which he is not the cause; in this way we must learn to expect and ask all things from him and thankfully ascribe to him whatever we receive. For this sense of the divine perfections is the proper master to teach us piety, out of which religion springs. By piety I mean that union of reverence and love to God which the knowledge of his benefits inspires. For, until men feel that they owe everything to God, that they are cherished by his paternal care, and that he is the author of all their blessings, so that nought is to be looked for away from him, they will never submit to him in voluntary obedience; nay, unless they place their entire happiness in him, they will never yield up their whole selves to him in truth and sincerity.

2. Those, therefore, who, in considering this question, propose to inquire what the essence of God is, only delude us with frigid speculations, it being much more our interest to know what kind of being God is and what things are agreeable to his nature. For of what use is it to join Epicurus in acknowledging some God who has cast off the care of the world and only delights himself in ease? What avails it, in short, to know a God with whom we have nothing to do? The effect of our knowledge rather ought to be, *first*, to teach us reverence and fear, and, *second*, to induce us, under its guidance and teaching, to ask every good thing from him, and,

when it is received, ascribe it to him. For how can the idea of God enter your mind without instantly giving rise to the thought that since you are his workmanship, you are bound, by the very law of creation, to submit to his authority? That your life is due to him? That whatever you do ought to have reference to him? If so, it undoubtedly follows that your life is sadly corrupted, if it is not framed in obedience to him, since his will ought to be the law of our lives. On the other hand, your idea of his nature is not clear unless you acknowledge him to be the origin and fountain of all goodness. Hence would arise both confidence in him and a desire of cleaving to him, did not the depravity of the human mind lead it away from the proper course of investigation.

For, first of all, the pious mind does not devise for itself any kind of God, but looks alone to the one true God; nor does it feign for him any character it pleases, but is contented to have him in the character in which he manifests himself always guarding, with the utmost diligences against transgressing his will, and wandering with daring presumptions from the right path. He by whom God is thus known perceiving how he governs all things confides in him as his guardian and protector and casts himself entirely upon his faithfulness, perceiving him to be the source of every blessing; if he is in any strait or feels any want, he instantly recurs to his protection and trusts to his aid, persuaded that he is good and merciful; he reclines upon him with sure confidence and doubts not that in the divine clemency, a remedy will be provided for his every time of need; acknowledging him as his Father and his Lord, he considers himself bound to have respect to his authority in all things, to reverence his majesty, aim at the advancement of his glory, and obey his commands, regarding him as a just judge, armed with severity to punish crimes; he keeps the judgment seat always in his view. Standing in awe of it, he curbs himself and fears to provoke his anger. Nevertheless, he is not so terrified by an apprehension of judgment as to wish he could withdraw himself, even if the means of escape lay before him; nay, he embraces him not less as the avenger of wickedness than as the rewarder of the righteous, because he perceives that it equally appertains to his glory to store up punishment for the one, and eternal life for the other. Besides, it is not the mere fear of punishment that restrains him from sin. Loving and revering God as his father, honoring and obeying him as his master, although there were no hell, he would revolt at the very idea of offending him.

Such is pure and genuine religion, namely, confidence in God coupled with serious fear—fear, which both includes in it willing reverence, and brings along with it such legitimate worship as is prescribed by the law. And it ought to be more carefully considered that all men promiscuously do homage to God, but very few truly reverence him. On all hands there is abundance of ostentatious ceremonies, but sincerity of heart is rare.

Chapter 3

THE KNOWLEDGE OF GOD NATURALLY IMPLANTED IN THE HUMAN MIND.

Sections

1. The knowledge of God being manifested to all makes the reprobate without excuse. Universal belief and acknowledgment of the existence of God.
2. Objection—that religion and the belief of a Deity are the inventions of crafty politicians. Refutation of the objection. This universal belief confirmed by the examples of wicked men and atheists.
3. Confirmed also by the vain endeavors of the wicked to banish all fear of God from their minds. Conclusion, that the knowledge of God is naturally implanted in the human mind.

1. That there exists in the human mind and indeed by natural instinct, some sense of Deity, we hold to be beyond dispute, since God himself, to prevent any man from pretending ignorance, has endued all men with some idea of his Godhead, the memory of which he constantly renews and occasionally enlarges, that all to a man being aware that there is a God, and that he is their Maker, may be condemned by their own conscience when they neither worship him nor consecrate their lives to his service. Certainly, if there is any quarter where it may be supposed that God is unknown, the most likely for such an instance to exist is among the dullest tribes farthest removed from civilization. But, as a hea-

then [Cicero] tells us, there is no nation so barbarous, no race so brutish, as not to be imbued with the conviction that there is a God. Even those who, in other respects, seem to differ least from the lower animals, constantly retain some sense of religion; so thoroughly has this common conviction possessed the mind, so firmly is it stamped on the breasts of all men. Since, then, there never has been, from the very first, any quarter of the globe, any city, any household even, without religion, this amounts to a tacit confession, that a sense of Deity is inscribed on every heart. Nay, even idolatry is ample evidence of this fact. For we know how reluctant man is to lower himself in order to set other creatures above him. Therefore, when he chooses to worship wood and stone rather than be thought to have no God, it is evident how very strong this impression of a Deity must be, since it is more difficult to obliterate it from the mind of man than to break down the feelings of his nature—these certainly being broken down, when, in opposition to his natural haughtiness, he spontaneously humbles himself before the meanest object as an act of reverence to God.

2. It is most absurd, therefore, to maintain, as some do, that religion was devised by the cunning and craft of a few individuals, as a means of keeping the body of the people in due subjection, while there was nothing which those very individuals, while teaching others to worship God, less believed than the existence of a God. I readily acknowledge that designing men have introduced a vast number of fictions into religion, with the view of inspiring the populace with reverence or striking them with terror and thereby rendering them more obsequious, but they never could have succeeded in this had the minds of men not been previously imbued with that uniform belief in God, from which, as from its seed, the religious propensity springs. And it is altogether incredible that those who, in the matter of religion, cunningly imposed on their ruder neighbors, were altogether devoid of a knowledge of God. For though in old times there were some, and in the present day not a few are found who deny the being of a God, yet, whether they will or not, they occasionally feel the truth which they are desirous not to know. We do not read of any man who broke out into more unbridled and audacious contempt of the Deity than [the Roman Emperor] Caligula, and yet none showed greater dread when any indication of divine wrath was manifested. Thus,

however unwilling, he shook with terror before the God whom he professedly studied to condemn. You may every day see the same thing happening to his modern imitators. The most audacious despiser of God is most easily disturbed, trembling at the sound of a falling leaf. How so, unless in vindication of the divine majesty, which smites their consciences the more strongly the more they endeavor to flee from it. They all, indeed, look out for hiding places where they may conceal themselves from the presence of the Lord, and again efface it from their minds, but after all their efforts they remain caught within the net. Though the conviction may occasionally seem to vanish for a moment, it immediately returns and rushes in with new impetuosity, so that any interval of relief from the gnawing of conscience is not unlike the slumber of the intoxicated or the insane, who have no quiet rest in sleep, but are continually haunted with dire horrific dreams. Even the wicked themselves, therefore, are an example of the fact that some idea of God always exists in every human mind.

3. All men of sound judgment will therefore hold that a sense of Deity is indelibly engraved on the human heart. And that this belief is naturally engendered in all, and thoroughly fixed as it were in our very bones, is strikingly attested by the contumacy of the wicked, who, though they struggle furiously, are unable to extricate themselves from the fear of God. Though Diagoras and others of like stamps make themselves merry with whatever has been believed in all ages concerning religion, and Dionysus scoffs at the judgment of heaven, it is but a Sardonian grin, for the worm of conscience, keener than burning steel, is gnawing them within. I do not say with Cicero that errors wear out by age, and that religion increases and grows better day by day. For the world (as will be shortly seen) labors as much as it can to shake off all knowledge of God, and corrupts his worship in innumerable ways. I only say that when the stupid hardness of heart, which the wicked eagerly court as a means of despising God, becomes enfeebled, the sense of Deity, which of all things they wished most to be extinguished, is still in vigor, and now and then breaks forth. Whence we infer that this is not a doctrine which is first learned at school, but one as to which every man is, from the womb, his own master; one which nature herself allows no individual to forget, though many, with all their might, strive to do so. Moreover, if all are born and live for

the express purpose of learning to know God, and if the knowledge of God, insofar as it fails to produce this effect, is fleeting and vain, it is clear that all those who do not direct the whole thoughts and actions of their lives to this end fail to fulfill the law of their being. This did not escape the observation even of philosophers. For it is the very thing which Plato meant (in *Phaedo* and *Theataetus*) when he taught, as he often does, that the chief good of the soul consists in resemblance to God; that is, when, by means of knowing him, she is wholly transformed into him. Thus Gryllus also, in Plutarch, reasons most skillfully when he affirms that if once religion is banished from the lives of men, they not only in no respect excel, but are, in many respects, much more wretched than the brutes, since, being exposed to so many forms of evil, they continually drag on a troubled and restless existence: that the only thing, therefore, which makes them superior is the worship of God, through which alone they aspire to immortality.

Chapter 4

THE KNOWLEDGE OF GOD STIFLED OR CORRUPTED, IGNORANTLY OR MALICIOUSLY.

Sections

1. The knowledge of God suppressed by ignorance, many falling away into superstition. Such persons, however, inexcusable, because their error is accompanied with pride and stubbornness.
2. Stubbornness the companion of impiety.
3. No pretext can justify superstition. This proved, first, from reason; and, second, from Scripture.
4. The wicked never willingly come into the presence of God. Hence their hypocrisy. Hence, too, their sense of Deity leads to no good result.

1. But though experience testifies that a seed of religion is divinely sown in all, scarcely one in a hundred is found who cherishes it in his heart, and not one in whom it grows to maturity so far is it from yielding fruit in its season. Moreover, while some lose

themselves in superstitious observances, and others, of set purpose, wickedly revolt from God, the result is that, in regard to the true knowledge of him, all are so degenerate that in no part of the world can genuine godliness be found. In saying that some fall away into superstition, I mean not to insinuate that their excessive absurdity frees them from guilt, for the blindness under which they labor is almost invariably accompanied with vain pride and stubbornness. Mingled vanity and pride appear in this, that when miserable men do seek after God, instead of ascending higher than themselves as they ought to do, they measure him by their own carnal stupidity, and, neglecting solid inquiry, fly off to indulge their curiosity in vain speculation. Hence, they do not conceive of him in the character in which he is manifested, but imagine him to be whatever their own rashness has devised. This abyss standing open, they cannot move one footstep without rushing headlong to destruction. With such an idea of God, nothing which they may attempt to offer in the way of worship or obedience can have any value in his sight, because it is not him they worship, but, instead of him, the dream and figment of their own heart. This corrupt procedure is admirably described by Paul, when he says, that *thinking to be wise, they became fools* (Rom. 1:22). He had previously said that *they became vain in their imaginations,* but lest any should suppose them blameless, he afterward adds that they were deservedly blinded, because, not contented with sober inquiry, because, arrogating to themselves more than they have any title to do, they of their own accord court darkness, nay, bewitch themselves with perverse, empty show. Hence it is that their folly, the result not only of vain curiosity, but of licentious desire and overweening confidence in the pursuit of forbidden knowledge, cannot be excused.

2. The expression of David (Ps. 14:1; 53:1), *The fool hath said in his heart, There is no God,* is primarily applied to those who, as will shortly further appear, stifle the light of nature and intentionally stupefy themselves. We see many, after they have become hardened in a daring course of sin, madly banishing all remembrance of God, though spontaneously suggested to them from within, by natural sense. To show how detestable this madness is, the psalmist introduces them as distinctly denying that there is a God, because although they do not disown his essence, they rob

him of his justice and Providence, and represent him as sitting idly in heaven. Nothing being less accordant with the nature of God than to cast off the government of the world, leaving it to chance, and so to wink at the crimes of men that they may wanton with impunity in evil courses; it follows, that every man who indulges in security, after extinguishing all fear of divine judgment, virtually denies that there is a God. As a just punishment of the wicked, after they have closed their own eyes, God makes their hearts dull and heavy, and hence, seeing, they see not. David, indeed, is the best interpreter of his own meaning, when he says elsewhere, the wicked has *no fear of God before his eyes* (Ps. 36:1); and, again, *He has said in his heart, God has forgotten; he hideth his face; he will never see it.* Thus although they are forced to acknowledge that there is some God, they, however, rob him of his glory by denying his power. For, as Paul declares, *If we believe not, he abideth faithful, he cannot deny himself* (2 Tim. 2:13); so those who feign to themselves a dead and dumb idol are truly said to deny God. It is, moreover, to be observed that though they struggle with their own convictions, and would fain not only banish God from their minds, but from heaven also, their stupefaction is never so complete as to secure them from being occasionally dragged before the divine tribunal. Still, as no fear restrains them from rushing violently in the face of God, so long as they are hurried on by that blind impulse, it cannot be denied that their prevailing state of mind in regard to him is brutish oblivion.

3. In this way, the vain pretext which many employ to clothe their superstition is overthrown. They deem it enough that they have some kind of zeal for religion, how preposterous soever it may be, not observing that true religion must be conformable to the will of God as its unerring standard; that he can never deny himself, and is no specter or phantom, to be metamorphosed at each individual's caprice. It is easy to see how superstition, with its false glosses, mocks God, while it tries to please him. Usually fastening merely on things on which he has declared he sets no value, it either contemptuously overlooks, or even undisguisedly rejects, the things which he expressly enjoins, or in which we are assured that he takes pleasure. Those, therefore, who set up a fictitious worship, merely worship and adore their own delirious fancies; indeed, they would never dare so to trifle with God, had they not

previously fashioned him after their own childish conceits. Hence that vague and wandering opinion of Deity is declared by an apostle to be ignorance of God: *Howbeit, then, when ye knew not God, ye did service unto them which by nature are no gods.* And he elsewhere declares that the Ephesians were *without God* (Eph. 2:12) at the time when they wandered without any correct knowledge of him. It makes little difference, at least in this respect, whether you hold the existence of one God or a plurality of gods, since in both cases alike, by departing from the true God, you have nothing left but an execrable idol. It remains, therefore, to conclude with Lactantius, "No religion is genuine that is not in accordance with truth."

4. To this fault they add a second, namely, that when they do think of God it is against their will; never approaching him without being dragged into his presence, and when there, instead of the voluntary fear flowing from reverence of the divine majesty, feeling only that forced and servile fear which divine judgment extorts judgment which, from the impossibility of escape, they are compelled to dread, but which, while they dread, they at the same time also hate. To impiety, and to it alone, the saying of Statius properly applies: "Fear first brought gods into the world." Those whose inclinations are at variance with the justice of God, knowing that his tribunal has been erected for the punishment of transgression, earnestly wish that that tribunal were overthrown. Under the influence of this feeling they are actually warring against God, justice being one of his essential attributes. Perceiving that they are always within reach of his power, that resistance and evasion are alike impossible, they fear and tremble. Accordingly, to avoid the appearance of condemning a majesty by which all are overawed, they have recourse to some species of religious observance, never ceasing meanwhile to defile themselves with every kind of vice, and add crime to crime, until they have broken the holy law of the Lord in every one of its requirements, and set his whole righteousness at nought; at all events, they are not so restrained by their semblance of fear as not to luxuriate and take pleasure in iniquity, choosing rather to indulge their carnal propensities than to curb them with the bridle of the Holy Spirit. But since this shadow of religion (it scarcely even deserves to be called a shadow) is false and vain, it is easy to infer how much this confused knowledge of God differs from that piety which is

instilled into the breasts of believers, and from which alone true religion springs. And yet hypocrites would fain, by means of tortuous windings, make a show of being near to God at the very time they are fleeing from him. For while the whole life ought to be one perpetual course of obedience, they rebel without fear in almost all their actions, and seek to appease him with a few paltry sacrifices; while they ought to serve him with integrity of heart and holiness of life, they endeavor to procure his favor by means of frivolous devices and punctilios of no value. Nay, they take greater license in their groveling indulgences, because they imagine that they can fulfill their duty to him by preposterous expiations; in short, while their confidence ought to have been fixed upon him, they put him aside, and rest in themselves or the creatures. At length they bewilder themselves in such a maze of error that the darkness of ignorance obscures, and ultimately extinguishes, those sparks which were designed to show them the glory of God. Still, however, the conviction that there is some Deity continues to exist, like a plant which can never be completely eradicated, though so corrupt that it is only capable of producing the worst of fruit. Nay, we have still stronger evidence of the proposition for which I now contend—namely, that a sense of Deity is naturally engraved on the human heart, in the fact that the very reprobate are forced to acknowledge it. When at their ease, they can jest about God, and talk pertly and loquaciously in disparagement of his power; but should despair, from any cause, overtake them, it will stimulate them to seek him, and dictate ejaculatory prayers, proving that they were not entirely ignorant of God, but had perversely suppressed feelings which ought to have been earlier manifested.

Chapter 5

THE KNOWLEDGE OF GOD CONSPICUOUS
IN THE CREATION AND CONTINUAL GOVERNMENT
OF THE WORLD.

This chapter consists of two parts: 1. The former, which occupies the first ten sections, divides all the works of God into two great classes, and elucidates the knowledge of God as displayed in each class. The one class is treated of in the first six, and the other in the four following sections; 2. The latter part of the chapter shows that, in consequence of the extreme stupidity of men, those manifestations of God, however perspicuous, lead to no useful result. This latter part, which commences at the eleventh section, is continued to the end of the chapter.

Sections

1. The invisible and incomprehensible essence of God, to a certain extent, made visible in his works.
2. This declared by the first class of works—namely, the admirable motions of the heavens and the earth, the symmetry of the human body, and the connection of its parts; in short, the various objects which are presented to every eye.
3. This more especially manifested in the structure of the human body.
4. The shameful ingratitude of disregarding God, who, in such a variety of ways, is manifested within us. The still more shameful ingratitude of contemplating the endowments of the soul, without ascending to him who gave them. No objection can be founded on any supposed organism in the soul.
5. The powers and actions of the soul, a proof of its separate existence from the body. Proofs of the soul's immortality. Objection that the whole world is quickened by one soul. Reply to the objection. Its impiety.
6. Conclusion from what has been said—namely, that the omnipotence, eternity, and goodness of God may be learned from the first class of works, that is, those which are in accordance with the ordinary course of nature.
7. The second class of works—namely, those above the ordinary course of nature, afford clear evidence of the perfections of God, especially his goodness, justice, and mercy.
8. Also his Providence, power, and wisdom.
9. Proofs and illustrations of the divine majesty. The use of them—namely, the acquisition of divine knowledge in combination with true piety.
10. The tendency of the knowledge of God to inspire the righteous with the hope of future life, and remind the wicked of the punishments reserved for them. Its tendency, moreover, to

keep alive in the hearts of the righteous a sense of the divine
goodness.

11. The second part of the chapter, which describes the stupidity
both of learned and unlearned, in ascribing the whole order of
things, and the admirable arrangements of divine Providence,
to fortune.

12. Hence polytheism, with all its abominations, and the endless
and irreconcilable opinions of the philosophers concerning
God.

13. All guilty of revolt from God, corrupting pure religion,
either by following general custom, or the impious consent of
antiquity.

14. Though irradiated by the wondrous glories of creation, we
cease not to follow our own ways.

15. Our conduct altogether inexcusable, the dullness of perception
being attributable to ourselves, while we are fully reminded of
the true path, both by the structure and the government of the
world.

1. Since the perfection of blessedness consists in the knowledge
of God, he has been pleased, in order that none might be excluded
from the means of obtaining felicity, not only to deposit in our
minds that seed of religion of which we have already spoken, but
so to manifest his perfections in the whole structure of the universe, and daily place himself in our view, that we cannot open our
eyes without being compelled to behold him. His essence, indeed,
is incomprehensible, utterly transcending all human thought; but
on each of his works his glory is engraved in characters so bright,
so distinct, and so illustrious, that none, however dull and illiterate, can plead ignorance as their excuse. Hence, with perfect truth,
the psalmist exclaims, *He covereth himself with light as with a garment* (Ps. 104:2); as if he had said that God for the first time was
arrayed in visible attire when, in the creation of the world, he displayed those glorious banners, on which, to whatever side we turn,
we behold his perfections visibly portrayed. In the same place, the
psalmist aptly compares the expanded heavens to his royal tent,
and says, *He layeth the beams of his chambers in the waters, maketh
the clouds his chariot, and walketh upon the wings of the wind,* send-

ing forth the winds and lightnings as his swift messengers. And because the glory of his power and wisdom is more refulgent in the firmament, it is frequently designated as his palace. And, first, wherever you turn your eyes, there is no portion of the world, however minute, that does not exhibit at least some sparks of beauty, while it is impossible to contemplate the vast and beautiful fabric as it extends around, without being overwhelmed by the immense weight of glory. Hence, the author of the Epistle to the Hebrews elegantly describes the visible worlds as images of the invisible (Heb. 11:3), the elegant structure of the world serving us as a kind of mirror, in which we may behold God, though otherwise invisible. For the same reason, the psalmist attributes language to celestial objects, a language which all nations understand (Ps. 19:1), the manifestation of the Godhead being too clear to escape the notice of any people, however obtuse. The Apostle Paul, stating this still more clearly, says, *That which may be known of God is manifest in them, for God has showed it unto them. For the invisible things of him from the creation of the world are clearly seen, being understood by the things that are made, even his eternal power and Godhead* (Rom. 1:20).

2. In attestation of his wondrous wisdom, both the heavens and the earth present us with innumerable proofs, not only those more recondite proofs, which astronomy, medicine, and all the natural sciences are designed to illustrate, but proofs which force themselves on the notice of the most illiterate peasant, who cannot open his eyes without beholding them. It is true, indeed, that those who are more or less intimately acquainted with those liberal studies are thereby assisted and enabled to obtain a deeper insight into the secret workings of divine wisdom. No man, however, though he be ignorant of these, is incapacitated for discerning such proofs of creative wisdom as may well cause him to break forth in admiration of the Creator. To investigate the motions of the heavenly bodies, to determine their positions, measure their distances, and ascertain their properties, demands skill, and a more careful examination; and where these are so employed, as the Providence of God is thereby more fully unfolded, so it is reasonable to suppose that the mind takes a loftier flight and obtains brighter views of his glory. Still, none who have the use of their

eyes can be ignorant of the divine skill manifested so conspicuously in the endless variety, yet distinct and well-ordered array, of the heavenly host; and, therefore, it is plain that the Lord has furnished every man with abundant proofs of his wisdom. The same is true in regard to the structure of the human frame. To determine the connection of its parts, its symmetry and beauty, with the skill of a Galen, requires singular acuteness; and yet all men acknowledge that the human body bears on its face such proofs of ingenious contrivance as are sufficient to proclaim the admirable wisdom of its Maker.

3. Hence certain of the philosophers [Aristotle, Macrobius, Boethius] have not improperly called man a *microcosm (miniature world)*, as being a rare specimen of divine power, wisdom, and goodness, and containing within himself wonders sufficient to occupy our minds, if we are willing so to employ them. Paul, accordingly, after reminding the Athenians that they *might feel after God and find him*, immediately adds, that *he is not far from every one of us* (Acts 17:27); every man having within himself undoubted evidence of the heavenly grace by which he lives, and moves, and has his being. But if, in order to apprehend God, it is unnecessary to go further than ourselves, what excuse can there be for the sloth of any man who will not take the trouble of descending into himself that he may find him? For the same reason, too, David, after briefly celebrating the wonderful name and glory of God, as everywhere displayed, immediately exclaims, *What is man, that thou art mindful of him?* and again, *Out of the mouths of babes and sucklings thou hast ordained strength* (Ps. 8:2, 4). Thus he declares not only that the human race is a bright mirror of the Creator's works, but that infants hanging on their mothers' breasts have tongues eloquent enough to proclaim his glory without the aid of other orators. Accordingly, he hesitates not to bring them forward as fully instructed to refute the madness of those who, from devilish pride, would fain extinguish the name of God. Hence, too, the passage which Paul quotes from Aratus, *We are his offspring* (Acts 17:28), the excellent gifts with which he has endued us attesting that he is our Father. In the same way also, from natural instinct, and, as it were, at the dictation of experience, heathen poets called him the father of men. No one, indeed, will voluntarily and willingly devote himself to the service of God unless he has

previously tasted his paternal love and been thereby allured to love and reverence him.

4. But herein appears the shameful ingratitude of men. Though they have in their own persons a factory where innumerable operations of God are carried on, and a magazine stored with treasures of inestimable value—instead of bursting forth in his praise, as they are bound to do, they, on the contrary, are the more inflated and swelled with pride. They feel how wonderfully God is working in them, and their own experience tells them of the vast variety of gifts which they owe to his liberality. Whether they will or not, they cannot but know that these are proofs of his Godhead, and yet they inwardly suppress them. They have no occasion to go further than themselves, provided they do not, by appropriating as their own that which has been given them from heaven, put out the light intended to exhibit God clearly to their minds. At this day, however, the earth sustains on her bosom many monster minds—minds which are not afraid to employ the seed of Deity deposited in human nature as a means of suppressing the name of God. Can anything be more detestable than this madness in man, who, finding God a hundred times both in his body and his soul, makes his excellence in this respect a pretext for denying that there is a God? He will not say that chance has made him differ from the brutes that perish; but, substituting nature as the architect of the universe, he suppresses the name of God. The swift motions of the soul, its noble faculties and rare endowments, bespeak the agency of God in a manner which would make the suppression of it impossible, did not the Epicureans, like so many Cyclops, use it as a vantage-ground, from which to wage more audacious war with God. Are so many treasures of heavenly wisdom employed in the guidance of such a worm as man, and shall the whole universe be denied the same privilege? To hold that there are organs in the soul corresponding to each of its faculties is so far from obscuring the glory of God that it rather illustrates it. Let Epicurus tell what concourse of atoms, cooking meat and drink, can form one portion into refuse and another portion into blood, and make all the members separately perform their office as carefully as if they were so many souls acting with common consent in the superintendence of one body.

5. But my business at present is not with that pigsty: I wish

rather to deal with those who, led away by absurd subtleties, are inclined, by giving an indirect turn to the frigid doctrine of Aristotle, to employ it for the purpose both of disproving the immortality of the soul, and robbing God of his rights. Under the pretext that the faculties of the soul are organized, they chain it to the body as if it were incapable of a separate existence, while they endeavor as much as in them lies, by pronouncing eulogies on nature, to suppress the name of God. But there is no ground for maintaining that the powers of the soul are confined to the performance of bodily functions. What has the body to do with your measuring the heavens, counting the number of the stars, ascertaining their magnitudes, their relative distances, the rate at which they move, and the orbits which they describe? I deny not that astronomy has its use; all I mean to show is that these lofty investigations are not conducted by organized symmetry, but by the faculties of the soul itself apart altogether from the body. The single example I have given will suggest many others to the reader. The swift and versatile movements of the soul in glancing from heaven to earth, connecting the future with the past, retaining the remembrance of former years, nay, forming creations of its own—its skill, moreover, in making astonishing discoveries, and inventing so many wonderful arts, are sure indications of the agency of God in man. What shall we say of its activity when the body is asleep, its many revolving thoughts, its many useful suggestions, its many solid arguments, nay, its presentiment of things yet to come? What shall we say but that man bears about with him a stamp of immortality which can never be effaced? But how is it possible for man to be divine, and yet not acknowledge his Creator? Shall we, by means of a power of judging implanted in our breast, distinguish between justice and injustice, and yet there be no judge in heaven? Shall some remains of intelligence continue with us in sleep, and yet no God keep watch in heaven? Shall we be deemed the inventors of so many arts and useful properties that God may be defrauded of his praise, though experience tells us plainly enough that whatever we possess is dispensed to us in unequal measures by another hand? The talk of certain persons concerning a secret inspiration quickening the whole world is not only silly, but altogether profane. Such persons are delighted with the following celebrated passage of Virgil:

Know, first, that heaven, and earth's compacted frame,
And flowing waters, and the starry flame,
And both the radiant lights, one common soul
Inspires and feeds—and animates the whole.
This active mind, infused through all the space,
Unites and mingles with the mighty mass:
Hence, men and beasts the breath of life obtain,
And birds of air, and monsters of the main.
Th' ethereal vigor is in all the same,
And every soul is filled with equal flame.
                    (*Aeneid*, Bk. 6, lines 724ff.; trans. Dryden)

The meaning of all this is that the world, which was made to display the glory of God, is its own creator. For the same poet has, in another place, adopted a view common to both Greeks and Latins:

Hence to the bee some sages have assigned
A portion of the God, and heavenly mind;
For God goes forth, and spreads throughout the whole,
Heaven, earth, and sea, the universal soul;
Each, at its birth, from him all beings share,
Both man and brute, the breath of vital air;
To him return, and, loosed from earthly chain,
Fly whence they sprung, and rest in God again;
Spurn at the grave, and, fearless of decay,
Dwell in high heaven, art star th' ethereal way.
                    (*Georgics*, Bk. 4, lines 220ff.)

Here we see how far that jejune speculation, of a universal mind animating and invigorating the world, is fitted to beget and foster piety in our minds. We have a still clearer proof of this in the profane verses which the licentious Lucretius has written as a deduction from the same principle. The plain object is to form an unsubstantial deity, and thereby banish the true God whom we ought to fear and worship. I admit, indeed, that the expression "Nature is God," may be piously used, if dictated by a pious mind; but as it is inaccurate and harsh (Nature being more properly the order which has been established by God), in matters which are so very important, and in regard to which special reverence is due, it does harm to confound the Deity with the inferior operations of his hands.

6. Let each of us, therefore, in contemplating his own nature, remember that there is one God who governs all natures, and, in governing, wishes us to have respect to himself, to make him the object of our faith, worship, and adoration. Nothing, indeed, can be more preposterous than to enjoy those noble endowments which bespeak the divine presence within us, and to neglect him who, of his own good pleasure, bestows them upon us. In regard to his power, how glorious the manifestations by which he urges us to the contemplation of himself; unless, indeed, we pretend not to know whose energy it is that by a word sustains the boundless fabric of the universe—at one time making heaven reverberate with thunder, sending forth the scorching lightning, and setting the whole atmosphere in a blaze; at another, causing the raging tempests to blow, and forthwith, in one moment, when it so pleases him, making a perfect calm; keeping the sea, which seems constantly threatening the earth with devastation, suspended as it were in air; at one time lashing it into fury by the impetuosity of the winds; at another, appeasing its rage and stilling all its waves. Here we might refer to those glowing descriptions of divine power, as illustrated by natural events, which occur throughout Scripture, but more especially in the book of Job, and the prophecies of Isaiah. These, however, I purposely omit, because a better opportunity of introducing them will be found when I come to treat of the scriptural account of the creation (*infra*, chap. 14, sect. 1, 2, 20, *seq.*). I only wish to observe here that this method of investigating the divine perfections, by tracing the lineaments of his countenance as shadowed forth in the firmament and on the earth, is common both to those within and to those without the pale of the Church. From the power of God we are naturally led to consider his eternity since that from which all other things derive their origin must necessarily be self-existent and eternal. Moreover, if it be asked what cause induced him to create all things at first, and now inclines him to preserve them, we shall find that there could be no other cause than his own goodness. But if this is the only cause, nothing more should be required to draw forth our love toward him; every creature, as the psalmist reminds

us, participating in his mercy. *His tender mercies are over all his works* (Ps. 145:9).

7. In the second class of God's works, namely those which are above the ordinary course of nature, the evidence of his perfections are in every respect equally clear. For in conducting the affairs of men, he so arranges the course of his Providence, as daily to declare, by the clearest manifestations, that though all are in innumerable ways the partakers of his bounty, the righteous are the special objects of his favor, the wicked and profane the special objects of his severity. It is impossible to doubt his punishment of crimes; while at the same time he, in no unequivocal manner, declares that he is the protector, and even the avenger of innocence, by shedding blessings on the good, helping their necessities, soothing and solacing their griefs, relieving their sufferings, and in all ways providing for their safety. And though he often permits the guilty to exult for a time with impunity, and the innocent to be driven to and fro in adversity, nay, even to be wickedly and iniquitously oppressed, this ought not to produce any uncertainty as to the uniform justice of all his procedure. Nay, an opposite inference should be drawn. When any one crime calls forth visible manifestations of his anger, it must be because he hates all crimes; and, on the other hand, his leaving many crimes unpunished only proves that there is a Judgment in reserve, when the punishment now delayed shall be inflicted. In like manner, how richly does he supply us with the means of contemplating his mercy when, as frequently happens, he continues to visit miserable sinners with unwearied kindness, until he subdues their depravity and woos them back with more than a parent's fondness?

8. To this purpose the psalmist (Ps. 107) mentioning how God, in a wondrous manner, often brings sudden and unexpected succor to the miserable when almost on the brink of despair, whether in protecting them when they stray in deserts, and at length leading them back into the right path, or supplying them with food when famishing for want, or delivering them when captive from iron fetters and foul dungeons, or conducting them safe into harbor after shipwreck, or bringing them back from the gates of death by curing their diseases, or, after burning up the fields with heat and drought, fertilizing them with the river of his grace, or exalting the meanest of the people, and casting down the mighty

from their lofty seats: the psalmist, after bringing forward examples of this description, infers that those things which men call fortuitous events are so many proofs of divine Providence, and more especially of paternal clemency, furnishing ground of joy to the righteous, and at the same time stopping the mouths of the ungodly. But as the greater part of mankind, enslaved by error, walk blindfold in this glorious theater, he exclaims that it is a rare and singular wisdom to meditate carefully on these works of God, which many, who seem most sharp-sighted in other respects, behold without profit. It is indeed true that the brightest manifestation of divine glory finds not one genuine spectator among a hundred. Still, neither his power nor his wisdom is shrouded in darkness. His power is strikingly displayed when the rage of the wicked, to all appearance irresistible, is crushed in a single moment; their arrogance subdued, their strongest bulwarks overthrown, their armor dashed to pieces, their strength broken, their schemes defeated without an effort, and audacity which set itself above the heavens is precipitated to the lowest depths of the earth. On the other hand, the poor are raised up out of the dust and the needy lifted out of the dung hill (Ps. 113:7), the oppressed and afflicted are rescued in extremity, the despairing animated with hope, the unarmed defeat the armed, the few the many, the weak the strong. The excellence of the divine wisdom is manifested in distributing everything in due season, confounding the wisdom of the world, and taking the wise in their own craftiness (1 Cor. 3:19); in short, conducting all things in perfect accordance with reason.

9. We see there is no need of a long and laborious train of argument in order to obtain proofs which illustrate and assert the divine majesty. The few which we have merely touched show them to be so immediately within our reach in every quarter that we can trace them with the eye or point to them with the finger. And here we must observe again (see chap. 2, sect. 2), that the knowledge of God which we are invited to cultivate is not that which, resting satisfied with empty speculation, only flutters in the brain, but a knowledge which will prove substantial and fruitful wherever it is duly perceived, and rooted in the heart. The Lord is manifested by his perfections. When we feel their power within us, and are conscious of their benefits, the knowledge must impress us much more vividly than if we merely imagined a God

whose presence we never felt. Hence it is obvious that in seeking God, the most direct path and the fittest method is not to attempt with presumptuous curiosity to pry into his essence, which is rather to be adored than minutely discussed, but to contemplate him in his works, by which he draws near, becomes familiar, and in a manner communicates himself to us. To this the apostle referred when he said that we need not go far in search of him (Acts 17:27), because, by the continual working of his power, he dwells in every one of us. Accordingly, David (Ps. 145), after acknowledging that his greatness is unsearchable, proceeds to enumerate his works, declaring that his greatness will thereby be unfolded. It therefore becomes us also diligently to prosecute that investigation of God which so enraptures the soul with admiration as, at the same time, to make an efficacious impression on it. And, as Augustine expresses it (in Ps. 144), since we are unable to comprehend him, and are, as it were, overpowered by his greatness, our proper course is to contemplate his works, and so refresh ourselves with his goodness.

10. By the knowledge thus acquired, we ought not only to be stimulated to worship God, but also aroused and elevated to the hope of future life. For, observing that the manifestations which the Lord gives both of his mercy and severity are only begun and incomplete, we ought to infer that these are doubtless only a prelude to higher manifestations, of which the full display is reserved for another state. Conversely, when we see the righteous brought into affliction by the ungodly, assailed with injuries, overwhelmed with calumnies, and lacerated by insult and contumely, while, on the contrary, the wicked flourish, prosper, acquire ease and honor, and all these with impunity, we ought forthwith to infer that there will be a future life in which iniquity shall receive its punishment and righteousness its reward. Moreover, when we observe that the Lord often lays his chastening rod on the righteous, we may the more surely conclude that far less will the righteous ultimately escape the scourges of his anger. There is a well-known passage in Augustine (*The City of God*, Bk. 1, chap. 8), "Were all sin now visited with open punishment, it might be thought that nothing was reserved for the final Judgment; and, on the other hand, were no sin now openly punished, it might be supposed there was no divine providence." It must be acknowledged, therefore, that in

each of the works of God, and more especially in the whole of them taken together, the divine perfections are delineated as in a picture, and the whole human race thereby invited and allured to acquire the knowledge of God, and, in consequence of this knowledge, true and complete felicity. Moreover, while his perfections are thus most vividly displayed, the only means of ascertaining their practical operation and tendency is to descend into ourselves and consider how it is that the Lord there manifests his wisdom, power, and energy—how he there displays his justice, goodness, and mercy. For although David (Ps. 92:6) justly complains of the extreme infatuation of the ungodly in not pondering the deep counsels of God, as exhibited in the government of the human race, what he elsewhere says (Ps. 40) is most true, that the wonders of the divine wisdom in this respect are more in number than the hairs of our head. But I leave this topic at present, as it will be more fully considered afterward in its own place (Bk. 1, chap. 16, sects. 6–9).

11. Bright, however, as is the manifestation which God gives both of himself and his immortal kingdom in the mirror of his works, so great is our stupidity, so dull are we in regard to these bright manifestations, that we derive no benefit from them. For in regard to the fabric and admirable arrangement of the universe, how few of us are there who, in lifting our eyes to the heavens or looking abroad on the various regions of the earth, ever think of the Creator? Do we not rather overlook him and sluggishly content ourselves with a view of his works? And then in regard to supernatural events, though these are occurring every day, how few are there who ascribe them to the ruling Providence of God—how many who imagine that they are casual results produced by the blind evolutions of the wheel of chance? Even when under the guidance and direction of these events, we are in a manner forced to the contemplation of God (a circumstance which all must occasionally experience), and are thus led to form some impressions of Deity, we immediately fly off to carnal dreams and depraved fictions, and so by our vanity corrupt heavenly truth. This far, indeed, we differ from each other, in that everyone appropriates to himself some peculiar error; but we are all alike in this, that we substitute monstrous fictions for the one living and true God—a disease not confined to obtuse and vulgar minds, but affecting the

noblest, and those who, in other respects, are singularly acute. How lavishly in this respect have the whole body of philosophers betrayed their stupidity and want of sense? To say nothing of the others whose absurdities are of a still grosser description, how completely does Plato, the soberest and most religious of them all, lose himself in his round globe? What must be the case with the rest, when the leaders, who ought to have set them an example, commit such blunders and labor under such hallucinations? In like manner, while the government of the world places the doctrine of Providence beyond dispute, the practical result is the same as if it were believed that all things were carried hither and thither at the caprice of chance, so prone are we to vanity and error. I am still referring to the most distinguished of the philosophers and not to the common herd whose madness in profaning the truth of God exceeds all bounds.

12. Hence that immense flood of error with which the whole world is overflowed. Every individual mind being a kind of labyrinth, it is not wonderful, not only that each nation has adopted a variety of fictions, but that almost every man has had his own god. To the darkness of ignorance have been added presumption and wantonness, and hence there is scarcely an individual to be found without some idol or phantom as a substitute for Deity. Like water gushing forth from a large and copious spring, immense crowds of gods have issued from the human mind, every man giving himself full license, and devising some peculiar form of divinity, to meet his own views. It is unnecessary here to attempt a catalog of the superstitions with which the world was overspread. The thing were endless; and the corruptions themselves, though not a word should be said, furnish abundant evidence of the blindness of the human mind. I say nothing of the rude and illiterate vulgar; but among the philosophers who attempted, by reason and learning, to pierce the heavens, what shameful disagreement! The higher anyone was endued with genius, and the more he was polished by science and art, the more specious was the coloring which he gave to his opinions. All these, however, if examined more closely, will be found to be vain show. The Stoics plumed themselves on their acuteness, when they said that the various names of God might be extracted from all the parts of nature, and yet that his unity was not thereby divided: as if

we were not already too prone to vanity and had no need of being presented with an endless multiplicity of gods to lead us further and more grossly into error. The mystic theology of the Egyptians shows how sedulously they labored to be thought rational on this subject. And, perhaps, at the first glance, some show of probability might deceive the simple and unwary, but never did any mortal devise a scheme by which religion was not foully corrupted. This endless variety and confusion emboldened the Epicureans, and other gross despisers of piety, to cut off all sense of God. For when they saw that the wisest contradicted each other they hesitated not to infer from their dissensions, and from the frivolous and absurd doctrines of each, that men foolishly, and to no purpose, brought torment upon themselves by searching for a God, there being none: and they thought this inference safe, because it was better at once to deny God altogether than to feign uncertain gods and thereafter engage in quarrels without end. They, indeed, argue absurdly, or rather weave a cloak for their impiety out of human ignorance; though ignorance surely cannot derogate from the prerogatives of God. But since all confess that there is no topic on which such difference exists, both among learned and unlearned, the proper inference is that the human mind, which thus errs in inquiring after God, is dull and blind in heavenly mysteries. Some praise the answer of Simonides, who being asked by King Hero what God was, asked a day to consider. When the king next day repeated the question, he asked two days; and after repeatedly doubling the number of days, at length replied, "The longer I consider, the darker the subject appears." He, no doubt, wisely suspended his opinion, when he did not see clearly: still his answer shows that if men are only naturally taught, instead of having any distinct, solid, or certain knowledge, they fasten only on contradictory principles, and, in consequence, worship an unknown God.

13. Hence we must hold that whosoever adulterates pure religion (and this must be the case with all who cling to their own views), makes a departure from the one God. No doubt, they will allege that they have a different intention; but it is of little consequence what they intend or persuade themselves to believe, since the Holy Spirit pronounces all to be apostates, who, in the blindness of their minds, substitute demons in the place of God. For

this reason Paul declares that the Ephesians were *without God* (Eph. 2:12), until they had learned from the Gospel what it is to worship the true God. Nor must this be restricted to one people only, since, in another place, he declares in general that all men *became vain in their imaginations*, after the majesty of the Creator was manifested to them in the structure of the world. Accordingly, in order to make way for the only true God, he condemns all the gods celebrated among the Gentiles as lying and false, leaving no Deity anywhere but in Mount Zion where the special knowledge of God was professed (Hab. 2:18, 20). Among the Gentiles in the time of Christ, the Samaritans undoubtedly made the nearest approach to true piety, yet we hear from his own mouth that they worshipped they knew not what (John 4:22); whence it follows that they were deluded by vain errors. In short, though all did not give way to gross vice or rush headlong into open idolatry, there was no pure and authentic religion founded merely on common belief. A few individuals may not have gone all insane lengths with the vulgar; still Paul's declaration remains true, that the wisdom of God was not apprehended by the princes of this world (1 Cor. 2:8). But if the most distinguished wandered in darkness, what shall we say of the refuse? No wonder, therefore, that all worship of man's device is repudiated by the Holy Spirit as degenerate. Any opinion which man can form in heavenly mysteries, though it may not beget a long train of errors, is still the parent of error. And though nothing worse should happen, even this is no light sin—to worship an unknown god at random. Of this sin, however, we hear from our Savior's own mouth (John 4:22), that all are guilty who have not been taught out of the law who the God is whom they ought to worship. Nay, even Socrates in Xenophon (Bk. 1, *Memorabilia*), lauds the response of Apollo enjoining every man to worship the gods according to the rites of his country, and the particular practice of his own city. But what right have mortals thus to decide of their own authority in a matter which is far above the world, or who can so acquiesce in the will of his forefathers, or the decrees of the people, as unhesitatingly to receive a god at their hands? Everyone will adhere to his own judgment sooner than submit to the dictation of others. Since, therefore, in regulating the worship of God, the custom of a city, or the consent of antiquity, is a too feeble and fragile bond of piety; it remains that God himself must bear witness to himself from heaven.

14. In vain for us, therefore, does Creation exhibit so many bright lamps lighted up to show forth the glory of its Author. Though they beam upon us from every quarter, they are altogether insufficient of themselves to lead us into the right path. Some sparks, undoubtedly, they do throw out; but these are quenched before they can give forth a brighter effulgence. Wherefore, the apostle, in the very place where he says that the worlds are images of invisible things, adds that it is *by faith* we understand that they were framed by the word of God (Heb. 11:3); thereby intimating that the invisible Godhead is indeed represented by such displays, but that we have no eyes to perceive it until they are enlightened through faith by internal revelation from God. When Paul says that that which may be known of God is manifested by the creation of the world, he does not mean such a manifestation as may be comprehended by the wit of man (Rom. 1:19); on the contrary, he shows that it has no further effect than to render us inexcusable (Acts 17:27). And though he says, elsewhere, that we have not far to seek for God, inasmuch as he dwells within us, he shows, in another passage, to what extent this nearness to God is availing. God, says he, *in times past, suffered all nations to walk in their own ways. Nevertheless, he left not himself without witness, in that he did good, and gave us rain from heaven, and fruitful seasons, filling our hearts with food and gladness* (Acts 14:16, 17). But though God is not left without a witness, while with numberless varied acts of kindness he woos men to the knowledge of himself, yet they cease not to follow their own ways, in other words, deadly errors.

15. But though we are deficient in natural powers which might enable us to rise to a pure and clear knowledge of God, still, as the dullness which prevents us is within, there is no room for excuse. We cannot plead ignorance without being at the same time convicted by our own consciences both of sloth and ingratitude. It were, indeed, a strange defense for man to pretend that he has no ears to hear the truth, while dumb creatures have voices loud enough to declare it; to allege that he is unable to see that which creatures without eyes demonstrate, to excuse himself on the ground of weakness of mind, while all creatures without reason

are able to teach. Wherefore, when we wander and go astray, we are justly shut out from every species of excuse, because all things point to the right path. But while man must bear the guilt of corrupting the seed of divine knowledge so wondrously deposited in his mind, and preventing it from bearing good and genuine fruit, it is still most true that we are not sufficiently instructed by that bare and simple but magnificent testimony which the creatures bear to the glory of their Creator. For no sooner do we, from a survey of the world, obtain some slight knowledge of Deity, than we pass by the true God, and set up in his stead the dream and phantom of our own brain, drawing away the praise of justice, wisdom, and goodness from the fountainhead, and transferring it to some other quarter. Moreover, by the erroneous estimate we form, we either so obscure or pervert his daily works, as at once to rob them of their glory and the author of them of his just praise.

THE LIFE OF A CHRISTIAN
BOOK 3

Chapter 6

THE LIFE OF A CHRISTIAN MAN.
SCRIPTURAL ARGUMENTS EXHORTING TO IT.

This and the four following chapters treat of the life of the Christian, and are so arranged as to admit of being classed under two principal heads. First, it must be held to be a universally acknowledged point that no man is a Christian who does not feel some special love for righteousness, chapter 6. Second, in regard to the standard by which every man ought to regulate his life, although it seems to be considered in chapter 7 only, yet the three following chapters also refer to it. For it shows that the Christian has two duties to perform. First, the observance being so arduous, he needs the greatest patience. Hence chapter 8 treats professedly of the utility of the cross, and chapter 9 invites to meditation on the future life. Last, chapter 10 clearly shows, as in no small degree conducive to this end, how we are to use this life and its comforts without abusing them.

This sixth chapter consists of two parts: I. Connection between this treatise on the Christian life and the doctrine of regeneration and repentance. Arrangement of the treatise, sects. 1–3. II. Extremes to be avoided; 1. False Christians denying Christ by their works condemned, sect. 4, 2. Christians should not despair, though they have not attained perfection, provided they make daily progress in piety and righteousness.

Sections

1. Connection between this chapter and the doctrine of regeneration. Necessity of the doctrine concerning the Christian life. The brevity of this treatise. The method of it. Plainness and unadorned simplicity of the Scripture system of morals.
2. Two divisions. First, personal holiness. 1. Because God is holy.

2. Because of our communion with his saints.

3. Second division, relating to our redemption. Admirable moral system of Scripture. Five special inducements or exhortations to a Christian life.

4. False Christians who are opposed to this life censured. 1. They have not truly learned Christ. 2. The Gospel not the guide of their words or actions. 3. They do not imitate Christ the Master. 4. They would separate the Spirit from his word.

5. Christians ought not to despond provided: 1. They take the word of God for their guide. 2. Sincerely cultivate righteousness. 3. Walk, according to their capacity, in the ways of the Lord. 4. Make some progress. 5. Persevere.

1. We have said that the object of regeneration is to bring the life of believers into concord and harmony with the righteousness of God, and so confirm the adoption by which they have been received as sons. But although the law comprehends within it that new life by which the image of God is restored in us, yet, as our sluggishness stands greatly in need both of helps and incentives, it will be useful to collect out of Scripture a true account of this reformation lest any who have a heartfelt desire of repentance should in their zeal go astray. Moreover, I am not unaware that, in undertaking to describe the life of the Christian, I am entering on a large and extensive subject, one which, when fully considered in all its parts, is sufficient to fill a large volume. We see the length to which the Fathers in treating of individual virtues extend their exhortations. This they do, not from mere loquaciousness, for whatever be the virtue which you undertake to recommend, your pen is spontaneously led by the copiousness of the matter so to amplify, that you seem not to have discussed it properly if you have not done it at length. My intention, however, in the plan of life which I now propose to give, is not to extend it so far as to treat of each virtue specially and expatiate in exhortation. This must be sought in the writings of others, and particularly in the Homilies of the Fathers. For me it will be sufficient to point out the method by which a pious man may be taught how to frame his life aright and briefly lay down some universal rule by which he may not improperly regulate his conduct. I shall one day possibly find time for more ample discourse or leave others to perform an office for

which I am not so fit. I have a natural love of brevity, and, perhaps, any attempt of mine at copiousness would not succeed. Even if I could gain the highest applause by being more prolix, I would scarcely be disposed to attempt it while the nature of my present work requires me to glance at simple doctrine with as much brevity as possible. As philosophers have certain definitions of rectitude and honesty from which they derive particular duties and the whole train of virtues, so in this respect Scripture is not without order, but presents a most beautiful arrangement, one, too, which is every way much more certain than that of philosophers. The only difference is that they, under the influence of ambition, constantly affect an exquisite perspicuity of arrangement, which may serve to display their genius, whereas the Spirit of God, teaching without affectation, is not so perpetually observant of exact method, and yet by observing it at times sufficiently intimates that it is not to be neglected.

2. The Scripture system of which we speak aims chiefly at two objects. The former is that the love of righteousness, to which we are by no means naturally inclined, may be instilled and implanted into our minds. The latter is (see chap. 7) to prescribe a rule which will prevent us while in the pursuit of righteousness from going astray. It has numerous admirable methods of recommending righteousness. Many have been already pointed out in different parts of this work, but we shall here also briefly advert to some of them. With what better foundation can it begin than by reminding us that we must be holy because *God is holy* (Lev. 19:1; 1 Pet. 1:16)? For when we were scattered abroad like lost sheep, wandering through the labyrinth of this world, he brought us back again to his own fold. When mention is made of our union with God, let us remember that holiness must be the bond; not that by the merit of holiness we come into communion with him (we ought rather first to cleave to him, in order that, pervaded with his holiness, we may follow whither he calls), but because it greatly concerns his glory not to have any fellowship with wickedness and impurity. Wherefore he tells us that this is the end of our calling, the end to which we ought ever to have respect, if we would answer the call of God. For to what end were we rescued from the iniquity and pollution of the world into which we were plunged, if we allow ourselves, during our whole lives, to wallow

in them? Besides, we are at the same time admonished that if we would be regarded as the Lord's people, we must inhabit the holy city Jerusalem, which, as he hath consecrated it to himself, it were impious for its inhabitants to profane by impurity. Hence the expressions, *Who shall abide in thy tabernacle? Who shall dwell in thy holy hill? He that walketh uprightly, and worketh righteousness* (Ps. 15:1, 2; 24:3, 4); for the sanctuary in which he dwells certainly ought not to be like an unclean stall.

3. The better to arouse us, it exhibits God the Father, who, as he hath reconciled us to himself in his Anointed, has impressed his image upon us, to which he would have us to be conformed (Rom. 5:4). Come, then, and let them show me a more excellent system among philosophers who think that they only have a moral philosophy duly and orderly arranged. They, when they would give excellent exhortations to virtue, can only tell us to live agreeably to nature. Scripture derives its exhortations from the true source when it not only enjoins us to regulate our lives with a view to God its author to whom it belongs, but after showing us that we have degenerated from our true origin—namely, the law of our Creator—adds that Christ, through whom we have returned to favor with God, is set before us as a model, the image of which our lives should express. What do you require more effectual than this? Nay, what do you require beyond this? If the Lord adopts us for his sons on the condition that our life be a representation of Christ, the bond of our adoption, then, unless we dedicate and devote ourselves to righteousness, we not only, with the utmost perfidy, revolt from our Creator, but also abjure the Savior himself. Then, from an enumeration of all the blessings of God, and each part of our salvation, it finds materials for exhortation. Ever since God exhibited himself to us as a Father, we must be convicted of extreme ingratitude if we do not in turn exhibit ourselves as his sons. Ever since Christ purified us by the laver of his blood and communicated this purification by baptism, it would ill become us to be defiled with new pollution. Ever since he ingrafted us into his body, we, who are his members, should anxiously beware of contracting any stain or taint. Ever since he who is our head ascended to heaven, it is befitting in us to withdraw our affections from the earth and with our whole soul aspire to heaven. Ever since the Holy Spirit dedicated us as temples to the

Lord, we should make it our endeavor to show forth the glory of God and guard against being profaned by the defilement of sin. Ever since our soul and body were destined to heavenly incorruptibility and an unfading crown, we should earnestly strive to keep them pure and uncorrupted against the day of the Lord. These, I say, are the surest foundations of a well-regulated life, and you will search in vain for anything resembling them among philosophers, who, in their commendation of virtue, never rise higher than the natural dignity of man.

4. This is the place to address those who, having nothing of Christ but the name and sign, would yet be called Christians. How dare they boast of this sacred name? None have intercourse with Christ but those who have acquired the true knowledge of him from the Gospel. The apostle denies that any man truly has learned Christ who has not learned to put off *the old man, which is corrupt according to the deceitful lusts, and put on Christ* (Eph. 4:22). They are convicted, therefore, of falsely and unjustly pretending a knowledge of Christ, whatever be the volubility and eloquence with which they can talk of the Gospel. Doctrine is not an affair of the tongue, but of the life; is not apprehended by the intellect and memory merely, like other branches of learning, but is received only when it possesses the whole soul and finds its seat and habitation in the inmost recesses of the heart. Let them, therefore, either cease to insult God, by boasting that they are what they are not, or let them show themselves not unworthy disciples of their divine Master. To doctrine in which our religion is contained we have given the first place, since by it our salvation commences; but it must be transfused into the breast, and pass into the conduct, and so transform us into itself, as not to prove unfruitful. If philosophers are justly offended, and banish from their company with disgrace those who, while professing an art which ought to be the mistress of their conduct, convert it into mere loquacious sophistry, with how much better reason shall we detest those flimsy Sophists who are contented to let the Gospel play upon their lips, when, from its efficacy, it ought to penetrate the inmost affections of the heart, fix its seat in the soul, and pervade the whole man a hundred times more than the frigid discourses of philosophers?

5. I insist not that the life of the Christian shall breathe nothing but the perfect Gospel, though this is to be desired and ought to be attempted. I insist not so strictly on evangelical perfection as to refuse to acknowledge as a Christian any man who has not attained it. In this way all would be excluded from the Church, since there is no man who is not far removed from this perfection, while many, who have made but little progress, would be undeservedly rejected. What then? Let us set this before our eye as the end at which we ought constantly to aim. Let it be regarded as the goal toward which we are to run. For you cannot divide the matter with God, undertaking part of what his word enjoins, and omitting part at pleasure. For, in the first place, God uniformly recommends integrity as the principal part of his worship, meaning by integrity real singleness of mind, devoid of gloss and fiction, and to this is opposed a double mind; as if it had been said that the spiritual commencement of a good life is when the internal affections are sincerely devoted to God, in the cultivation of holiness and justice. But seeing that in this earthly prison of the body no man is supplied with strength sufficient to hasten in his course with due alacrity, while the greater number are so oppressed with weakness that hesitating, and halting, and even crawling on the ground they make little progress, let every one of us go as far as his humble ability enables him and prosecute the journey once begun. No one will travel so badly as not daily to make some degree of progress. This, therefore, let us never cease to do, that we may daily advance in the way of the Lord; and let us not despair because of the slender measure of success. How little soever the success may correspond with our wish, our labor is not lost when today is better than yesterday, provided with true singleness of mind we keep our aim and aspire to the goal, not speaking flattering things to ourselves, nor indulging our vices, but making it our constant endeavor to become better, until we attain to goodness itself. If during the whole course of our life we seek and follow, we shall at length attain it, when relieved from the infirmity of flesh we are admitted to full fellowship with God.

Chapter 7

A SUMMARY OF THE CHRISTIAN LIFE.
OF SELF-DENIAL.

The divisions of the chapter are: I. The rule which permits us not to go astray in the study of righteousness, requires two things—namely, that man, abandoning his own will, devote himself entirely to the service of God; whence it follows that we must seek not our own things, but the things of God, sects. 1, 2. II. A description of this renovation or Christian life taken from the Epistle to Titus, and accurately explained under certain special heads, sect. 3 to end.

Sections

1. Consideration of the second general division in regard to the Christian life. Its beginning and sum. A twofold respect. 1. We are not our own. Respect to both the fruit and the use. Unknown to philosophers, who have placed reason on the throne of the Holy Spirit.

2. Since we are not our own, we must seek the glory of God and obey his will. Self-denial recommended to the disciples of Christ. He who neglects it, deceived either by pride or hypocrisy, rushes on destruction.

3. Three things to be followed, and two to be shunned in life. Impiety and worldly lusts to be shunned. Sobriety, justice, and piety to be followed. An inducement to right conduct.

4. Self-denial the sum of Paul's doctrine. Its difficulty. Qualities in us which make it difficult. Cures for these qualities. 1. Ambition to be suppressed. 2. Humility to be embraced. 3. Candor to be esteemed. 4. Mutual charity to be preserved. 5. Modesty to be sincerely cultivated.

5. The advantage of our neighbor to be promoted. Here self-denial most necessary, and yet most difficult. Here a double remedy. 1. The benefits bestowed upon us are for the common benefit of the Church. 2. We ought to do all we can for our neighbor. This illustrated by analogy from the members of

the human body. This duty of charity founded on the divine command.

6. Charity ought to have for its attendants patience and kindness. We should consider the image of God in our neighbors, and especially in those who are of the household of faith. Hence a fourfold consideration which refutes all objections. A common objection refuted.

7. Christian life cannot exist without charity. Remedies for the vices opposed to charity. 1. Mercy. 2. Humility. 3. Modesty. 4. Diligence. 5. Perseverance.

8. Self-denial, in respect of God, should lead to equanimity and tolerance. 1. We are always subject to God. 2. We should shun avarice and ambition. 3. We should expect all prosperity from the blessing of God and entirely depend on him.

9. We ought not to desire wealth or honors without the divine blessing, nor follow the arts of the wicked. We ought to cast all our care upon God and never envy the prosperity of others.

10. We ought to commit ourselves entirely to God. The necessity of this doctrine. Various uses of affliction. Heathen abuse and corruption.

1. Although the Law of God contains a perfect rule of conduct admirably arranged, it has seemed proper to our divine Master to train his people by a more accurate method, to the rule which is enjoined in the Law; and the leading principle in the method is that it is the duty of believers to present their *bodies a living sacrifice, holy and acceptable unto God, which is their reasonable service* (Rom. 12:1). Hence he draws the exhortation: *Be not conformed to this world: but be ye transformed by the renewing of your mind, that ye may prove what is that good, and acceptable, and perfect will of God.* The great point, then, is that we are consecrated and dedicated to God, and, therefore, should not henceforth think, speak, design, or act without a view to his glory. What he hath made sacred cannot, without signal insult to him, be applied to profane use. But if we are not our own, but the Lord's, it is plain both what error is to be shunned, and to what end the actions of our lives ought to be directed. We are not our own; therefore, neither is our own reason or will to rule our acts and counsels. We are not our own; there-

fore, let us not make it our end to seek what may be agreeable to our carnal nature. We are not our own; therefore, as far as possible, let us forget ourselves and the things that are ours. On the other hand, we are God's; let us, therefore, live and die to him (Rom. 14:8). We are God's; therefore, let his wisdom and will preside over all our actions. We are God's; to him, then, as the only legitimate end, let every part of our life be directed. O how great the proficiency of him who, taught that he is not his own, has withdrawn the dominion and government of himself from his own reason that he may give them to God! For as the surest source of destruction to men is to obey themselves, so the only haven of safety is to have no other will, no other wisdom, than to follow the Lord wherever he leads. Let this, then, be the first step, to abandon ourselves and devote the whole energy of our minds to the service of God. By service, I mean not only that which consists in verbal obedience, but that by which the mind, divested of its own carnal feelings, implicitly obeys the call of the Spirit of God. This transformation (which Paul calls *the renewing of the mind*, Rom. 12:2; Eph. 4:23), though it is the first entrance to life, was unknown to all the philosophers. They give the government of man to reason alone, thinking that she alone is to be listened to; in short, they assign to her the sole direction of the conduct. But Christian philosophy bids her give place and yield complete submission to the Holy Spirit, so that the man himself no longer lives, but Christ lives and reigns in him (Gal. 2:20).

2. Hence follows the other principle, that we are not to seek our own, but the Lord's will, and act with a view to promote his glory. Great is our proficiency, when, almost forgetting ourselves, certainly postponing our own reason, we faithfully make it our study to obey God and his commandments. For when Scripture enjoins us to lay aside private regard to ourselves, it not only divests our minds of an excessive longing for wealth, or power, or human favor, but eradicates all ambition and thirst for worldly glory, and other more secret pests. The Christian ought, indeed, to be so trained and disposed as to consider that during his whole life he has to do with God. For this reason, as he will bring all things to the disposal and estimate of God, so he will religiously direct his whole mind to him. For he who has learned to look to God in everything he does is at the same time diverted from all vain

thoughts. This is that self-denial which Christ so strongly enforces on his disciples from the very outset (Matt. 16:24), which, as soon as it takes hold of the mind, leaves no place either, first, for pride, show, and ostentation; or, second, for avarice, lust, luxury, effeminacy, or other vices which are engendered by self-love. On the contrary, wherever it reigns not, the foulest vices are indulged in without shame; or, if there is some appearance of virtue, it is vitiated by a depraved longing for applause. Show me, if you can, an individual who, unless he has renounced himself in obedience to the Lord's command, is disposed to do good for its own sake. Those who have not so renounced themselves have followed virtue at least for the sake of praise. The philosophers who have contended most strongly that virtue is to be desired on her own account were so inflated with arrogance as to make it apparent that they sought virtue for no other reason than as a ground for indulging in pride. So far, therefore, is God from being delighted with these hunters after popular applause with their swollen breasts that he declares they have received their reward in this world (Matt. 6:2), and that harlots and publicans are nearer the kingdom of heaven than they (Matt. 21:31). We have not yet sufficiently explained how great and numerous are the obstacles by which a man is impeded in the pursuit of rectitude, so long as he has not renounced himself. The old saying is true, "There is a world of iniquity treasured up in the human soul." Nor can you find any other remedy for this than to deny yourself, renounce your own reason, and direct your whole mind to the pursuit of those things which the Lord requires of you, and which you are to seek only because they are pleasing to him.

3. In another passage, Paul gives a brief, indeed, but more distinct account of each of the parts of a well-ordered life: *The grace of God that bringeth salvation hath appeared to all men, teaching us that, denying ungodliness and worldly lusts, we should live soberly, righteously, and godly, in this present world; looking for that blessed hope, and the glorious appearance of the great God and our Savior Jesus Christ; who gave himself for us, that he might redeem us from all iniquity, and purify to himself a peculiar people, zealous of good works* (Titus 2:11–14). After holding forth the grace of God to animate us and pave the way for his true worship, he removes the two greatest obstacles which stand in the way—namely, ungodliness,

to which we are by nature too prone, and worldly lusts, which are of still greater extent. Under *ungodliness*, he includes not merely superstition, but everything at variance with the true fear of God. *Worldly lusts* are equivalent to the lusts of the flesh. Thus he enjoins us, in regard to both tables of the Law, to lay aside our own mind, and renounce whatever our own reason and will dictate. Then he reduces all the actions of our lives to three branches: sobriety, righteousness, and godliness. *Sobriety* undoubtedly denotes as well chastity and temperance as the pure and frugal use of temporal goods and patient endurance of want. *Righteousness* comprehends all the duties of equity, in every one his due. Next follows *godliness*, which separates us from the pollutions of the world, and connects us with God in true holiness. These, when connected together by an indissoluble chain, constitute complete perfection. But as nothing is more difficult than to bid adieu to the will of the flesh, subdue, nay, abjure our lusts, devote ourselves to God and our brethren, and lead an angelic life amid the pollutions of the world, Paul, to set our minds free from all entanglements, recalls us to the hope of a blessed immortality, justly urging us to contend, because as Christ has once appeared as our Redeemer, so on his final advent he will give full effect to the salvation obtained by him. And in this way he dispels all the allurements which becloud our path and prevent us from aspiring as we ought to heavenly glory; nay, he tells us that we must be pilgrims in the world, that we may not fail of obtaining the heavenly inheritance.

4. Moreover, we see by these words that self-denial has respect partly to men and partly (more especially) to God (sects. 8–10). For when Scripture enjoins us, in regard to our fellow men, to prefer them in honor to ourselves, and sincerely labor to promote their advantages (Rom. 12:10; Phil. 2:3), he gives us commands which our mind is utterly incapable of obeying until its natural feelings are suppressed. For so blindly do we all rush in the direction of self-love that everyone thinks he has a good reason for exalting himself and despising all others in comparison. If God has bestowed on us something not to be repented of, trusting to it, we immediately become elated, and not only swell, but almost burst with pride. The vices with which we abound we both carefully conceal from others and flatteringly represent to ourselves as

minute and trivial, nay, sometimes hug them as virtues. When the same qualities which we admire in ourselves are seen in others, even though they should be superior, we, in order that we may not be forced to yield to them, maliciously lower and carp at them; in like manner, in the case of vices, not contented with severe and keen animadversion, we studiously exaggerate them. Hence the insolence with which each, as if exempted from the common lot, seeks to exalt himself above his neighbor, confidently and proudly despising others, or at least looking down upon them as his inferiors. The poor man yields to the rich, the plebeian to the noble, the servant to the master, the unlearned to the learned, and yet everyone inwardly cherishes some idea of his own superiority. Thus each flattering himself sets up a kind of kingdom in his breast; the arrogant, to satisfy themselves, pass censure on the minds and manners of other men, and when contention arises, the full venom is displayed. Many bear about with them some measure of mildness so long as all things go smoothly and lovingly with them, but how few are there who, when stung and irritated, preserve the same tenor of moderation? For this there is no other remedy than to pluck up by the roots those most noxious pests, self-love and love of victory (φιλονεικία καί φιλαυτία). This the doctrine of Scripture does. For it teaches us to remember that the endowments which God has bestowed upon us are not our own, but his free gifts, and that those who plume themselves upon them betray their ingratitude. *Who maketh thee to differ,* saith Paul, *and what hast thou that thou didst not receive? now if thou didst receive it, why dost thou glory, as if thou hadst not received it?* (1 Cor. 4:7). Then by a diligent examination of our faults let us keep ourselves humble. Thus while nothing will remain to swell our pride, there will be much to subdue it. Again, we are enjoined, whenever we behold the gifts of God in others, so to reverence and respect the gifts, as also to honor those in whom they reside. God having been pleased to bestow honor upon them, it would ill become us to deprive them of it. Then we are told to overlook their faults, not, indeed, to encourage by flattering them, but not because of them to insult those whom we ought to regard with honor and goodwill. In this way, with regard to all with whom we have intercourse, our behavior will be not only moderate and modest, but courteous and friendly. The only way by which you can ever attain to true meekness is to have your heart imbued with a humble opinion of yourself and respect for others.

5. How difficult it is to perform the duty of seeking the good of our neighbor! Unless you leave off all thought of yourself and in a manner cease to be yourself, you will never accomplish it. How can you exhibit those works of charity which Paul describes unless you renounce yourself and become wholly devoted to others? *Charity* (says he, 1 Cor. 13:4) *suffereth long, and is kind; charity envieth not; charity vaunteth not itself, is not puffed up, doth not behave itself unseemly, seeketh not her own, is not easily provoked,* et cetera. Were it the only thing required of us to seek not our own, nature would not have the least power to comply: she so inclines us to love ourselves only, that she will not easily allow us carelessly to pass by ourselves and our own interests that we may watch over the interests of others, nay, spontaneously to yield our own rights and resign it to another. But Scripture, to conduct us to this, reminds us that whatever we obtain from the Lord is granted on the condition of our employing it for the common good of the Church, and that, therefore, the legitimate use of all our gifts is a kind and liberal communication of them with others. There cannot be a surer rule, nor a stronger exhortation to the observance of it, than when we are taught that all the endowments which we possess are divine deposits entrusted to us for the very purpose of being distributed for the good of our neighbor. But Scripture proceeds still further when it likens these endowments to the different members of the body (1 Cor. 12:12). No member has its function for itself, or applies it for its own private use, but transfers it to its fellow-members; nor does it derive any other advantage from it than that which it receives in common with the whole body. Thus, whatever the pious man can do, he is bound to do for his brethren, not consulting his own interest in any other way than by striving earnestly for the common edification of the Church. Let this, then, be our method of showing goodwill and kindness, considering that, in regard to everything which God has bestowed upon us, and by which we can aid our neighbor, we are his stewards and are bound to give account of our stewardship; moreover, that the only right mode of administration is that which is regulated by love. In this way, we shall not only unite the study of our neighbor's advantage with a regard to our own, but make the latter subordinate to the

former. And lest we should have omitted to perceive that this is the law for duly administering every gift which we receive from God, he of old applied that law to the minutest expressions of his own kindness. He commanded the firstfruits to be offered to him as an attestation by the people that it was impious to reap any advantage from goods not previously consecrated to him (Exod. 22:29; 23:19). But if the gifts of God are not sanctified to us until we have with our own hand dedicated them to the Giver, it must be a gross abuse that does not give signs of such dedication. It is in vain to contend that you cannot enrich the Lord by your offerings. Though, as the psalmist says, *Thou art my Lord: my goodness extendeth not unto thee,* yet you can extend it *to the saints that are in the earth* (Ps. 16:2, 3); and therefore a comparison is drawn between sacred oblations and alms as now corresponding to the offerings under the Law.

6. Moreover, that we may not weary in well-doing (as would otherwise forthwith and infallibly be the case), we must add the other quality in the apostle's enumeration, *Charity suffereth long, and is kind, is not easily provoked* (1 Cor. 13:4). The Lord enjoins us to do good to all without exception, though the greater part, if estimated by their own merit, are most unworthy of it. But Scripture subjoins a most excellent reason when it tells us that we are not to look to what men in themselves deserve, but to attend to the image of God, which exists in all, and to which we owe all honor and love. But in those who are of the household of faith, the same rule is to be more carefully observed, inasmuch as that image is renewed and restored in them by the Spirit of Christ. Therefore, whoever be the man that is presented to you as needing your assistance, you have no ground for declining to give it to him. Say he is a stranger. The Lord has given him a mark which ought to be familiar to you: for which reason he forbids you to despise your own flesh (Gal. 6:10). Say he is mean and of no consideration. The Lord points him out as one whom he has distinguished by the luster of his own image (Isa. 58:7). Say that you are bound to him by no ties of duty. The Lord has substituted him as it were into his own place, that in him you may recognize the many great obligations under which the Lord has laid you to himself. Say that he is unworthy of your least exertion on his account; but the image of God, by which he is recommended to you, is worthy of yourself

and all your exertions. But if he not only merits no good, but has provoked you by injury and mischief, still this is no good reason why you should not embrace him in love, and visit him with offices of love. He has deserved very differently from me, you will say. But what has the Lord deserved? Whatever injury he has done you, when he enjoins you to forgive him, he certainly means that it should be imputed to himself. In this way only we attain to what is not to say difficult but altogether against nature, to love those that hate us, render good for evil, and blessing for cursing, remembering that we are not to reflect on the wickedness of men, but look to the image of God in them, an image which, covering and obliterating their faults, should by its beauty and dignity allure us to love and embrace them.

7. We shall thus succeed in mortifying ourselves if we fulfill all the duties of charity. Those duties, however, are not fulfilled by the mere discharge of them, though none be omitted, unless it is done from a pure feeling of love. For it may happen that one may perform every one of these offices, insofar as the external act is concerned, and be far from performing them aright. For you see some who would be thought very liberal, and yet accompany everything they give with insult, by the haughtiness of their looks or the violence of their words. And to such a calamitous condition have we come in this unhappy age, that the greater part of men almost never give alms without contumely. Such conduct ought not to have been tolerated even among the heathen, but from Christians something more is required than to carry cheerfulness in their looks and give attractiveness to the discharge of their duties by courteous language. First, they should put themselves in the place of him whom they see in need of their assistance and pity his misfortune as if they felt and bore it, so that a feeling of pity and humanity should incline them to assist him just as they would themselves. He who is thus minded will go and give assistance to his brethren and not only not taint his acts with arrogance or upbraiding, but will neither look down upon the brother to whom he does a kindness, as one who needed his help, or keep him in subjection as under obligation to him, just as we do not insult a diseased member when the rest of the body labors for its recovery, nor think it under special obligation to the other members because it has required more exertion than it has returned. A communica-

tion of offices between members is not regarded as at all gratuitous, but rather as the payment of that which being due by the law of nature it were monstrous to deny. For this reason, he who has performed one kind of duty will not think himself thereby discharged, as is usually the case when a rich man, after contributing somewhat of his substance, delegates remaining burdens to others as if he had nothing to do with them. Everyone should rather consider that however great he is, he owes himself to his neighbors, and that the only limit to his beneficence is the failure of his means. The extent of these should regulate that of his charity.

8. The principal part of self-denial, that which as we have said has reference to God, let us again consider more fully. Many things have already been said with regard to it which it were superfluous to repeat; and, therefore, it will be sufficient to view it as forming us to equanimity and endurance. First, then, in seeking the convenience or tranquillity of the present life, Scripture calls us to resign ourselves, and all we have, to the disposal of the Lord, to give him up the affections of our heart, that he may tame and subdue them. We have a frenzied desire, an infinite eagerness, to pursue wealth and honor, intrigue for power, accumulate riches, and collect all those frivolities which seem conducive to luxury and splendor. On the other hand, we have a remarkable dread, a remarkable hatred of poverty, mean birth, and a humble condition, and feel the strongest desire to guard against them. Hence, in regard to those who frame their life after their own counsel, we see how restless they are in mind, how many plans they try, to what fatigues they submit, in order that they may gain what avarice or ambition desires, or, on the other hand, escape poverty and meanness. To avoid similar entanglements, the course which Christian men must follow is this: first, they must not long for, or hope for, or think of any kind of prosperity apart from the blessing of God; on it they must cast themselves and there safely and confidently recline. For, however much the carnal mind may seem sufficient for itself when in the pursuit of honor or wealth, it depends on its own industry and zeal or is aided by the favor of men, it is certain that all this is nothing, and that neither intellect nor labor will be of the least avail, except insofar as the Lord prospers both. On the contrary, his blessing alone makes a way through all obstacles and brings everything to a joyful and favorable issue. Second, though

without this blessing we may be able to acquire some degree of fame and opulence (as we daily see wicked men loaded with honors and riches), yet since those on whom the curse of God lies do not enjoy the least particle of true happiness, whatever we obtain without his blessing must turn out ill. But surely men ought not to desire what adds to their misery.

9. Therefore, if we believe that all prosperous and desirable success depends entirely on the blessing of God, and that when it is wanting all kinds of misery and calamity await us, it follows that we should not eagerly contend for riches and honors, trusting to our own dexterity and assiduity, or leaning on the favor of men, or confiding in any empty imagination of fortune; but should always have respect to the Lord, that under his auspices we may be conducted to whatever lot he has provided for us. First, the result will be that instead of rushing on regardless of right and wrong, by wiles and wicked arts, and with injury to our neighbors, to catch at wealth and seize upon honors, we will only follow such fortune as we may enjoy with innocence. Who can hope for the aid of the divine blessing amid fraud, rapine, and other iniquitous arts? As this blessing attends him only who thinks purely and acts uprightly, so it calls off all who long for it from sinister designs and evil actions. Second, a curb will be laid upon us, restraining a too-eager desire of becoming rich, or an ambitious striving after honor. How can anyone have the effrontery to expect that God will aid him in accomplishing desires at variance with his word? What God with his own lips pronounces cursed never can be prosecuted with his blessing. Last, if our success is not equal to our wish and hope, we shall, however, be kept from impatience and detestation of our condition, whatever it be, knowing that so to feel were to murmur against God, at whose pleasure riches and poverty, contempt and honors, are dispensed. In short, he who leans on the divine blessing in the way which has been described, will not, in the pursuit of those things which men are wont most eagerly to desire, employ wicked arts which he knows would avail him nothing; nor when anything prosperous befalls him will he impute it to himself and his own diligence, or industry, or fortune, instead of ascribing it to God as its author. If, while the affairs of others flourish, his make little progress, or even retrograde, he will bear his humble lot with greater equanimity and moderation than

any irreligious man does the moderate success which only falls short of what he wished, for he has a solace in which he can rest more tranquilly than at the very summit of wealth or power, because he considers that his affairs are ordered by the Lord in the manner most conducive to his salvation. This, we see, is the way in which David was affected, who, while he follows God and gives up himself to his guidance, declares, *Neither do I exercise myself in great matters, or in things too high for me. Surely I have behaved and quieted myself as a child that is weaned of his mother* (Ps. 131:1, 2).

10. Nor is it in this respect only that pious minds ought to manifest this tranquillity and endurance; it must be extended to all the accidents to which this present life is liable. He alone, therefore, has properly denied himself, who has resigned himself entirely to the Lord, placing all the course of his life entirely at his disposal. Happen what may, he whose mind is thus composed will neither deem himself wretched nor murmur against God because of his lot. How necessary this disposition is will appear, if you consider the many accidents to which we are liable. Various diseases ever and anon attack us: at one time pestilence rages; at another we are involved in all the calamities of war. Frost and hail, destroying the promise of the year, cause sterility, which reduces us to penury; wife, parents, children, relatives, are carried off by death; our house is destroyed by fire. These are the events which make men curse their life, detest the day of their birth, execrate the light of heaven, even censure God, and (as they are eloquent in blasphemy) charge him with cruelty and injustice. The believer must in these things also contemplate the mercy and truly paternal indulgence of God. Accordingly, should he see his house by the removal of kindred reduced to solitude even then he will not cease to bless the Lord; his thought will be, "Still the grace of the Lord, which dwells within my house, will not leave it desolate." If his crops are blasted, mildewed, or cut off by frost, or struck down by hail, and he sees famine before him, he will not however despond or murmur against God, but maintain his confidence in him; *We thy people, and sheep of thy pasture, will give thee thanks forever* (Ps. 79:13); he will supply me with food, even in the extreme of sterility. If he is afflicted with disease, the sharpness of the pain will not so overcome him as to make him break out with impatience and expostulate with God; but, recognizing justice and

lenity in the rod, will patiently endure. In short, whatever happens, knowing that it is ordered by the Lord, he will receive it with a placid and grateful mind and will not contumaciously resist the government of him at whose disposal he has placed himself and all that he has. Especially let the Christian breast eschew that foolish and most miserable consolation of the heathen, who, to strengthen their mind against adversity, imputed it to fortune, at which they deemed it absurd to feel indignant, as she was ἄσκοπος (aimless) and rash, and blindly wounded the good equally with the bad. On the contrary, the rule of piety is that the hand of God is the ruler and arbiter of the fortunes of all, and, instead of rushing on with thoughtless violence, dispenses good and evil with perfect regularity.

Chapter 8

OF BEARING THE CROSS —
ONE BRANCH OF SELF-DENIAL.

The four divisions of this chapter are—I. The nature of the cross, its necessity and dignity, sects. 1, 2. II. The manifold advantages of the cross described, sects. 3–6. III. The form of the cross the most excellent of all, and yet it by no means removes all sense of pain, sects. 7, 8. IV. A description of warfare under the cross, and of true patience (not that of philosophers), after the example of Christ, sects. 9–11.

Sections

1. What the cross is. By whom, and on whom, and for what cause imposed. Its necessity and dignity.
2. The cross necessary. a. To humble our pride. b. To make us apply to God for aid. Example of David.
3. To give us experience of God's presence. c. Manifold uses of the cross. i. Produces patience, hope, and firm confidence in God, gives us victory and perseverance. Faith invincible.
4. ii. Frames us to obedience. Example of Abraham. This training how useful.
5. The cross necessary to subdue the wantonness of the flesh.

This portrayed by an apposite simile. Various forms of the cross.

6. iii. God permits our infirmities, and corrects past faults, that he may keep us in obedience. This confirmed by a passage from Solomon and an apostle.

7. Singular consolation under the cross, when we suffer persecution for righteousness. Some parts of this consolation.

8. This form of the cross most appropriate to believers, and should be borne willingly and cheerfully. This cheerfulness is not unfeeling hilarity, but, while groaning under the burden, waits patiently for the Lord.

9. A description of this conflict. Opposed to the vanity of the Stoics. Illustrated by the authority and example of Christ.

10. Proved by the testimony and uniform experience of the elect. Also by the special example of the Apostle Peter. The nature of the patience required of us.

11. Distinction between the patience of Christians and philosophers. The latter pretend a necessity which cannot be resisted. The former hold forth the justice of God and his care of our safety. A full exposition of this difference.

1. The pious mind must ascend still higher, namely, whither Christ calls his disciples when he says that every one of them must *take up his cross* (Matt. 16:24). Those whom the Lord has chosen and honored with his intercourse must prepare for a hard, laborious, troubled life, a life full of many and various kinds of evils; it being the will of our heavenly Father to exercise his people in this way while putting them to the proof. Having begun this course with Christ the firstborn, he continues it toward all his children. For though that Son was dear to him above others, the Son in whom he was *well pleased*, yet we see that far from being treated gently and indulgently, we may say that not only was he subjected to a perpetual cross while he dwelled on earth, but his whole life was nothing else than a kind of perpetual cross. The apostle assigns the reason, *Though he was a Son, yet learned he obedience by the things which he suffered* (Heb. 5:8). Why then should we exempt ourselves from that condition to which Christ our Head felt behooved to submit, especially since he submitted on our account, that he might in his own person exhibit a model of patience?

Wherefore, the apostle declares that all the children of God are destined to be conformed to him. Hence it affords us great consolation in hard and difficult circumstances, which men deem evil and adverse, to think that we are holding fellowship with the sufferings of Christ; that as he passed to celestial glory through a labyrinth of many woes, so we too are conducted thither through various tribulations. For, in another passage, Paul himself thus speaks, *we must through much tribulation enter the kingdom of God* (Acts 14:22); and again, *that I may know him, and the power of his resurrection, and the fellowship of his sufferings, being made conformable unto his death* (Rom 8:29). How powerfully should it soften the bitterness of the cross, to think that the more we are afflicted with adversity, the surer we are made of our fellowship with Christ; by communion with whom our sufferings are not only blessed to us, but tend greatly to the furtherance of our salvation.

2. We may add that the only thing which made it necessary for our Lord to undertake to bear the cross was to testify and prove his obedience to the Father; whereas there are many reasons which make it necessary for us to live constantly under the cross. Feeble as we are by nature, and prone to ascribe all perfection to our flesh, unless we receive as it were ocular demonstration of our weakness, we readily estimate our virtue above its proper worth, and doubt not that, whatever happens, it will stand unimpaired and invincible against all difficulties. Hence we indulge a stupid and empty confidence in the flesh, and then trusting to it wax proud against the Lord himself; as if our own faculties were sufficient without his grace. This arrogance cannot be better repressed than when he proves to us by experience, not only how great our weakness, but also our frailty is. Therefore, he visits us with disgrace, or poverty, or bereavement, or disease, or other afflictions. Feeling altogether unable to support them, we forthwith, insofar as regards ourselves, give way, and thus humbled learn to invoke his strength, which alone can enable us to bear up under a weight of affliction. Nay, even the holiest of men, however well aware that they stand not in their own strength, but by the grace of God, would feel too secure in their own fortitude and constancy were they not brought to a more thorough knowledge of themselves by the trial of the

cross. This feeling gained even upon David, *In my prosperity I said, I shall never be moved. Lord, by thy favor thou hast made my mountain to stand strong: thou didst hide thy face, and I was troubled* (Ps. 30:6, 7). He confesses that in prosperity his feelings were dulled and blunted, so that, neglecting the grace of God, on which alone he ought to have depended, he leaned to himself, and promised himself perpetuity. If it so happened to this great prophet, who of us should not fear and study caution? Though in tranquillity they flatter themselves with the idea of greater constancy and patience, yet, humbled by adversity, they learn the deception. Believers, I say, warned by such proofs of their diseases, make progress in humility, and, divesting themselves of a depraved confidence in the flesh, betake themselves to the grace of God, and, when they have so betaken themselves, experience the presence of the divine power, in which is ample protection.

3. This Paul teaches when he says that tribulation worketh patience, and patience experience. God having promised that he will be with believers in tribulation, they feel the truth of the promise; while supported by his hand, they endure patiently. This they could never do by their own strength. Patience, therefore, gives the saints an experimental proof that God in reality furnishes the aid which he has promised whenever there is need. Hence also their faith is confirmed, for it were very ungrateful not to expect that in future the truth of God will be, as they have already found it, firm and constant. We now see how many advantages are at once produced by the cross. Overturning the overweening opinion we form of our own virtue, and detecting the hypocrisy in which we delight, it removes our pernicious carnal confidence, teaching us, when thus humbled, to recline on God alone, so that we neither are oppressed nor despond. Then victory is followed by hope, inasmuch as the Lord, by performing what he has promised, establishes his truth in regard to the future. Were these the only reasons, it is surely plain how necessary it is for us to bear the cross. It is of no little importance to be rid of your self-love and made fully conscious of your weakness; so impressed with a sense of your weakness as to learn to distrust yourself—to distrust yourself so as to transfer your confidence to God, reclining on him with such heartfelt confidence as to trust in his aid, and

continue invincible to the end, standing by his grace so as to perceive that he is true to his promises, and so assured of the certainty
of his promises as to be strong in hope.

4. Another end which the Lord has in afflicting his people is to
try their patience and train them to obedience—not that they can
yield obedience to him except insofar as he enables them; but he is
pleased thus to attest and display striking proofs of the graces
which he has conferred upon his saints, lest they should remain
within unseen and unemployed. Accordingly, by bringing forward openly the strength and constancy of endurance with which
he has provided his servants, he is said to try their patience. Hence
the expressions that God tempted Abraham (Gen. 21:1, 12), and
made proof of his piety by not declining to sacrifice his only son.
Hence, too, Peter tells us that our faith is proved by tribulation,
just as gold is tried in a furnace of fire. But who will say it is
not expedient that the most excellent gift of patience which the
believer has received from his God should be applied to uses by
being made sure and manifest? Otherwise men would never value
it according to its worth. But if God himself, to prevent the virtues
which he has conferred upon believers from lurking in obscurity,
nay, lying useless and perishing, does aright in supplying materials
for calling them forth, there is the best reason for the afflictions of
the saints, since without them their patience could not exist. I say
that by the cross they are also trained to obedience, because they
are thus taught to live not according to their own wish, but at the
disposal of God. Indeed, did all things proceed as they wish, they
would not know what it is to follow God. Seneca mentions (*De
Vita Beata*, chap. 15) that there was an old proverb when anyone
was exhorted to endure adversity, "Follow God"; thereby intimating that men truly submitted to the yoke of God only when they
gave their back and hand to his rod. But if it is most right that we
should in all things prove our obedience to our heavenly Father,
certainly we ought not to decline any method by which he trains
us to obedience.

5. Still, however, we see not how necessary that obedience is,
unless we at the same time consider how prone our carnal nature
is to shake off the yoke of God whenever it has been treated with
some degree of gentleness and indulgence. It just happens to it
as with refractory horses, which, if kept idle for a few days at

hack and manger, become ungovernable and no longer recognize the rider, whose command before they implicitly obeyed. And we invariably become what God complains of in the people of Israel—waxing gross and fat, we kick against him who reared and nursed us (Deut. 32:15). The kindness of God should allure us to ponder and love his goodness, but since such is our malignity that we are invariably corrupted by his indulgence, it is more than necessary for us to be restrained by discipline from breaking forth into such petulance. Thus, lest we become emboldened by an overabundance of wealth; lest elated with honor, we grow proud; lest inflated with other advantages of body, or mind, or fortune, we grow insolent, the Lord himself interferes as he sees to be expedient by means of the cross, subduing and curbing the arrogance of our flesh, and that in various ways, as the advantage of each requires. For as we do not all equally labor under the same disease, so we do not all need the same difficult cure. Hence we see that all are not exercised with the same kind of cross. While the heavenly Physician treats some more gently, in the case of others he employs harsher remedies, his purpose being to provide a cure for all. Still none is left free and untouched, because he knows that all, without a single exception, are diseased.

6. We may add that our most merciful Father requires not only to prevent our weakness, but often to correct our past faults, that he may keep us in due obedience. Therefore, whenever we are afflicted we ought immediately to call to mind our past life. In this way we will find that the faults which we have committed are deserving of such castigation. And yet the exhortation to patience is not to be founded chiefly on the acknowledgment of sin. For Scripture supplies a far better consideration when it says that in adversity *we are chastened of the Lord, that we should not be condemned with the world* (1 Cor. 11:32). Therefore, in the very bitterness of tribulation we ought to recognize the kindness and mercy of our Father, since even then he ceases not to further our salvation. For he afflicts, not that he may ruin or destroy, but rather that he may deliver us from the condemnation of the world. Let this thought lead us to what Scripture elsewhere teaches: *My son, despise not the chastening of the Lord; neither be weary of his correction: For whom the Lord loveth he correcteth; even as a father the son in whom he delighteth* (Prov. 3:11, 12). When we perceive our

Father's rod, is it not our part to behave as obedient docile sons rather than rebelliously imitate desperate men who are hardened in wickedness? God dooms us to destruction, if he does not, by correction, call us back when we have fallen off from him, so that it is truly said, *If ye be without chastisement, then are ye bastards, and not sons* (Heb. 12:8). We are most perverse then if we cannot bear him while he is manifesting his goodwill to us, and the care which he takes of our salvation. Scripture states the difference between believers and unbelievers to be that the latter, as the slaves of inveterate and deep-seated iniquity, only become worse and more obstinate under the lash; whereas the former, like freeborn sons, turn to repentance. Now, therefore, choose your class. But as I have already spoken of this subject, it is sufficient to have here briefly adverted to it.

7. There is singular consolation, moreover, when we are persecuted for righteousness' sake. For our thought should then be, "How high the honor which God bestows upon us in distinguishing us by the special badge of his soldiers." By suffering persecution for righteousness' sake, I mean not only striving for the defense of the Gospel, but for the defense of righteousness in any way. Whether, therefore, in maintaining the truth of God against the lies of Satan, or defending the good and innocent against the injuries of the bad, we are obliged to incur the offense and hatred of the world, so as to endanger life, fortune, or honor, let us not grieve or decline so far to spend ourselves for God; let us not think ourselves wretched in those things in which he with his own lips has pronounced us blessed (Matt. 5:10). Poverty, indeed considered in itself, is misery; so are exile, contempt, imprisonment, ignominy: in fine, death itself is the last of all calamities. But when the favor of God breathes upon us, there is none of these things which may not turn out to our happiness. Let us then be contented with the testimony of Christ rather than with the false estimate of the flesh, and then, after the example of the apostles, we will rejoice in being *counted worthy to suffer shame for his name* (Acts 5:41). For why? If, while conscious of our innocence, we are deprived of our substance by the wickedness of man, we are, no doubt, humanly speaking, reduced to poverty, but in truth our riches in heaven are increased: if driven from our homes we have a more welcome reception into the family of God; if vexed and

despised, we are more firmly rooted in Christ; if stigmatized by disgrace and ignominy, we have a higher place in the kingdom of God; and if we are slain, entrance is thereby given us to eternal life. The Lord having set such a price upon us, let us be ashamed to estimate ourselves at less than the shadowy and evanescent allurements of the present life.

8. Since by these, and similar considerations, Scripture abundantly solaces us for the ignominy or calamities which we endure in defense of righteousness, we are very ungrateful if we do not willingly and cheerfully receive them at the hand of the Lord, especially since this form of the cross is the most appropriate to believers, being that by which Christ desires to be glorified in us, as Peter also declares (1 Pet. 4:11, 14). But as to ingenuous natures, it is more bitter to suffer disgrace than a hundred deaths. Paul expressly reminds us that not only persecution, but also disgrace awaits us, *because we trust in the living God* (1 Tim. 4:10). So in another passage he bids us, after his example, walk *by evil report and good report* (2 Cor. 6:8). The cheerfulness required, however, does not imply a total insensibility to pain. The saints could show no patience under the cross if they were not both tortured with pain and grievously molested. Were there no hardship in poverty, no pain in disease, no sting in ignominy, no fear in death, where would be the fortitude and moderation in enduring them? But while every one of these, by its inherent bitterness, naturally vexes the mind, the believer in this displays his fortitude, that though fully sensible of the bitterness and laboring grievously, he still withstands and struggles boldly; in this displays his patience, that though sharply stung, he is however curbed by the fear of God from breaking forth into any excess; in this displays his alacrity, that though pressed with sorrow and sadness, he rests satisfied with spiritual consolation from God.

9. This conflict which believers maintain against the natural feeling of pain, while they study moderation and patience, Paul elegantly describes in these words: *We are troubled on every side, yet not distressed; we are perplexed, but not in despair; persecuted, but not forsaken; cast down, but not destroyed* (2 Cor. 4:8, 9). You see that to bear the cross patiently is not to have your feelings altogether blunted, and to be absolutely insensible to pain, according to the absurd description which the Stoics of old gave of their hero as

one who, divested of humanity, was affected in the same way by adversity and prosperity, grief and joy; or rather, like a stone, was not affected by anything. And what did they gain by that sublime wisdom? They exhibited a shadow of patience, which never did, and never can, exist among men. Nay, rather by aiming at a too exact and rigid patience, they banished it altogether from human life. Now also we have among Christians a new kind of Stoics, who hold it vicious not only to groan and weep, but even to be sad and anxious. These paradoxes are usually started by indolent men who, employing themselves more in speculation than in action, can do nothing else for us than beget such paradoxes. But we have nothing to do with that iron philosophy which our Lord and Master condemned—not only in word, but also by his own example. For he both grieved and shed tears for his own and others' woes. Nor did he teach his disciples differently: *Ye shall weep and lament, but the world shall rejoice* (John 16:20). And lest anyone should regard this as vicious, he expressly declares, *Blessed are they that mourn* (Matt. 5:4). And no wonder. If all tears are condemned, what shall we think of our Lord himself, whose *sweat was as it were great drops of blood falling down to the ground* (Luke 22:44; Matt. 26:38)? If every kind of fear is a mark of unbelief, what place shall we assign to the dread which, it is said, in no slight degree amazed him; if all sadness is condemned, how shall we justify him when he confesses, *My soul is exceeding sorrowful, even unto death*?

10. I wished to make these observations to keep pious minds from despair, lest, from feeling it impossible to divest themselves of the natural feeling of grief, they might altogether abandon the study of patience. This must necessarily be the result with those who convert patience into stupor, and a brave and firm man into a block. Scripture gives saints the praise of endurance when, though afflicted by the hardships they endure, they are not crushed; though they feel bitterly, they are at the same time filled with spiritual joy; though pressed with anxiety, breathe exhilarated by the consolation of God. Still there is a certain degree of repugnance in their hearts, because natural sense shuns and dreads what is adverse to it, while pious affection, even through these difficulties, tries to obey the divine will. This repugnance the Lord expressed when he thus addressed Peter: *Verily, verily, I say unto thee, When*

thou wast young, thou girdedst thyself and walkedst whither thou wouldst; but when thou shalt be old, thou shalt stretch forth thy hands, and another shall gird thee; and carry thee whither thou wouldest not (John 21:18). It is not probable, indeed, that when it became necessary to glorify God by death he was driven to it unwilling and resisting; had it been so, little praise would have been due to his martyrdom. But though he obeyed the divine ordination with the greatest alacrity of heart, yet, as he had not divested himself of humanity, he was distracted by a double will. When he thought of the bloody death which he was to die, struck with horror, he would willingly have avoided it: on the other hand, when he considered that it was God who called him to it, his fear was vanquished and suppressed, and he met death cheerfully. It must therefore be our study, if we would be disciples of Christ, to imbue our minds with such reverence and obedience to God as may tame and subjugate all affections contrary to his appointment. In this way, whatever be the kind of cross to which we are subjected, we shall in the greatest straits firmly maintain our patience. Adversity will have its bitterness and sting us. When afflicted with disease, we shall groan and be disquieted and long for health; pressed with poverty, we shall feel the stings of anxiety and sadness, feel the pain of ignominy, contempt, and injury, and pay the tears due to nature at the death of our friends: but our conclusion will always be, "The Lord so willed it, therefore let us follow his will." Nay, amid the pungency of grief, among groans and tears this thought will necessarily suggest itself and incline us cheerfully to endure the things for which we are so afflicted.

11. But since the chief reason for enduring the cross has been derived from a consideration of the divine will, we must in few words explain wherein lies the difference between philosophical and Christian patience. Indeed, very few of the philosophers advanced so far as to perceive that the hand of God tries us by means of affliction, and that we ought in this matter to obey God. The only reason which they adduce is that *so it must be*. But is not this just to say that we must yield to God because it is in vain to contend against him? For if we obey God only because it is necessary, provided we can escape, we shall cease to obey him. But what Scripture calls us to consider in the will of God is very different, namely, first justice and equity, and then a regard to our own

salvation. Hence Christian exhortations to patience are of this nature. Whether poverty, or exile, or imprisonment, or contumely, or disease, or bereavement, or any such evil affects us, we must think that none of them happens except by the will and Providence of God; moreover, that everything he does is in the most perfect order. What! Do not our numberless daily faults deserve to be chastised, more severely, and with a heavier rod than his mercy lays upon us? Is it not most right that our flesh should be subdued, and be, as it were, accustomed to the yoke, so as not to rage and wanton as it lists? Are not the justice and the truth of God worthy of our suffering on their account? But if the equity of God is undoubtedly displayed in affliction, we cannot murmur or struggle against them without iniquity. We no longer hear the frigid cant, "Yield, because it is necessary"; but a living and energetic precept, "Obey, because it is unlawful to resist; bear patiently, because impatience is rebellion against the justice of God." Then as that only seems to us attractive which we perceive to be for our own safety and advantage, here also our heavenly Father consoles us, by the assurance that in the very cross with which he afflicts us, he provides for our salvation. But if it is clear that tribulations are salutary to us, why should we not receive them with calm and grateful minds? In bearing them patiently we are not submitting to necessity but resting satisfied with our own good. The effect of these thoughts is that to whatever extent our minds are contracted by the bitterness which we naturally feel under the cross, to the same extent will they be expanded with spiritual joy. Hence arises thanksgiving, which cannot exist unless joy be felt. But if the praise of the Lord and thanksgiving can emanate only from cheerful and gladdened breasts and there is nothing which ought to interrupt these feelings in us, it is clear how necessary it is to temper the bitterness of the cross with spiritual joy.

Chapter 9

OF MEDITATING ON THE FUTURE LIFE.

The three divisions of this chapter—I. The principal use of the cross is that it in various ways accustoms us to despise the present and excites us to aspire to the future life, sects. 1, 2. II. In withdrawing from the present life we must neither shun it nor feel hatred for it, but desiring the future life, gladly quit the present at the command of our sovereign Master, sects. 3, 4. III. Our infirmity in dreading death described. The correction and safe remedy, sect. 6.

Sections

1. The design of God in afflicting his people. 1. To accustom us to despise the present life. Our infatuated love of it. Afflictions employed as the cure. 2. To lead us to aspire to heaven.
2. Excessive love of the present life prevents us from duly aspiring to the other. Hence the disadvantages of prosperity. Blindness of the human judgment. Our philosophizing on the vanity of life only of momentary influence. The necessity of the cross.
3. The present life an evidence of the divine favor to his people; and, therefore, not to be detested. On the contrary, should call forth thanksgiving. The crown of victory in heaven after the contest on earth.
4. Weariness of the present life how to be tempered. The believer's estimate of life. Comparison of the present and the future life. How far the present life should be hated.
5. Christians should not tremble at the fear of death. Two reasons. Objection. Answer. Other reasons.
6. Reasons continued. Conclusion.

1. Whatever be the kind of tribulation with which we are afflicted, we should always consider the end of it to be that we may be trained to despise the present and thereby stimulated to aspire to the future life. For since God well knows how strongly we are inclined by nature to a slavish love of this world, in order to prevent us from clinging too strongly to it, he employs the fittest reason for calling us back and shaking off our lethargy. Every one of us, indeed, would be thought to aspire and aim at heavenly immortality during the whole course of his life. For we would be ashamed in no respect to excel the lower animals, whose condition would not be at all inferior to ours had we not a hope of immortality beyond the grave. But when you attend to the plans, wishes, and actions of each, you see nothing in them but the earth. Hence

our stupidity; our minds being dazzled with the glare of wealth, power, and honors, that they can see no farther. The heart also, engrossed with avarice, ambition, and lust, is weighed down and cannot rise above them. In short, the whole soul, ensnared by the allurements of the flesh, seeks its happiness on the earth. To meet this disease, the Lord makes his people sensible of the vanity of the present life, by a constant proof of its miseries. Thus, that they may not promise themselves deep and lasting peace in it, he often allows them to be assailed by war, tumult, or rapine, or to be disturbed by other injuries. That they may not long with too much eagerness after fleeting and fading riches, or rest in those which they already possess, he reduces them to want, or, at least, restricts them to a moderate allowance, at one time by exile, at another by sterility, at another by fire, or by other means. That they may not indulge too complacently in the advantages of married life, he either vexes them by the misconduct of their partners, or humbles them by the wickedness of their children, or afflicts them by bereavement. But if in all these he is indulgent to them, lest they should either swell with vainglory or be elated with confidence, by diseases and dangers he sets palpably before them how unstable and evanescent are all the advantages competent to mortals. We duly profit by the discipline of the cross when we learn that this life, estimated in itself, is restless, troubled, in numberless ways wretched, and plainly in no respect happy; that what are estimated its blessings are uncertain, fleeting, vain, and vitiated by a great admixture of evil. From this we conclude that all we have to seek or hope for here is contest; that when we think of the crown we must raise our eyes to heaven. For we must hold that our mind never rises seriously to desire and aspire after the future until it has learned to despise the present life.

2. For there is no medium between the two things: the earth must either be worthless in our estimation or keep us enslaved by an intemperate love of it. Therefore, if we have any regard to eternity, we must carefully strive to disencumber ourselves of these fetters. Moreover, since the present life has many enticements to allure us, and great semblance of delight, grace, and sweetness to soothe us, it is of great consequence to us to be now and then called off from its fascinations. For what, pray, would happen, if we here enjoyed an uninterrupted course of honor and felicity, when even

the constant stimulus of affliction cannot arouse us to a due sense of our misery? That human life is like smoke or a shadow is not only known to the learned; there is not a more trite proverb among the vulgar. Considering it a fact most useful to be known, they have recommended it in many well-known expressions. Still there is no fact which we ponder less carefully, or less frequently remember. For we form all our plans just as if we had fixed our immortality on the earth. If we see a funeral, or walk among graves, as the image of death is then present to the eye, I admit we philosophize admirably on the vanity of life. We do not indeed always do so, for those things often have no effect upon us at all. But, at the best, our philosophy is momentary. It vanishes as soon as we turn our back, and leaves not the vestige of remembrance behind; in short, it passes away, just like the applause of a theater at some pleasant spectacle. Forgetful not only of death, but also of mortality itself, as if no rumor of it had ever reached us, we indulge in supine security as expecting a terrestrial immortality. Meanwhile, if anyone breaks in with the proverb, that man is the creature of a day, we indeed acknowledge its truth, but, so far from giving heed to it, the thought of perpetuity still keeps hold of our minds. Who then can deny that it is of the highest importance to us all, I say not, to be admonished by words, but convinced by all possible experience of the miserable condition of our earthly life; since even when convinced we scarcely cease to gaze upon it with vicious, stupid admiration, as if it contained within itself the sum of all that is good? But if God finds it necessary so to train us, it must be our duty to listen to him when he calls and shakes us from our torpor, that we may hasten to despise the world and aspire with our whole heart to the future life.

3. Still, the contempt which believers should train themselves to feel for the present life must not be of a kind to beget hatred of it or ingratitude to God. This life, though abounding in all kinds of wretchedness, is justly classed among divine blessings which are not to be despised. Wherefore, if we do not recognize the kindness of God in it, we are chargeable with no little ingratitude toward him. To believers, especially, it ought to be a proof of divine benevolence, since it is wholly destined to promote their salvation. Before openly exhibiting the inheritance of eternal glory, God is pleased to manifest himself to us as a Father by minor proofs—

namely, the blessings which he daily bestows upon us. Therefore, while this life serves to acquaint us with the goodness of God, shall we disdain it as if it did not contain one particle of good? We ought, therefore, to feel and be affected toward it in such a manner as to place it among those gifts of the divine benignity which are by no means to be despised. Were there no proofs in Scripture (they are most numerous and clear), yet nature herself exhorts us to return thanks to God for having brought us forth into light, granted us the use of it, and bestowed upon us all the means necessary for its preservation. And there is a much higher reason when we reflect that here we are in a manner prepared for the glory of the heavenly kingdom. For the Lord hath ordained that those who are ultimately to be crowned in heaven must maintain a previous warfare on the earth, that they may not triumph before they have overcome the difficulties of war, and obtained the victory. Another reason is that we here begin to experience in various ways a foretaste of the divine benignity, in order that our hope and desire may be whetted for its full manifestation. When once we have concluded that our earthly life is a gift of the divine mercy, of which, agreeably to our obligation, it behooves us to have a grateful remembrance, we shall then properly descend to consider its most wretched condition, and thus escape from that excessive fondness for it, to which, as I have said, we are naturally prone.

4. In proportion as this improper love diminishes, our desire of a better life should increase. I confess, indeed, that a most accurate opinion was formed by those who thought that the best thing was not to be born, the next best to die early. For, being destitute of the light of God and of true religion, what could they see in it that was not of dire and evil omen? Nor was it unreasonable for those who felt sorrow and shed tears at the birth of their kindred to keep holiday at their deaths. But this they did without profit; because, devoid of the true doctrine of faith, they saw not how that which in itself is neither happy nor desirable turns to the advantage of the righteous: and hence their opinion issued in despair. Let believers, then, in forming an estimate of this mortal life, and perceiving that in itself it is nothing but misery, make it their aim to exert themselves with greater alacrity, and less hindrance, in aspiring to the future and eternal life. When we contrast the two, the

former may not only be securely neglected, but, in comparison of the latter, be disdained and contemned. If heaven is our country, what can the earth be but a place of exile? If departure from the world is entrance into life, what is the world but a sepulchre, and what is residence in it but immersion in death? If to be freed from the body is to gain full possession of freedom, what is the body but a prison? If it is the very summit of happiness to enjoy the presence of God, is it not miserable to want it? But *whilst we are at home in the body, we are absent from the Lord* (2 Cor. 5:6). Thus when the earthly is compared with the heavenly life, it may undoubtedly be despised and trampled underfoot. We ought never, indeed, to regard it with hatred, except insofar as it keeps us subject to sin; and even this hatred ought not to be directed against life itself. At all events, we must stand so affected toward it in regard to weariness or hatred as, while longing for its termination, to be ready at the Lord's will to continue in it, keeping far from everything like murmuring and impatience. For it is as if the Lord had assigned us a post, which we must maintain till he recalls us. Paul, indeed, laments his condition, in being still bound with the fetters of the body, and sighs earnestly for redemption (Rom. 7:24); nevertheless, he declared that, in obedience to the command of God he was prepared for both courses, because he acknowledges it as his duty to God to glorify his name whether by life or by death, while it belongs to God to determine what is most conducive to his glory (Phil. 1:20–24). Wherefore, if it becomes us to live and die to the Lord, let us leave the period of our life and death at his disposal. Still let us ardently long for death, and constantly meditate upon it, and in comparison with future immortality, let us despise life, and, on account of the bondage of sin, long to renounce it whenever it shall so please the Lord.

5. But, most strange to say, many who boast of being Christians, instead of thus longing for death, are so afraid of it that they tremble at the very mention of it as a thing ominous and dreadful. We cannot wonder, indeed, that our natural feelings should be somewhat shocked at the mention of our dissolution. But it is altogether intolerable that the light of piety should not be so powerful in a Christian breast as with greater consolation to overcome and suppress that fear. For if we reflect that this our tabernacle, unsta-

ble, defective, corruptible, fading, pining, and putrid, is dissolved, in order that it may forthwith be renewed in sure, perfect, incorruptible, in fine, in heavenly glory, will not faith compel us eagerly to desire what nature dreads? If we reflect that by death we are recalled from exile to inhabit our native country, a heavenly country, shall this give us no comfort? But everything longs for permanent existence. I admit this, and therefore contend that we ought to look to future immortality, where we may obtain that fixed condition which nowhere appears on the earth. For Paul admirably enjoins believers to hasten cheerfully to death, not because they *would be unclothed, but clothed upon* (2 Cor. 5:2). Shall the lower animals, and inanimate creatures themselves, even wood and stone, as conscious of their present vanity, long for the final resurrection, that they may with the sons of God be delivered from vanity (Rom. 8:19); and shall we, endued with the light of intellect, and more than intellect, enlightened by the Spirit of God, when our essence is in question, rise no higher than the corruption of this earth? But it is not my purpose, nor is this the place, to plead against this great perverseness. At the outset, I declared that I had no wish to engage in a diffuse discussion of commonplaces. My advice to those whose minds are thus timid is to read the short treatise of Cyprian, *De Mortalitate*, unless it be more accordant with their deserts to send them to the philosophers, that by inspecting what they say on the contempt of death, they may begin to blush. This, however, let us hold as fixed, that no man has made much progress in the school of Christ who does not look forward with joy to the day of death and final resurrection (2 Tim. 4:18; Titus 2:13), for Paul distinguishes all believers by this mark; and the usual course of Scripture is to direct us thither whenever it would furnish us with an argument for substantial joy. *Look up,* says our Lord, *and lift up your heads: for your redemption draweth nigh* (Luke 21:28). Is it reasonable, I ask, that what he intended to have a powerful effect in stirring us up to alacrity and exultation should produce nothing but sadness and consternation? If it is so, why do we still glory in him as our Master? Therefore, let us come to a sounder mind, and how repugnant soever the blind and stupid longing of the flesh may be, let us doubt not to desire the advent of the Lord not in wish only, but with earnest sighs, as the most propitious of all events. He will come as a Redeemer to deliver us from an immense abyss of evil and misery, and lead us to the blessed inheritance of his life and glory.

6. Thus, indeed, it is; the whole body of the faithful, so long as they live on the earth, must be like sheep for the slaughter, in order that they may be conformed to Christ their head (Rom. 8:36). Most deplorable, therefore, would their situation be did they not, by raising their mind to heaven, become superior to all that is in the world, and rise above the present aspect of affairs (1 Cor. 15:19). On the other hand, when once they have raised their head above all earthly objects, though they see the wicked flourishing in wealth and honor, and enjoying profound peace, indulging in luxury and splendor, and reveling in all kinds of delights, though they should moreover be wickedly assailed by them, suffer insult from their pride, be robbed by their avarice, or assailed by any other passion, they will have no difficulty in bearing up under these evils. They will turn their eye to that day (Isa. 25:8; Rev. 7:17), on which the Lord will receive his faithful servants, wipe away all tears from their eyes, clothe them in a robe of glory and joy, feed them with the ineffable sweetness of his pleasures, exalt them to share with him in his greatness; in fine, admit them to a participation in his happiness. But the wicked who may have flourished on the earth, he will cast forth in extreme ignominy, will change their delights into torments, their laughter and joy into wailing and gnashing of teeth, their peace into the gnawing of conscience, and punish their luxury with unquenchable fire. He will also place their necks under the feet of the godly, whose patience they abused. For, as Paul declares, *it is a righteous thing with God to recompense tribulation to them that trouble you; and to you who are troubled rest with us, when the Lord Jesus shall be revealed from heaven* (2 Thess. 1:6, 7). This, indeed, is our only consolation; deprived of it, we must either give way to despondency or resort to our destruction to the vain solace of the world. The psalmist confesses, *My feet were almost gone: my steps had well nigh slipped: for I was envious at the foolish when I saw the prosperity of the wicked* (Ps. 73:3, 4); and he found no resting-place until he entered the sanctuary, and considered the latter end of the righteous and the wicked. To conclude in one word, the cross of Christ then

only triumphs in the breasts of believers over the devil and the flesh, sin and sinners, when their eyes are directed to the power of his resurrection.

Chapter 10

HOW TO USE THE PRESENT LIFE,
AND THE COMFORTS OF IT.

The divisions of this chapter are: The necessity and useful-ness of this doctrine. Extremes to be avoided, if we would rightly use the present life and its comforts, sects. 1, 2. II. One of these extremes—namely, the intemperance of the flesh—to be carefully avoided. Four methods of doing so described in order, sects. 3–6.

Sections

1. Necessity of this doctrine. Use of the goods of the present life. Extremes to be avoided. 1. Excessive austerity. 2. Carnal intem-perance and lasciviousness.
2. God, by creating so many mercies, consulted not only for our necessities, but also for our comfort and delight. Confirmation from a passage in the Psalms, and from experience.
3. Excessive austerity, therefore, to be avoided. So also must the wantonness of the flesh. 1. The creatures invite us to know, love, and honor the Creator. 2. This not done by the wicked, who only abuse these temporal mercies.
4. All earthly blessings to be despised in comparison of the heav-enly life. Aspiration after this life destroyed by an excessive love of created objects. First, intemperance.
5. Second, impatience and immoderate desire. Remedy of these evils. The creatures assigned to our use. Man still accountable for the use he makes of them.
6. God requires us in all our actions to look to his calling. Use of this doctrine. It is full of comfort.

1. By such rudiments we are at the same time well instructed by Scripture in the proper use of earthly blessings, a subject which, in forming a scheme of life, is by no means to be neglected. For if we

are to live, we must use the necessary supports of life; nor can we even shun those things which seem more subservient to delight than to necessity. We must therefore observe a mean, that we may use them with a pure conscience, whether for necessity or for pleasure. This the Lord prescribes by his word, when he tells us that to his people the present life is a kind of pilgrimage by which they hasten to the heavenly kingdom. If we are only to pass through the earth, there can be no doubt that we are to use its blessings only insofar as they assist our progress, rather than retard it. Accordingly, Paul, not without cause, admonishes us to use this world without abusing it, and to buy possessions as if we were selling them (1 Cor. 7:30, 31). But as this is a slippery place, and there is great danger of falling on either side, let us fix our feet where we can stand safely. There have been some good and holy men who, when they saw intemperance and luxury perpetually carried to excess, if not strictly curbed, and were desirous to correct so pernicious an evil, imagined that there was no other method than to allow man to use corporeal goods only insofar as they were necessaries: a counsel pious indeed, but unnecessarily austere; for it does the very dangerous thing of binding consciences in closer fetters than those in which they are bound by the word of God. Moreover, necessity, according to them, was abstinence from everything which could be wanted, so that they held it scarcely lawful to make any addition to bread and water. Others were still more austere, as is related of Cratetes the Theban, who threw his riches into the sea because he thought that unless he destroyed them, they would destroy him. Many also in the present day, while they seek a pretext for carnal intemperance in the use of external things, and at the same time would pave the way for licentiousness, assume for granted, what I by no means concede, that this liberty is not to be restrained by any modification, but that it is to be left to every man's conscience to use them as far as he thinks lawful. I indeed confess that here consciences neither can nor ought to be bound by fixed and definite laws; but that Scripture having laid down general rules for the legitimate uses, we should keep within the limits which they prescribe.

2. Let this be our principle, that we err not in the use of the gifts of Providence when we refer them to the end for which their author made and destined them, since he created them for our

good and not for our destruction. No man will keep the true path better than he who shall have this end carefully in view. Now then, if we consider for what end he created food, we shall find that he consulted not only for our necessity, but also for our enjoyment and delight. Thus, in clothing, the end was, in addition to necessity, comeliness and honor; and in herbs, fruits, and trees, besides their various uses, gracefulness of appearance and sweetness of smell. Were it not so, the prophet [sic; i.e., the psalmist] would not enumerate among the mercies of God *wine that maketh glad the heart of man, and oil to make his face to shine* (Ps. 104:15). The Scriptures would not everywhere mention, in commendation of his benignity, that he had given such things to men. The natural qualities of things themselves demonstrate to what end, and how far, they may be lawfully enjoyed. Has the Lord adorned flowers with all the beauty which spontaneously presents itself to the eye and the sweet odor which delights the sense of smell, and shall it be unlawful for us to enjoy that beauty and this odor? What? Has he not so distinguished colors as to make some more agreeable than others? Has he not given qualities to gold and silver, ivory and marble, thereby rendering them precious above other metals or stones? In short, has he not given many things a value without having any necessary use?

3. Have done, then, with that inhuman philosophy which, in allowing no use of the creatures but for necessity, not only maliciously deprives us of the lawful fruit of the divine beneficence, but cannot be realized without depriving man of all his senses, and reducing him to a block. But, on the other hand, let us with no less care guard against the lusts of the flesh, which, if not kept in order, break through all bounds, and are, as I have said, advocated by those who, under pretense of liberty, allow themselves every sort of license. First one restraint is imposed when we hold that the object of creating all things was to teach us to know their author and feel grateful for his indulgence. Where is the gratitude if you so gorge or stupefy yourself with feasting and wine as to be unfit for offices of piety or the duties of your calling? Where the recognition of God, if the flesh, boiling forth in lust through excessive indulgences infects the mind with its impurity, so as to lose the discernment of honor and rectitude? Where thankfulness to God for clothing, if on account of sumptuous raiment we both admire our-

selves and disdain others? If, from a love of show and splendor, we pave the way for immodesty? Where our recognition of God, if the glare of these things captivates our minds? For many are so devoted to luxury in all their senses that their mind lies buried: many are so delighted with marble, gold, and pictures that they become marble-hearted—are changed as it were into metal, and made like painted figures. The kitchen, with its savory smells, so engrosses them that they have no spiritual savor. The same thing may be seen in other matters. Wherefore, it is plain that there is here great necessity for curbing licentious abuse, and conforming to the rule of Paul, *make not provision for the flesh to fulfill the lusts thereof* (Rom. 13:14). Where too much liberty is given to them, they break forth without measure or restraint.

4. There is no surer or quicker way of accomplishing this than by despising the present life and aspiring to celestial immortality. For hence two rules arise: First, *it remaineth, that both they that have wives be as though they had none; . . . and they that use this world, as not abusing it* (1 Cor. 7:29, 31). Second, we must learn to be no less placid and patient in enduring penury, than moderate in enjoying abundance. He who makes it his rule to use this world as if he used it not, not only cuts off all gluttony in regard to meat and drink, and all effeminacy, ambition, pride, excessive shows, and austerity, in regard to his table, his house, and his clothes, but removes every care and affection which might withdraw or hinder him from aspiring to the heavenly life and cultivating the interest of his soul. It was well said by Cato: "Luxury causes great care, and produces great carelessness as to virtue"; and it is an old proverb—"Those who are much occupied with the care of the body, usually give little care to the soul." Therefore while the liberty of the Christian in external matters is not to be tied down to a strict rule, it is, however, subject to this law—he must indulge as little as possible; on the other hand, it must be his constant aim not only to curb luxury, but to cut off all show of superfluous abundance, and carefully beware of converting a help into a hindrance.

5. Another rule is that those in narrow and slender circumstances should learn to bear their wants patiently, that they may not become immoderately desirous of things, the moderate use of which implies no small progress in the school of Christ. For in addition to the many other vices which accompany a longing for

earthly good, he who is impatient under poverty almost always betrays the contrary disease in abundance. By this I mean that he who is ashamed of a sordid garment will be vainglorious of a splendid one; he who not contented with a slender, feels annoyed at the want of a more luxurious supper, will intemperately abuse his luxury if he obtains it; he who has a difficulty, and is dissatisfied in submitting to a private and humble condition, will be unable to refrain from pride if he attain to honor. Let it be the aim of all who have any unfeigned desire for piety to learn, after the example of the apostle, *both to be full and to be hungry, both to abound and to suffer need* (Phil. 4:12). Scripture, moreover, has a third rule for modifying the use of earthly blessings. We have already adverted to it when considering the offices of charity. For it declares that they have all been given us by the kindness of God and appointed for our use under the condition of being regarded as trusts, of which we must one day give account. We must, therefore, administer them as if we constantly heard the words sounding in our ears, *Give an account of your stewardship.* At the same time, let us remember by whom the account is to be taken—namely, by him who, while he so highly commends abstinence, sobriety, frugality, and moderation, abominates luxury, pride, ostentation, and vanity; who approves of no administration but that which is combined with charity, who with his own lips has already condemned all those pleasures which withdraw the heart from chastity and purity, or darken the intellect.

6. The last thing to be observed is that the Lord enjoins every one of us, in all the actions of life, to have respect to our own calling. He knows the boiling restlessness of the human mind, the fickleness with which it is borne hither and thither, its eagerness to hold opposites at one time in its grasp, its ambition. Therefore, lest all things should be thrown into confusion by our folly and rashness, he has assigned distinct duties to each in the different modes of life. And that no one may presume to overstep his proper limits, he has distinguished the different modes of life by the name of callings. Every man's mode of life, therefore, is a kind of station assigned him by the Lord, that he may not be always driven about at random. So necessary is this distinction, that all our actions are thereby estimated in his sight, and often in a very different way from that in which human reason or philosophy would estimate

them. There is no more illustrious deed even among philosophers than to free one's country from tyranny, and yet the private individual who stabs the tyrant is openly condemned by the voice of the heavenly Judge. But I am unwilling to dwell on particular examples; it is enough to know that in everything the call of the Lord is the foundation and beginning of right action. He who does not act with reference to it will never, in the discharge of duty, keep the right path. He will sometimes be able, perhaps, to give the semblance of something laudable, but whatever it may be in the sight of man, it will be rejected before the throne of God; and besides, there will be no harmony in the different parts of his life. Hence, he only who directs his life to this end will have it properly framed, because free from the impulse of rashness, he will not attempt more than his calling justifies, knowing that it is unlawful to overleap the prescribed bounds. He who is obscure will not decline to cultivate a private life, that he may not desert the post at which God has placed him. Again, in all our cares, toils, annoyances, and other burdens, it will be no small alleviation to know that all these are under the superintendence of God. The magistrate will more willingly perform his office, and the father of a family confine himself to his proper sphere. Everyone in his particular mode of life will, without repining, suffer its inconveniences, cares, uneasiness, and anxiety, persuaded that God has laid on the burden. This, too, will afford admirable consolation, that in following your proper calling, no work will be so mean and sordid as not to have a splendor and value in the eye of God.

OF PRAYER

BOOK 3

Chapter 20

OF PRAYER — A PERPETUAL EXERCISE OF FAITH.
THE DAILY BENEFITS DERIVED FROM IT.

The principal divisions of this chapter are: I. Connection of the subject of prayer with the previous chapters. The nature of prayer and its necessity as a Christian exercise, sects. 1, 2. II. To whom prayer is to be offered. Refutation of an objection which is too apt to present itself to the mind, sect. 3. III. Rules to be observed in prayer, sects. 4–11. IV. The nature of prayer, and some of its accidents, sects. 28–29. V. A perfect form of invocation, or an exposition of the Lord's Prayer, sects. 34–50. VI. Some rules to be observed with regard to prayer, as time, perseverance, the feeling of the mind, and the assurance of faith, sects. 50–52.

Sections

1. A general summary of what is contained in the previous part of the work. A transition to the doctrine of prayer. Its connection with the subject of faith.
2. Prayer defined. Its necessity and use.
3. Objection, that prayer seems useless, because God already knows our wants. Answer, from the institution and end of prayer. Confirmation by example. Its necessity and propriety. Perpetually reminds us of our duty and leads to meditation on divine Providence. Conclusion. Prayer a most useful exercise. This proved by three passages of Scripture.
4. Rules to be observed in prayer. First, reverence to God. How the mind ought to be composed.
5. All giddiness of mind must be excluded, and all our feelings seriously engaged. This confirmed by the form of lifting the hand in prayer. We must ask only insofar as God permits. To help our weakness, God gives the Spirit to be our guide in

35. Lord's Prayer divided into six petitions. Subdivision into two principal parts, the former referring to the glory of God, the latter to our salvation.

36. The use of the term Father implies, 1. That we pray to God in the name of Christ alone. 2. That we lay aside all distrust. 3. That we expect everything that is for our good.

37. Objection, that our sins exclude us from the presence of him whom we have made a Judge, not a Father. Answer, from the nature of God, as described by an apostle, the parable of the prodigal son, and from the expression, Our Father. Christ the earnest, the Holy Spirit the witness, of our adoption.

38. Why God is called generally, Our Father.

39. We may pray specially for ourselves and certain others, provided we have in our mind a general reference to all.

40. In what sense God is said to be in heaven. A threefold use of this doctrine for our consolation. Three cautions. Summary of the preface to the Lord's Prayer.

41. The necessity of the first petition a proof of our unrighteousness. What meant by the name of God. How it is hallowed. Parts of this hallowing. A deprecation of the sins by which the name of God is profaned.

42. Distinction between the first and second petitions. The kingdom of God, what. How said to come. Special exposition of this petition. It reminds us of three things. Advent of the kingdom of God in the world.

43. Distinction between the second and third petitions. The will here meant not the secret will or good pleasure of God, but that manifested in the word. Conclusion of the three first petitions.

44. A summary of the second part of the Lord's Prayer. Three petitions. What contained in the first. Declares the exceeding kindness of God and our distrust. What meant by bread. Why the petition for bread precedes that for the forgiveness of sins. Why it is called ours. Why to be sought *this day*, or *daily*. The doctrine resulting from this petition, illustrated by an example. Two classes of men sin in regard to this petition. In what sense it is called, our bread. Why we ask God to give it to us.

45. Close connection between this and the subsequent petition. Why our sins are called debts. This petition violated, 1. By

1. From the previous part of the work we clearly see how completely destitute man is of all good, how devoid of every means of procuring his own salvation. Hence, if he would obtain succor in his necessity, he must go beyond himself and procure it in some other quarter. It has further been shown that the Lord kindly and spontaneously manifests himself in Christ, in whom he offers all happiness for our misery, all abundance for our want, opening up

the treasures of heaven to us, so that we may turn with full faith to his beloved Son, depend upon him with full expectation, rest in him, and cleave to him with full hope. This, indeed, is that secret and hidden philosophy which cannot be learned by syllogisms: a philosophy thoroughly understood by those whose eyes God has so opened as to see light in his light (Ps. 36:9). But after we have learned by faith to know that whatever is necessary for us or defective in us is supplied in God and in our Lord Jesus Christ, in whom it hath pleased the Father that all fullness should dwell, that we may thence draw as from an inexhaustible fountain, it remains for us to seek and in prayer implore of him what we have learned to be in him. To know God as the sovereign disposer of all good, inviting us to present our requests, and yet not to approach or ask of him, were so far from availing us, that it were just as if one told of a treasure were to allow it to remain buried in the ground. Hence the apostle, to show that a faith unaccompanied with prayer to God cannot be genuine, states this to be the order: As faith springs from the Gospel, so by faith our hearts are framed to call upon the name of God (Rom. 10:14). And this is the very thing which he had expressed sometime before—namely, that the *Spirit of adoption*, which seals the testimony of the Gospel on our hearts, gives us courage to make our requests known unto God, calls forth groanings which cannot be uttered, and enables us to cry, Abba, Father (Rom. 8:26). This last point, as we have hitherto only touched upon it slightly in passing, must now be treated more fully.

2. To *prayer*, then, are we indebted for penetrating to those riches which are treasured up for us with our heavenly Father. For there is a kind of intercourse between God and men, by which, having entered the upper sanctuary, they appear before him and appeal to his promises, that when necessity requires they may learn by experiences that what they believed merely on the authority of his word was not in vain. Accordingly, we see that nothing is set before us as an object of expectation from the Lord which we are not enjoined to ask of him in prayer, so true it is that prayer digs up those treasures which the Gospel of our Lord discovers to the eye of faith. The necessity and utility of this exercise of prayer no words can sufficiently express. Assuredly it is not without cause our heavenly Father declares that our only safety is in calling upon

his name, since by it we invoke the presence of his Providence to watch over our interests, of his power to sustain us when weak and almost fainting, of his goodness to receive us into favor, though miserably loaded with sin; in fine, call upon him to manifest himself to us in all his perfections. Hence, admirable peace and tranquillity are given to our consciences; for the straits by which we were pressed being laid before the Lord, we rest fully satisfied with the assurance that none of our evils are unknown to him, and that he is both able and willing to make the best provision for us.

3. But honor will say, "Does he not know without a monitor both what our difficulties are, and what is meet for our interest, so that it seems in some measure superfluous to solicit him by our prayers, as if he were winking, or even sleeping, until aroused by the sound of our voice?" Those who argue thus attend not to the end for which the Lord taught us to pray. It was not so much for his sake as for ours. He wills indeed, as is just, that due honor be paid him by acknowledging that all which men desire or feel to be useful, and pray to obtain, is derived from him. But even the benefit of the homage which we thus pay him redounds to ourselves. Hence the holy patriarchs, the more confidently they proclaimed the mercies of God to themselves and others, felt the stronger incitement to prayer. It will be sufficient to refer to the example of Elijah, who being assured of the purpose of God had good ground for the promise of rain which he gives to Ahab, and yet prays anxiously upon his knees and sends his servant seven times to inquire (1 Kings 18:42); not that he discredits the oracle, but because he knows it to be his duty to lay his desires before God, lest his faith should become drowsy or torpid. Wherefore, although it is true that while we are listless or insensible to our wretchedness, he wakes and watches for us and sometimes even assists us unasked; it is very much for our interest to be constantly supplicating him; first, that our heart may always be inflamed with a serious and ardent desire of seeking, loving, and serving him, while we accustom ourselves to have recourse to him as a sacred anchor in every necessity; second, that no desires, no longing whatever, of which we are ashamed to make him the witness, may enter our minds, while we learn to place all our wishes in his sight, and thus pour out our heart before him; and, last, that we may be prepared to

receive all his benefits with true gratitude and thanksgiving, while our prayers remind us that they proceed from his hand. Moreover, having obtained what we asked, being persuaded that he has answered our prayers, we are led to long more earnestly for his favor, and at the same time have greater pleasure in welcoming the blessings which we perceive to have been obtained by our prayers. Last, use and experience confirm the thought of his Providence in our minds in a manner adapted to our weakness, when we understand that he not only promises that he will never fail us, and spontaneously gives us access to approach him in every time of need, but has his hand always stretched out to assist his people, not amusing them with words, but proving himself to be a present aid. For these reasons, though our most merciful Father never slumbers nor sleeps, he very often seems to do so, that thus he may exercise us, when we might otherwise be listless and slothful, in asking, entreating, and earnestly beseeching him to our great good. It is very absurd, therefore, to dissuade men from prayer by pretending that divine Providence, which is always watching over the government of the universes, is in vain importuned by our supplications, when, on the contrary, the Lord himself declares that he is *nigh unto all that call upon him, to all that call upon him in truth* (Ps. 145:18). No better is the frivolous allegation of others, that it is superfluous to pray for things which the Lord is ready of his own accord to bestow, since it is his pleasure that those very things which flow from his spontaneous liberality should be acknowledged as conceded to our prayers. This is testified by that memorable sentence in the Psalms to which many others correspond: *The eyes of the Lord are upon the righteous, and his ears are open unto their cry* (Ps. 34:15). This passage, while extolling the care which divine Providence spontaneously exercises over the safety of believers, omits not the exercise of faith by which the mind is aroused from sloth. The eyes of God are awake to assist the blind in their necessity, but he is likewise pleased to listen to our groans, that he may give us the better proof of his love. And thus both things are true, *He that keepeth Israel shall neither slumber nor sleep* (Ps. 121:4); and yet whenever he sees us dumb and torpid, he withdraws as if he had forgotten us.

4. Let the first rule of right prayer then be to have our heart and mind framed as becomes those who are entering into converse

with God. This we shall accomplish in regard to the mind, if, laying aside carnal thoughts and cares which might interfere with the direct and pure contemplation of God, it not only be wholly intent on prayer, but also, as far as possible, be borne and raised above itself. I do not here insist on a mind so disengaged as to feel none of the gnawings of anxiety; on the contrary, it is by much anxiety that the fervor of prayer is inflamed. Thus we see that the holy servants of God betray great anguish, not to say solicitude, when they cause the voice of complaint to ascend to the Lord from the deep abyss and the jaws of death. What I say is that all foreign and extraneous cares must be dispelled by which the mind might be driven to and fro in vague suspense, be drawn down from heaven, and kept groveling on the earth. When I say it must be raised above itself, I mean that it must not bring into the presence of God any of those things which our blind and stupid reason is wont to devise, nor keep itself confined within the little measure of its own vanity, but rise to a purity worthy of God.

5. Both things are specially worthy of notice. First, let everyone in professing to pray turn thither all his thoughts and feelings, and be not (as is usual) distracted by wandering thoughts, because nothing is more contrary to the reverence due to God than that levity which bespeaks a mind too much given to license and devoid of fear. In this matter we ought to labor the more earnestly the more difficult we experience it to be, for no man is so intent on prayer as not to feel many thoughts creeping in, and either breaking off the tenor of his prayer, or retarding it by some turning or digression. Here let us consider how unbecoming it is when God admits us to familiar intercourse to abuse his great condescension by mingling things sacred and profane, reverence for him not keeping our minds under restraint; but just as if in prayer we were conversing with one like ourselves forgetting him, and allowing our thoughts to run to and fro. Let us know, then, that none duly prepare themselves for prayer but those who are so impressed with the majesty of God that they engage in it free from all earthly cares and affections. The ceremony of lifting up our hands in prayer is designed to remind us that we are far removed from God, unless our thoughts rise upward: as it is said in the psalm, *Unto thee, O Lord, do I lift up my soul* (Ps. 25:1). And Scripture repeatedly uses the expression to *raise our prayer*, meaning that

those who would be heard by God must not grovel in the mire. The sum is that the more liberally God deals with us, condescendingly inviting us to disburden our cares into his bosom, the less excusable we are if this admirable and incomparable blessing does not in our estimation outweigh all other things, and win our affection, that prayer may seriously engage our every thought and feeling. This cannot be unless our mind, strenuously exerting itself against all impediments, rise upward. Our second proposition was that we are to ask only insofar as God permits. For though he bids us pour out our hearts (Ps. 62:8), he does not indiscriminately give loose reins to foolish and depraved affections; and when he promises that he will grant believers their wish, his indulgence does not proceed so far as to submit to their caprice. In both matters grievous delinquencies are everywhere committed. For not only do many without modesty, without reverence, presume to invoke God concerning their frivolities, but impudently bring forward their dreams, whatever they may be, before the tribunal of God. Such is the folly or stupidity under which they labor that they have the hardihood to obtrude upon God desires so vile that they would blush exceedingly to impart them to their fellow men. Profane writers have derided and even expressed their detestation of this presumption, and yet the vice has always prevailed. Hence, as the ambitious adopted Jupiter as their patron; the avaricious, Mercury; the literary aspirants, Apollo and Minerva; the warlike, Mars; the licentious, Venus: so in the present day, as I lately observed, men in prayer give greater license to their unlawful desires than if they were telling jocular tales among their equals. God does not suffer his condescension to be thus mocked, but vindicating his own light, places our wishes under the restraint of his authority. We must, therefore, attend to the observation of John: *This is the confidence that we have in him, that if we ask anything according to his will, he heareth us* (1 John 5:14). But as our faculties are far from being able to attain to such high perfection, we must seek for some means to assist them. As the eye of our mind should be intent upon God, so the affection of our heart ought to follow in the same course. But both fall far beneath this, or rather, they faint and fail and are carried in a contrary direction. To assist this weakness, God gives us the guidance of the Spirit in our prayers to dictate what is right, and regulate our affections. For seeing *we*

*know not what we should pray for as we ought, . . . the Spirit itself
maketh intercession for us with groanings which cannot be uttered*
(Rom. 8:26), not that he actually prays or groans, but he excites in
us sighs, and wishes, and confidence, which our natural powers
are not at all able to conceive. Nor is it without cause Paul gives the
name of *groanings which cannot be uttered* to the prayers which
believers send forth under the guidance of the Spirit. For those
who are truly exercised in prayer are not unaware that blind anxieties so restrain and perplex them that they can scarcely find what
it becomes them to utter; nay, in attempting to lisp they halt and
hesitate. Hence it appears that to pray aright is a special gift. We
do not speak thus in indulgence to our sloth, as if we were to leave
the office of prayer to the Holy Spirit, and give way to that carelessness to which we are too prone. Thus we sometimes hear the
impious expression that we are to wait in suspense until he take
possession of our minds while otherwise occupied. Our meaning
is that, weary of our own heartlessness and sloth, we are to long for
the aid of the Spirit. Nor, indeed, does Paul, when he enjoins us to
pray *in the Spirit* (1 Cor. 14:15), cease to exhort us to vigilance, intimating that while the inspiration of the Spirit is effectual to the
formation of prayer, it by no means impedes or retards our own
endeavors; since in this matter God is pleased to try how efficiently
faith influences our hearts.

6. Another rule of prayer is that in asking we must always truly
feel our wants, and seriously considering that we need all the
things which we ask, accompany the prayer with a sincere, nay,
ardent desire of obtaining them. Many repeat prayers in a perfunctory manner from a set form, as if they were performing a
task to God, and though they confess that this is a necessary remedy for the evils of their condition, because it were fatal to be left
without the divine aid which they implore, it still appears that they
perform the duty from custom, because their minds are meanwhile cold, and they ponder not what they ask. A general and confused feeling of their necessity leads them to pray, but it does not
make them solicitous as in a matter of present consequence, that
they may obtain the supply of their need. Moreover, can we suppose anything more hateful or even more execrable to God than
this fiction of asking the pardon of sins, while he who asks at the
very time either thinks that he is not a sinner, or, at least, is not

thinking that he is a sinner; in other words, a fiction by which God is plainly held in derision? But mankind, as I have lately said, are full of depravity, so that in the way of perfunctory service they often ask many things of God which they think come to them without his beneficence, or from some other quarter, or are already certainly in their possession. There is another fault which seems less heinous, but is not to be tolerated. Some murmur out prayers without meditation, their only principle being that God is to be propitiated by prayer. Believers ought to be specially on their guard never to appear in the presence of God with the intention of presenting a request unless they are under some serious impression, and are, at the same time, desirous to obtain it. Nay, although in these things which we ask only for the glory of God, we seem not at first sight to consult for our necessity, yet we ought not to ask with less fervor and vehemence of desire. For instance, when we pray that his name be hallowed—that hallowing must, so to speak, be earnestly hungered and thirsted after.

7. If it is objected that the necessity which urges us to pray is not always equal, I admit it, and this distinction is profitably taught us by James: *Is any among you afflicted? let him pray. Is any merry? let him sing psalms* (James 5:13). Therefore, common sense itself dictates that as we are too sluggish, we must be stimulated by God to pray earnestly whenever the occasion requires. This David calls a time when God *may be found* (a seasonable time); because, as he declares in several other passages, that the more hardly grievances, annoyances, fears, and other kinds of trial press us, the freer is our access to God, as if he were inviting us to himself. Still not less true is the injunction of Paul to pray *always* (Eph. 6:18); because, however prosperously, according to our view, things proceed, and however we may be surrounded on all sides with grounds of joy, there is not an instant of time during which our want does not exhort us to prayer. A man abounds in wheat and wine, but as he cannot enjoy a morsel of bread, unless by the continual bounty of God, his granaries or cellars will not prevent him from asking for daily bread. Then, if we consider how many dangers impend every moment, fear itself will teach us that no time ought to be without prayer. This, however, may be better known in spiritual matters. For when will the many sins of which we are conscious allow us to sit secure without suppliantly entreating freedom from

guilt and punishment? When will temptation give us a truce, making it unnecessary to hasten for help? Moreover, zeal for the kingdom and glory of God ought not to seize us by starts, but urge us without intermission, so that every time should appear seasonable. It is not without cause, therefore, that assiduity in prayer is so often enjoined. I am not now speaking of perseverance, which shall afterward be considered; but Scripture, by reminding us of the necessity of constant prayer, charges us with sloth, because we feel not how much we stand in need of this care and assiduity. By this rule hypocrisy and the device of lying to God are restrained, nay, altogether banished from prayer. God promises that he will be near to those who call upon him in truth and declares that those who seek him with their whole heart will find him: those, therefore, who delight in their own pollution cannot surely aspire to him. One of the requisites of legitimate prayer is repentance. Hence the common declaration of Scripture, that God does not listen to the wicked; that their prayers, as well as their sacrifices, are an abomination to him. For it is right that those who seal up their hearts should find the ears of God closed against them, that those who, by their hard-heartedness, provoke his severity should find him inflexible. In Isaiah he thus threatens: *When ye make many prayers, I will not hear: your hands are full of blood* (Isa. 1:15). In like manner, in Jeremiah, *Though they shall cry unto me, I will not hearken unto them* (Jer. 11:7, 8, 11); because he regards it as the highest insult for the wicked to boast of his covenant while profaning his sacred name by their whole lives. Hence he complains in Isaiah: *This people draw near to me with their mouth, and with their lips do honor me; but have removed their heart far from me* (Isa. 29:13). Indeed, he does not confine this to prayers alone, but declares that he abominates pretense in every part of his service. Hence the words of James, *Ye ask and receive not because ye ask amiss, that ye may consume it upon your lusts* (James 4:3). It is true, indeed (as we shall again see in a little), that the pious, in the prayers which they utter, trust not to their own worth; still the admonition of John is not superfluous: *Whatsoever we ask, we receive of him, because we keep his commandments* (1 John 3:22); an evil conscience shuts the door against us. Hence it follows that none but the sincere worshippers of God pray aright, or are listened to. Let everyone, therefore, who prepares to pray feel dissatisfied with what is wrong in his condition, and assume, which he cannot do without repentance, the character and feelings of a poor suppliant.

8. The third rule to be added is that he who comes into the presence of God to pray must divest himself of all vainglorious thoughts, lay aside all idea of worth; in short, discard all self-confidence, humbly giving God the whole glory, lest by arrogating anything, however little, to himself, vain pride cause him to turn away his face. Of this submission, which casts down all haughtiness, we have numerous examples in the servants of God. The holier they are, the more humbly they prostrate themselves when they come into the presence of the Lord. Thus Daniel, on whom the Lord himself bestowed such high commendation, says, *We do not present our supplications before thee for our righteousness but for thy great mercies. O Lord, hear; O Lord, forgive; O Lord, hearken and do; defer not, for thine own sake, O my God: for thy city and thy people are called by thy name.* This he does not indirectly in the usual manner, as if he were one of the individuals in a crowd: he rather confesses his guilt apart, and as a suppliant betaking himself to the asylum of pardon, he distinctly declares that he was confessing his own sin and the sin of his people Israel (Dan. 9:18–20). David also sets us an example of this humility: *Enter not into judgment with thy servant: for in thy sight shall no man living be justified* (Ps. 143:2). In like manner, Isaiah prays, *Behold, thou art wroth; for we have sinned: in those is continuance, and we shall be saved. But we are all as an unclean thing, and all our righteousnesses are as filthy rags; and we all do fade as a leaf; and our iniquities, like the wind, have taken us away. And there is none that calleth upon thy name, that stirreth up himself to take hold of thee: for thou hast hid thy face from us, and hast consumed us, because of our iniquities. But now, O Lord, thou art our Father; we are the clay, and thou our potter; and we all are the work of thy hand. Be not wroth very sore, O Lord, neither remember iniquity forever: Behold, see, we beseech thee, we are all thy people* (Isa. 64:5–9). You see how they put no confidence in anything but this: considering that they are the Lord's, they despair not of being the objects of his care. In the same way, Jeremiah says, *O Lord, though our iniquities testify against us, do thou it for thy name's sake* (Jer. 14:7). For it was most truly and piously written by the uncertain author (whoever he may have been) that wrote the book

which is attributed to the prophet Baruch, *But the soul that is greatly vexed, which goeth stooping and feeble, and the eyes that fail, and the hungry soul, will give thee praise and righteousness, O Lord. Therefore, we do not make our humble supplication before thee, O Lord our God, for the righteousness of our fathers, and of our kings . . . Hear, O Lord, and have mercy; for thou art merciful: and have pity upon us, because we have sinned before thee* (Bar. 2:18, 19; 3:2).

9. In fine, supplication for pardon, with humble and ingenuous confession of guilt, forms both the preparation and commencement of right prayer. For the holiest of men cannot hope to obtain anything from God until he has been freely reconciled to him. God cannot be propitious to any but those whom he pardons. Hence it is not strange that this is the key by which believers open the door of prayer, as we learn from several passages in the Psalms. David, when presenting a request on a different subject, says, *Remember not the sins of my youth, nor my transgressions; according to thy mercy remember me, for thy goodness sake, O Lord* (Ps. 25:7). Again, *Look upon my affliction and my pain, and forgive my sins* (Ps. 25:18). Here also we see that it is not sufficient to call ourselves to account for the sins of each passing day; we must also call to mind those which might seem to have been long before buried in oblivion. For in another passage the same prophet, confessing one grievous crime, takes occasion to go back to his very birth, *I was shapen in iniquity, and in sin did my mother conceive me* (Ps. 51:5); not to extenuate the fault by the corruption of his nature, but as it were to accumulate the sins of his whole life, that the stricter he was in condemning himself, the more placable God might be. But although the saints do not always in express terms ask forgiveness of sins, yet if we carefully ponder those prayers as given in Scripture, the truth of what I say will readily appear; namely, that their courage to pray was derived solely from the mercy of God, and that they always began with appeasing him. For when a man interrogates his conscience, so far is he from presuming to lay his cares familiarly before God that if he did not trust to mercy and pardon, he would tremble at the very thought of approaching him. There is, indeed, another special confession. When believers long for deliverance from punishment, they at the same time pray that their sins may be pardoned, for it were absurd to wish that the effect should be taken away while the cause remains. For we must

beware of imitating foolish patients who, anxious only about curing accidental symptoms, neglect the root of the disease. Nay, our endeavor must be to have God propitious even before he attests his favor by external signs, both because this is the order which he himself chooses, and it were of little avail to experience his kindness, did not conscience feel that he is appeased, and thus enable us to regard him as altogether lovely. Of this we are even reminded by our Savior's reply. Having determined to cure the paralytic, he says, *Thy sins are forgiven thee;* in other words, he raises our thoughts to the object which is especially to be desired—namely, admission into the favor of God, and then gives the fruit of reconciliation by bringing assistance to us. But besides that special confession of present guilt which believers employ, in supplicating for pardon of every fault and punishment, that general introduction which procures favor for our prayers must never be omitted, because prayers will never reach God unless they are founded on free mercy. To this we may refer the words of John, *If we confess our sins, he is faithful and just to forgive us our sins and to cleanse us from all unrighteousness* (1 John 1:9). Hence, under the law it was necessary to consecrate prayers by the expiation of blood, both that they might be accepted, and that the people might be warned that they were unworthy of the high privilege until, being purged from their defilements, they founded their confidence in prayer entirely on the mercy of God.

10. Sometimes, however, the saints in supplicating God, seem to appeal to their own righteousness, as when David says, *Preserve my soul; for I am holy* (Ps. 86:2). Also Hezekiah, *Remember now, O Lord, I beseech thee how I have walked before thee in truth, and with a perfect heart, and have done that which is good in thy sight* (Isa. 38:2). All they mean by such expressions is that regeneration declares them to be among the servants and children to whom God engages that he will show favor. We have already seen how he declares by the psalmist that his eyes *are upon the righteous, and his ears are open unto their cry* (Ps. 34:16) and again by the apostle, that whatsoever we ask of him we obtain, because we keep his commandments (John 3:22). In these passages he does not fix a value on prayer as a meritorious work, but designs to establish the confidence of those who are conscious of an unfeigned integrity and innocence, such as all believers should possess. For the saying

of the blind man who had received his sight is in perfect accordance with divine truth, *And God heareth not sinners* (John 9:31); provided we take the term sinners in the sense commonly used by Scripture to mean those who, without any desire for righteousness, are sleeping secure in their sins; since no heart will ever rise to genuine prayer that does not at the same time long for holiness. Those supplications in which the saints allude to their purity and integrity correspond to such promises, that they may thus have, in their own experience, a manifestation of that which all the servants of God are made to expect. Thus they almost always use this mode of prayer when before God they compare themselves with their enemies, from whose injustice they long to be delivered by his hand. When making such comparisons, there is no wonder that they bring forward their integrity and simplicity of heart, that thus, by the justice of their cause, the Lord may be the more disposed to give them succor. We rob not the pious breast of the privilege of enjoying a consciousness of purity before the Lord, and thus feeling assured of the promises with which he comforts and supports his true worshippers, but we would have them to lay aside all thought of their own merits and found their confidence of success in prayer solely on the divine mercy.

11. The fourth rule of prayer is that notwithstanding of our being thus abased and truly humbled, we should be animated to pray with the sure hope of succeeding. There is, indeed, an appearance of contradiction between the two things, between a sense of the just vengeance of God and firm confidence in his favor, and yet they are perfectly accordant, if it is the mere goodness of God that raises up those who are overwhelmed by their own sins. For, as we have formerly shown (chap. 3, sects. 1, 2) that repentance and faith go hand in hand, being united by an indissoluble tie, the one causing terror, the other joy, so in prayer they must both be present. This concurrence David expresses in a few words: *But as for me, I will come into thy house in the multitude of thy mercy, and in thy fear will I worship toward thy holy temple* (Ps. 5:7). Under the goodness of God he comprehends faith, at the same time not excluding fear; for not only does his majesty compel our reverence, but our own unworthiness also divests us of all pride and confidence and keeps us in fear. The confidence of which I speak is not one which frees the mind from all anxiety and

soothes it with sweet and perfect rest; such rest is peculiar to those who, while all their affairs are flowing to a wish are annoyed by no care, stung with no regret, agitated by no fear. But the best stimulus which the saints have to prayer is when, in consequence of their own necessities, they feel the greatest disquietude, and are all but driven to despair, until faith seasonably comes to their aid; because in such straits the goodness of God so shines upon them that while they groan, burdened by the weight of present calamities and tormented with the fear of greater, they yet trust to this goodness, and in this way both lighten the difficulty of endurance and take comfort in the hope of final deliverance. It is necessary, therefore, that the prayer of the believer should be the result of both feelings, and exhibit the influence of both; namely, that while he groans under present and anxiously dreads new evils, he should, at the same time, have recourse to God, not at all doubting that God is ready to stretch out a helping hand to him. For it is not easy to say how much God is irritated by our distrust when we ask what we expect not of his goodness. Hence, nothing is more accordant to the nature of prayer than to lay it down as a fixed rule, that it is not to come forth at random, but is to follow in the footsteps of faith. To this principle Christ directs all of us in these words, *Therefore, I say unto you, What things soever ye desire, when ye pray, believe that ye receive them, and ye shall have them* (Mark 11:24). The same thing he declares in another passage, *All things, whatsoever ye shall ask in prayer, believing, ye shall receive* (Matt. 21:22). In accordance with this are the words of James, *If any of you lack wisdom, let him ask of God, that giveth to all men liberally, and upbraideth not, and it shall be given him. But let him ask in faith, nothing wavering* (James 1:5). He most aptly expresses the power of faith by opposing it to wavering. No less worthy of notice is his additional statement, that those who approach God with a doubting, hesitating mind, without feeling assured whether they are to be heard or not, gain nothing by their prayers. Such persons he compares to a wave of the sea, driven with the wind and tossed. Hence, in another passage he terms genuine prayer *the prayer of faith* (James 5:15). Again, since God so often declares that he will give to every man according to his faith, he intimates that we cannot obtain anything without faith. In short, it is faith which obtains everything that is granted to prayer. This is the meaning of Paul in the well-known passage to which dull men give too little heed, *How then shall they call upon him in whom they have not believed? And how shall they believe in him of whom they have not heard? . . . So then faith cometh by hearing, and hearing by the word of God* (Rom. 10:14, 17). Gradually deducing the origin of prayer from faith, he distinctly maintains that God cannot be invoked sincerely except by those to whom, by the preaching of the Gospel, his mercy and willingness have been made known, nay, familiarly explained.

28. But though prayer is properly confined to vows and supplications, yet so strong is the affinity between petition and thanksgiving that both may be conveniently comprehended under one name. For the forms which Paul enumerates (1 Tim. 2:1) fall under the first member of this division. By prayer and supplication we pour out our desires before God, asking as well those things which tend to promote his glory and display his name, as the benefits which contribute to our advantage. By thanksgiving we duly celebrate his kindnesses toward us, ascribing to his liberality every blessing which enters into our lot. David accordingly includes both in one sentence, *Call upon me in the day of trouble: I will deliver thee, and thou shalt glorify me* (Ps. 50:15). Scripture, not without reason, commands us to use both continually. We have already described the greatness of our want, while experience itself proclaims the straits which press us on every side to be so numerous and so great that all have sufficient ground to send forth sighs and groans to God without intermission and suppliantly implore him. For even should they be exempt from adversity, still the holiest ought to be stimulated first by their sins, and, second, by the innumerable assaults of temptation, to long for a remedy. The sacrifice of praise and thanksgiving can never be interrupted without guilt, since God never ceases to load us with favor upon favor, so as to force us to gratitude, however slow and sluggish we may be. In short, so great and widely diffused are the riches of his liberality toward us, so marvelous and wondrous the miracles which we behold on every side, that we never can want a subject and materials for praise and thanksgiving. To make this somewhat clearer: since all our hopes and resources are placed in God (this has already been fully proved), so that neither our persons nor our interests can prosper without his blessing, we must constantly submit ourselves and our all to him. Then whatever we deliberate,

speak, or do should be deliberated, spoken, and done under his hand and will; in fine, under the hope of his assistance. God has pronounced a curse upon all who, confiding in themselves or others, form plans and resolutions, who, without regarding his will, or invoking his aid, either plan or attempt to execute (James 4:14; Isa. 30:1; 31:1). And since, as has already been observed, he receives the honor which is due when he is acknowledged to be the author of all good, it follows that, in deriving all good from his hand, we ought continually to express our thankfulness, and that we have no right to use the benefits which proceed from his liberality, if we do not assiduously proclaim his praise, and give him thanks, these being the ends for which they are given. When Paul declares that every creature of God *is sanctified by the word of God and prayers* (1 Tim. 4:5), he intimates that without the word and prayers none of them are holy and pure, *word* being used metonymically for *faith*. Hence David, on experiencing the loving-kindness of the Lord, elegantly declares, *He hath put a new song in my mouth* (Ps. 40:3), intimating that our silence is malignant when we leave his blessings unpraised, seeing every blessing he bestows is a new ground of thanksgiving. Thus Isaiah, proclaiming the singular mercies of God, says, *Sing unto the Lord a new song* (Isa. 42:10). In the same sense David says in another passage, *O Lord, open thou my lips; and my mouth shall show forth thy praise* (Ps. 51:15). In like manner, Hezekiah and Jonah declare that they will regard it as the end of their deliverance *to celebrate the goodness of God with songs in his temple* (Isa. 38:20; Jon. 2:10). David lays down a general rule for all believers in these words, *What shall I render unto the Lord for all his benefits toward me? I will take the cup of salvation, and call upon the name of the Lord* (Ps. 116:12, 13). This rule the Church follows in another psalm, *Save us, O Lord our God, and gather us from among the heathen, to give thanks unto thy holy name, and to triumph in thy praise* (Ps. 106:47). Again, *He will regard the prayer of the destitute, and not despise their prayer. This shall be written for the generation to come: and the people which shall be created shall praise the Lord. . . . To declare the name of the Lord in Zion, and his praise in Jerusalem* (Ps. 102:18, 21). Nay, whenever believers beseech the Lord to do anything *for his own name's sake*, as they declare themselves unworthy of obtaining it in their own name, so they oblige themselves to give thanks and promise to make the right use of his loving-kindness by being the heralds of it. Thus Hosea, speaking of the future redemption of the Church, says, *Take away all iniquity, and receive us graciously; so will we render the calves of our lips* (Hos. 14:2). Not only do our tongues proclaim the kindness of God, but they naturally inspire us with love to him. *I love the Lord, because he hath heard my voice and my supplications* (Ps. 116:1). In another passage, speaking of the help which he had experienced, he says, *I will love thee, O Lord, my strength* (Ps. 18:1). No praise will ever please God that does not flow from this feeling of love. Nay, we must attend to the declaration of Paul, that all wishes are vicious and perverse which are not accompanied with thanksgiving. His words are, *In everything by prayer and supplication with thanksgiving let your requests be made known unto God* (Phil. 4:6). Because many, under the influence of moroseness, weariness, impatience, bitter grief, and fear, use murmuring in their prayers, he enjoins us so to regulate our feelings as cheerfully to bless God even before obtaining what we ask. But if this connection ought always to subsist in full vigor between things that are almost contrary, the more sacred is the tie which binds us to celebrate the praises of God whenever he grants our requests. And as we have already shown that our prayers, which otherwise would be polluted, are sanctified by the intercession of Christ, so the apostle, by enjoining us *to offer the sacrifice of praise to God continually* by Christ (Heb. 13:15), reminds us that without the intervention of his priesthood our lips are not pure enough to celebrate the name of God. Hence we infer that a monstrous delusion prevails among papists, the great majority of whom wonder when Christ is called an intercessor. The reason why Paul enjoins, *Pray without ceasing; in everything give thanks* (1 Thess. 5:17, 18) is because he would have us with the utmost assiduity, at all times, in every place, in all things, and under all circumstances, direct our prayers to God, to expect all the things which we desire from him, and when obtained ascribe them to him, thus furnishing perpetual grounds for prayer and praise.

29. This assiduity in prayer, though it specially refers to the peculiar private prayers of individuals, extends also in some measure to the public prayers of the Church. These, it may be said, cannot be continual, and ought not to be made, except in the manner which, for the sake of order, has been established by public

consent. This I admit, and hence certain hours are fixed before-hand, hours which, though indifferent in regard to God, are nec-essary for the use of man, that the general convenience may be consulted, and all things be done in the Church, as Paul enjoins, *decently and in order* (1 Cor. 14:40). But there is nothing in this to prevent each church from being now and then stirred up to a more frequent use of prayer and being more zealously affected under the impulse of some greater necessity. Of perseverance in prayer, which is much akin to assiduity, we shall speak toward the close of the chapter (sects. 51, 52). This assiduity, moreover, is very differ-ent from the βαττολογίαν, *vain speaking*, which our Savior has prohibited (Matt. 6:7). For he does not there forbid us to pray long or frequently, or with great fervor, but warns us against supposing that we can extort anything from God by importuning him with garrulous loquacity, as if he were to be persuaded after the manner of men. We know that hypocrites, because they consider not that they have to do with God, offer up their prayers as pompously as if it were part of a triumphal show. The Pharisee, who thanked God that he was not as other men, no doubt proclaimed his praises before men, as if he had wished to gain a reputation for sanctity by his prayers. Hence that *vain speaking*, which for a similar reason prevails so much in the papacy in the present day, some vainly spinning out the time by a reiteration of the same frivolous prayers, and others employing a long series of verbiage for vul-gar display. This childish garrulity being a mockery of God, it is not strange that it is prohibited in the Church, in order that every feeling there expressed may be sincere, proceeding from the inmost heart. Akin to this abuse is another which our Savior also condemns, namely, when hypocrites for the sake of ostentation court the presence of many witnesses and would sooner pray in the marketplace than pray without applause. The true object of prayer being, as we have already said (sects. 4, 5), to carry our thoughts directly to God, whether to celebrate his praise or implore his aid, we can easily see that its primary seat is in the mind and heart, or rather that prayer itself is properly an effu-sion and manifestation of internal feeling before him who is the searcher of hearts. Hence (as has been said), when our divine Mas-ter was pleased to lay down the best rule for prayer, his injunction was, *Enter into thy closet, and when thou hast shut thy door, pray to thy Father which is in secret, and thy Father which seeth in secret shall reward thee openly* (Matt. 6:6). Dissuading us from the example of hypocrites, who sought the applause of men by an ambitious ostentation in prayer, he adds the better course—enter thy chamber, shut thy door, and there pray. By these words (as I understand them) he taught us to seek a place of retirement which might enable us to turn all our thoughts inward and enter deeply into our hearts, promising that God would hold converse with the feelings of our mind, of which the body ought to be the temple. He meant not to deny that it may be expedient to pray in other places also, but he shows that prayer is somewhat of a secret nature, having its chief seat in the mind, and requiring a tranquillity far removed from the turmoil of ordinary cares. And hence it was not without cause that our Lord himself, when he would engage more earnestly in prayer, withdrew into a retired spot beyond the bustle of the world, thus reminding us by his example that we are not to neglect those helps which enable the mind, in itself too much disposed to wander, to become sincerely intent on prayer. Meanwhile, as he abstained not from prayer when the occasion required it, though he were in the midst of a crowd, so must we, whenever there is need, lift up *pure hands* (1 Tim. 2:8) at all places. And hence we must hold that he who declines to pray in the public meeting of the saints knows not what it is to pray apart, in retirement, or at home. On the other hand, he who neglects to pray alone and in private, however sedulously he frequents public meetings, there gives his prayers to the wind, because he defers more to the opinion of man than to the secret judgment of God. Still, lest the public prayers of the Church should be held in contempt, the Lord anciently bestowed upon them the most honorable appellation, especially when he called the temple the *house of prayer* (Isa. 56:7). For by this expression he both showed that the duty of prayer is a principal part of his worship, and that to enable believers to engage in it with one consent his temple is set up before them as a kind of banner. A noble promise was also added, *Praise waiteth for thee, O God, in Sion: and unto thee shall the vow be performed* (Ps. 65:1). By these words the psalmist reminds us that the prayers of the Church are never in vain because God always furnishes his people with materials for a song of joy. But although the shadows of the law have ceased, yet because God was pleased by this ordinance to foster the unity of the faith among us also, there can be no doubt that the same promise belongs to us—a promise which Christ sanctioned with his own lips, and which Paul declares to be perpetually in force.

34. We must now attend not only to a surer method, but also form of prayer, that, namely, which our heavenly Father has delivered to us by his beloved Son, and in which we may recognize his boundless goodness and condescension (Matt. 6:9; Luke 11:2). Besides admonishing and exhorting us to seek him in our every necessity (as children are wont to betake themselves to the protection of their parents when oppressed with any anxiety), seeing that we were not fully aware how great our poverty was, or what was right or for our interest to ask, he has provided for this ignorance; that wherein our capacity failed he has sufficiently supplied. For he has given us a form in which is set before us as in a picture everything which it is lawful to wish, everything which is conducive to our interest, everything which it is necessary to demand. From his goodness in this respect we derive the great comfort of knowing that as we ask almost in his words, we ask nothing that is absurd, or foreign, or unseasonable; nothing, in short, that is not agreeable to him. Plato, seeing the ignorance of men in presenting their desires to God, desires which if granted would often be most injurious to them, declares the best form of prayer to be that which an ancient poet has furnished: "O king Jupiter, give what is best, whether we wish it or wish it not; but avert from us what is evil even though we ask it" (Plato, *Alcibiades*, 2). This heathen shows his wisdom in discerning how dangerous it is to ask of God what our own passion dictates; while, at the same time, he reminds us of our unhappy condition in not being able to open our lips before God without dangers unless his Spirit instruct us how to pray aright (Rom. 8:26). The higher value, therefore, ought we to set on the privilege, when the only-begotten Son of God puts words into our lips, and thus relieves our minds of all hesitation.

35. This form or rule of prayer is composed of *six petitions*. For I am prevented from agreeing with those who divide it into *seven* by the adversative mode of diction used by the evangelist, who appears to have intended to unite the two members together; as if he had said, "Do not allow us to be overcome by temptation, but rather bring assistance to our frailty, and deliver us that we may

not fall." Ancient writers also agree with us, that what is added by Matthew as a seventh head is to be considered as explanatory of the sixth petition. But though in every part of the prayer the first place is assigned to the glory of God, still this is more especially the object of the three first petitions, in which we are to look to the glory of God alone, without any reference to what is called our own advantage. The three remaining petitions are devoted to our interest, and properly relate to things which it is useful for us to ask. When we ask that the name of God may be hallowed, as God wishes to prove whether we love and serve him freely, or from the hope of reward, we are not to think at all of our own interest; we must set his glory before our eyes, and keep them intent upon it alone. In the other similar petitions, this is the only manner in which we ought to be affected. It is true that in this way our own interest is greatly promoted, because, when the name of God is hallowed in the way we ask, our own sanctification also is thereby promoted. But in regard to this advantage, we must, as I have said, shut our eyes, and be in a manner blind, so as not even to see it; and hence were all hope of our private advantage cut off, we still should never cease to wish and pray for this hallowing, and every-thing else which pertains to the glory of God. We have examples in Moses and Paul, who did not count it grievous to turn away their eyes and minds from themselves, and with intense and fer-vent zeal long for death, if by their loss the kingdom and glory of God might be promoted (Exod. 32:32; Rom. 9:3). On the other hand, when we ask for daily bread, although we desire what is advantageous for ourselves, we ought also especially to seek the glory of God, so much so that we would not ask at all unless it were to turn to his glory. Let us now proceed to an exposition of the Prayer.

Our Father which art in Heaven.

36. The first thing suggested at the very outset is that all our prayers to God ought only to be presented in the name of Christ, as there is no other name which can recommend them. In calling God our Father, we certainly plead the name of Christ. For with what confidence could any man call God his Father? Who would have the presumption to arrogate to himself the honor of a son of God were we not gratuitously adopted as his sons in Christ? He being the true Son has been given to us as a brother, so that that

which he possesses as his own by nature becomes ours by adoption, if we embrace this great mercy with firm faith. As John says, *As many as received him, to them gave he power to become the sons of God, even to them that believe in his name* (John 1:12). Hence he both calls himself our Father and is pleased to be so called by us, by this delightful name relieving us of all distrust, since nowhere can a stronger affection be found than in a father. Hence, too, he could not have given us a stronger testimony of his boundless love than in calling us his sons. But his love toward us is so much the greater and more excellent than that of earthly parents, the further he surpasses all men in goodness and mercy (Isa. 63:16). Earthly parents, laying aside all paternal affection, might abandon their offspring; he will never abandon us (Ps. 27:10), seeing he cannot deny himself. For we have his promise, *If ye then, being evil, know how to give good gifts unto your children, how much more shall your Father which is in heaven give good things to them that ask him?* (Matt. 7:11). In like manner in the prophet, *Can a woman forget her sucking child, that she should not have compassion on the son of her womb? Yea, they may forget, yet will not I forget thee* (Isa. 49:15). But if we are his sons, then as a son cannot betake himself to the protection of a stranger and a foreigner without at the same time complaining of his father's cruelty or poverty, so we cannot ask assistance from any other quarter than from him, unless we would upbraid him with poverty, or want of means, or cruelty and excessive austerity.

37. Nor let us allege that we are justly rendered timid by a consciousness of sin, by which our Father, though mild and merciful, is daily offended. For if among men a son cannot have a better advocate to plead his cause with his father, and cannot employ a better intercessor to regain his lost favor, than if he come himself suppliant and downcast, acknowledging his fault, to implore the mercy of his father, whose paternal feelings cannot but be moved by such entreaties, what will that *Father of all mercies, and God of all comfort*, do? (2 Cor. 1:3). Will he not rather listen to the tears and groans of his children, when supplicating for themselves (especially seeing he invites and exhorts us to do so), than to any advocacy of others to whom the timid have recourse, not without some semblance of despair, because they are distrustful of their father's mildness and clemency? The exuberance of his paternal

kindness he sets before us in the parable (Luke 15:20), when the father with open arms receives the son who had gone away from him, wasted his substance in riotous living, and in all ways grievously sinned against him. He waits not till pardon is asked in words, but, anticipating the request, recognizes him afar off, runs to meet him, consoles him, and restores him to favor. By setting before us this admirable example of mildness in a man, he designed to show in how much greater abundance we may expect it from him who is not only a Father, but the best and most merciful of all fathers, however ungrateful, rebellious, and wicked sons we may be, provided only we throw ourselves upon his mercy. And the better to assure us that he is such a Father if we are Christians, he has been pleased to be called not only a Father, but our Father, as if we were pleading with him after this manner, "O Father, who art possessed of so much affection for thy children, and art so ready to forgive, we thy children approach thee and present our requests, fully persuaded that thou hast no other feelings toward us than those of a father, though we are unworthy of such a parent." But as our narrow hearts are incapable of comprehending such boundless favor, Christ is not only the earnest and pledge of our adoption, but also gives us the Spirit as a witness of this adoption, that through him we may freely cry aloud, "Abba, Father." Whenever, therefore, we are restrained by any feeling of hesitation, let us remember to ask of him that he may correct our timidity, and placing us under the magnanimous guidance of the Spirit, enable us to pray boldly.

38. The instruction given us, however, is not that every individual in particular is to call him Father, but rather that we are all in common to call him Our Father. By this we are reminded how strong the feeling of brotherly love between us ought to be, since we are all alike, by the same mercy and free kindness, the children of such a Father. For if he from whom we all obtain whatever is good is our common Father (Matt. 23:9), everything which has been distributed to us we should be prepared to communicate to each other, as far as occasion demands. But if we are thus desirous as we ought, to stretch out our hands and give assistance to each other, there is nothing by which we can more benefit our brethren than by committing them to the care and protection of the best of parents, since if he is propitious and favorable nothing more can

be desired. And, indeed, we owe this also to our Father. For as he who truly and from the heart loves the father of a family, extends the same love and goodwill to all his household, so the zeal and affection which we feel for our heavenly Parent it becomes us to extend toward his people, his family, and, in fine, his heritage, which he has honored so highly as to give them the appellation of the *fullness* of his only begotten Son (Eph. 1:23). Let the Christian, then, so regulate his prayers as to make them common, and embrace all who are his brethren in Christ; not only those whom at present he sees and knows to be such, but all men who are alive upon the earth. What God has determined with regard to them is beyond our knowledge, but to wish and hope the best concerning them is both pious and humane. Still, it becomes us to regard with special affection those who are of the household of faith, and whom the apostle has in express terms recommended to our care in everything (Gal. 6:10). In short, all our prayers ought to bear reference to that community which our Lord has established in his kingdom and family.

39. This, however, does not prevent us from praying specially for ourselves and certain others, provided our mind is not withdrawn from the view of this community, does not deviate from it, but constantly refers to it. For prayers, though couched in special terms, keeping that object still in view, cease not to be common. All this may easily be understood by analogy. There is a general command from God to relieve the necessities of all the poor, and yet this command is obeyed by those who with that view give succor to all whom they see or know to be in distress, although they pass by many whose wants are not less urgent, either because they cannot know or are unable to give supply to all. In this way there is nothing repugnant to the will of God in those who, giving heed to this common society of the Church, yet offer up particular prayers, in which, with a public mind, though in special terms, they commend to God themselves or others, with whose necessity he has been pleased to make them more familiarly acquainted. It is true that prayer and the giving of our substance are not in all respects alike. We can only bestow the kindness of our liberality on those of whose wants we are aware, whereas in prayer we can assist the greatest strangers, how wide soever the space which may separate them from us. This is done by that general form of prayer which,

including all the sons of God, includes them also. To this we may refer the exhortation which Paul gave to the believers of his age, to lift up *holy hands without wrath and doubting* (1 Tim. 2:8). By reminding them that dissension is a bar to prayer, he shows it to be his wish that they should with one accord present their prayers in common.

40. The next words are, *which art in Heaven.* From this we are not to infer that he is enclosed and confined within the circumference of heaven, as by a kind of boundary. Hence Solomon confesses, *The heaven of heavens cannot contain thee* (1 Kings 8:27); and he himself says by the prophet, *The heaven is my throne, and the earth is my footstool* (Isa. 66:1); thereby intimating that his presence, not confined to any region, is diffused over all space. But as our gross minds are unable to conceive of his ineffable glory, it is designated to us by *heaven*, nothing which our eyes can behold being so full of splendor and majesty. While, then, we are accustomed to regard every object as confined to the place where our senses discern it, no place can be assigned to God; and hence, if we would seek him, we must rise higher than all corporeal or mental discernment. Again, this form of expression reminds us that he is far beyond the reach of change or corruption, that he holds the whole universe in his grasp and rules it by his power. The effect of the expressions, therefore, is the same as if it had been said that he is of infinite majesty, incomprehensible essence, boundless power, and eternal duration. When we thus speak of God, our thoughts must be raised to their highest pitch; we must not ascribe to him anything of a terrestrial or carnal nature, must not measure him by our little standards or suppose his will to be like ours. At the same time, we must put our confidence in him, understanding that heaven and earth are governed by his Providence and power. In short, under the name of Father is set before us that God who hath appeared to us in his own image, that we may invoke him with sure faith; the familiar name of Father being given not only to inspire confidence, but also to curb our minds and prevent them from going astray after doubtful or fictitious gods. We thus ascend from the only-begotten Son to the supreme Father of angels and of the Church. Then when his throne is fixed in heaven, we are reminded that he governs the world, and, therefore, that it is not in vain to approach him whose present care we actually experi-

ence. *He that cometh to God,* says the apostle, *must believe that he is, and that he is a rewarder of them that diligently seek him* (Heb. 11:6). Here Christ makes both claims for his Father, *first,* that we place our faith in him; and, *second,* that we feel assured that our salvation is not neglected by him, inasmuch as he condescends to extend his Providence to us. By these elementary principles Paul prepares us to pray aright; for before enjoining us to make our requests known unto God, he premises in this way, *The Lord is at hand. Be careful for nothing* (Phil. 4:5, 6). Whence it appears that doubt and perplexity hang over the prayers of those in whose minds the belief is not firmly seated, that *the eyes of the Lord are upon the righteous* (Ps. 34:15).

41. The first petition is, *hallowed be Thy Name.* The necessity of presenting it bespeaks our great disgrace. For what can be more unbecoming than that our ingratitude and malice should impair, our audacity and petulance should as much as in them lies destroy, the glory of God? But though all the ungodly should burst with sacrilegious rage, the holiness of God's name still shines forth. Justly does the psalmist exclaim, *According to thy name, O God, so is thy praise unto the ends of the earth* (Ps. 48:10). For wherever God hath made himself known, his perfections must be displayed, his power, goodness, wisdom, justice, mercy, and truth, which fill us with admiration, and incite us to show forth his praise. Therefore, as the name of God is not duly hallowed on the earth, and we are otherwise unable to assert it, it is at least our duty to make it the subject of our prayers. The sum of the whole is, it must be our desire that God may receive the honor which is his due: that men may never think or speak of him without the greatest reverence. The opposite of this reverence is profanity, which has always been too common in the world, and is very prevalent in the present day. Hence the necessity of the petition, which, if piety had any proper existence among us, would be superfluous. But if the name of God is duly hallowed only when separated from all other names it alone is glorified, we are in the petition enjoined to ask not only that God would vindicate his sacred name from all contempt and insult, but also that he would compel the whole human race to reverence it. Then since God manifests himself to us partly by his word, and partly by his works, he is not sanctified unless in regard to both of these we ascribe to him what is due, and thus embrace

whatever has proceeded from him, giving no less praise to his justice than to his mercy. On the manifold diversity of his works he
has inscribed the marks of his glory, and these ought to call forth
from every tongue an ascription of praise. Thus Scripture will
obtain its due authority with us, and no event will hinder us from
celebrating the praises of God, in regard to every part of his government. On the other hand, the petition implies a wish that all
impiety which pollutes this sacred name may perish and be extinguished, that everything which obscures or impairs his glory,
all detraction and insult, may cease; that all blasphemy being
suppressed, the divine majesty may be more and more signally
displayed.

42. The second petition is, *Thy Kingdom come*. This contains
nothing new, and yet there is good reason for distinguishing it
from the first. For if we consider our lethargy in the greatest of all
matters, we shall see how necessary it is that what ought to be in
itself perfectly known should be inculcated at greater length.
Therefore, after the injunction to pray that God would reduce to
order and at length completely efface every stain which is thrown
on his sacred name, another petition, containing almost the same
wish, is added—namely, *Thy kingdom come*. Although a definition
of this kingdom has already been given, I now briefly repeat that
God reigns when men, in denial of themselves and contempt of
the world and this earthly life, devote themselves to righteousness
and aspire to heaven. Thus this kingdom consists of two parts; the
first is when God by the agency of his Spirit corrects all the
depraved lusts of the flesh, which in bands war against him; and
the second, when he brings all our thoughts into obedience to his
authority. This petition, therefore, is duly presented only by those
who begin with themselves; in other words, who pray that they
may be purified from all the corruptions which disturb the tranquillity and impair the purity of God's kingdom. Then as the
word of God is like his royal scepter, we are here enjoined to
pray that he would subdue all minds and hearts to voluntary obedience. This is done when by the secret inspiration of his Spirit he
displays the efficacy of his word, and raises it to the place of honor
which it deserves. We must next descend to the wicked, who
perversely and with desperate madness resist his authority. God,
therefore, sets up his kingdom by humbling the whole world,

though in different ways, taming the wantonness of some and breaking the ungovernable pride of others. We should desire this to be done every day, in order that God may gather churches to himself from all quarters of the world, may extend and increase their numbers, enrich them with his gifts, establish due order among them; on the other hand, beat down all the enemies of pure doctrine and religion, dissipate their counsels, defeat their attempts. Hence it appears that there is good ground for the precept which enjoins daily progress, for human affairs are never so prosperous as when the impurities of vice are purged away and integrity flourishes in full vigor. The completion, however, is deferred to the final advent of Christ, when, as Paul declares, *God will be all in all* (1 Cor. 15:28). This prayer, therefore, ought to withdraw us from the corruptions of the world which separate us from God and prevent his kingdom from flourishing within us; second, it ought to inflame us with an ardent desire for the mortification of the flesh; and, last, it ought to train us to the endurance of the cross, since this is the way in which God would have his kingdom to be advanced. It ought not to grieve us that the outward man decays provided the inner man is renewed. For such is the nature of the kingdom of God, that while we submit to his righteousness he makes us partakers of his glory. This is the case when continually adding to his light and truth, by which the lies and the darkness of Satan and his kingdom are dissipated, extinguished, and destroyed, he protects his people, guides them aright by the agency of his Spirit, and confirms them in perseverance; while, on the other hand, he frustrates the impious conspiracies of his enemies, dissipates their wiles and frauds, prevents their malice and curbs their petulance, until at length he consumes Antichrist *with the spirit of his mouth* and destroys all impiety *with the brightness of his coming* (2 Thess. 2:8).

43. The third petition is, *Thy will be done on earth as it is in heaven.* Though this depends on his kingdom, and cannot be disjoined from it, yet a separate place is not improperly given to it on account of our ignorance, which does not at once or easily apprehend what is meant by God reigning in the world. This, therefore, may not improperly be taken as the explanation, that God will be King in the world when all shall subject themselves to his will. We are not here treating of that secret will by which he governs all

things, and destines them to their end. For although devils and men rise in tumult against him, he is able by his incomprehensible counsel not only to turn aside their violence, but make it sub-servient to the execution of his decrees. What we here speak of is another will of God, namely, that of which voluntary obedience is the counterpart; and, therefore, heaven is expressly contrasted with earth, because, as is said in the Psalms, the angels *do his com-mandments, hearkening unto the voice of his word* (Ps. 103:20). We are, therefore, enjoined to pray that as everything done in heaven is at the command of God, and the angels are calmly disposed to do all that is right, so the earth may be brought under his au-thority, all rebellion and depravity having been extinguished. In presenting this request we renounce the desires of the flesh, because he who does not entirely resign his affections to God does as much as in him lies to oppose the divine will, since everything which proceeds from us is vicious. Again, by this prayer we are taught to deny ourselves, that God may rule us according to his pleasure; and not only so, but also having annihilated our own may create new thoughts and new minds so that we shall have no desire save that of entire agreement with his will; in short, wish nothing of ourselves, but have our hearts governed by his Spirit, under whose inward teaching we may learn to love those things which please and hate those things which displease him. Hence also we must desire that he would nullify and suppress all affec-tions which are repugnant to his will. Such are the three first heads of the prayer, in presenting which we should have the glory of God only in view, taking no account of ourselves and paying no respect to our own advantage, which, though it is thereby greatly promoted, is not here to be the subject of request. And though all the events prayed for must happen in their own time, without being either thought of, wished, or asked by us, it is still our duty to wish and ask for them. And it is of no slight importance to do so, that we may testify and profess that we are the servants and children of God, desirous by every means in our power to promote the honor due to him as our Lord and Father, and truly and thor-oughly devoted to his service. Hence if men, in praying that the name of God may be hallowed, that his kingdom may come, and his will be done, are not influenced by this zeal for the promotion of his glory, they are not to be accounted among the servants and

children of God; and as all these things will take place against
their will, so they will turn out to their confusion and destruction.

44. Now comes the second part of the prayer, in which we
descend to our own interests, not, indeed, that we are to lose sight
of the glory of God (to which, as Paul declares, we must have
respect even in meat and drink, 1 Cor. 10:31), and ask only what is
expedient for ourselves; but the distinction, as we have already
observed, is this: God claiming the three first petitions as specially
his own, carries us entirely to himself, that in this way he may
prove our piety. Next he permits us to look to our own advantage,
but still on the condition that when we ask anything for ourselves
it must be in order that all the benefits which he confers may show
forth his glory, there being nothing more incumbent on us than to
live and die to him. By the first petition of the second part, *give us
this day our daily bread,* we pray in general that God would give us
all things which the body requires in this sublunary state, not only
food and clothing, but everything which he knows will assist us to
eat our bread in peace. In this way we briefly cast our care upon
him and commit ourselves to his Providence, that he may feed,
foster, and preserve us. For our heavenly Father disdains not to
take our body under his charge and protection, that he may exercise our faith in those minute matters, while we look to him for
everything, even to a morsel of bread and a drop of water. For
since, owing to some strange inequality, we feel more concern for
the body than for the soul, many who can trust the latter to God
still continue anxious about the former, still hesitate as to what
they are to eat, as to how they are to be clothed, and are in trepida-
tion whenever their hands are not filled with corn, and wine, and
oil, so much more value do we set on this shadowy, fleeting life,
than on a blessed immortality. But those who, trusting to God,
have once cast away that anxiety about the flesh, immediately look
to him for greater gifts, even salvation and eternal life. It is no
slight exercise of faith, therefore, to hope in God for things which
would otherwise give us so much concern; nor have we made little
progress when we get quit of this unbelief, which cleaves, as it
were, to our very bones. The speculations of some concerning
supersubstantial bread seem to be very little accordant with our
Savior's meaning; for our prayer would be defective were we not
to ascribe to God the nourishment even of this fading life. The

reason which they give is heathenish—namely, that it is inconsistent with the character of sons of God who ought to be spiritual, not only to occupy their mind with earthly cares, but to suppose God also occupied with them. As if his blessing and paternal favor were not eminently displayed in giving us food, or as if there were nothing in the declaration that godliness hath *the promise of the life that now is, and of that which is to come* (1 Tim. 4:8). But although the forgiveness of sins is of far more importance than the nourishment of the body, yet Christ has set down the inferior in the prior place, in order that he might gradually raise us to the other two petitions, which properly belong to the heavenly life—in this providing for our sluggishness. We are enjoined to ask *our bread*, that we may be contented with the measure which our heavenly Father is pleased to dispense, and not strive to make gain by illicit arts. Meanwhile, we must hold that the title by which it is ours is donation, because, as Moses says (Lev. 26:20, Deut. 8:17), neither our industry, nor labor, nor hands acquire anything for us, unless the blessing of God be present; nay, not even would abundance of bread be of the least avail were it not divinely converted into nourishment. And hence this liberality of God is not less necessary to the rich than the poor, because, though their cellars and barns were full, they would be parched and pine with want did they not enjoy his favor along with their bread. The terms *this day*, or, as it is in another evangelist, *daily*, and also the epithet *daily*, lay a restraint on our immoderate desire of fleeting good—a desire which we are extremely apt to indulge to excess, and from which other evils ensue: for when our supply is in richer abundance we ambitiously squander it in pleasure, luxury, ostentation, or other kinds of extravagance. Wherefore, we are only enjoined to ask as much as our necessity requires, and as it were for each day, confiding that our heavenly Father, who gives us the supply of today, will not fail us on the morrow. How great soever our abundance may be, however well filled our cellars and granaries, we must still always ask for daily bread, for we must feel assured that all substance is nothing, unless insofar as the Lord, by pouring out his blessing, make it fruitful during its whole progress; for even that which is in our hand is not ours except insofar as he every hour portions it out and permits us to use it. As nothing is more difficult to human pride than the admission of this truth, the Lord declares that he gave a special proof for all ages when he fed his people with manna in the desert (Deut. 8:3), that he might remind us that *man shall not live by bread alone, but by every word that proceedeth out of the mouth of God* (Matt. 4:4). It is thus intimated that by his power alone our life and strength are sustained, though he ministers supply to us by bodily instruments. In like manner, whenever it so pleases, he gives us a proof of an opposite description, by breaking the strength, or, as he himself calls it, the *staff* of bread (Lev. 26:26), and leaving us even while eating to pine with hunger, and while drinking to be parched with thirst. Those who, not contented with daily bread, indulge an unrestrained insatiable cupidity, or those who are full of their own abundance and trust in their own riches, only mock God by offering up this prayer. For the former ask what they would be unwilling to obtain, nay, what they most of all abominate, namely, daily bread only, and as much as in them lies disguise their avarice from God, whereas true prayer should pour out the whole soul and every inward feeling before him. The latter, again, ask what they do not at all expect to obtain, namely, what they imagine that they in themselves already possess. In its being called *ours*, God, as we have already said, gives a striking display of his kindness, making that to be ours to which we have no just claim. Nor must we reject the view to which I have already adverted—namely, that this name is given to what is obtained by just and honest labor, as contrasted with what is obtained by fraud and rapine, nothing being our own which we obtain with injury to others. When we ask God to *give us*, the meaning is that the thing asked is simply and freely the gift of God, whatever be the quarter from which it comes to us, even when it seems to have been specially prepared by our own art and industry and procured by our hands, since it is to his blessing alone that all our labors owe their success.

45. The next petition is, *forgive us our debts*. In this and the following petition our Savior has briefly comprehended whatever is conducive to the heavenly life, as these two members contain the spiritual covenant which God made for the salvation of his Church, *I will put my law in their inward parts, and write it on their hearts. . . . I will pardon all their iniquities* (Jer. 31:33; 33:8). Here our Savior begins with the forgiveness of sins and then adds the subsequent blessing—namely, that God would protect us by the power

and support us by the aid of his Spirit, so that we may stand invincible against all temptations. To sins he gives the name of *debts*, because we owe the punishment due to them, a debt which we could not possibly pay were we not discharged by this remission, the result of his free mercy, when he freely expunges the debt, accepting nothing in return, but of his own mercy receiving satisfaction in Christ, who gave himself a ransom for us (Rom. 3:24). Hence, those who expect to satisfy God by merits of their own or of others, or to compensate and purchase forgiveness by means of satisfactions, have no share in this free pardon, and while they address God in this petition, do nothing more than subscribe their own accusation and seal their condemnation by their own testimony. For they confess that they are debtors, unless they are discharged by means of forgiveness. This forgiveness, however, they do not receive, but rather reject, when they obtrude their merits and satisfactions upon God, since by so doing they do not implore his mercy, but appeal to his justice. Let those, again, who dream of a perfection which makes it unnecessary to seek pardon find their disciples among those whose itching ears incline them to imposture; only let them understand that those whom they thus acquire have been carried away from Christ, since he, by instructing all to confess their guilt, receives none but sinners, not that he may soothe and so encourage them in their sins, but because he knows that believers are never so divested of the sins of the flesh as not to remain subject to the justice of God. It is, indeed, to be wished, it ought even to be our strenuous endeavor, to perform all the parts of our duty, so as truly to congratulate ourselves before God as being pure from every stain; but as God is pleased to renew his image in us by degrees, so that to some extent there is always a residue of corruption in our flesh, we ought by no means to neglect the remedy. But if Christ, according to the authority given him by his Father, enjoins us, during the whole course of our lives, to implore pardon, who can tolerate those new teachers who, by the phantom of perfect innocence, endeavor to dazzle the simple and make them believe that they can render themselves completely free from guilt? This, as John declares, is nothing else than to make God a liar (1 John 1:10). In like manner, those foolish men mutilate the covenant in which we have seen that our salvation is contained by concealing one head of it, and so destroying it entirely; being guilty not only of profanity in that they separate things which ought to be indissolubly connected; but also of wickedness and cruelty in overwhelming wretched souls with despair—of treachery also to themselves and their followers, in that they encourage themselves in a carelessness diametrically opposed to the mercy of God. It is excessively childish to object that when they long for the advent of the kingdom of God, they at the same time pray for the abolition of sin. In the former division of the prayer absolute perfection is set before us; but in the latter our own weakness. Thus the two fitly correspond to each other— we strive for the goal, and at the same time neglect not the remedies which our necessities require. In the next part of the petition we pray to be forgiven, *as we forgive our debtors*; that is, as we spare and pardon all by whom we are in any way offended, either in deed by unjust or in word by contumelious treatment. Not that we can forgive the guilt of a fault or offense; this belongs to God only; but we can forgive to this extent: we can voluntarily divest our minds of wrath, hatred, and revenge, and efface the remembrance of injuries by a voluntary oblivion. Wherefore, we are not to ask the forgiveness of our sins from God unless we forgive the offenses of all who are or have been injurious to us. If we retain any hatred in our minds, if we meditate revenge, and devise the means of hurting; nay, if we do not return to a good understanding with our enemies, perform every kind of friendly office, and endeavor to effect a reconciliation with them, we by this petition beseech God not to grant us forgiveness. For we ask him to do to us as we do to others. This is the same as asking him not to do unless we do also. What, then, do such persons obtain by this petition but a heavier judgment? Last, it is to be observed that the condition of being forgiven as we forgive our debtors is not added because by forgiving others we deserve forgiveness, as if the cause of forgiveness were expressed; but by the use of this expression the Lord has been pleased partly to solace the weakness of our faith, using it as a sign to assure us that our sins are as certainly forgiven as we are certainly conscious of having forgiven others, when our mind is completely purged from all envy, hatred, and malice; and partly using as a badge by which he excludes from the number of his children all who, prone to revenge and reluctant to forgive, obstinately keep up their enmity, cherishing against others that indignation which they deprecate from themselves; so that they should not venture to invoke him as a Father. In the Gospel of Luke, we have this distinctly stated in the words of Christ.

46. The sixth petition corresponds (as we have observed) to the promise of *writing the law upon our hearts*; but because we do not obey God without a continual warfare, without sharp and arduous contests, we here pray that he would furnish us with armor, and defend us by his protection, that we may be able to obtain the victory. By this we are reminded that we not only have need of the gift of the Spirit inwardly to soften our hearts and turn and direct them to the obedience of God, but also of his assistance, to render us invincible by all the wiles and violent assaults of Satan. The forms of temptation are many and various. The depraved conceptions of our minds provoking us to transgress the law—conceptions which our concupiscence suggests or the devil excites are temptations; and things which in their own nature are not evil become temptations by the wiles of the devil when they are presented to our eyes in such a way that the view of them makes us withdraw or decline from God. These temptations are both on the right hand and on the left. On the right, when riches, power, and honors, which by their glare, and the semblance of good which they present, generally dazzle the eyes of men, and so entice by their blandishments, that, caught by their snares and intoxicated by their sweetness, they forget their God: on the left, when offended by the hardship and bitterness of poverty, disgrace, contempt, afflictions, and other things of that description, they despond, cast away their confidence and hope, and are at length totally estranged from God. In regard to both kinds of temptation, which either enkindled in us by concupiscence or presented by the craft of Satan's war against us, we pray God the Father not to allow us to be overcome, but rather to raise and support us by his hand, that strengthened by his mighty power we may stand firm against all the assaults of our malignant enemy, whatever be the thoughts which he sends into our minds; next we pray that whatever of either description is allotted us, we may turn to good, that is, may neither be inflated with prosperity, nor cast down by adversity. Here, however, we do not ask to be altogether exempted from temptation, which is very necessary to excite, stimulate, and urge us on, that we may not become too lethargic. It was not with-

out reason that David wished to be tried, nor is it without cause that the Lord daily tries his elect, chastising them by disgrace, poverty, tribulation, and other kinds of cross. But the temptations of God and Satan are very different: Satan tempts, that he may destroy, condemn, confound, throw headlong; God, that by proving his people he may make trial of their sincerity, and by exercising their strength confirm it; may mortify, tame, and cauterize their flesh, which, if not curbed in this manner, would wanton and exult above measure. Besides, Satan attacks those who are unarmed and unprepared that he may destroy them unawares; whereas whatever God sends, he *will with the temptation also make a way to escape, that ye may be able to bear it.* Whether by the term evil we understand the devil or sin is not of the least consequence. Satan is indeed the very enemy who lays snares for our life, but it is by sin that he is armed for our destruction. Our petition, therefore, is that we may not be overcome or overwhelmed with temptation, but in the strength of the Lord may stand firm against all the powers by which we are assailed; in other words, may not fall under temptation: that being thus taken under his charge and protection, we may remain invincible by sin, death, the gates of hell, and the whole power of the devil; in other words, be delivered from evil. Here it is carefully to be observed that we have no strength to contend with such a combatant as the devil, or to sustain the violence of his assault. Were it otherwise, it would be mockery of God to ask of him what we already possess in ourselves. Assuredly those who in self-confidence prepare for such a fight do not understand how bold and well-equipped the enemy is with whom they have to do. Now we ask to be delivered from his power, as from the mouth of some furious raging lion who would instantly tear us with his teeth and claws and swallow us up, did not the Lord rescue us from the midst of death; at the same time knowing that if the Lord is present and will fight for us while we stand by, through him *we shall do valiantly* (Ps. 60:12). Let others if they will confide in the powers and resources of their free will which they think they possess; enough for us that we stand and are strong in the power of God alone. But the prayer comprehends more than at first sight it seems to do. For if the Spirit of God is our strength in waging the contest with Satan, we cannot gain the victory unless we are filled with him and thereby freed from all infirmity of the flesh. Therefore, when we pray to be delivered from sin and Satan, we at the same time desire to be enriched with new supplies of divine grace, until completely replenished with them, we triumph over every evil. To some it seems rude and harsh to ask God not to lead us into temptation, since, as James declares (James 1:13), it is contrary to his nature to do so. This difficulty has already been partly solved by the fact that our concupiscence is the cause, and therefore properly bears the blame of all the temptations by which we are overcome. All that James means is that it is vain and unjust to ascribe to God vices which our own consciousness compels us to impute to ourselves. But this is no reason why God may not when he sees it meet bring us into bondage to Satan, give us up to a reprobate mind and shameful lusts, and so by a just, indeed, but often hidden judgment, lead us into temptation. Though the cause is often concealed from men, it is well known to him. Hence we may see that the expression is not improper, if we are persuaded that it is not without cause he so often threatens to give sure signs of his vengeance, by blinding the reprobate and hardening their hearts.

47. These three petitions, in which we specially commend ourselves and all that we have to God, clearly show what we formerly observed (sects. 38, 39), that the prayers of Christians should be public and have respect to the public edification of the Church and the advancement of believers in spiritual communion. For no one requests that anything should be given to him as an individual, but we all ask in common for daily bread and the forgiveness of sins, not to be led into temptation, but delivered from evil. Moreover, there is subjoined the reason for our great boldness in asking and confidence of obtaining (sects. 11, 36). Although this does not exist in the Latin copies, yet as it accords so well with the whole, we cannot think of omitting it. The words are, *Thine is the Kingdom, and the Power, and the Glory, forever and ever.* Here is the calm and firm assurance of our faith. For were our prayers to be commended to God by our own worth, who would venture even to whisper before him? Now, however wretched we may be, however unworthy, however devoid of commendation, we shall never want a reason for prayer, nor a ground of confidence, since the kingdom, power, and glory can never be wrested from our Father. The last word is *Amen*, by which is expressed the eagerness of

our desire to obtain the things which we ask, while our hope is confirmed, that all things have already been obtained and will assuredly be granted to us, seeing they have been promised by God, who cannot deceive. This accords with the form of expression to which we have already adverted: "Grant, O Lord, for thy name's sake, not on account of us or of our righteousness." By this the saints not only express the end of their prayers, but confess that they are unworthy of obtaining did not God find the cause in himself and were not their confidence founded entirely on his nature.

48. All things that we ought, indeed all that we are able, to ask of God are contained in this formula, and as it were rule, of prayer delivered by Christ, our divine Master, whom the Father has appointed to be our teacher, and to whom alone he would have us to listen (Matt. 17:5). For he ever was the eternal wisdom of the Father, and being made man, was manifested as the Wonderful, the Counselor (Isa. 11:2). Accordingly, this prayer is complete in all its parts, so complete that whatever is extraneous and foreign to it, whatever cannot be referred to it, is impious and unworthy of the approbation of God. For he has here summarily prescribed what is worthy of him, what is acceptable to him, and what is necessary for us; in short, whatever he is pleased to grant. Those, therefore, who presume to go further and ask something more from God first seek to add of their own to the wisdom of God (this it is insane blasphemy to do); second, refusing to confine themselves within the will of God, and despising it, they wander as their cupidity directs; last, they will never obtain anything, seeing they pray without faith. For there cannot be a doubt that all such prayers are made without faith, because at variance with the word of God, on which if faith do not always lean it cannot possibly stand. Those who, disregarding the Master's rule, indulge their own wishes, not only have not the word of God, but as much as in them lies oppose it. Hence Tertullian (*De fuga in persecutione*) has not less truly than elegantly termed it *Lawful Prayer*, tacitly intimating that all other prayers are lawless and illicit.

49. By this, however, we would not have it understood that we are so restricted to this form of prayer as to make it unlawful to change a word or syllable of it. For in Scripture we meet with many prayers differing greatly from it in word, yet written by the same Spirit, and capable of being used by us with the greatest

advantage. Many prayers also are continually suggested to believers by the same Spirit, though in expression they bear no great resemblance to it. All we mean to say is that no man should wish, expect, or ask anything which is not summarily comprehended in this prayer. Though the words may be very different, there must be no difference in the sense. In this way, all prayers, both those which are contained in the Scripture and those which come forth from pious breasts, must be referred to it, certainly none can ever equal it, far less surpass it in perfection. It omits nothing which we can conceive in praise of God, nothing which we can imagine advantageous to man, and the whole is so exact that all hope of improving it may well be renounced. In short, let us remember that we have here the doctrine of heavenly wisdom. God has taught what he willed; he willed what was necessary.

50. But although it has been said above (sect. 7, e.g.), that we ought always to raise our minds upward toward God and pray without ceasing, yet such is our weakness, which requires to be supported, such our torpor, which requires to be stimulated, that it is requisite for us to appoint special hours for this exercise, hours which are not to pass away without prayer, and during which the whole affections of our minds are to be completely occupied; namely, when we rise in the morning, before we commence our daily work, when we sit down to food, when by the blessing of God we have taken it, and when we retire to rest. This, however, must not be a superstitious observance of hours, by which, as it were, performing a task to God, we think we are discharged as to other hours; it should rather be considered as a discipline by which our weakness is exercised and ever and anon stimulated. In particular, it must be our anxious care whenever we are ourselves pressed or see others pressed by any strait, instantly to have recourse to him not only with quickened pace, but with quickened minds; and again, we must not in any prosperity of ourselves or others omit to testify our recognition of his hand by praise and thanksgiving. Last, we must in all our prayers carefully avoid wishing to confine God to certain circumstances or prescribe to him the time, place, or mode of action. In like manner, we are taught by this prayer not to fix any law or impose any condition upon him, but leave it entirely to him to adopt whatever course of procedure seems to him best, in respect of method, time, and

place. For before we offer up any petition for ourselves, we ask that his will may be done, and by so doing place our will in subordination to his, just as if we had laid a curb upon it, that, instead of presuming to give law to God, it may regard him as the ruler and disposer of all its wishes.

51. If, with minds thus framed to obedience, we allow ourselves to be governed by the laws of divine Providence, we shall easily learn to persevere in prayer, and suspending our own desires wait patiently for the Lord, certain, however little the appearance of it may be, that he is always present with us and will in his own time show how very far he was from turning a deaf ear to prayers, though to the eyes of men they may seem to be disregarded. This will be a very present consolation, if at any time God does not grant an immediate answer to our prayers, preventing us from fainting or giving way to despondency, as those are wont to do who, in invoking God, are so borne away by their own fervor that unless he yield on their first importunity and give present help, they immediately imagine that he is angry and offended with them and abandoning all hope of success cease from prayer. On the contrary, deferring our hope with well-tempered equanimity, let us insist with that perseverance which is so strongly recommended to us in Scripture. We may often see in the Psalms how David and other believers, after they are almost weary of praying and seem to have been beating the air by addressing a God who would not hear, yet cease not to pray because due authority is not given to the word of God, unless the faith placed in it is superior to all events. Again, let us not tempt God, and by wearying him with our importunity provoke his anger against us. Many have a practice of formally bargaining with God on certain conditions, and, as if he were the servant of their lust, binding him to certain stipulations; with which if he does not immediately comply, they are indignant and fretful, murmur, complain, and make a noise. Thus offended, he often in his anger grants to such persons what in mercy he kindly denies to others. Of this we have a proof in the children of Israel, for whom it had been better not to have been heard by the Lord than to swallow his indignation with their flesh (Num. 11:18, 33).

52. But if our sense is not able till after long expectation to perceive what the result of prayer is, or experience any benefit from it,

still our faith will assure us of that which cannot be perceived by sense—namely, that we have obtained what was fit for us, the Lord having so often and so surely engaged to take an interest in all our troubles from the moment they have been deposited in his bosom. In this way we shall possess abundance in poverty and comfort in affliction. For though all things fail, God will never abandon us, and he cannot frustrate the expectation and patience of his people. He alone will suffice for all, since in himself he comprehends all good, and will at last reveal it to us on the day of judgment, when his kingdom shall be plainly manifested. We may add that although God complies with our request, he does not always give an answer in the very terms of our prayers but while apparently holding us in suspense, yet in an unknown way, shows that our prayers have not been in vain. This is the meaning of the words of John, *If we know that he hear us, whatsoever we ask, we know that we have the petitions that we desired of him* (1 John 5:15). It might seem that there is here a great superfluity of words, but the declaration is most useful, namely, that God, even when he does not comply with our requests, yet listens and is favorable to our prayers, so that our hope founded on his word is never disappointed. But believers have always need of being supported by this patience, as they could not stand long if they did not lean upon it. For the trials by which the Lord proves and exercises us are severe, nay, he often drives us to extremes, and when driven allows us long to stick fast in the mire before he gives us any taste of his sweetness. As Hannah says, *The Lord killeth, and maketh alive; he bringeth down to the grave, and bringeth up* (1 Sam. 2:6). What could they here do but become dispirited and rush on despair, were they not, when afflicted, desolate, and half dead, comforted with the thought that they are regarded by God, and that there will be an end to their present evils. But however secure their hopes may stand, they in the meantime cease not to pray, since prayer unaccompanied by perseverance leads to no result.

Commentary
on Scripture

The Old Testament

To the godly and ingenuous readers, greeting.

If the reading of these my commentaries confer as much benefit on the Church of God as I myself have reaped advantage from the composition of them, I shall have no reason to regret that I have undertaken this work. Having expounded here, in our small school, the book of Psalms, about three years ago, I thought that I had by this means sufficiently discharged my duty, and had resolved not to publish to the world what I had familiarly taught those of my own household. And, in fact, before I had undertaken to expound this book in my lectures, at the request of my brethren, I said what was true, that I had kept away from this subject, because that most faithful teacher of the Church of God, Martin Bucer, had labored in this field with such singular learning, diligence, fidelity, and success, that at least there was not so great need that I should put my hand to the work. And had the commentaries of Wolphangus Musculus at that time been published, I would not have omitted to do them justice by mentioning them in the same way, since he, too, in the judgment of good men, has earned no small praise by his diligence and industry in this walk. I had not yet come to the end of the book, when, lo! I am urged by renewed solicitations not to suffer my lectures, which certain persons had carefully, faithfully, and not without great labor, taken down, to be lost to the world. My purpose still remained unaltered; only I promised what for a long time I had been thinking of, to write something on the subject in the French language, that my countrymen might not be without the means of being enabled to understand so useful a book when perusing it. While I am thinking of making this attempt, suddenly, and contrary to my first design, it occurred to me, by what impulse I know not, to compose in Latin, only as it were in the way of trial, an exposition of one psalm. When I found that my success corresponded to my desire far beyond what I had ventured to anticipate, I was encouraged, and accordingly began to make the same attempt in a few other psalms. On perceiving this, my intimate friends, as if in this way they held me bound, urged me with the greater confidence not to desist from my course. One reason which made me comply with their solicitations, and which also had from the commencement induced me to make this first attempt, was an apprehension that at some future period that which had been taken down from my lectures might be published to the world contrary to my wishes or at least without my knowledge. I can truly say that I was drawn to execute this work rather from such an apprehension, than led to it from my own free will. At the same time, as I continued to prosecute the work, I began to perceive more distinctly that this was by no means a superfluous undertaking, and I have also felt from my own individual experience that to readers who are not so exercised, I would furnish important assistance in understanding the Psalms.

The varied and resplendent riches which are contained in this treasury it is no easy matter to express in words; so much so that I well know that whatever I shall be able to say will be far from approaching the excellence of the subject. But as it is better to give to my readers some taste, however small, of the wonderful advantages they will derive from the study of this book than to be entirely silent on the point, I may be permitted briefly to advert to a matter, the greatness of which does not admit of being fully unfolded. I have been accustomed to call this book, I think not inappropriately, "An Anatomy of All the Parts of the Soul"; for there is not an emotion of which anyone can be conscious that is not here represented as in a mirror. Or rather, the Holy Spirit has here drawn to the life all the griefs, sorrows, fears, doubts, hopes, cares, perplexities, in short, all the distracting emotions with which the minds of men are wont to be agitated. The other parts of Scripture contain the commandments which God enjoined his servants to announce to us. But here the prophets themselves, seeing they are exhibited to us as speaking to God, and laying open all their inmost thoughts and affections, call, or rather draw, each of us to the examination of himself in particulars in order that none of the many infirmities to which we are subject, and of the many vices with which we abound, may remain concealed. It is certainly a rare and singular advantage, when all lurking places are discovered, and the heart is brought into the light, purged from that most baneful infection, hypocrisy. In short, as calling upon God is one of the principal means of securing our safety, and as a better and more unerring rule for guiding us in this exercise cannot be found elsewhere than in the Psalms, it follows that in proportion to the proficiency which a man shall have attained in understanding them, will be his knowledge of the most important part of celestial doctrine. Genuine and earnest prayer proceeds first from a sense of our need, and next, from faith in the promises of God. It is by perusing these inspired compositions that men will be most effectually awakened to a sense of their maladies, and, at the same time, instructed in seeking remedies for their cure. In a word, whatever may serve to encourage us when we are about to pray to God is taught us in this book. And not only are the promises of God presented to us in it, but oftentimes there is exhibited to us one standing, as it were, amid the invitations of God on the one hand and the impediments of the flesh on the other, girding and preparing himself for prayer: thus teaching us, if at any time we are agitated with a variety of doubts, to resist and fight against them, until the soul, freed and disentangled from all these impediments, rise up to God; and not only so, but even when in the midst of doubts, fears, and apprehensions, let us put forth our efforts in prayer until we experience some consolation which may calm and bring contentment to our minds. Although distrust may shut the gate against our prayers, yet we must not allow ourselves to give way, whenever our hearts waver or are agitated with inquietude, but must persevere until faith finally come forth victorious from these conflicts. In many places we may perceive the exercise of the servants of God in prayer so fluctuating that they are almost overwhelmed by the alternate hope of success and apprehension of failure, and gain the prize only by strenuous exertions. We see on the one hand, the flesh manifesting its infirmity; and on the other, faith putting forth its power; and if it is not so valiant and courageous as might be desired, it is at least prepared to fight until by degrees it acquire perfect strength. But as those things which serve to teach us the true method of praying aright will be found scattered through the whole of this commentary, I will not now stop to treat of topics which it will be necessary afterward to repeat, nor detain my readers from proceeding to the work itself. Only it appeared to me to be requisite to show in passing that this book makes known to us this privilege, which is desirable above all others—that not only is there opened up to us familiar access to God, but also that we have permission and freedom granted us to lay open before him our infirmities which we would be ashamed to confess before men. Besides there is also here prescribed to us an infallible rule for directing us with respect to the right manner of offering to God the sacrifice of praise, which he declares to be most precious in his sight, and of the sweetest odor. There is no other book in which there is to be found more express and magnificent commendations, both of the unparalleled liberality of God toward his Church, and of all his works; there is no other book in which there is recorded so many deliverances nor one in which the evidences and experiences of the fatherly Providence and solicitude which God exercises toward us are celebrated with such splendor of diction, and yet with the strictest adherence to truth; in short, there is no other book in which we are more perfectly taught the right manner of praising God, or in which we are more powerfully stirred up to the performance of this religious exercise. Moreover although the Psalms are replete with all the precepts which serve to frame our life to every part of holiness, piety, and righteousness, yet they will principally teach and train us to bear the cross; and the bearing of the cross is a genuine proof of our obedience, since by doing this, we renounce the guidance of our own affections and submit ourselves entirely to God, leaving him to govern us and to dispose of our life according to his will, so that the afflictions which are the bitterest and most severe to our nature become sweet to us, because they proceed from him. In one word, not only will we here find general commendations of the goodness of God, which may teach men to repose themselves in him alone and to seek all their happiness solely in him, and which are intended to teach true believers with their whole hearts confidently to look to him for help in all their necessities, but we will also find that the free remission of sins, which alone reconciles God toward us and procures for us settled peace with him, is so set forth and magnified as that here there is nothing wanting which relates to the knowledge of eternal salvation.

Now, if my readers derive any fruit and advantage from the labor which I have bestowed in writing these commentaries, I would have them to understand that the small measure of experience which I have had by the conflicts with which the Lord has exercised me has in no ordinary degree assisted me, not only in applying to present use whatever instruction could be gathered from these divine compositions, but also in more easily comprehending the design of each of the writers. And as David holds the principal place among them, it has greatly aided me in understanding more fully the complaints made by him of the internal afflictions which the Church had to sustain through those who gave themselves out to be her members, that I had suffered the same or similar things from the domestic enemies of the Church. For although I follow David at a great distance, and come far short of equaling him, or rather, although in aspiring slowly and with great difficulty to attain to the many virtues in which he excelled, I still feel myself tarnished with the contrary vices, yet if I have any things in common with him, I have no hesitation in comparing myself with him. In reading the instances of his faith, patience, fervor, zeal, and integrity, it has, as it ought, drawn from me unnumbered groans and sighs, that I am so far from approaching them; but it has, notwithstanding, been of very great advantage to me to behold in him as in a mirror, both the commencement of my calling and the continued course of my function; so that I know the more assuredly, that whatever that most illustrious king and prophet suffered was exhibited to me by God as an example for imitation. My condition no doubt is much inferior to his, and it is unnecessary for me to stay to show this. But as he was taken from the sheepfold and elevated to the rank of supreme authority, so God having taken me from my originally obscure and humble condition has reckoned me worthy of being invested with the honorable office of a preacher and minister of the Gospel. When I was as yet a very little boy, my father had destined me for the study of theology. But afterward when he considered that the legal profession commonly raised those who followed it to wealth, this prospect induced him suddenly to change his purpose. Thus it came to pass that I was withdrawn from the study of philosophy, and was put to the study of law. To this pursuit I endeavored faithfully to apply myself in obedience to the will of my father, but God, by the secret guidance of his Providence, at length gave a different direction to my course. And first, since I was too obstinately devoted to the superstitions of popery to be easily extricated from so profound an abyss of mire, God by a sudden conversion subdued and brought my mind to a teachable frame, which was more hardened in such matters than might have been expected from one at my early period of life. Having thus received some taste and knowledge of true godliness, I was immediately inflamed with so intense a desire to make progress therein that although I did not altogether leave off other studies, I yet pursued them with less ardor.

I was quite surprised to find that before a year had elapsed, all who had any desire after purer doctrine were continually coming to me to learn, although I myself was as yet but a mere novice and tyro. Being of a disposition somewhat unpolished and bashful, which led me always to love the shade and retirement, I then began to seek some secluded corner where I might be withdrawn from the public view; but so far from being able to accomplish the object of my desire, all my retreats were like public schools. In short, while my one great object was to live in seclusion without being known, God so led me about through different turnings and changes that he never permitted me to rest in any place, until, in spite of my natural disposition, he brought me forth to public notice. Leaving my native country, France, I in fact retired into Germany, expressly for the purpose of being able there to enjoy in some obscure corner the repose which I had always desired, and which had been so long denied me. But lo! While I lay hidden at Basle, and known only to a few people, many faithful and holy persons were burned alive in France; and the report of these burnings having reached foreign nations, they excited the strongest disapprobation among a great part of the Germans, whose indignation was kindled against the authors of such tyranny. In order to allay this indignation, certain wicked and lying pamphlets were circulated, stating that none were treated with such cruelty but Anabaptists and seditious persons, who by their perverse ravings and false opinions were overthrowing not only religion but also all civil order. Observing that the object which these instruments of the court aimed at by their disguises was not only that the disgrace of shedding so much innocent blood might remain buried under the false charges and calumnies which they brought against the holy martyrs after their death, but also that afterward they might be able to proceed to the utmost extremity in murdering the poor saints without exciting compassion toward them in the breasts of any, it appeared to me, that unless I opposed them to the utmost of my ability, my silence could not be vindicated from the charge of cowardice and treachery. This was the consideration which induced me to publish my *Institutes of the Christian Religion.* My objects were, first, to prove that these reports were false and calumnious, and thus to vindicate my brethren, whose death was precious in the sight of the Lord; and next, that as the same cruelties might very soon after be exercised against many unhappy individuals, foreign nations might be touched with at least some compassion toward them and solicitude about them. When it was then published, it was not that copious and labored work which it now is, but only a small treatise containing a summary of the principal truths of the Christian religion, and it was published with no other design than that men might know what was the faith held by those whom I saw basely and wickedly defamed by those flagitious and perfidious flatterers. That my object was not to acquire fame appeared from this, that immediately after I left Basle, and particularly from the fact that nobody there knew that I was the author.

Wherever else I have gone, I have taken care to conceal that I was the author of that performance, and I had resolved to continue in the same privacy and obscurity until at length William Farel* detained me at Geneva, not so much by counsel and exhortation as by a dreadful imprecation, which I felt to be as if God had from heaven laid his mighty hand upon me to arrest me. As the

---

* Guillaume Farel (1489–1565) was, like Calvin, a Frenchman. He was one of the circle of Reformers who gathered around Bishop Briçonnet at Meaux near Paris. When, after much struggle in which Farel was active, the Reformed faith was established in Geneva in 1535, he was the leader of the church and induced Calvin to work with him. He was ousted with Calvin in 1538, and returned with him in 1541, but he left in 1542, and in 1544 settled in Neuchâtel. He remained Calvin's close friend, and died a year after Calvin in 1565 in Metz.

most direct road to Strasbourg, to which I then intended to retire, was as shut up by the wars, I had resolved to pass quickly by Geneva, without staying longer than a single night in that city. A little before this, popery had been driven from it by the exertions of the excellent person whom I have named, and Pierre Viret;* but matters were not yet brought to a settled state, and the city was divided into unholy and dangerous factions. Then an individual who now basely apostasized and returned to the papists, discovered me and made me known to others. Upon this, Farel, who burned with an extraordinary zeal to advance the Gospel, immediately strained every nerve to detain me. And after having learned that my heart was set upon devoting myself to private studies for which I wished to keep myself free from other pursuits, and finding that he gained nothing by entreaties, he proceeded to utter an imprecation that God would curse my retirement and the tranquillity of the studies which I sought if I should withdraw and refuse to give assistance when the necessity was so urgent. By this imprecation I was so stricken with terror that I desisted from the journey which I had undertaken; but sensible of my natural bashfulness and timidity, I would not bring myself under obligation to discharge any particular office. After that, four months had scarcely elapsed, when, on the one hand, the Anabaptists began to assail us, and, on the other, a certain wicked apostate, who being secretly supported by the influence of some of the magistrates of the city, was thus enabled to give us a great deal of trouble. At the same time, a succession of dissensions fell out in the city which strangely afflicted us. Being, as I acknowledge, naturally of a timid, softer, and pusillanimous disposition, I was compelled to encounter these violent tempests as part of my early training; and although I did not sink under themes, yet I was not sustained by such greatness of mind as not to rejoice more than it became me, when, in consequence of certain commotions, I was banished from Geneva.

---

* Pierre Viret (1511–71), Swiss-born Reformer, helped Farel in Geneva and stayed in the city when Farel and Calvin were expelled (1538–41). Thereafter he worked in Lausanne, his birthplace, and also lectured on the New Testament in Bern, until he was ousted in 1559 and returned to Geneva. After a checkered career in France and much controversy with French Catholics, he died at Orthez (south of Bordeaux) in 1571. He was an extensive and respected writer as well as an effective preacher.

By this means set at liberty and loosed from the tie of my vocation I resolved to live in a private station, free from the burden and cares of any public charge, when that most excellent servant of Christ, Martin Bucer,* employing a similar kind of remonstrance and protestation as that to which Farel had recourse before, drew me back to a new station. Alarmed by the example of Jonas which he set before me, I still continued in the work of teaching. And although I always continued like myself, studiously avoiding celebrity, yet I was carried, I know not how, as it were by force to the Imperial assemblies, where, willing or unwilling, I was under the necessity of appearing before the eyes of many.† Afterward, when the Lord having compassion on this city had allayed the hurtful agitations and broils which prevailed in it, and by his wonderful power had defeated both the wicked counsels and the sanguinary attempts of the disturbers of the Republic, necessity was imposed upon me of returning to my former charge, contrary to my desire and inclination. The welfare of this Church, it is true, lay so near my heart that for its sake I would not have hesitated to lay down my life; but my timidity nevertheless suggested to me many reasons for excusing myself from again willingly taking upon my shoulders so heavy a burden. At length, however, a solemn and conscientious regard to my duty prevailed with me to consent to return to the flock from which I had been torn; but with what grief, tears, great anxiety, and distress I did this, the Lord is my best witness, and many godly persons who would have wished to see me delivered from this painful state, had it not been that that which I feared, and which made me give my consent, prevented them and shut their mouths.

Were I to narrate the various conflicts by which the Lord has exercised me since that time, and by what trials he has proved me,

---

* Martin Bucer (1491–1551) was the Protestant Reformer in Strasbourg, where Calvin stayed for three years (1538–41) when he was forced out of Geneva. A man zealous for Christian unity, he had considerable influence upon Calvin, especially during this early period in the latter's activity. He commented extensively upon the Bible and did his best-known work on the Gospels. His commentary on Romans was published in Strasbourg in 1536, shortly before Calvin began to work on his own.

† At Worms in 1540 and at Regensburg in 1541, where the Catholics and the Protestants entered into futile discussions on reunion.

it would make a long history. But that I may not become tedious to my readers by a waste of words, I shall content myself with repeating briefly what I have touched upon a little before, that in considering the whole course of the life of David, it seemed to me that by his own footsteps he showed me the way, and from this I have experienced no small consolation. As that holy king was harassed by the Philistines and other foreign enemies with continual wars, while he was much more grievously afflicted by the malice and wickedness of some perfidious men among his own people, so I can say as to myself that I have been assailed on all sides and have scarcely been able to enjoy repose for a single moment, but have always had to sustain some conflict either from enemies without or within the Church. Satan has made many attempts to overthrow the fabric of this Church; and once it came to this, that I, altogether feeble and timorous as I am, was compelled to break and put a stop to his deadly assaults by putting my life in danger and opposing my person to his blows. Afterward, for the space of five years, when some wicked libertines were furnished with undue influence, and also some of the common people, corrupted by the allurements and perverse discourse of such persons, desired to obtain the liberty of doing whatever they pleased, without controls I was under the necessity of fighting without ceasing to defend and maintain the discipline of the Church. To these irreligious characters and despisers of the heavenly doctrine, it was a matter of entire indifference, although the Church should sink into ruin, provided they obtained what they sought—the power of acting just as they pleased. Many, too, harassed by poverty and hunger, and others impelled by insatiable ambition or avarice and a desire of dishonest gain, were become so frantic that they chose rather, by throwing all things into confusion, to involve themselves and us in one common ruin, than to remain quiet by living peaceably and honestly. During the whole of this lengthened period, I think that there is scarcely any of the weapons which are forged in the workshop of Satan, which has not been employed by them in order to obtain their object. And at length matters had come to such a state that an end could be put to their machinations in no other way than cutting them off by an ignominious death; which was indeed a painful and pitiable spectacle to me. They no doubt deserved the severest punishment, but I always rather desired that they might live in prosperity and continue safe and untouched, which would have been the case had they not been altogether incorrigible and obstinately refused to listen to wholesome admonition.

The trial of these five years was grievous and hard to bear, but I experienced not less excruciating pain from the malignity of those who ceased not to assail myself and my ministry with their envenomed calumnies. A great proportion of them, it is true, are so blinded by a passion for slander and detraction that to their great disgracers they betray at once their impudence, while others, however crafty and cunning, cannot so cover or disguise themselves as to escape being shamefully convicted and disgraced; yet when a man has been a hundred times found innocent of a charge brought against him, and when the charge is again repeated without any cause or occasion, it is an indignity hard to bear. Because I affirm and maintain that the world is managed and governed by the secret Providence of God, a multitude of presumptuous men rise up against me and allege that I represent God as the author of sin. This is so foolish a calumny that it would of itself quickly come to nothing did it not meet with persons who have tickled ears and who take pleasure in feeding upon such discourse. But there are many whose minds are so filled with envy and spleen, or ingratitude, or malignity, that there is no falsehood, however preposterous, yea, even monstrous, which they do not receive, if it is spoken to them. Others endeavor to overthrow God's eternal purpose of predestination, by which he distinguishes between the reprobate and the elect; others take upon them to defend free will, and forthwith many throw themselves into their ranks, not so much through ignorance as by a perversity of zeal which I know not how to characterize. If they were open and avowed enemies who brought these troubles upon me, the thing might in some way be borne. But that those who shroud themselves under the name of brethren, and not only eat Christ's sacred bread, but also administer it to others, that those, in short, who loudly boast of being preachers of the Gospel, should wage such nefarious war against me, how detestable is it? In this matter I may very justly complain with David,

> Yea, mine own familiar friend, in whom I trusted, who did
>   eat of my bread, hath lifted up his heel against me.
>
> (Ps. 41:9)
>
> For it was not an enemy that reproached me;
> but it was thou, a man mine equal, my guide, and mine
>   acquaintance.
> We took sweet counsel together, and walked unto the house
>   of God in company.
>
> (Ps. 55:12, 13, 14)

Others circulated ridiculous reports concerning my treasures; others, of the extravagant authority and enormous influence which they say I possess; others speak of my delicacies and magnificence. But when a man is content with scanty food and common clothing and does not require from the humblest more frugality than he shows and practices himself, shall it be said that such a one is too sumptuous and lives in too high a style? As to the power and influence of which they envy me, I wish I could discharge this burden upon them; for they estimate my power by the multitude of affairs and the vast weight of labors with which I am overwhelmed. And if there are some whom I cannot persuade while I am alive that I am not rich, my death at length will prove it. I confess, indeed, that I am not poor, for I desire nothing more than what I have. All these are invented stories, and there is no color whatever for any one of them; but many nevertheless are very easily persuaded of their truth and applaud them; and the reason is because the greatest part judge that the only means of cloaking their enormities is to throw all things into disorder and to confound black and white; and they think that the best and shortest way by which they can obtain full liberty to live with impunity just as they please is to destroy the authority of Christ's servants.

In addition to these, there are *the hypocritical mockers in feasts*, of whom David complains (Ps. 35:16), and I mean by these not only plate-licking characters who seek a meal to fill their belly, but all those who by false reports seek to obtain the favor of the great. Having been long accustomed to swallow such wrongs as these, I have become almost hardened; yet when the insolence of such characters increases I cannot but sometimes feel my heart wounded with bitter pangs. Nor was it enough that I should be so inhumanly treated by my neighbors. In addition to this, in a distant country toward the frozen ocean, there was raised I know not how, by the frenzy of a few, a storm which afterward stirred up against me a vast number of persons, who are too much at leisure, and have nothing to do but by their bickering to hinder those who are laboring for the edification of the Church. I am still speaking of the internal enemies of the Church—of those who, boasting mightily of the Gospel of Christ, nevertheless rush against me with greater impetuosity than against the open adversaries of the Church, because I do not embrace their gross and fictitious notion concerning a carnal way of eating Christ in the sacrament; and of whom I may protest, after the example of David, *I am for peace; but when I speak, they are for war* (Ps. 120:7). Moreover, the cruel ingratitude of all of them is manifest in this, that they scruple not to assail both in flank and rear a man who strenuously exerts himself to maintain a cause which they have in common with him and whom therefore they ought to aid and succor. Certainly, if such persons were possessed of even a small portion of humanity, the fury of the papists which is directed against me with such unbridled violence would appease the most implacable animosity which they may bear toward me. But since the condition of David was such that though he had deserved well of his own people, he was nevertheless bitterly hated by many without a cause, as he complains in Psalm 69:4, *I restored that which I took not away,* it afforded me no small consolation when I was groundlessly assailed by the hatred of those who ought to have assisted and solaced me, to conform myself to the example of so great and so excellent a person. This knowledge and experience have been of much service in enabling me to understand the Psalms, so that in my meditations upon them, I did not wander, as it were, in an unknown region.

My readers, too, if I mistake not, will observe that in unfolding the internal affections both of David and of others I discourse upon them as matters of which I have familiar experience. Moreover, since I have labored faithfully to open up this treasure for the use of all the people of God, although what I have done has not been equal to my wishes, yet the attempt which I have made deserves to be received with some measure of favor. Still, I only ask that each may judge of my labors with justice and candor, according to the advantage and fruit which he shall derive from them. Certainly, as I have said before, in reading these commentaries, it will be clearly seen that I have not sought to please, unless insofar as I might at the same time be profitable to others. And, therefore, I have not only observed throughout a simple style of teaching, but in order to be removed the further from all ostentation, I have also generally abstained from refuting the opinions of others, although this presented a more favorable opportunity for plausible display, and of acquiring the applause of those who shall favor my book with a perusal. I have never touched upon opposite opinions, unless where there was reason to fear that by being silent respecting them, I might leave my readers in doubt and perplexity. At the same time, I am sensible that it would have been much more agreeable to the taste of many had I heaped together a great mass of materials which has great show, and acquires fame for the writer; but I have felt nothing to be of more importance than to have a regard to the edification of the Church. May God, who has implanted this desire in my heart, grant by his grace that the success may correspond thereto!

GENEVA

JULY 22, 1557

PSALM 16

Mictam. A Psalm of David.

¹Keep me, O God! *For* in thee do I trust.

²Thou shalt say unto Jehovah, "Thou art my Lord; my well-doing *extendeth* not unto thee."

³Unto the saints who are on the earth, and to the excellent; all my delight is in them.

⁴Multiplied shall be their sorrows who offer to a stranger; I will not taste their libations of blood, Nor will I take their names in my lips.

⁵Jehovah is the portion of my inheritance, and of my cup; Thou maintainest my lot.

⁶The lines have fallen to me in pleasant *places*; Yea, an inheritance that is goodly hath fallen to me.

⁷I will magnify Jehovah, who giveth me counsel; Even in the nights instruct me do my reins.

⁸I have set Jehovah before me continually; Since he is at my right hand, I shall not be moved.

⁹Therefore glad is my heart, rejoice doth my tongue; Also my flesh dwelleth in confidence.

¹⁰For thou wilt not leave my soul in the grave; Nor wilt thou make thy Holy One to see the pit.

¹¹Thou wilt make known to me the way of life; Fullness of joy *is* in thy countenance; Pleasures *are* at thy right hand for evermore.

In the beginning David commends himself to the protection of God. He then meditates upon the benefits which he received from God and thereby stirs himself up to thanksgiving. By his service, it is true, he could in no respect be profitable to God, but he, notwithstanding, surrenders and devotes himself entirely to him, protesting that he will have nothing to do with superstitions. He also states the reason of this to be that full and substantial happiness consists in resting in God alone, who never suffers his own people to want any good thing.

Mictam of David.

As to the meaning of the word *mictam*, the Jewish expositors are not of one mind. Some derive it from כתם, *catham*, as if it were a golden crest or jewel. Others think it is the beginning of a song, which at that time was very common. To others it seems rather to be some kind of tune, and this opinion I am inclined to adopt.

¹Keep [or guard] me, O God; for in thee do I trust.

1. This is a prayer in which David commits himself to the protection of God. He does not, however, here implore the aid of God in some particular emergency as he often does in other psalms, but he beseeches him to show himself his protector during the whole course of his life, and indeed our safety both in life and in death depends entirely upon our being under the protection of God. What follows concerning *trust* signifies much the same thing as if the Holy Spirit assured us by the mouth of David that God is ready to succor all of us, provided we rely upon him with a sure and steadfast faith; and that he takes under his protection none but those who commit themselves to him with their whole heart. At the same time, we must be reminded that David, supported by this trust, continued firm and unmoved amid all the storms of adversity with which he was buffeted.

²Thou shalt say unto Jehovah, "Thou art my Lord, my well-doing extendeth not unto thee." ³Unto the saints who are on the earth, and to the excellent; all my delight is in them.

2. *Thou shalt say unto Jehovah.* David begins by stating that he can bestow nothing upon God, not only because God stands in no need of anything, but also because mortal man cannot merit the favor of God by any service which he can perform to him. At the same time, however, he takes courage, and, as God accepts our devotion and the service which we yield to him, David protests that he will be one of his servants. To encourage himself the more effectually to this duty, he speaks to his own soul; for the Hebrew word, which is rendered *Thou shalt say*, is of the feminine gender, which can refer only to the soul. Some may prefer reading the word in the past tense, *Thou hast said*, which I think is unobjectionable, for the psalmist is speaking of an affliction which had a continued abode in his soul. The import of his language is: I am, indeed, fully convinced in my heart and know assuredly that God can derive no profit or advantage from me; but notwithstanding

this, I will join myself in fellowship with the saints, that with one accord we may worship him by the sacrifices of praise. Two things are distinctly laid down in this verse. The first is that God has a right to require of us whatever he pleases, seeing we are wholly bound to him as our rightful proprietor and Lord. David, by ascribing to him the power and the dominion of *Lord*, declares that both himself and all he possessed are the property of God. The other particular contained in this verse is the acknowledgment which the psalmist makes of his own indigence. *My well-doing extendeth not unto thee.* Interpreters expound this last clause in two ways. As עָלֶיךָ, *aleyḳa*, may be rendered *upon thee*, some draw from it this sense, that God is not brought under obligation, or in the least degree indebted to us, by any good deeds which we may perform to him; and they understand the term *goodness* in a passive sense, as if David affirmed that whatever goodness he received from God did not proceed from any obligation he had laid God under, or from any merit which he possessed. But I think the sentence has a more extensive meaning, namely, that let men strive ever so much to lay themselves out for God, yet they can bring no advantage to him. Our goodness extendeth not to him, not only because, having in himself alone an all-sufficiency, he stands in need of nothing, but also because we are empty and destitute of all good things and have nothing with which to show ourselves liberal toward him. From this doctrine, however, the other point which I have before touched upon will follow, namely, that it is impossible for men, by any merits of their own, to bring God under obligation to them so as to make him their debtor. The sum of the discourse is that when we come before God, we must lay aside all presumption. When we imagine that there is any good thing in us, we need not wonder if he reject us, as we thus take away from him a principal part of the honor which is his due. But, on the contrary, if we acknowledge that all the services which we can yield him are in themselves things of nought and undeserving of any recompense, this humility is as a perfume of a sweet odor, which will procure for them acceptance with God.

3. *Unto the saints who are on the earth.* Almost all are agreed in understanding this place, as if David, after the sentence which we have just now been considering, had added, "The only way of serving God aright is to endeavor to do good to his holy servants."

And the truth is that God, as our good deeds cannot extend to him, substitutes the saints in his place, toward whom we are to exercise our charity. When men, therefore, mutually exert themselves in doing good to one another, this is to yield to God right and acceptable service. We ought, doubtless, to extend our charity even to those who are unworthy of it, as our heavenly Father *maketh his sun to rise on the evil and on the good* (Matt. 5:45); but David justly prefers the saints to others and places them in a higher rank. This, then, as I have said in the commencement, is the common opinion of almost all interpreters. But although I do not deny that this doctrine is comprehended under the words of David, I think he goes somewhat further and intimates that he will unite himself with the devout worshippers of God and be their associate or companion, even as all the children of God ought to be joined together by the bond of fraternal unity, that they may all serve and call upon their common Father with the same affection and zeal. We thus see that David, after having confessed that he can find nothing in himself to bring to God, seeing he is indebted to him for everything which he has, sets his affections upon the saints, because it is the will of God that, in this world, he should be magnified and exalted in the assembly of the just, whom he has adopted into his family for this end, that they may live together with one accord under his authority and under the guidance of his Holy Spirit. This passage, therefore, teaches us that there is no sacrifice more acceptable to God than when we sincerely and heartily connect ourselves with the society of the righteous, and being knit together by the sacred bond of godliness cultivate and maintain with them brotherly goodwill. In this consists the communion of saints which separates them from the degrading pollutions of the world that they may be the holy and peculiar people of God. He expressly speaks of *the saints who are on the earth*, because it is the will of God that even in this world, there should be conspicuous marks and, as it were, visible escutcheons of his glory, which may serve to conduct us to himself. The faithful, therefore, bear his image, that, by their example, we may be stirred up to meditation upon the heavenly life. For the same reason, the psalmist calls them *excellent* or honorable, because there is nothing which ought to be more precious to us than righteousness and holiness, in which the brightness of God's Spirit shines forth; just as we are commanded in the preceding psalm to prize and honor those who fear God. We ought, therefore, highly to value and esteem the true and devoted servants of God, and to regard nothing as of greater importance than to connect ourselves with their society; and this we will actually do if we wisely reflect in what true excellence and dignity consist, and do not allow the vain splendor of the world and its deceitful pomps to dazzle our eyes.

4Their sorrows shall be multiplied who offer to a stranger. I will not taste their libations of blood, nor will I take their names in my lips.

The psalmist now describes the true way of maintaining brotherly concord with the saints, by declaring that he will have nothing to do with unbelievers and the superstitious. We cannot be united into the one body of the Church under God if we do not break off all the bonds of impiety, separate ourselves from idolaters, and keep ourselves pure and at a distance from all the pollutions which corrupt and vitiate the holy service of God. This is certainly the general drift of David's discourse. But as to the words there is a diversity of opinion among expositors. Some translate the first word of the verse עַצְּבוֹת, *atsboth*, by *idols*, and according to this rendering the meaning is that after men in their folly have once begun to make to themselves false gods, their madness breaks forth without measure until they accumulate an immense multitude of deities. As, however, this word is here put in the feminine gender, I prefer translating it *sorrows* or *troubles*, although it may still have various meanings. Some think it is an imprecation, and they read, *Let their sorrows be multiplied;* as if David, inflamed with a holy zeal, denounced the just vengeance of God against the superstitious. Others, whose opinions I prefer, do not change the tense of the verb, which in the Hebrew is future, *Their sorrows shall be multiplied,* but to me they do not seem to express, with sufficient clearness, what kind of sorrows David intends. They say, indeed, that wretched idolaters are perpetually adding to their new inventions, in doing which they miserably torment themselves. But I am of opinion that by this word there is, at the same time, denoted the end and issue of the pains which they take in committing it; it points out that they not only put themselves to trouble without any profit or advantage, but also miserably harass and busy themselves to accomplish their own destruction. As an incitement to him to withdraw himself further from their company, he takes this as an incontrovertible principle, that, so far from deriving any advantage from their vain superstitions, they only, by their strenuous efforts in practicing them, involve themselves in greater misery and wretchedness. For what must be the issue with respect to those miserable men who willingly surrender themselves as bond-slaves to the devil, but to be disappointed of their hope? Even as God complains in Jeremiah (2:13), *They have forsaken me the fountain of living waters, and hewed them out cisterns, broken cisterns, that can hold no water.*

In the next clause there is also some ambiguity. The Hebrew word מָהַר, *mahar*, which we have translated *to offer*, in the conjugation *kal* signifies *to endow* or *to give*. But as in the conjugation *hiphil*, it is more frequently taken for *to run* or *to make haste*, many have preferred this latter meaning and interpret the clause thus, that superstitious persons eagerly hasten after strange gods. And in fact we see them rushing into their idolatries with all the impetuosity and recklessness of madmen running in the fields; and the prophets often upbraid them for this inconsiderate frenzy with which they are fired. I would, therefore, be much disposed to adopt this sense were it supported by the common usage of the language; but as grammarians observe that there is not to be found another similar passage in Scripture, I have followed, in my translation, the first opinion. In short, the sum of what the psalmist says is this: That unbelievers, who lavish and squander away their substance upon their idols, not only lose all the gifts and offerings which they present to them, but also, by provoking the wrath of God against themselves, are continually increasing the amount of their miseries. Perhaps, also, the prophet has an allusion to the common doctrine of Scripture, that idolaters violate the promise of the spiritual marriage contracted with the true God and enter into covenant with idols. Ezekiel (16:33) justly upbraids the Jews, in that while the custom is for the lover to allure the harlot with presents, they, on the contrary, offered rewards to the idols to whom they prostituted and abandoned themselves. But the meaning which we have above given brings out the spirit of the passage, namely, that unbelievers, who honor their false gods by offering to them gifts, not only lose what is thus expended, but also heap up for themselves sorrows upon sorrows, because at last the issue will be miserable and ruinous to them.

I will not taste their libations of blood. By libations of blood some understand that there is a reference to sacrifices made of things acquired by murder or rapine. As, however, the prophet is not here inveighing against cruel and bloodthirsty men, but condemns, in general, all false and corrupt religious worship; and again, as he does not directly name sacrifices, but expressly speaks of the ceremony of taking the cup, and tasting a little of it, which was observed in offering sacrifices, I have no doubt but that to this ceremony, as it was observed according to the law of God, he here tacitly opposes the drinking of blood in heathen sacrifices. We know that God, in order to teach his ancient people to hold in greater abhorrence murder and all cruelty, forbade them to eat or to drink blood either in their common food or in sacrifices. On the contrary, the histories of the heathen nations bear testimony that the custom of tasting the blood in their sacrifices prevailed among them. David, therefore, protests that he will not only keep himself uncontaminated by the corrupt and false opinions by which idolaters are seduced, but that he will also take care not to show outwardly any token of his complying with or approving them. In the same sense we are to understand what follows immediately after, *I will not take their names in my lips.* This implies that he will hold idols in such hatred and detestation, as to keep himself from naming them as from execrable treason against the majesty of heaven. Not that it is unlawful to pronounce their names, which we frequently meet with in the writings of the prophets, but David felt he could not otherwise more forcibly express the supreme horror and detestation with which the faithful ought to regard false gods. This is also shown by the form of expression which he employs, using the relative only, *their names,* although he has not expressly stated before that he is speaking of idols. Thus, by his example, he enjoins believers not only to beware of errors and wicked opinions, but also to abstain from all appearance of giving their consent to them. He evidently speaks of external ceremonies, which indicate either the true religion or some perverse superstition. If, then, it is unlawful for the faithful to show any token of consenting to or complying with the superstitions of idolaters, Nicodemuses (who falsely call themselves by this name) must not think to shelter themselves under the frivolous pretext that they have not renounced the faith, but keep it hidden within their hearts, when they join in the observance of the profane superstitions of the papists. Some understand the words *strangers* and *their names* as denoting the worshippers of false gods; but in my judgment David rather means the false gods themselves. The scope of his discourse is this: The earth is filled with an immense accumulation of superstitions in every possible variety, and idolaters are lavish beyond all bounds in ornamenting their idols; but the good and the holy will ever regard all their superstitious inventions with abhorrence.

5Jehovah is the portion of mine inheritance, and of my cup; thou sustainest my lot. 6The lines have fallen to me in pleasant places; yea, I have a goodly heritage.

5. *The Lord is the portion of mine inheritance.* Here the psalmist explains his sentiments more clearly. He shows the reason why he separates himself from idolaters and resolves to continue in the Church of God; why he shuns, with abhorrence, all participation in their errors and cleaves to the pure worship of God; namely, because he rests in the only true God as his portion. The unhappy restlessness of those blind idolaters whom we see going astray and running about as if stricken and impelled by madness is doubtless to be traced to their destitution of the true knowledge of God. All who have not their foundation and trust in God must necessarily be often in a state of irresolution and uncertainty; and those who do not hold the true faith in such a manner as to be guided and governed by it must be often carried away by the overflowing floods of errors which prevail in the world. This passage teaches us that none are taught aright in true godliness but those who reckon God alone sufficient for their happiness. David, by calling God *the portion of his lot*, and *his inheritance*, and *his cup*, protests that he is so fully satisfied with him alone as neither to covet anything besides him, nor to be excited by any depraved desires. Let us therefore learn, when God offers himself to us, to embrace him with the whole heart and to seek in him only all the ingredients and the fullness of our happiness. All the superstitions which have ever prevailed in the world have undoubtedly proceeded from this source, that superstitious men have not been contented with possessing God alone. But we do not actually possess him unless "he is the portion of our inheritance"; in other words, unless we are wholly devoted to him, so as no longer to have any desire unfaith-

fully to depart from him. For this reason, God, when he upbraids the Jews who had wandered from him as apostates, with having run about after idols, addresses them thus, "Let them be thine inheritance, and thy portion." By these words he shows that if we do not reckon him alone an all-sufficient portion for us, and if we will have idols along with him, he gives place entirely to them, and lets them have the full possession of our hearts. David here employs three metaphors; he first compares God to an inheritance; second, to a cup; and third, he represents him as he who defends and keeps him in possession of his inheritance. By the first metaphor he alludes to the heritages of the land of Canaan, which we know were divided among the Jews by divine appointment, and the law commanded everyone to be content with the portion which had fallen to him. By the word *cup* is denoted either the revenue of his own proper inheritance, or by synecdoche, ordinary food by which life is sustained, seeing drink is a part of our nourishment. It is as if David had said, "God is mine both in respect of property and enjoyment." Nor is the third comparison superfluous. It often happens that rightful owners are put out of their possession because no one defends them. But while God has given himself to us for an inheritance, he has engaged to exercise his power in maintaining us in the safe enjoyment of a good so inconceivably great. It would be of little advantage to us to have once obtained him as ours, if he did not secure our possession of him against the assaults which Satan daily makes upon us. Some explain the third clause as if it had been said, *Thou art my ground in which my portion is situated*, but this sense appears to me to be cold and unsatisfactory.

6. *The lines* have fallen to me. The psalmist confirms more fully what he had already said in the preceding verse with respect to his resting, with a composed and tranquil mind, in God alone; or rather, he so glories in God as nobly to despise all that the world imagines to be excellent and desirable without him. By magnifying God in such honorable and exalted strains, he gives us to

---

* The Hebrew is *measuring lines*. There is here an allusion to the ancient division of the land of Canaan among God's chosen people. This was done by lot, and the length and breadth of the portion of each tribe was ascertained by cords or measuring lines. Hence they came to signify the land so measured out.

understand that he does not desire anything more as his portion and felicity. This doctrine may be profitable to us in many ways. It ought to draw us away not only from all the perverse inventions of superstition, but also from all the allurements of the flesh and of the world. Whenever, therefore, those things present themselves to us which would lead us away from resting in God alone, let us make use of this sentiment as an antidote against them, that we have sufficient cause for being contented, since he who has in himself an absolute fullness of all good has given himself to be enjoyed by us. In this way we will experience our condition to be always pleasant and comfortable; for he who has God as his portion is destitute of nothing which is requisite to constitute a happy life.

7 *I will magnify Jehovah, who giveth me counsel; even in the nights my reins instruct me.*

Last of all, David confesses that it was entirely owing to the pure grace of God that he had come to possess so great a good, and that he had been made a partaker of it by faith. It would be of no advantage to us for God to offer himself freely and graciously to us if we did not receive him by faith, seeing he invites to himself both the reprobate and the elect in common; but the former, by their ingratitude, defraud themselves of this inestimable blessing. Let us, therefore, know that both these things proceed from the free liberality of God; first, his being our inheritance, and next, our coming to the possession of him by faith. The *counsel* of which David makes mention is the inward illumination of the Holy Spirit, by which we are prevented from rejecting the salvation to which he calls us, which we would otherwise certainly do, considering the blindness of our flesh. Whence we gather that those who attribute to the free will of man the choice of accepting or rejecting the grace of God basely mangle that grace, and show as much ignorance as impiety. That this discourse of David ought not to be understood of external teaching appears clearly from the words, for he tells us that *he was instructed in the night* when he was removed from the sight of men. Again, when he speaks of this being done *in his reins*, he doubtless means secret inspirations. Further, it ought to be carefully observed that in speaking of the time when he was instructed, he uses the plural number, saying, it was done in the *nights*. By this manner of speaking, he not only ascribes to God the beginning of faith, but acknowledges that he is contin-

ually making progress under his tuition; and, indeed, it is necessary for God, during the whole of our life, to continue to correct
the vanity of our minds, to kindle the light of faith into a brighter
flame, and by every means to advance us higher in the attainments
of spiritual wisdom.

*8I have set Jehovah continually before me; because he is at my right
hand, I shall not be moved. 9Therefore my heart is glad, my tongue
rejoiceth; my flesh also dwelleth in confidence [or in security].*

8. *I have set Jehovah*, et cetera. The psalmist again shows the
firmness and stability of his faith. To set God before us is nothing
else than to keep all our senses bound and captive, that they may
not run out and go astray after any other object. We must look to
him with other eyes than those of the flesh, for we shall seldom be
able to perceive him unless we elevate our minds above the world;
and faith prevents us from turning our back upon him. The
meaning, therefore, is that David kept his mind so intently fixed
upon the Providence of God, as to be fully persuaded that whenever any difficulty or distress should befall him, God would be
always at hand to assist him. He adds, also, *continually*, to show us
how he constantly depended upon the assistance of God, so that,
amid the various conflicts with which he was agitated, no fear of
danger could make him turn his eyes to any other quarter than to
God in search of succor. And thus we ought so to depend upon
God as to continue to be fully persuaded of his being near to us,
even when he seems to be removed to the greatest distance from
us. When we shall have thus turned our eyes toward him, the
masks and the vain illusions of this world will no longer deceive us.

Because he is at my right hand. I read this second clause as a distinct sentence from the preceding. To connect them together as
some do in this way, *I have set the Lord continually before me,
because he is at my right hand* would give a meager meaning to the
words and take away much of the truth which is taught in them,
as it would make David to say that he measured God's presence
according to the experience he had of it; a mode of speaking which
would not be at all becoming. I consider, therefore, the words,
I have set the Lord continually before me as a complete sentence,
and David set the Lord before him for the purpose of constantly
repairing to him in all his dangers. For his greater encouragement
to hope well, he sets before himself what it is to have God's assis-

tance and fatherly care, namely, that it implies his keeping firm
and unmoved his own people with whom he is present. David
then reckons himself secure against all dangers and promises himself certain safety, because, with the eyes of faith, he beholds God
as present with him. From this passage we are furnished with an
argument which overthrows the fabrication of the doctors of the
Sorbonne in Paris, *that the faithful are in doubt with respect to their
final perseverance,* for David, in very plain terms, extends his
reliance on the grace of God to the time to come. And, certainly, it
would be a very miserable condition to be in, to tremble in uncertainty every moment, having no assurance of the continuance of
the grace of God toward us.

9. *Therefore my heart is glad.* In this verse the psalmist commends the inestimable fruit of faith, of which Scripture everywhere makes mention, in that, by placing us under the protection
of God, it makes us not only to live in the enjoyment of mental
tranquillity, but, what is more, to live joyful and cheerful. The
principal, the essential part of a happy life, as we know, is to possess tranquillity of conscience and of mind; as, on the contrary,
there is no greater infelicity than to be tossed amid a multiplicity of
cares and fears.

But the ungodly, however much intoxicated with the spirit of
thoughtlessness or stupidity, never experience true joy or serene
mental peace; they rather feel terrible agitations within, which
often come upon them and trouble them, so much as to constrain
them to awake from their lethargy. In short, calmly to rejoice is
the lot of no man but of him who has learned to place his confidence in God alone and to commit his life and safety to his protection. When, therefore, encompassed with innumerable troubles
on all sides, let us be persuaded that the only remedy is to direct
our eyes toward God; and if we do this, faith will not only tran-
quilize our minds, but also replenish them with fullness of joy.
David, however, not only affirms that he is glad inwardly; he also
makes his *tongue*, yea, even his *flesh*, sharers of this joy. And not
without cause, for true believers not only have this spiritual joy in
the secret affection of their heart, but also manifest it by the
tongue, inasmuch as they glory in God as he who protects them
and secures their salvation. The word כָּבוֹד, *kabod*, properly signifies glory and excellence. I have, however, no doubt of its being

here taken for *the tongue*, as it is in Genesis 49:6; for otherwise the division which is obviously made in this verse of the person into three parts is not so distinct and evident. Further, although the body is not free from inconveniences and troubles, yet as God defends and maintains not only our souls, but also our bodies, David does not speak groundlessly when he represents the blessing of dwelling in safety as extending to his flesh in common with his soul.

¹⁰For thou wilt not leave my soul in the grave; neither wilt thou make thy Holy One to see the pit.

The psalmist goes on to explain still more fully the preceding doctrine by declaring that as he is not afraid of death, there is nothing wanting which is requisite to the completion of his joy. Whence it follows that no one truly trusts in God but he who takes such hold of the salvation which God has promised him as to despise death. Moreover, it is to be observed that David's language is not to be limited to some particular kind of deliverance, as in Psalm 49:15, where he says, *God hath redeemed my soul from the power of the grave,* and in other similar passages; but he entertains the undoubted assurance of eternal salvation, which freed him from all anxiety and fear. It is as if he had said, "There will always be ready for me a way of escape from the grave, that I may not remain in corruption." God, in delivering his people from any danger, prolongs their life only for a short time; but how slender and how empty a consolation would it be to obtain some brief respite and to take breath for a short time, until death, coming at last, should terminate the course of our life and swallow us up without any hope of deliverance? Hence it appears that when David spake thus, he raised his mind above the common lot of mankind. As the sentence has been pronounced upon all the children of Adam, *Dust thou art, and unto dust shalt thou return* (Gen. 3:19), the same condition in this respect awaits them all without exception. If, therefore, Christ, who is the firstfruits of those who rise again, does not come forth from the grave, they will remain forever under the bondage of corruption. From this Peter justly concludes (Acts 2:30) that David could not have gloried in this manner but by the spirit of prophecy; and unless he had had a special respect to the Author of life, who was promised to him, who alone was to be honored with this privilege in its fullest sense.

This, however, did not prevent David from assuring himself of exemption from the dominion of death by right, seeing Christ, by his rising from the dead, obtained immortality not for himself individually, but for us all. As to the point, that Peter (Acts 2:30) and Paul (Acts 13:33) contend that this prophecy was fulfilled in the person of Christ alone, the sense in which we must understand them is this, that he was wholly and perfectly exempted from the corruption of the grave that he might call his members into his fellowship and make them partakers of this blessing, although by degrees, and each according to his measure. As the body of David, after death, was, in the course of time, reduced to dust, the apostles justly conclude that he was not exempted from corruption. It is the same with respect to all the faithful, not one of whom becomes a partaker of incorruptible life without being first subjected to corruption. From this it follows that the fullness of life which resides in the head alone, namely, in Christ, falls down upon the members only in drops, or in small portions. The question, however, may be asked, as Christ descended into the grave, was not he also subject to corruption? The answer is easy. The etymology or derivation of the two words here used to express the grave should be carefully attended to. The grave is called שְׁאוֹל, *sheol*, being as it were an insatiable gulf, which devours and consumes all things, and the pit is called שַׁחַת, *shachath*, which signifies *corruption*. These words, therefore, here denote not so much the place as the quality and condition of the place, as if it had been said, the life of Christ will be exempted from the dominion of the grave, inasmuch as his body, even when dead, will not be subject to corruption. Besides, we know that the grave of Christ was filled and, as it were, embalmed with the life-giving perfume of his Spirit that it might be to him the gate to immortal glory. Both the Greek and Latin fathers, I confess, have strained these words to a meaning wholly different, referring them to the bringing back of the soul of Christ from hell. But it is better to adhere to the natural simplicity of the interpretation which I have given, that we may not make ourselves objects of ridicule to the Jews; and further, that one subtlety, by engendering many others, may not involve us in a labyrinth. In the second clause mention is without doubt made of the body; and we know it to be a mode of speaking very common with David intentionally to repeat the same thing twice, making a slight variation as to words. It is true, we translate **נֶפֶשׁ**, *nephesh* by *soul*, but in Hebrew it only signifies *the vital breath* or *life itself.*

¹¹Thou wilt make me to know the path of life; fullness of joy is in thy countenance, pleasures are at thy right hand for evermore.

The psalmist confirms the statement made in the preceding verse and explains the way in which God will exempt him from the bondage of death, namely, by conducting and bringing him at length safely to the possession of eternal life. Whence we again learn what I have already observed, that this passage touches upon the difference which there is between true believers and aliens, or reprobates, with respect to their everlasting state. It is a mere cavil to say that when David here speaks of *the path of life* being shown to him, it means the prolongation of his natural life. It is to form a very low estimate, indeed, of the grace of God to speak of him as a guide to his people in the path of life only for a very few years in this world. In this case, they would differ nothing from the reprobate, who enjoy the light of the sun in common with them. If, therefore, it is the special grace of God which he communicates to none but his own children, that David here magnifies and exalts, the showing of the way of life, of which he speaks, must undoubtedly be viewed as extending to a blessed immortality; and, indeed, he only knows the way of life who is so united to God that he lives in God and cannot live without him.

David next adds that when God is reconciled to us, we have all things which are necessary to perfect happiness. The phrase, *the countenance of God*, may be understood either of our being beheld by him or of our beholding him; but I consider both these ideas as included, for his fatherly favor, which he displays in looking upon us with a serene countenance, precedes this joy, and is the first cause of it, and yet this does not cheer us until, on our part, we behold it shining upon us. By this clause David also intended distinctly to express to whom those *pleasures* belong, of which God has in his hand a full and an overflowing abundance. As there are with God pleasures sufficient to replenish and satisfy the whole world, whence comes it to pass that a dismal and deadly darkness envelopes the greater part of mankind, but because God does not look upon all men equally with his friendly and fatherly countenance, nor opens the eyes of all men to seek the matter of their joy in him, and nowhere else? *Fullness of joy* is contrasted with the evanescent allurements and pleasures of this transitory world, which, after having diverted their miserable votaries for a time, leave them at length unsatisfied, famished, and disappointed. They may intoxicate and glut themselves with pleasures to the greatest excess, but, instead of being satisfied, they rather become wearied of them through loathing; and, besides, the pleasures of this world vanish away like dreams. David, therefore, testifies that true and solid joy in which the minds of men may rest will never be found anywhere else but in God; and that, therefore, none but the faithful, who are contented with his grace alone, can be truly and perfectly happy.

PSALM 23

A Psalm of David.

¹Jehovah is my shepherd, I shall not want.

²He maketh me to lie down in pastures of grass; he leadeth me to gently flowing waters.

³He restoreth my soul; he leadeth me by the paths of righteousness for his name's sake.

⁴Though I should walk in the valley of the shadow of death, I will fear no evil: for thou art with me; thy staff and thy crook comfort me.

⁵Thou wilt prepare a table before me in the presence of my persecutors: thou wilt anoint my head with oil; my cup overflows.

⁶Surely goodness and mercy will follow me all the days of my life; and I shall dwell in the house of Jehovah for a length of days.

This psalm is neither intermingled with prayers, nor does it complain of miseries for the purpose of obtaining relief; but it contains simply a thanksgiving, from which it appears that it was composed when David had obtained peaceable possession of the kingdom, and lived in prosperity, and in the enjoyment of all he could desire. That he might not, therefore, in the time of his great prosperity, be like worldly men, who, when they seem to themselves to be fortunate, bury God in forgetfulness, and luxuriously plunge themselves into their pleasures, he delights himself in God, the author of all the blessings which he enjoyed. And he not only acknowledges that the state of tranquillity in which he now lives, and his exemption from all inconveniences and troubles, is owing to the goodness of God, but he also trusts that through his Providence he will continue happy even to the close of his life, and for this end that he may employ himself in his pure worship.

A Psalm of David.

¹Jehovah is my shepherd, I shall not want. ²He maketh me to lie down in pastures of grass; he leadeth me to gently flowing waters. ³He restoreth my soul; he leadeth me by the paths of righteousness for his name's sake. ⁴Though I should walk in the valley of the shadow of death, I will fear no evil: for thou art with me; thy staff and thy crook comfort me.

1. *Jehovah is my shepherd.* Although God, by his benefits, gently allures us to himself, as it were by a taste of his fatherly sweetness, yet there is nothing into which we more easily fall than into a forgetfulness of him, when we are in the enjoyment of peace and comfort. Yea, prosperity not only so intoxicates many, as to carry them beyond all bounds in their mirth, but it also engenders insolence, which makes them proudly rise up and break forth against God. Accordingly, there is scarcely a hundredth part of those who enjoy in abundance the good things of God, who keep themselves in his fear and live in the exercise of humility and temperance, which would be so becoming. For this reason, we ought the more carefully to mark the example which is here set before us by David, who, elevated to the dignity of sovereign power, surrounded with the splendor of riches and honors, possessed of the greatest abundance of temporal good things, and in the midst of princely pleasures, not only testifies that he is mindful of God, but calling to remembrance the benefits which God had conferred upon him, makes them ladders by which he may ascend nearer to him. By this means he not only bridles the wantonness of his flesh, but also excites himself with the greater earnestness to gratitude, and the other exercises of godliness, as appears from the concluding sentence of the psalm, where he says, "I shall dwell in the house of Jehovah for a length of days." In like manner, in the Eighteenth Psalm, which was composed at a period of his life when he was applauded on every side, by calling himself the servant of God, he showed the humility and simplicity of heart to which he had attained, and, at the same time, openly testified his gratitude by applying himself to the celebration of the praises of God.

Under the similitude of a shepherd, he commends the care which God, in his Providence, had exercised toward him. His language implies that God had no less care of him than a shepherd has of the sheep who are committed to his charge. God, in the Scripture, frequently takes to himself the name and puts on the character of a shepherd, and this is no mean token of his tender love toward us. As this is a lowly and homely manner of speaking, he who does not disdain to stoop so low for our sake must bear a singularly strong affection toward us. It is therefore wonderful that when he invites us to himself with such gentleness and familiarity, we are not drawn or allured to him, that we may rest in safety and peace under his guardianship. But it should be observed that God is a shepherd only to those who, touched with a sense of their own weakness and poverty, feel their need of his protection, and who willingly abide in his sheepfold and surrender themselves to be governed by him. David, who excelled both in power and riches, nevertheless frankly confessed himself to be a poor sheep, that he might have God for his shepherd. Who is there, then, among us, who would exempt himself from this necessity, seeing our own weakness sufficiently shows that we are more than miserable if we do not live under the protection of this shepherd? We ought to bear in mind that our happiness consists in this, that his hand is stretched forth to govern us, that we live under his shadow, and that his Providence keeps watch and ward over our welfare. Although, therefore, we have abundance of all temporal good things, yet let us be assured that we cannot be truly happy unless God vouchsafe to reckon us among the number of his flock. Besides, we then only attribute to God the office of a shepherd with due and rightful honor when we are persuaded that his Providence alone is sufficient to supply all our necessities. As those who enjoy the greatest abundance of outward good things are empty and famished if God is not their Shepherd; so it is beyond all doubt that those whom he has taken under his charge shall not want a full abundance of all good things. David, therefore, declares that he is not afraid of wanting anything, because God is his Shepherd.

2. *He maketh me to lie down in pastures of grass.* With respect to the words, it is in the Hebrew, *pastures*, or *fields of grass*, for *grassy and rich grounds*. Some, instead of translating the word נאות, *neoth*, which we have rendered *pastures*, render it *shepherds' cots* or *lodges*. If this translation is considered preferable, the meaning of the psalmist will be that sheep-cots were prepared in rich pasture grounds, under which he might be protected from the heat of the sun. If even in cold countries the immoderate heat which sometimes occurs is troublesome to a flock of sheep, how could they bear the heat of the summer in Judea, a warm region, without sheepfolds? The verb רבץ, *rabats*, *to lie down* or *repose*, seems to have a reference to the same thing. David has used the phrase, *the*

quiet waters, to express gently flowing waters; for rapid streams are inconvenient for sheep to drink in and are also for the most part hurtful. In this verse, and in the verses following, he explains the last clause of the first verse, *I shall not want.* He relates how abundantly God had provided for all his necessities, and he does this without departing from the comparison which he employed at the commencement. The amount of what is stated is that the heavenly Shepherd had omitted nothing which might contribute to make him live happily under his care. He, therefore, compares the great abundance of all things requisite for the purposes of the present life which he enjoyed, to meadows richly covered with grass, and to gently flowing streams of water; or he compares the benefit or advantage of such things to sheep-cots; for it would not have been enough to have been fed and satisfied in rich pasture had there not also been provided waters to drink and the shadow of the sheep-cot to cool and refresh him.

3. *He restoreth my soul.* As it is the duty of a good shepherd to cherish his sheep, and when they are diseased or weak to nurse and support them, David declares that this was the manner in which he was treated by God. *The restoring of the soul,* as we have translated it, or *the conversion of the soul,* as it is literally rendered, is of the same import as *to make anew* or *to recover,* as has been already stated in the Nineteenth Psalm, at the seventh verse. By *the paths of righteousness,* he means easy and plain paths. As he still continues his metaphor, it would be out of place to understand this as referring to the direction of the Holy Spirit. He has stated a little before that God liberally supplies him with all that is requisite for the maintenance of the present life, and now he adds that he is defended by him from all trouble. The amount of what is said is that God is in no respect wanting to his people, seeing he sustains them by his power, invigorates and quickens them, and averts from them whatever is hurtful, that they may walk at ease in plain and straight paths. That, however, he may not ascribe anything to his own worth or merit, David represents the goodness of God as the cause of so great liberality, declaring that God bestows all these things upon him *for his own name's sake.* And certainly his choosing us to be his sheep, and his performing toward us all the offices of a shepherd, is a blessing which proceeds entirely from his free and sovereign goodness, as we shall see in the Sixty-fifth Psalm.

4. *Though I should walk.* True believers, although they dwell safely under the protection of God, are, notwithstanding, exposed to many dangers, or rather they are liable to all the afflictions which befall mankind in common, that they may the better feel how much they need the protection of God. David, therefore, here expressly declares that if any adversity should befall him, he would lean upon the Providence of God. Thus he does not promise himself continual pleasures, but he fortifies himself by the help of God courageously to endure the various calamities with which he might be visited. Pursuing his metaphor, he compares the care which God takes in governing true believers to a shepherd's staff and crook, declaring that he is satisfied with this as all-sufficient for the protection of his life. As a sheep, when it wanders up and down through a dark valley is preserved safe from the attacks of wild beasts and from harm in other ways, by the presence of the shepherd alone, so David now declares that as often as he shall be exposed to any danger, he will have sufficient defense and protection in being under the pastoral care of God.

We thus see how, in his prosperity, he never forgot that he was a man, but even then seasonably meditated on the adversities which afterward might come upon him. And certainly, the reason why we are so terrified when it pleases God to exercise us with the cross is because every man, that he may sleep soundly and undisturbed, wraps himself up in carnal security. But there is a great difference between this sleep of stupidity and the repose which faith produces. Since God tries faith by adversity, it follows that no one truly confides in God, but he who is armed with invincible constancy for resisting all the fears with which he may be assailed. Yet David did not mean to say that he was devoid of all fear, but only that he would surmount it so as to go without fear wherever his shepherd should lead him. This appears more clearly from the context. He says, in the first place, *I will fear no evil,* but immediately adding the reason of this, he openly acknowledges that he seeks a remedy against his fear in contemplating, and having his eyes fixed on, the staff of his shepherd: *For thy staff and thy crook comfort me.* What need would he have had of that consolation, if he had not been disquieted and agitated with fear? It ought, therefore, to be kept in mind that when David reflected on the adversities which might befall him, he became victorious over fear and temptations, in no other way than by casting himself on the protection of God. This he had also stated before, although a little more obscurely, in these words, *For thou art with me.* This implies that he had been afflicted with fear. Had not this been the case, for what purpose could he desire the presence of God? Besides, it is not against the common and ordinary calamities of life only that he opposes the protection of God, but against those which distract and confound the minds of men with the darkness of death. For the Jewish grammarians think that צלמות, *tsalmaveth,* which we have translated *the shadow of death,* is a compound word, as if one should say *deadly shade.* David here makes an allusion to the dark recesses or dens of wild beasts, to which when an individual approaches he is suddenly seized at his first entrance with an apprehension and fear of death. Now, since God, in the person of his only-begotten Son, has exhibited himself to us as our shepherd, much more clearly than he did in old time to the Fathers who lived under the Law, we do not render sufficient honor to his protecting care, if we do not lift our eyes to behold it, and keeping them fixed upon it, tread all fears and terrors under our feet.

⁵*Thou wilt prepare a table before me in the presence of my persecutors: thou wilt anoint my head with oil; my cup overflows.* ⁶*Surely goodness and mercy will follow me all the days of my life; and I shall dwell in the house of Jehovah for a length of days.*

5. *Thou wilt prepare.* These words, which are put in the future tense, here denote a continued act. David, therefore, now repeats, without a figure, what he has hitherto declared concerning the beneficence of God under the similitude of a shepherd. He tells us that by his liberality he is supplied with all that is necessary for the maintenance of this life. When he says, *Thou preparest a table before me,* he means that God furnished him with sustenance without trouble or difficulty on his part, just as if a father should stretch forth his hand to give food to his child. He enhances this benefit from the additional consideration that although many malicious persons envy his happiness, and desire his ruin, yea, endeavor to defraud him of the blessing of God, yet God does not desist from showing himself liberal toward him and from doing him good. What he subjoins concerning *oil* has a reference to a custom which then prevailed. We know that in old time, ointments were used at the more magnificent feasts, and no man

thought he had honorably received his guests if he had not perfumed them therewith. Now, this exuberant store of *oil*, and also this overflowing *cup*, ought to be explained as denoting the abundance which goes beyond the mere supply of the common necessaries of life; for it is spoken in commendation of the royal wealth with which, as the sacred historian records, David had been amply furnished. All men, it is true, are not treated with the same liberality with which David was treated; but there is not an individual who is not under obligation to God by the benefits which God has conferred upon him, so that we are constrained to acknowledge that he is a kind and liberal Father to all his people. In the meantime, let each of us stir up himself to gratitude to God for his benefits, and the more abundantly these have been bestowed upon us, our gratitude ought to be the greater. If he is ungrateful who, having only a coarse loaf, does not acknowledge in that the fatherly Providence of God, how much less can the stupidity of those be tolerated who glut themselves with the great abundance of the good things of God which they possess, without having any sense or taste of his goodness toward them? David, therefore, by his own example, admonishes the rich of their duty that they may be the more ardent in the expression of their gratitude to God, the more delicately he feeds them. Further, let us remember that those who have greater abundance than others are bound to observe moderation not less than if they had only as much of the good things of this life as would serve for their limited and temperate enjoyment. We are too much inclined by nature to excess, and, therefore, when God is, in respect of worldly things, bountiful to his people, it is not to stir up and nourish in them this disease. All men ought to attend to the rule of Paul, which is laid down in Philippians 4:12, that they *may know both how to be abased, and how to abound.* That want may not sink us into despondency, we need to be sustained by patient endurance; and, on the other hand, that too great abundance may not elate us above measure, we need to be restrained by the bridle of temperance. Accordingly, the Lord, when he enriches his own people, restrains, at the same time, the licentious desires of the flesh by the spirit of confidence so that, of their own accord, they prescribe to themselves rules of temperance. Not that it is unlawful for rich men to enjoy more freely the abundance which they possess than if God had given them a smaller portion; but all men ought to beware (and much more kings), lest they should be dissolved in voluptuous pleasures. David, no doubt, as was perfectly lawful, allowed himself larger scope than if he had been only one of the common people, or than if he had still dwelt in his father's cottage, but he so regulated himself in the midst of his delicacies, as not at all to take pleasure in stuffing and fattening the body. He knew well how to distinguish between the table which God had prepared for him and a trough for swine. It is also worthy of particular notice that although David lived upon his own lands, the tribute money, and other revenues of the kingdom, he gave thanks to God just as if God had daily given him his food with his own hand. From this we conclude that he was not blinded with his riches, but always looked upon God as his householder, who brought forth meat and drink from his own store and distributed it to him at the proper season.

6. *Surely goodness and mercy.* Having recounted the blessings which God had bestowed upon him, he now expresses his undoubted persuasion of the continuance of them to the end of his life. But whence proceeded this confidence, by which he assures himself that the beneficence and mercy of God will accompany him forever, if it did not arise from the promise by which God is accustomed to season the blessings which he bestows upon true believers, that they may not inconsiderately devour them without having any taste or relish for them? When he said to himself before that even amid the darkness of death he would keep his eyes fixed in beholding the Providence of God, he sufficiently testified that he did not depend upon outward things, nor measured the grace of God according to the judgment of the flesh, but that even when assistance from every earthly quarter failed him, his faith continued shut up in the word of God. Although, therefore, experience led him to hope well, yet it was principally on the promise by which God confirms his people with respect to the future that he depended. If it is objected that it is presumption for a man to promise himself a continued course of prosperity in this uncertain and changing world, I answer that David did not speak in this manner with the view of imposing on God a law; but he hoped for such exercise of God's beneficence toward him as the condition of this world permits, with which he would be con-

tented. He does not say, My cup shall be always full, or, My head shall be always perfumed with oil; but in general he entertains the hope that as the goodness of God never fails, he will be favorable toward him even to the end.

I will dwell in the house of Jehovah. By this concluding sentence he manifestly shows that he does not confine his thoughts to earthly pleasures or comforts, but that the mark at which he aims is fixed in heaven, and to reach this was his great object in all things. It is as if he had said, "I do not live for the mere purpose of living, but rather to exercise myself in the fear and service of God and to make progress daily in all the branches of true godliness." He makes a manifest distinction between himself and ungodly men, who take pleasure only in filling their bellies with luxuriant fare. And not only so, but he also intimates that to live to God is, in his estimation, of so great importance that he valued all the comforts of the flesh only in proportion as they served to enable him to live to God. He plainly affirms that the end which he contemplated in all the benefits which God had conferred upon him was that he might dwell in the house of the Lord. Whence it follows that when deprived of the enjoyment of this blessing, he made no account of all other things; as if he had said, I would take no pleasure in earthly comforts, unless I at the same time belonged to the flock of God, as he also writes in another place, *Happy is that people that is in such a case: yea, happy is that people whose God is the Lord* (Ps. 144:15).

Why did he desire so greatly to frequent the temple, but to offer sacrifices there along with his fellow-worshippers and to improve by the other exercises of religion in meditation upon the celestial life? It is, therefore, certain that the mind of David, by the aid of the temporal prosperity which he enjoyed, was elevated to the hope of the everlasting inheritance. From this we conclude that those men are brutish who propose to themselves any other felicity than that which arises from drawing near to God.

PSALM 51

To the Chief Musician. A Psalm of David, when Nathan the prophet came to him, after he had gone in to Bathsheba.

¹Have mercy upon me, O God: according to thy loving-kindness; According to the multitude of thy compassions, blot out my transgressions.

²Multiply to wash me from my iniquity, And cleanse me from my sin.

³For my sins I know, And my wickedness is before me continually.

⁴Against thee, against thee only, have I sinned, And that which was displeasing in thy sight have I done; That thou mayest be justified when thou speakest, And be pure in giving judgment.

⁵Behold in iniquity I was born, And in sin conceive me did my mother.

⁶Behold, truth thou hast loved in the inmost parts, And in secret, wisdom thou hast made me know.

⁷Thou shalt purge me with hyssop, and I shall be clean; Thou shalt wash me, and I shall be whiter than snow.

⁸Make me to hear joy and gladness; And the bones which thou hast broken shall rejoice.

⁹Hide thy face from my sins, And all my iniquities blot out.

¹⁰Create in me a clean heart, O God! And renew a right spirit in my inward parts.

¹¹Cast me not away from thy presence, And take not the Spirit of thy holiness from me.

¹²Restore unto me the joy of thy salvation, And uphold me with a free spirit.

¹³I will teach transgressors thy ways, the ungodly to time shall be converted.

¹⁴Deliver me from bloods, O God! O God of my salvation! And sing aloud shall my tongue of thy righteousness.

¹⁵O Lord! my lips do thou open, And my mouth shall show forth thy praise.

¹⁶For thou wilt not accept a sacrifice; Though I should give a burnt-offering, it would not please thee.

¹⁷The sacrifices of God are an afflicted spirit: A heart afflicted and contrite, O God! thou wilt not despise.

¹⁸Do good in thy good pleasure to Zion; Build thou the walls of Jerusalem.

¹⁹Then shalt thou accept the sacrifices of righteousness, The burnt-offering and oblation; Then shall come upon thy altar calves.

We learn the cause which led to the composition of this psalm from the title appended to it, and which will immediately come under our consideration. For a long period after his melancholy fall, David would seem to have sunk into a spiritual lethargy; but when roused from it by the expostulation of Nathan, he was filled with self-loathing and humiliation in the sight of God and was anxious both to testify his repentance to all around him and leave some lasting proof of it to posterity. In the commencement of the psalm, having his eyes directed to the heinousness of his guilt, he encourages himself to hope for pardon by considering the infinite mercy of God. This he extols in high terms, and with a variety of expressions, as one who felt that he deserved multiplied condemnation. In the after part of the psalm, he prays for restoration to the favor of God, being conscious that he deserved to have been cast off forever and deprived of all the gifts of the Holy Spirit. He promises, should forgiveness be bestowed upon him, to retain a deep and grateful sense of it. Toward the conclusion, he declares it to be for the good of the Church that God should grant his request; and, indeed, when the peculiar manner in which God had deposited his covenant of grace with David is considered, it could not but be felt that the common hope of the salvation of all must have been shaken on the supposition of his final rejection.

To the Chief Musician. A Psalm of David, when Nathan the prophet came to him, after he had gone in to Bathsheba.

When Nathan the prophet came to him. Express mention is made of the prophet having come before the psalm was written, proving, as it does, the deep lethargy into which David must have fallen. It was a wonderful circumstance that so great a man, and one so eminently gifted with the Spirit, should have continued in this dangerous state for upward of a year. Nothing but satanic influence can account for that stupor of conscience which could lead him to despise or slight the divine judgment, which he had incurred. It serves additionally to mark the supineness into which he had fallen, that he seems to have had no compunction for his sin till the prophet came to him. We have here a striking illustration, at the same time, of the mercy of God in sending the prophet to reclaim him when he had wandered. In this view, there is an antithesis in the repetition of the word *came.* It was when David came in to Bathsheba that Nathan came to him. By that sinful step he had placed himself at a distance from God; and the divine goodness was signally displayed in contemplating his restoration. We do not imagine that David, during this interval, was so wholly deprived of the sense of religion as no longer to acknowledge the supremacy of the divine Being. In all probability he continued to pray daily, engaged in the acts of divine worship, and aimed at conforming his life to the law of God. There is no reason to think that grace was wholly extinct in his heart; but only that he was possessed by a spirit of infatuation upon one particular point and labored under a fatal insensibility as to his present exposure to divine wrath. Grace, whatever sparks it might emit in other directions, was smothered, so to speak, in this. Well may we tremble to contemplate the fact that so holy a prophet and so excellent a king should have sunk into such a condition! That the sense of religion was not altogether extinguished in his mind is proved by the manner in which he was affected immediately upon receiving the prophet's reproof. Had such been the case, he could not have cried out as he did, *I have sinned against the Lord* (2 Sam. 12:13); nor would he have so readily submitted himself, in the spirit of meekness, to admonition and correction. In this respect, he has set an example to all such as may have sinned against God, teaching them the duty of humbly complying with the calls to repentance, which may be addressed to them by his servants, instead of remaining under sin till they be surprised by the final vengeance of heaven.

¹Have mercy upon me, O God: according to thy loving-kindness; according to the multitude of thy compassions, blot out my transgressions. ²Multiply to wash me from mine iniquity, and cleanse me from my sin.

1. *Have mercy upon me.* David begins, as I have already remarked, by praying for pardon; and his sin having been of an aggravated description, he prays with unwonted earnestness. He does not satisfy himself with one petition. Having mentioned the *loving-kindness* of the Lord, he adds *the multitude of his compassions*, to intimate that mercy of an ordinary kind would not suffice for so great a sinner. Had he prayed God to be favorable, simply according to his clemency or goodness, even that would have amounted to a confession that his case was a bad one; but when he speaks of his sin as remissible only through the countless multitude of the compassions of God, he represents it as peculiarly atrocious. There is an implied antithesis between the greatness of the mercies sought for, and the greatness of the transgression which required them. Still more emphatical is the expression which follows, *multiply to wash me.* Some take הרבה, *herebeh*, for a noun, but this is too great a departure from the idiom of the language. The sense, on that supposition, would indeed remain the same, that God would wash him abundantly, and with multiplied washing; but I prefer that form of expression which agrees best with the Hebrew idiom. This, at least, is certain from the expression which he employs, that he felt the stain of his sin to be deep and to require multiplied washings. Not as if God could experience any difficulty in cleansing the worst sinner, but the more aggravated a man's sin is, the more earnest naturally are his desires to be delivered from the terrors of conscience.

The figure itself, as all are aware, is one of frequent occurrence in Scripture. Sin resembles filth or uncleanness, as it pollutes us and makes us loathsome in the sight of God, and the remission of it is therefore aptly compared to *washing.* This is a truth which should both commend the grace of God to us and fill us with detestation of sin. Insensible, indeed, must that heart be which is not affected by it!

3For I know my transgressions, and my sin is continually before me. 4Against thee, thee only, have I sinned, and done evil in thy sight; that thou mayest be justified when thou speakest, and be clear when thou judgest. 5Behold, I was born in iniquity, and in sin did my mother conceive me. 6Behold, thou hast desired truth in the inward parts, and hast shown me wisdom in secret.

3. *For I know my sins.* He now discovers his reason for imploring

pardon with so much vehemency, and this was the painful disquietude which his sins caused him, and which could only be relieved by his obtaining reconciliation with God. This proves that his prayer did not proceed from dissimulation, as many will be found commending the grace of God in high terms, although, in reality, they care little about it, having never felt the bitterness of being exposed to his displeasure. David, on the contrary, declares that he is subjected by his sin to constant anguish of mind, and that it is this which imparts such an earnestness to his supplications. From his example we may learn who they are that can alone be said to seek reconciliation with God in a proper manner. They are such as have had their consciences wounded with a sense of sin and who can find no rest until they have obtained assurance of his mercy. We will never seriously apply to God for pardon until we have obtained such a view of our sins as inspires us with fear. The more easily satisfied we are under our sins, the more do we provoke God to punish them with severity, and if we really desire absolution from his hand, we must do more than confess our guilt in words; we must institute a rigid and formidable scrutiny into the character of our transgressions. David does not simply say that he will confess his sins to man, but declares that he has a deep inward feeling of them, such a feeling of them as filled him with the keenest anguish. His was a very different spirit from that of the hypocrite, who displays a complete indifference upon this subject, or when it intrudes upon him, endeavors to bury the recollection of it. He speaks of his *sins* in the plural number. His transgression, although it sprung from one root, was complicated, including, besides adultery, treachery, and cruelty; nor was it one man only whom he had betrayed, but the whole army which had been summoned to the field in defense of the Church of God. He accordingly recognizes many particular sins as wrapped up in it.

4. *Against thee, thee only, have I sinned.* It is the opinion of some that he here adverts to the circumstance of his sin, although it was committed against man, being concealed from every eye but that of God. None was aware of the double wrong which he had inflicted upon Uriah, nor of the wanton manner in which he had exposed his army to danger; and his crime being thus unknown to men might be said to have been committed exclusively against God. According to others, David here intimates that

however deeply he was conscious of having injured men, he was chiefly distressed for having violated the law of God. But I conceive his meaning to be that though all the world should pardon him, he felt that God was the Judge with whom he had to do, that conscience hailed him to his bar, and that the voice of man could administer no relief to him, however much he might be disposed to forgive, or to excuse, or to flatter. His eyes and his whole soul were directed to God, regardless of what man might think or say concerning him. To one who is thus overwhelmed with a sense of the dreadfulness of being obnoxious to the sentence of God, there needs no other accuser. God is to him instead of a thousand. There is every reason to believe that David, in order to prevent his mind from being soothed into a false peace by the flatteries of his court, realized the judgment of God upon his offense and felt that this was in itself an intolerable burden, even supposing that he should escape all trouble from the hands of his fellow-creatures. This will be the exercise of every true penitent. It matters little to obtain our acquittal at the bar of human judgment or to escape punishment through the connivance of others, provided we suffer from an accusing conscience and an offended God. And there is, perhaps, no better remedy against deception in the matter of our sins than to turn our thoughts inward upon ourselves, to concentrate them upon God, and lose every self-complacent imagination in a sharp sense of his displeasure. By a violent process of interpretation, some would have us read the second clause of this verse, *That thou mayest be justified when thou speakest,* in connection with the first verse of the psalm, and consider that it cannot be referred to the sentence immediately preceding. But not to say that this breaks in upon the order of the verses, what sense could any attach to the prayer as it would then run, *have mercy upon me, that thou mayest be clear when thou judgest?* et cetera. Any doubt upon the meaning of the words, however, is completely removed by the connection in which they are cited in Paul's Epistle to the Romans, *For what if some did not believe? Shall God be unjust? God forbid: yea, let God be true, but every man a liar; as it is written, That thou mayest be justified in thy sayings, and mightest overcome when thou art judged* (3:3, 4).

Here the words before us are quoted in proof of the doctrine that God's righteousness is apparent even in the sins of men, and his truth in their falsehood. To have a clear apprehension of their meaning, it is necessary that we reflect upon the covenant which God had made with David. The salvation of the whole world having been in a certain sense deposited with him by this covenant, the enemies of religion might take occasion to exclaim upon his fall, "Here is the pillar of the Church gone, and what is now to become of the miserable remnant whose hopes rested upon his holiness? Once nothing could be more conspicuous than the glory by which he was distinguished, but mark the depth of disgrace to which he has been reduced! Who, after so gross a fall, would look for salvation from his seed?" Aware that such attempts might be made to impugn the righteousness of God, David takes this opportunity of justifying it and charging himself with the whole guilt of the transaction. He declares that God was justified *when he spoke*—not when he spoke the promises of the covenant, although some have so understood the words, but justified should he have spoken the sentence of condemnation against him for his sin, as he might have done but for his gratuitous mercy. Two forms of expression are here employed which have the same meaning, *that thou mayest be justified when thou speakest, and be clear when thou judgest.* As Paul, in the quotation already referred to, has altered the latter clause, and may even seem to have given a new turn to the sentiment contained in the verse, I shall briefly show how the words were applicable to the purpose for which they were cited by him. He adduces them to prove that God's faithfulness remained unaffected by the fact that the Jews had broken his covenant, and fallen from the grace which he had promised. Now, at first sight it may not appear how they contain the proof alleged. But their appositeness will at once be seen if we reflect upon the circumstance to which I have already adverted. Upon the fall of one who was so great a pillar in the Church, so illustrious both as a prophet and a king, as David, we cannot but believe that many were shaken and staggered in the faith of the promises. Many must have been disposed to conclude, considering the close connection into which God had adopted David, that he was implicated in some measure in his fall. David, however, repels an insinuation so injurious to the divine honor and declares that although God should cast him headlong into everlasting destruction, his mouth would be shut, or opened only to acknowledge his unimpeachable justice. The sole departure which the apostle has made from the passage in his quotation consists in his using the verb *to judge* in a passive sense, and reading, *that thou mightest overcome*, instead of, *that thou mightest be clear.* In this he follows the Septuagint, and it is well known that the apostles do not study verbal exactness in their quotations from the Old Testament. It is enough for us to be satisfied that the passage answers the purpose for which it was adduced by the apostle. The general doctrine which we are taught from the passage is that whatever sins men may commit are chargeable entirely upon themselves and never can implicate the righteousness of God. Men are ever ready to arraign his administration when it does not correspond with the judgment of sense and human reason. But should God at any time raise persons from the depth of obscurity to the highest distinction, or, on the other hand, allow persons who occupied a most conspicuous station to be suddenly precipitated from it, we should learn from the example which is here set before us to judge of the divine procedure with sobriety, modesty, and reverence, and to rest satisfied that it is holy, and that the works of God, as well as his words, are characterized by unerring rectitude. The conjunction in the verse, *that—that thou mayest be justified*, denotes not so much cause as consequence. It was not the fall of David, properly speaking, which caused the glory of God's righteousness to appear. And yet, although men when they sin seem to obscure his righteousness, it emerges from the foul attempt only more bright than ever, it being the peculiar work of God to bring light out of darkness.

5. *Behold, I was born in iniquity*, et cetera. He now proceeds further than the mere acknowledgment of one or of many sins, confessing that he brought nothing but sin with him into the world, and that his nature was entirely depraved. He is thus led by the consideration of one offense of peculiar atrocity to the conclusion that he was born in iniquity and was absolutely destitute of all spiritual good. Indeed, every sin should convince us of the general truth of the corruption of our nature. The Hebrew word יֶחֱמַתְנִי, *yechemathni*, signifies literally, *hath warmed herself of me*, from יָחַם, *yacham*, or חָמַם, *chamam*, *to warm*; but interpreters have very properly rendered it *hath conceived me.* The expression intimates that we are cherished in sin from the first moment that we are in the womb. David, then, is here brought, by reflecting on one par-

ticular transgression, to cast a retrospective glance upon his whole past life and to discover nothing but sin in it. And let us not imagine that he speaks of the corruption of his nature, merely as hypocrites will occasionally do, to excuse their faults, saying, "I have sinned it may be, but what could I do? We are men, and prone by nature to everything which is evil." David has recourse to no such stratagems for evading the sentence of God and refers to original sin with the view of aggravating his guilt, acknowledging that he had not contracted this or that sin for the first time lately, but had been born into the world with the seed of every iniquity.

The passage affords a striking testimony in proof of original sin entailed by Adam upon the whole human family. It not only teaches the doctrine, but may assist us in forming a correct idea of it. The Pelagians, to avoid what they considered the absurdity of holding that all were ruined through one man's transgression, maintained of old that sin descended from Adam only through force of imitation. But the Bible, both in this and other places, clearly asserts that we are born in sin, and that it exists within us as a disease fixed in our nature. David does not charge it upon his parents, nor trace his crime to them, but sits himself before the divine tribunal, confesses that he was formed in sin, and that he was a transgressor ere he saw the light of this world. It was therefore a gross error in Pelagius to deny that sin was hereditary, descending in the human family by contagion. The papists, in our own day, grant that the nature of man has become depraved, but they extenuate original sin as much as possible, and represent it as consisting merely in an inclination to that which is evil. They restrict its seat besides to the inferior part of the soul and the gross appetites, and while nothing is more evident from experience than that corruption adheres to men through life, they deny that it remains in them subsequently to baptism. We have no adequate idea of the dominion of sin, unless we conceive of it as extending to every part of the soul, and acknowledge that both the mind and heart of man have become utterly corrupt. The language of David sounds very differently from that of the papists, *I was formed in iniquity, and in sin did my mother conceive me.* He says nothing of his grosser appetites, but asserts that sin cleaved by nature to every part of him without exception.

Here the question has been stated, how is sin transmitted from the parents to the children? And this question has led to another regarding the transmission of the soul, many denying that corruption can be derived from the parent to the child, except on the supposition of one soul being begotten of the substance of another. Without entering upon such mysterious discussions, it is enough that we hold that Adam, upon his fall, was despoiled of his original righteousness, his reason darkened, his will perverted, and that, being reduced to this state of corruption, he brought children into the world resembling himself in character. Should any object that generation is confined to bodies, and that souls can never derive anything in common from one another, I would reply that Adam, when he was endued at his creation with the gifts of the Spirit, did not sustain a private character, but represented all mankind, who may be considered as having been endued with these gifts in his person; and from this view it necessarily follows that when he fell, we all forfeited along with him our original integrity.

6. *Behold, thou hast desired truth*, et cetera. This verse confirms the remark which we already made, that David was far from seeking to invent an apology for his sin, when he traced it back to the period of his conception, and rather intended by this to acknowledge that from his very infancy he was an heir of eternal death. He thus represents his whole life to have been obnoxious to condemnation. So far is he from imitating those who arraign God as the author of sin, and impiously suggest that he might have given man a better nature, that in the verse now before us he opposes God's judgment to our corruption, insinuating that every time we appear before him, we are certain of being condemned, inasmuch as we are born in sin, while he delights in holiness and uprightness. He goes further and asserts that in order to meet the approval of God, it is not enough that our lives be conformed to the letter of his law, unless our heart be clean and purified from all guile. He tells us that God desires truth in *the inward parts*, intimating to us that secret as well as outward and gross sins excite his displeasure. In the second clause of the verse, he aggravates his offense by confessing that he could not plead the excuse of ignorance. He had been sufficiently instructed by God in his duty. Some interpret בסתם, *besathum*, as if he here declared that God had discovered secret mysteries to him or things hidden from the human under-

standing. He seems rather to mean that wisdom had been discovered to his mind in a secret and intimate manner. The one member of the verse responds to the other. He acknowledges that it was not a mere superficial acquaintance with divine truth which he had enjoyed, but that it had been closely brought home to his heart. This rendered his offense the more inexcusable. Though privileged so highly with the saving knowledge of the truth, he had plunged into the commission of brutish sin, and by various acts of iniquity had almost ruined his soul.

We have thus set before us the exercise of the psalmist at this time. First, we have seen that he is brought to a confession of the greatness of his offense; this leads him to a sense of the complete depravity of his nature: to deepen his convictions, he then directs his thoughts to the strict judgment of God, who looks not to the outward appearance but the heart; and, last, he adverts to the peculiarity of his case, as one who had enjoyed no ordinary measure of the gifts of the Spirit and deserved on that account the severer punishment. The exercise is such as we should all strive to imitate. Are we conscious of having committed any one sin, let it be the means of recalling others to our recollection until we are brought to prostrate ourselves before God in deep self-abasement. And if it has been our privilege to enjoy the special teaching of the Spirit of God, we ought to feel that our guilt is additionally heavy, having sinned in this case against light and having trampled underfoot the precious gifts with which we were entrusted.

7Thou shalt purge me with hyssop, and I shall be clean; thou shalt wash me, and I shall be whiter than snow. 8Make me to hear joy and gladness; and the bones which thou hast broken shall rejoice. 9Hide thy face from my sins, and blot out all mine iniquities.

7. *Thou shalt purge me with hyssop.* He still follows out the same strain of supplication, and the repetition of his requests for pardon proves how earnestly he desired it. He speaks of *hyssop,** in allusion to the ceremonies of the law; and though he was far from

---

* Hyssop was much used by the Hebrews in their sacred purifications and sprinklings. The allusion here probably is to the ceremony of sprinkling such as had been infected with leprosy. Two birds were to be taken, cedarwood, scarlet, and hyssop; one of the birds was to be killed, and the priest having dipped the living bird, the cedarwood, scarlet, and hyssop in the blood of the bird that was killed, sprinkled the leper (Lev. 14). This ceremony, it is to be observed, was not to be

putting his trust in the mere outward symbol of purification, he knew that, like every other legal rite, it was instituted for an important end. The sacrifices were seals of the grace of God. In them, therefore, he was anxious to find assurance of his reconciliation, and it is highly proper that when our faith is disposed at any time to waver, we should confirm it by improving such means of divine support. All which David here prays for is that God would effectually accomplish, in his experience, what he had signified to his Church and people by these outward rites, and in this he has set us a good example for our imitation. It is no doubt to the blood of Christ alone that we must look for the atonement of our sins, but we are creatures of sense who must see with our eyes and handle with our hands, and it is only by improving the outward symbols of propitiation that we can arrive at a full and assured persuasion of it. What we have said of the *hyssop* applies also to the *washings* referred to in this verse and which were commonly practiced under the Law. They figuratively represented our being purged from all iniquity in order to our reception into the divine favor. I need not say that it is the peculiar work of the Holy Spirit to sprinkle our consciences inwardly with the blood of Christ, and, by removing the sense of guilt, to secure our access into the presence of God.

In the two verses which follow, the psalmist prays that God would be pacified toward him. Those put too confined a meaning upon the words who have suggested that in praying *to hear the voice of joy and gladness*, he requests some prophet to be sent who might assure him of pardon. He prays, in general, for testimonies of the divine favor. When he speaks of his *bones* as having been *broken*, he alludes to the extreme grief and overwhelming distress

---

performed until the person was cured; and it was intended as a declaration to the people, that, God having healed him of a disease which no human means could remove, he might with safety be restored to society and to the privileges of which he had been deprived. David, polluted with the crimes of adultery and murder, regarded himself as a man affected with the dreadful disease of leprosy, and he prays that God would sprinkle him with hyssop, as the leper was sprinkled, using this figurative language to express his ardent desires to obtain forgiveness and cleansing by the application of the blood of Christ, and that God would show to the people that he had pardoned his sin, restored him to favor, and purified his soul.

to which he had been reduced. The joy of the Lord would reani-
mate his soul, and this joy he describes as to be obtained by *hearing*;
for it is the word of God alone which can first and effectually
cheer the heart of any sinner. There is no true or solid peace to be
enjoyed in the world except in the way of reposing upon the
promises of God. Those who do not resort to them may succeed
for a time in hushing or evading the terrors of conscience, but they
must ever be strangers to true inward comfort. And, granting that
they may attain to the peace of insensibility, this is not a state
which could satisfy any man who has seriously felt the fear of the
Lord. The joy which he desires is that which flows from hearing
the word of God, in which he promises to pardon our guilt and
readmit us into his favor. It is this alone which supports the
believer amid all the fears, dangers, and distresses of his earthly
pilgrimage; for the joy of the Spirit is inseparable from faith.
When God is said, in the ninth verse, to *hide his face* from our sins,
this signifies his pardoning them, as is explained in the clause
immediately annexed—*Blot out all my sins.* This represents our
justification as consisting in a voluntary act of God, by which he
condescends to forget all our iniquities; and it represents our
cleansing to consist in the reception of a gratuitous pardon. We
repeat the remark which has been already made, that David, in
thus reiterating his one request for the mercy of God, evinces the
depth of that anxiety which he felt for a favor which his conduct
had rendered difficult of attainment. The man who prays for pardon in a mere formal manner is proved to be a stranger to the
dreadful desert of sin. *Happy is the man,* said Solomon, *that feareth
alway* (Prov. 28:14).

But here it may be asked why David needed to pray so earnestly
for the joy of remission when he had already received assurance
from the lips of Nathan that his sin was pardoned (2 Sam. 12:13)?
Why did he not embrace this absolution? And was he not chargeable with dishonoring God by disbelieving the word of his
prophet? We cannot expect that God will send us angels in order
to announce the pardon which we require. Was it not said by
Christ that whatever his disciples remitted on earth would be
remitted in heaven (John 20:23)? And does not the apostle declare
that ministers of the Gospel are ambassadors to reconcile men to
God (2 Cor. 5:20)? From this it might appear to have argued unbe-

lief in David, that, notwithstanding the announcement of Nathan, he should evince a remaining perplexity or uncertainty regarding his forgiveness. There is a twofold explanation which may be given of the difficulty. We may hold that Nathan did not immediately make him aware of the fact that God was willing to be reconciled to him. In Scripture, it is well known, things are not always stated according to the strict order of time in which they occurred. It is quite conceivable that, having thrown him into this situation of distress, God might keep him in it for a considerable interval, for his deeper humiliation; and that David expresses in these verses the dreadful anguish which he endured when challenged with his crime, and not yet informed of the divine determination to pardon it. Let us take the other supposition, however, and it by no means follows that a person may not be assured of the favor of God, and yet show great earnestness and importunity in praying for pardon. David might be much relieved by the announcement of the prophet and yet be visited occasionally with fresh convictions, influencing him to have recourse to the throne of grace. However rich and liberal the offers of mercy may be which God extends to us, it is highly proper on our part that we should reflect upon the grievous dishonor which we have done to his name and be filled with due sorrow on account of it. Then our faith is weak, and we cannot at once apprehend the full extent of the divine mercy; so that there is no reason to be surprised that David should have once and again renewed his prayers for pardon, the more to confirm his belief in it. The truth is that we cannot properly pray for the pardon of sin until we have come to a persuasion that God will be reconciled to us. Who can venture to open his mouth in God's presence unless he be assured of his fatherly favor? And pardon being the first thing we should pray for, it is plain that there is no inconsistency in having a persuasion of the grace of God, and yet proceeding to supplicate his forgiveness. In proof of this, I might refer to the Lord's Prayer, in which we are taught to begin by addressing God as our Father, and yet afterward to pray for the remission of our sins. God's pardon is full and complete, but our faith cannot take in his overflowing goodness, and it is necessary that it should distill to us drop by drop. It is owing to this infirmity of our faith that we are often found repeating and repeating again the same petition, not with the view surely of gradually softening the heart of God to compassion, but because we advance by slow and difficult steps to the requisite fullness of assurance. The mention which is here made of *purging with hyssop* and of *washing* or *sprinkling* teaches us, in all our prayers for the pardon of sin, to have our thoughts directed to the great sacrifice by which Christ has reconciled us to God. *Without shedding of blood,* says Paul, *is no remission* (Heb. 9:22); and this, which was intimated by God to the ancient Church under figures, has been fully made known by the coming of Christ. The sinner, if he would find mercy, must look to the sacrifice of Christ, which expiated the sins of the world, glancing, at the same time, for the confirmation of his faith, to baptism and the Lord's Supper; for it were vain to imagine that God, the Judge of the world, would receive us again into his favor in any other way than through a satisfaction made to his justice.

10Create in me a clean heart, O God! and renew a right spirit in my inward parts. 11Cast me not away from thy presence, and take not the Spirit of thy holiness from me. 12Restore unto me the joy of thy salvation, and uphold me with a free spirit.

10. *Create in me a clean heart, O God!* In the previous part of the psalm David has been praying for pardon. He now requests that the grace of the Spirit, which he had forfeited, or deserved to have forfeited, might be restored to him. The two requests are quite distinct, though sometimes confounded together, even by men of learning. He passes from the subject of the gratuitous remission of sin to that of sanctification. And to this he was naturally led with earnest anxiety, by the consciousness of his having merited the loss of all the gifts of the Spirit, and of his having actually, in a great measure, lost them. By employing the term *create*, he expresses his persuasion that nothing less than a miracle could effect his reformation, and emphatically declares that repentance is the gift of God. The Sophists grant the necessity of the aids of the Spirit and allow that assisting grace must both go before and come after; but by assigning a middle place to the free will of man, they rob God of a great part of his glory. David, by the word which he here uses, describes the work of God in renewing the heart in a manner suitable to its extraordinary nature, representing it as the formation of a new creature.

As he had already been endued with the Spirit, he prays in the latter part of the verse that *God would renew a right spirit within him*. But by the term *create*, which he had previously employed, he acknowledges that we are indebted entirely to the grace of God, both for our first regeneration, and, in the event of our falling, for subsequent restoration. He does not merely assert that his heart and spirit were weak, requiring divine assistance, but that they must remain destitute of all purity and rectitude till these be communicated from above. By this it appears that our nature is entirely corrupt: for were it possessed of any rectitude or purity, David would not, as in this verse, have called the one *a gift of the Spirit* and the other *a creation*.

In the verse which follows, he presents the same petition, in language which implies the connection of pardon with the enjoyment of the leading of the Holy Spirit. If God reconciles us gratuitously to himself, it follows that he will guide us by the Spirit of adoption. It is only such as he loves, and has numbered among his own children, that he blesses with a share of his Spirit; and David shows that he was sensible of this when he prays for the continuance of the grace of adoption as indispensable to the continued possession of the Spirit. The words of this verse imply that the Spirit had not altogether been taken away from him, however much his gifts had been temporarily obscured. Indeed, it is evident that he could not be altogether divested of his former excellencies, for he seems to have discharged his duties as a king with credit, to have conscientiously observed the ordinances of religion, and to have regulated his conduct by the divine law. Upon one point he had fallen into a deadly lethargy, but he was not given over to a reprobate mind; and it is scarcely conceivable that the rebuke of Nathan the prophet should have operated so easily and so suddenly in arousing him, had there been no latent spark of godliness still remaining in his soul. He prays, it is true, that his spirit may be *renewed*, but this must be understood with a limitation. The truth on which we are now insisting is an important one, as many learned men have been inconsiderately drawn into the opinion that the elect, by falling into mortal sin, may lose the Spirit altogether, and be alienated from God. The contrary is clearly declared by Peter, who tells us that the word by which we are born again is an incorruptible seed (1 Pet. 1:23); and John is equally explicit in informing us that the elect are preserved from falling away altogether (1 John 3:9).

However much they may appear for a time to have been cast off by God, it is afterward seen that grace must have been alive in their breast, even during that interval when it seemed to be extinct. Nor is there any force in the objection that David speaks as if he feared that he might be deprived of the Spirit. It is natural that the saints, when they have fallen into sin, and have thus done what they could to expel the grace of God, should feel an anxiety upon this point; but it is their duty to hold fast the truth that grace is the incorruptible seed of God, which never can perish in any heart where it has been deposited. This is the spirit displayed by David. Reflecting upon his offense, he is agitated with fears, and yet rests in the persuasion that, being a child of God, he would not be deprived of what indeed he had justly forfeited.

12. *Restore unto me the joy of thy salvation.* He cannot dismiss his grief of mind until he will have obtained peace with God. This he declares once and again, for David had no sympathy with those who can indulge themselves in ease when they are lying under the divine displeasure. In the latter clause of the verse, he prays as in the verses preceding, that the Holy Spirit might not be taken away from him. There is a slight ambiguity in the words. Some take תסמכני, *thismecheni*, to be the third person of the verb, because רוח, *ruach*, is feminine, and translate, *let the Spirit uphold me.* The difference is immaterial, and does not affect the meaning of the passage. There is more difficulty in fixing the sense of the epithet נדיבה, *nedibah*, which I have translated *free.* As the verb נדב, *nadab*, signifies *to deal liberally*, princes are in the Hebrew called, by way of eminence, נדיבים, *nedibim*, which has led several learned men to think that David speaks here of a *princely* or *royal* spirit. . . . The prayer, in this sense, would no doubt be a suitable one for David, who was a king, and required a heroical courage for the execution of his office. But it seems better to adopt the more extensive meaning, and to suppose that David, under a painful consciousness of the bondage to which he had been reduced by a sense of guilt, prays for a free and cheerful spirit. This invaluable attainment, he was sensible, could only be recovered through divine grace.

13*I will teach transgressors thy ways, and sinners shall be converted unto thee.* 14*Deliver me from bloods, O God! thou God of my salvation,*

and my tongue shall sing aloud with joy of thy righteousness. ¹⁵*O Lord!
open thou my lips, and my mouth shall show forth thy praise.*

13. *I will teach transgressors thy ways.* Here he speaks of the gratitude which he would feel should God answer his prayer and
engages to show it by exerting himself in effecting the conversion
of others by his example. Those who have been mercifully recovered from their falls will feel inflamed by the common law of
charity to extend a helping hand to their brethren; and in general,
such as are partakers of the grace of God are constrained by religious principle, and regard for the divine glory, to desire that others should be brought into the participation of it. The sanguine
manner in which he expresses his expectation of converting others
is not unworthy of our notice. We are too apt to conclude that our
attempts at reclaiming the ungodly are vain and ineffectual and
forget that God is able to crown them with success.

14. *Deliver me from bloods.* His recurring so often to petitions for
pardon proves how far David was from flattering himself with
unfounded hopes and what a severe struggle he sustained with
inward terrors. According to some, he prays in this verse to be
delivered from the guilt of the blood of Uriah, and, in general, of
the whole army. But the term *bloods* in Hebrew may denote any
capital crime, and, in my opinion, he is here to be considered as
alluding to the sentence of death, to which he felt himself to be
obnoxious, and from which he requests deliverance. By *the righteousness of God*, which he engages to celebrate, we are to understand his goodness; for this attribute, as usually ascribed to God in
the Scriptures, does not so much denote the strictness with which
he exacts vengeance, as his faithfulness in fulfilling the promises
and extending help to all who seek him in the hour of need. There
is much emphasis and vehemence in the mode of his address,
O God! the God of my salvation, intimating at once how tremblingly
he was alive to the danger of his situation, and how strongly his
faith terminated upon God as the ground of his hope. Similar is
the strain of the verse which follows. He prays that *his lips may be
opened*; in other words, that God would afford him matter of
praise. The meaning usually attached to the expression is that God
would so direct his tongue by the Spirit as to fit him for singing his
praises. But though it is true that God must supply us with words,

and that if he does not, we cannot fail to be silent in his praise, David seems rather to intimate that his mouth must be shut until God called him to the exercise of thanksgiving by extending pardon. In another place we find him declaring that a new song had been put in his mouth (Ps. 40:3), and it seems to be in this sense that he here desires his lips to be opened. He again signifies the gratitude which he would feel, and which he would express, intimating that he sought the mercy of God with no other view than that he might become the herald of it to others. *My mouth*, he says emphatically, *shall show forth thy praise.*

16For thou wilt not accept a sacrifice; though I should give* a burnt-offering, it would not please thee. 17The sacrifices of God are a broken spirit: a broken and a contrite heart, O God! thou wilt not despise. 18Do good in thy good pleasure unto Zion; build thou the walls of Jerusalem. 19Thou shalt then accept the sacrifices of righteousness, even the burnt-offering and whole oblation; then shall calves come upon thine altar.

16. *For thou wilt not accept a sacrifice.* By this language he expresses his confidence of obtaining pardon, although he brought nothing to God in the shape of compensation, but relied entirely upon the riches of divine mercy. He confesses that he comes to God both poor and needy, but is persuaded that this will not prevent the success of his suit because God attaches no importance to sacrifices. In this he indirectly reproves the Jews for an error which prevailed among them in all ages. In proclaiming that the sacrifices made expiation for sin, the Law had designed to withdraw them from all trust in their own works to the one satisfaction of Christ; but they presumed to bring their sacrifices to the altar as a price by which they hoped to procure their own redemption. In opposition to this proud and preposterous notion, David declares

---

* There may be another reason why David here affirms that God would not accept a sacrifice, nor be pleased with a burnt-offering. No particular sacrifices were appointed by the Law of Moses to expiate the guilt of murder and adultery. The person who had perpetrated these crimes was, according to the divine law, to be punished with death. David therefore may be understood as declaring that it was utterly vain for him to think of resorting to sacrifices and burnt-offerings with a view to the expiation of his guilt; that his criminality was of such a character that the ceremonial law made no provision for his deliverance from the doom which his deeds of horror deserved; and that the only sacrifices which would avail were those mentioned in the succeeding verse, "The sacrifices of a broken heart."

that God had no delight in sacrifices, and that he had nothing to present which could purchase his favor. God had enjoined the observance of sacrifice, and David was far from neglecting it. He is not to be understood as asserting that the rite might warrantably be omitted, or that God would absolutely reject the sacrifices of his own institution, which, along with the other ceremonies of the Law, proved important helps, as we have already observed, both to David and the whole Church of God. He speaks of them as observed by the proud and the ignorant, under an impression of meriting the divine favor. Diligent as he was, therefore, in the practice of sacrifice, resting his whole dependence upon the satisfaction of Christ, who atoned for the sins of the world, he could yet honestly declare that he brought nothing to God in the shape of compensation, and that he trusted entirely to a gratuitous reconciliation. The Jews, when they presented their sacrifices, could not be said to bring anything of their own to the Lord, but must rather be viewed as borrowing from Christ the necessary purchase-money of redemption. They were passive, not active, in this divine service.

17. *The sacrifices of God are a broken spirit.* He had shown that sacrifices have no such efficacy in procuring the divine favor as the Jews imagined; and now he declares that he needed to bring nothing whatever to God but a contrite and humbled heart. Nothing more is necessary on the part of the sinner than to prostrate himself in supplication for divine mercy. The plural number is used in the verse to express more forcibly the truth that the sacrifice of repentance is enough in itself without any other. Had he said no more than that this kind of sacrifice was peculiarly acceptable to God, the Jews might easily have evaded his argument by alleging that this might be true, and yet other sacrifices be equally agreeable in his sight; just as the papists in our own day mix up the grace of God with their own works rather than submit to receive a gratuitous pardon for their sins. In order to exclude every idea of a pretended satisfaction, David represents contrition of heart as comprehending in itself the whole sum of acceptable sacrifices. And in using the term *sacrifices of God*, he conveys a tacit reproof to the proud hypocrite, who sets a high value upon such sacrifices as are of his own unauthorized fancy, when he imagines that by means of them he can propitiate God. But here a difficulty may be

started. "If the contrite heart," it may be said, "hold a higher place in the estimation of God than all sacrifices, does it not follow that we acquire pardon by our penitence, and that thus it ceases to be gratuitous?" In reply to this, I might observe that David is not speaking at this time of the meritorious condition by which pardon is procured, but, on the contrary, asserting our absolute destitution of merit by enjoining humiliation and contrition of spirit, in opposition to everything like an attempt to render a compensation to God. The man of broken spirit is one who has been emptied of all vainglorious confidence and brought to acknowledge that he is nothing. The contrite heart abjures the idea of merit and has no dealings with God upon the principle of exchange. Is it objected that faith is a more excellent sacrifice that that which is here commended by the psalmist, and of greater efficacy in procuring the divine favor, as it presents to the view of God that Savior who is the true and only propitiation? I would observe that faith cannot be separated from the humility of which David speaks. This is such a humility as is altogether unknown to the wicked. They may tremble in the presence of God, and the obstinacy and rebellion of their hearts may be partially restrained, but they still retain some remainders of inward pride. Where the spirit has been broken, on the other hand, and the heart has become contrite, through a felt sense of the anger of the Lord, a man is brought to genuine fear and self-loathing, with a deep conviction that of himself he can do or deserve nothing and must be indebted unconditionally for salvation to divine mercy. That this should be represented by David as constituting all which God desires in the shape of sacrifice need not excite our surprise. He does not exclude faith, he does not condescend upon any nice division of true penitence into its several parts, but asserts in general that the only way of obtaining the favor of God is by prostrating ourselves with a wounded heart at the feet of his divine mercy, and supplicating his grace with ingenuous confessions of our own helplessness.

18. *Do good to Zion in thy good pleasure: build thou the walls of Jerusalem.* From prayer in his own behalf he now proceeds to offer up supplications for the collective Church of God, a duty which he may have felt to be the more incumbent upon him from the circumstance of his having done what he could by his fall to ruin it. Raised to the throne, and originally anointed to be king for the

very purpose of fostering the Church of God, he had by his disgraceful conduct nearly accomplished its destruction. Although chargeable with this guilt, he now prays that God would restore it in the exercise of his free mercy. He makes no mention of the righteousness of others, but rests his plea entirely upon the good pleasure of God, intimating that the Church, when at any period it has been brought low, must be indebted for its restoration solely to divine grace. Jerusalem was already built, but David prays that God would build it still further for he knew that it fell far short of being complete, so long as it wanted the temple, where he had promised to establish the Ark of his Covenant and also the royal palace. We learn from the passage that it is God's own work to build the Church. *His foundation*, says the psalmist elsewhere, *is in the holy mountains* (Ps. 87:1). We are not to imagine that David refers simply to the Church as a material structure, but must consider him as having his eye fixed upon the spiritual temple, which cannot be raised by human skill or industry. It is true, indeed, that men will not make progress even in the building of material walls unless their labor be blessed from above; but the Church is in a peculiar sense the erection of God, who has founded it upon the earth in the exercise of his mighty power, and who will exalt it higher than the heavens. In this prayer David does not contemplate the welfare of the Church for a short period merely, but prays that God would preserve and advance it till the coming of Christ. And here, may it not justly excite our surprise to find one who, in the preceding part of the psalm, had employed the language of distress and almost of despair, now inspired with the confidence necessary for commending the whole Church to the care of God? How comes it about, may we not ask, that one who so narrowly escaped destruction himself should now appear as a guide to conduct others to salvation? In this we have a striking proof that, provided we obtain reconciliation with God, we may not only expect to be inspired with confidence in praying for our own salvation, but may hope to be admitted as intercessors in behalf of others, and even to be advanced to the higher honor still, of commending into the hands of God the glory of the Redeemer's kingdom.

19. *Then shalt thou accept sacrifices of righteousness.* In these words there is an apparent, but only an apparent, inconsistency

with others which he had used in the preceding context. He had declared sacrifices to be of no value when considered in themselves, but now he acknowledges them to be acceptable to God when viewed as expressions or symbols of faith, penitence, and thanksgiving. He calls them distinctly *sacrifices of righteousness*, right, warrantable, and such as are offered in strict accordance with the commandment of God. The expression is the same employed in Psalm 4:5, where David uses it with a tacit condemnation of those who gloried in the mere outward form of ceremonies. We find him again exciting himself and others by his example to the exercise of gratitude, and to the expression of it openly in the solemn assembly. Besides sacrifices in general, two particular kinds of sacrifice are specified. Although some consider כָּלִיל, *calil*, and עוֹלָה, *olah*, to be both of one signification, others maintain with more correctness that the first is to be understood as meaning the priest's sacrifice, because in it the offering was consumed or burned with fire. In the enumeration which he makes, David designs to teach us that none of all the legal rites can find acceptance with God unless they be used with a reference to the proper end of their institution. The whole of this verse has been figuratively applied by some to the kingdom of Christ, but the interpretation is unnatural and too refined. Thanksgivings are indeed called by Hosea *the calves of the lips* (Hos. 14:2), but it seems evident that in the passage before us there are conjoined along with the frame or disposition of the heart those solemn ceremonies which constituted part of the ancient worship.

PSALM 90

A Psalm of Moses, the man of God.

¹O Lord! thou hast been our dwelling-place, from generation to generation.

²Before the mountains were brought forth, And *before* thou hadst formed the earth and the world, Even from everlasting to everlasting, thou art God.

³Thou shalt turn man to destruction, And shalt say, "Return ye sons of Adam."

⁴For a thousand years in thy sight *are* as yesterday when it is past, And *as* a watch in the night.

⁵Thou overflowest them; they will be a sleep: In the morning as grass he shall grow.

⁶In the morning he [*or* it] shall flourish and grow: At the evening he [*or* it] shall be cut down, and shall wither.

⁷For we fail by thy anger, And by thy indignation are we affrighted.

⁸Thou hast set our iniquities before thee, Our secret sins in the light of thy countenance.

⁹For all our days are passed away in thy indignation: We have spent our years as if a thought.

¹⁰In the days of our years *there are* seventy years; And if through strength, eighty years, Yet is their pride [*but*] grief and labor; For it passeth by quickly, and we fly away.

¹¹Who knoweth the power of thy anger? And according to thy fear is thy wrath.

¹²Teach us so to number our days, And we shall apply our heart to wisdom.

¹³Return, O Jehovah! how long? Be pacified toward thy servants.

¹⁴Satiate us early with thy goodness, And we will exult and rejoice all our days.

¹⁵Make us joyful according to the days of our affliction; *According* to the years in which we have seen evil.

¹⁶Let thy work appear toward thy servants, And thy glory upon their children.

¹⁷And let there be the beauty of the Lord our God upon us; And the work of our hands direct thou upon us; Yea, the work of our hands direct thou.

As Moses is about to treat as well of the brevity and miseries of human life, as of the punishments inflicted upon the people of Israel, in order to minister some consolation for assuaging the grief and fear which the faithful might have entertained upon observing the operation of the common law, to which all mankind are subject, and especially, upon considering their own afflictions, he opens the psalm by speaking of the peculiar grace which God had vouchsafed to his chosen tribes. He next briefly recites how wretched the condition of men is, if they allow their hearts to rest in this world, especially when God summons them as guilty sinners to his judgment seat. And after he has bewailed that even the children of Abraham had experienced for a time such severity that they were almost consumed with sorrow, confiding in God's free favor, by which he had adopted them to himself, he prays that he would deal toward them in a merciful and gracious manner, as he had done in times past, and that he would continue even to the end the ordinary course of his grace.

A Prayer of Moses, the man of God.

It is uncertain whether this psalm was composed by Moses, or whether someone of the prophets framed it into a song for the use of the people from a formula of prayer written by Moses and handed down from age to age. It is, however, highly probable that it is not without some ground ascribed to Moses in the title; and since psalms were in use even in his time, I have no doubt that he was its author. Some maintain that the reason why his name appears in the inscription is that it was sung by his posterity; but I cannot see why they should have recourse to such a groundless conceit. The epithet, *the man of God*, given to Moses, which is immediately added, clearly confutes them. This honorable designation is expressly applied to him that his doctrine may have the greater authority. If conjectures are to be admitted, it is probable that when the time of his death drew near, he composed this prayer to assuage the prolonged sorrow under which the people had almost pined away, and to comfort their hearts under the accumulation of adversities with which they were oppressed. Although the wonderful goodness of God shone brightly in their deliverance from Egypt, which, burying the miseries formerly endured by them might have filled them with joy, yet we know that, soon after, it was extinguished by their ingratitude; so that for the space of not less than forty years, they were consumed with continual languor in the wilderness. It was therefore very seasonable for Moses at that time to beseech God that he would deal mercifully and gently with his people, according to the number of the years in which he had afflicted them.

¹O Lord! thou hast been our dwelling-place, from generation to generation. ²Before the mountains were brought forth, and before thou hadst formed the earth and the world, even from everlasting to everlasting, thou art God.

1. *O Lord! thou hast been our dwelling-place.* In separating the seed of Abraham by special privilege from the rest of the human family, the psalmist magnifies the grace of adoption, by which God had embraced them as his children. The object which he has in view in this exordium is that God would now renew the grace which he had displayed in old time toward the holy patriarchs, and continue it toward their offspring. Some commentators think that he alludes to the tabernacle, because in it the majesty of God was not less conspicuous than if he had dwelt in the midst of the people; but this seems to me to be altogether out of place. He rather comprehends the whole time in which the Fathers sojourned in the land of Canaan. As the tabernacle had not yet continued for the space of forty years, the long duration here mentioned—*our dwelling-place from generation to generation*—would not at all be applicable to it. It is not then intended to recount what God showed himself to be toward the Israelites from the time that he delivered them from Egypt, but what their fathers had experienced him to be in all ages, even from the beginning. Now it is declared that as they had always been pilgrims and wanderers, so God was to them instead of a dwelling-place. No doubt, the condition of all men is unstable upon earth, but we know that Abraham and his posterity were, above all others, sojourners and, as it were, exiles. Since, then, they wandered in the land of Canaan till they were brought into Egypt, where they lived only by suffer-

ance from day to day, it was necessary for them to seek for themselves a dwelling-place under the shadow of God, without which they could hardly be accounted inhabitants of the world since they continued everywhere strangers and were afterward led about through many windings and turnings. The grace which the Lord displayed in sustaining them in their wanderings, and shielding them with his hand when they sojourned among savage and cruel nations, and were exposed to injurious treatment at their hands— this grace is extolled by Moses in very striking terms, when he represents God as an abode or dwelling-place to these poor fugitives who were continually wandering from one place to another in quest of lodgings. This grace he magnifies from the length of time during which it had been exercised, for God ceased not to preserve and defend them for the space of more than four hundred years, during which time they dwelt under the wings of his protection.

2. *Before the mountains were brought forth.* Moses designs to set forth some high and hidden mystery, and yet he seems to speak feebly, and, as it were, in a puerile manner. For who does not know that God existed before the world? This we grant is a truth which all men admit, but we will scarcely find one in a hundred who is thoroughly persuaded that God remains unchangeably the same. God is here contrasted with created beings, who, as all know, are subject to continual changes, so that there is nothing stable under heaven. As, in a particular manner, nothing is fuller of vicissitude than human life, that men may not judge of the nature of God by their own fluctuating condition, he is here placed in a state of settled and undisturbed tranquillity. Thus the everlastingness of which Moses speaks is to be referred not only to the essence of God, but also to his Providence, by which he governs the world. Although he subjects the world to many alterations, he remains unmoved; and that not only in regard to himself, but also in regard to the faithful, who find from experience that instead of being wavering, he is steadfast in his power, truth, righteousness, and goodness, even as he has been from the beginning. This eternal and unchangeable steadfastness of God could not be perceived prior to the creation of the world, since there were as yet no eyes to be witnesses of it. But it may be gathered *a posteriori*; for while all things are subject to revolution and incessant vicissitude, his nature continues always the same. There may be also here a con-

trast between him and all the false gods of the heathen, who have, by little and little, crept into the world in such vast numbers, through the error and folly of men. But I have already shown the object which Moses has in view, which is that we mistake if we measure God by our own understanding, and that we must mount above the earth, yea, even above heaven itself, whenever we think upon him.

³*Thou shalt turn man to destruction, and shalt say, Return, ye sons of Adam. ⁴For a thousand years in thy sight are as yesterday when it is gone, and as a watch in the night. ⁵Thou carriest them away as with a flood, they will be a sleep: in the morning he shall grow as grass: ⁶In the morning it shall flourish and grow: at the evening it shall be cut down, and shall wither. ⁷For we fail by thy anger, and are affrighted by thy indignation. ⁸Thou hast set our iniquities before thee, and our secret sins in the light of thy countenance.*

3. *Thou shalt turn man to destruction.* Moses, in the first place, mentions how frail and transitory is the life of man, and bewails its miseries. This he does, not for the purpose of quarreling with God, but as an argument to induce him the more readily to exercise his mercy, even as he is elsewhere said to pardon mortal men, when he considers of what they are made and remembers that they are but dust and grass (Ps. 103:14); he compares the course of our life to a ring or circle, because God, placing us upon the earth, turns us about within a narrow circuit, and when we have reached the last point, draws us back to himself in a moment. Others give a different interpretation, namely, that God leads men forth to death and afterward restores them at the resurrection. But this subtlety is farfetched and does not harmonize with the context. We have here laid down a simple definition of our life, that it is, as it were, a short revolution in which we quickly complete our circle, the last point of which is the termination of our earthly course. This account of human life sets in a clearer light the gracious manner in which God deals with his servants, in adopting them to be his peculiar people, that he may at length gather them together into his everlasting inheritance. Nor is it in vain that it is added, by way of contrast (verse 4), *that a thousand years in God's sight are as yesterday.* Although we are convinced from experience that men, when they have completed their circle, are forthwith taken out of the world, yet the knowledge of this frailty fails in making a deep

impression upon our hearts because we do not lift our eyes above the world. Whence proceeds the great stupidity of men, who, bound fast to the present state of existence, proceed in the affairs of life as if they were to live two thousand years, but because they do not elevate their conceptions above visible objects? Each man, when he compares himself with others, flatters himself that he will live to a great age. In short, men are so dull as to think that thirty years, or even a smaller number, are, as it were, an eternity; nor are they impressed with the brevity of their life so long as this world keeps possession of their thoughts. This is the reason why Moses awakens us by elevating our minds to the eternity of God, without the consideration of which we perceive not how speedily our life vanishes away. The imagination that we shall have a long life resembles a profound sleep in which we are all benumbed, until meditation upon the heavenly life swallow up this foolish fancy respecting the length of our continuance upon earth.

As men are thus blinded, Moses sets before their view God as their judge. O Lord! as if he had said, if men would duly reflect upon that eternity from which thou beholdest these inconstant cir-clings of the world, they would not make so great account of the present life. But as, instead of seriously considering what is true duration, they rather willfully turn away their eyes from heaven, this explains why they are so stupid and look upon one day as if it were a hundred years. Moses' apostrophe to God is emphatic, implying that his patience being exhausted at seeing us so thoughtless, he addresses himself to God; and that it was labor to no purpose for him to speak to the deaf, who would not be taught that they were mortal, no, not even by the proofs of this, which experience was constantly presenting before them. This text is quoted by the Apostle Peter in a sense somewhat different (2 Pet. 3:8), while at the same time he does not pervert it, for he aptly and judiciously applies the testimony of Moses in illustration of the subject of which he is there treating. The design of Moses is to elevate the minds of men to heaven by withdrawing them from their own gross conceptions. And what is the object of Peter? As many, because Christ does not hasten his coming according to their desire, cast off the hope of the resurrection through the weariness of long delay, he corrects this preposterous impatience by a very suitable remedy. He perceives men's faith in the divine promises fainting and failing, from their thinking that Christ delays his coming too long. Whence does this proceed, but because they grovel upon the earth? Peter therefore appropriately applies these words of Moses to cure this vice. As the indulgence in pleasures to which unbelievers yield themselves is to be traced to this, that having their hearts too much set upon the world, they do not taste the pleasures of a celestial eternity, so impatience proceeds from the same source. Hence we learn the true use of this doctrine. To what is it owing that we have so great anxiety about our life that nothing suffices us, and that we are continually molesting ourselves, but because we foolishly imagine that we shall nestle in this world forever? Again, to what are we to ascribe that extreme fretfulness and impatience, which make our hearts fail in waiting for the coming of Christ, but to their groveling upon the earth? Let us learn then not to judge according to the understanding of the flesh, but to depend upon the judgment of God; and let us elevate our minds by faith, even to his heavenly throne, from which he declares that this earthly life is nothing. Nor does Moses simply contrast a thousand years with one day, but he contrasts them with *yesterday*, which is already gone; for whatever is still before our eyes has a hold upon our minds, but we are less affected with the recollection of what is past. In regard to the word *watch*, the ancients, as is well known, were accustomed to divide the night into four watches, consisting of three hours each. To express still more forcibly how inconsiderable that which appears to us a long period is in God's eyes, this similitude is added: That a thousand years in his sight differ nothing from three hours of the night, in which men scarcely know whether they are awake or asleep.

5. *Thou carriest them away as with a flood.* Moses confirms what he had previously said, that men, so long as they are sojourners in this world, perform, as it were, a revolution which lasts only for a moment. I do not limit the expression to *carry away as with a flood to* calamities of a more grievous kind, but consider that death is simply compared in general to a flood; for when we have staid a little while in the world, we forthwith fall into the grave and are covered with earth. Thus death, which is common to all, is with propriety called *an inundation.* While we are breathing the breath of life, the Lord overflows us by death, just as those who perish in a shipwreck are engulfed in the ocean; so that death may be fitly

called an invisible deluge. And Moses affirms that it is then evidently seen that men who flatter themselves that they are possessed of wonderful vigor in their earthly course are only as a sleep. The comparison of *grass*, which is added, amounts to this: That men come forth in the morning as grass springs up, that they become green, or pass away within a short time, when being cut down, they wither and decay. The verbs in the sixth verse being in the singular number, it is better to connect them with the word *grass*. But they may also be appropriately referred to each man; and as it makes little difference as to the sense of the text, whether we make *grass* or *each man* the nominative to the verbs, I am not disposed to expend much labor upon the matter. This doctrine requires to be continually meditated upon; for although we all confess that nothing is more transitory than our life, yet each of us is soon carried away, as it were, by a frantic impulse to picture to his own imagination an earthly immortality. Whoever bears in mind that he is mortal restrains himself, that instead of having his attention and affections engrossed beyond measure with earthly objects, he may advance with haste to his mark. When we set no limit to our cares, we require to be urged forward by continual goadings, that we may not dream of a thousand lives instead of one, which is but as a shadow that quickly vanishes away.

7. *For we fail by thy anger.* Moses makes mention of the anger of God advisedly, for it is necessary that men be touched with the feeling of this, in order to their considering in good earnest what experience constrains them to acknowledge, how soon they finish their course and pass away. He had, however, still another reason for joining together the brevity of human life and the anger of God. While men are by nature so transitory, and, as it were, shadowy, the Israelites were afflicted by the hostile hand of God; and his anger is less supportable by our frail natures, which speedily vanish away, than it would be were we furnished with some tolerable degree of strength.

8. *Thou hast set our iniquities before thee.* To show that by this complaint he is far from intending to murmur against God, he asserts that the divine anger, however terrible it had been, was just, inasmuch as the people had provoked it by their iniquities; for those who, when stricken by the divine hand, are not brought to genuine humiliation, harden themselves more and more. The

true way to profit, and also to subdue our pride, is to feel that he is a righteous judge. Accordingly Moses, after having briefly taught that men by nature vanish away like smoke, gathers from thence that it is not to be wondered at if God exanimates and consumes those whom he pursues with his wrath. The manner of the expression by which God is described as showing the tokens of his anger is to be observed—*he sets the iniquities of men before his eyes.* Hence it follows that whatever intermission of punishment we experience ought in justice to be ascribed to the forbearance of God, who buries our sins that he may spare us. The word עלומים, *alumim*, which I have rendered *our secret sins*, is translated by some, *our youth*, as if Moses had said that the faults committed in youth are brought to remembrance. But this is too forced and inconsistent with the scope of the passage, for it would destroy the contrast between *secret sins* and *the light of God's countenance*, by which Moses intimates that men hide themselves in darkness and wrap themselves in many deceits, so long as God does not shine upon them with the light of his judgment; whereas, when he draws them back from their subterfuges, by which they endeavor to escape from him, and sets before his eyes the sins which they hide by hypocrisy, being subdued by fear and dread, they are brought sincerely to humble themselves before him.

9*For all our days are passed away in thy indignation: we have spent our years as if a thought.* 10*In the days of our years there are threescore years and ten: and if through strength they are fourscore years, yet is their pride but labor and grief; for it swiftly passes by, and we fly away.*

9. *For all our days are passed away in thy indignation.* This might be viewed as a general confirmation of the preceding sentence, that the whole course of man's life is suddenly brought to an end as soon as God shows himself displeased. But in my opinion Moses rather amplifies what he has said above concerning the rigor of God's wrath and his strict examination of every case in which he punishes sin. He asserts that this terror which God brought upon his people was not only for a short time, but that it was extended without intermission even to death. He complains that the Jews had almost wasted away by continual miseries because God neither remitted nor mitigated his anger. It is therefore not surprising to find him declaring that their years passed away like a *tale*, when God's anger rested upon them so unremittingly.

10. *In the days of our years there are threescore years and ten.* He again returns to the general doctrine respecting the precariousness of the condition of men, although God may not openly display his wrath to terrify them. "What," says he, "is the duration of life? Truly, if we reckon all our years, we will at length come to three-score and ten, or, if there be some who are stronger and more vigorous, they will bring us even to fourscore." Moses uses the expression, *the days of our years,* for the sake of emphasis, for when the time is divided into small portions, the very number itself deceives us, so that we flatter ourselves that life is long. With the view of overthrowing these vain delusions, he permits men to sum up the many thousand days which are in a few years, while he at the same time affirms that this great heap is soon brought to nothing. Let men then extend the space of their life as much as they please, by calculating that each year contains three hundred and sixty-five days; yet assuredly they will find that the term of seventy years is short. When they have made a lengthened calculation of the days, this is the sum in which the process ultimately results. He who has reached the age of fourscore years hastens to the grave. Moses himself lived longer (Deut. 34:7), and so perhaps did others in his time; but he speaks here of the ordinary term. And even then, those were accounted old men, and in a manner decrepit, who attained to the age of fourscore years, so that he justly declares that it is the robust only who arrive at that age. He puts *pride* for *the strength* or *excellence* of which men boast so highly. The sense is that before men decline and come to old age, even in the very bloom of youth, they are involved in many troubles, and that they cannot escape from the cares, weariness, sorrows, fears, griefs, inconveniences, and anxieties, to which this mortal life is subject. Moreover, this is to be referred to the whole course of our existence in the present state. And assuredly, he who considers what is the condition of our life from our infancy until we descend into the grave, will find troubles and turmoil in every part of it. The two Hebrew words עָמָל, *amal,* and אָוֶן, *aven,* which are joined together, are taken passively for *inconveniences* and *afflictions,* implying that the life of man is full of labor and fraught with many torments, and that even at the time when men are in the height of their pride. The reason which is added, *for it swiftly passes by, and we fly away,* seems hardly to suit the scope of the pas-

sage, for felicity may be brief, and yet on that account it does not cease to be felicity. But Moses means that men foolishly glory in their excellence, since, whether they will or no, they are constrained to look to the time to come. And as soon as they open their eyes, they see that they are dragged and carried forward to death with rapid haste, and that their excellence is every moment vanishing away.

¹¹Who knoweth the power of thy anger? And according to thy fear, so is thy wrath. ¹²Teach us so to number our days, and we shall apply our hearts to wisdom. ¹³Return, O Jehovah! how long? Be pacified toward thy servants.

11. *Who knoweth the power of thy anger?* Moses again returns to speak of the peculiar afflictions of the Israelites; for he had also on this occasion complained before of the common frailty and miseries of mankind. He justly exclaims that the power of God's wrath is immeasurably great. So long as God withholds his hand, men wantonly leap about like runaway slaves who are no longer afraid at the sight of their master; nor can their rebellious nature be reduced to obedience in any other way than by his striking them with the fear of his judgment. The meaning then is that while God hides himself, and, so to speak, dissembles his displeasure, men are inflated with pride and rush upon sin with reckless impetuosity, but when they are compelled to feel how dreadful his wrath is, they forget their loftiness and are reduced to nothing. What follows, *According to thy fear, so is thy wrath,* is commonly explained as denoting that the more a man is inspired with reverence toward God, the more severely and sternly is he commonly dealt with, for *judgment begins at the house of God* (1 Pet. 4:17). While he pampers the reprobate with the good things of this life, he wastes his chosen ones with continual troubles; and in short, *whom he loveth he chasteneth* (Heb. 12:6). It is then a true and profitable doctrine that he deals more roughly with those who serve him than with the reprobate. But Moses, I think, has here a different meaning, which is that it is a holy awe of God, and that alone, which makes us truly and deeply feel his anger. We see that the reprobate, although they are severely punished, only chafe upon the bit, or kick against God, or become exasperated, or are stupefied, as if they were hardened against all calamities, so far are they from being subdued. And though they are full of trouble

and cry aloud, yet the divine anger does not so penetrate their hearts as to abate their pride and fierceness. The minds of the godly alone are wounded with the wrath of God, nor do they wait for his thunderbolts, to which the reprobate hold out their hard and iron necks, but they tremble the very moment when God moves only his little finger. This I consider to be the true meaning of the prophet. He had said that the human mind could not sufficiently comprehend the dreadfulness of the divine wrath. And we see how, although God shakes heaven and earth, many notwithstanding, like the giants of old, treat this with derision and are actuated by such brutish arrogance that they despise him when he brandishes his bolts. But as the psalmist is treating of a doctrine which properly belongs to true believers, he affirms that they have a strongly sensitive feeling of the wrath of God which makes them quietly submit themselves to his authority. Although to the wicked their own conscience is a tormentor which does not suffer them to enjoy repose, yet so far is this secret dread from teaching them to humble themselves that it excites them to clamor against God with increasing forwardness. In short, the faithful alone are sensible of God's wrath, and being subdued by it, they acknowledge that they are nothing and with true humility devote themselves wholly to him. This is wisdom to which the reprobate cannot attain, because they cannot lay aside the pride with which they are inflated. They are not touched with the feeling of God's wrath, because they do not stand in awe of him.

12. *Teach us so to number our days.* Some translate to *the number of our days*, which gives the same sense. As Moses perceived that what he had hitherto taught is not comprehended by the understandings of men until God shine upon them by his Spirit, he now sets himself to prayer. It indeed seems at first sight absurd to pray that we may know the number of our years. What? Since even the strongest scarcely reach the age of fourscore years, is there any difficulty in reckoning up so small a sum? Children learn numbers as soon as they begin to prattle, and we do not need a teacher in arithmetic to enable us to count the length of a hundred upon our fingers. So much the fouler and more shameful is our stupidity in never comprehending the short term of our life. Even he who is most skillful in arithmetic, and who can precisely and accurately understand and investigate millions of millions, is nevertheless

unable to count fourscore years in his own life. It is surely a monstrous thing that men can measure all distances without themselves, that they know how many feet the moon is distant from the center of the earth, what space there is between the different planets, and, in short, that they can measure all the dimensions both of heaven and earth, while yet they cannot number threescore and ten years in their own case. It is therefore evident that Moses had good reason to beseech God for ability to perform what requires a wisdom which is very rare among mankind. The last clause of the verse is also worthy of special notice. By it he teaches us that we then truly apply our hearts to wisdom when we comprehend the shortness of human life. What can be a greater proof of madness than to ramble about without proposing to one's self any end? True believers alone, who know the difference between this transitory state and a blessed eternity, for which they were created, know what ought to be the aim of their life. No man then can regulate his life with a settled mind, but he who, knowing the end of it, that is to say death itself, is led to consider the great purpose of man's existence in this world, that he may aspire after the prize of the heavenly calling.

13. *Return, O Jehovah! how long?* After having spoken in the language of complaint, Moses adds a prayer that God, who had not ceased for a long time severely to punish his people, would at length be inclined to deal gently with them. Although God daily gave them in many ways some taste of his love, yet their banishment from the land of promise was a very grievous affliction, for it admonished them that they were unworthy of that blessed inheritance which he had appointed for his children. They could not fail often to remember that dreadful oath which he had thundered out against them, *Surely they shall not see the land which I swore unto their fathers, neither shall any of them that provoked me see it: But as for you, your carcases, they shall fall in this wilderness* (Num. 14:23, 32).

Moses, no doubt, combines that sore bondage which they had suffered in Egypt with their wanderings in the wilderness, and therefore he justly bewails their protracted languishing in the words *how long?* As God is said to turn his back upon us or to depart to a distance from us when he withdraws the tokens of his favor, so by his return we are to understand the manifestation of his grace. The word **נחם**, *nacham*, which we have translated *be pacified*, signifies to *repent*, and may therefore not improperly be explained thus: Let it repent thee concerning thy servants. According to the not infrequent and well-known phraseology of Scripture, God is said to repent; when putting away men's sorrow and affording new ground of gladness, he appears, as it were, to be changed. Those, however, seem to come nearer the mind of the psalmist, who translates, *Comfort thyself over thy servants,* for God, in cherishing us tenderly, takes no less pleasure in us than does a father in his own children. Now that is nothing else than to be pacified or propitious, as we have translated it, to make the meaning the more obvious.

14Satiate us early with thy goodness, and we will be glad and rejoice all our days. 15Make us joyful according to the days of our affliction; according to the years in which we have seen evil. 16Let thy work appear toward thy servants, and thy glory upon their children. 17And let the beauty of the Lord our God be upon us; and direct the work of our hands upon us; yea, direct thou the work of our hands.

16. *Let thy work appear toward thy servants.* As God, when he forsakes his Church, puts on, as it were, a character different from his own, Moses, with much propriety, calls the blessing of protection which had been divinely promised to the children of Abraham *God's proper work.* Although, therefore, God's work was manifest in all the instances in which he had punished the perfidiousness, ingratitude, obstinacy, unruly lusts, and unhallowed desires of his people, yet Moses, by way of eminence, prefers before all other proofs of God's power that care which he exercised in maintaining the welfare of the people, by which it was his will that he should be principally known. This is the reason why Paul (Rom. 9:23) especially applies to the divine goodness the honorable title of *glory.* God indeed maintains his glory by judging the world; but as nothing is more natural to him than to show himself gracious, his glory on that account is said to shine forth chiefly in his benefits. With respect to the present passage, God had then only begun to deliver his people, for they had still to be put in possession of the land of Canaan. Accordingly, had they gone no farther than the wilderness, the luster of their deliverance would have been obscured. Besides, Moses estimates the work of God

according to the divine promise, and doing this he affirms that it will be imperfect and incomplete unless he continue his grace even to the end. This is expressed still more plainly in the second clause of the verse, in which he prays not only for the welfare of his own age, but also for the welfare of the generation yet unborn. His exercise thus corresponds with the form of the covenant, *And I will establish my covenant between me and thee, and thy seed after thee, in their generations, for an everlasting covenant to be a God unto thee, and to thy seed after thee* (Gen. 17:7).

By this example we are taught that in our prayers we ought to extend our care to those who are to come after us. As God has promised that the Church will be perpetuated even to the end of the world—a subject which was brought under our notice in the preceding psalm—this ought, in a special manner, to lead us in all the prayers by which we commend the welfare of the Church to him, to include, at the same time, our posterity who are yet unborn. Further, the words *glory* and *beauty* are to be particularly noticed, from which we learn that the love which God bears toward us is unparalleled. Although, in enriching us with his gifts he gains nothing for himself, yet he would have the splendor and beauty of his character manifested in dealing bountifully with us, as if his beauty were obscured when he ceases to do us good. In the clause immediately succeeding, *Direct the work of our hands upon us,* Moses intimates that we cannot undertake or attempt anything with the prospect of success unless God become our guide and counselor and govern us by his Spirit. Whence it follows that the reason why the enterprises and efforts of worldly men have a disastrous issue is because, in not following God, they pervert all order and throw everything into confusion. Nor is the word עָלֵינוּ, *alenu, upon us,* superfluous; for although God converts to good in the end whatever Satan and the reprobate plot and practice against him or his people, yet the Church, in which God rules with undisturbed sway, has in this respect a special privilege. By his Providence, which to us is incomprehensible, he directs his work in regard to the reprobate externally, but he governs his believing people internally by his Holy Spirit; and therefore he is properly said to order or direct the work of their hands. The repetition shows that a continual course of perseverance in the grace of God is required. It would not be enough for us to be brought to the midst of our journey. He must enable us to complete the whole course. Some translate, *confirm* or *establish*, and this sense may be admitted. I have, however, followed that translation which was more agreeable to the context, conceiving the prayer to be that God would direct to a prosperous issue all the actions and undertakings of his people.

¹Ho, every one that thirsteth, come ye to the waters, and he that hath no money; come ye, buy, and eat; yea, come, buy wine and milk without money and without price. ²Wherefore do ye spend money for *that which is* not bread? and your labor for *that which* satisfieth not? hearken diligently unto me, and eat ye *that which is* good, and let your soul delight itself in fatness. ³Incline your ear, and come unto me: hear, and your soul shall live; and I will make an everlasting covenant with you, *even* the sure mercies of David. ⁴Behold, I have given him *for* a witness to the people, a leader and commander to the people. ⁵Behold, thou shalt call a nation *that* thou knowest not, and nations *that* knew not thee shall run unto thee because of the Lord thy God, and for the Holy One of Israel; for he hath glorified thee. ⁶Seek ye the Lord while he may be found, call ye upon him while he is near: ⁷Let the wicked forsake his way, and the unrighteous man his thoughts: and let him return unto the Lord, and he will have mercy upon him; and to our God, for he will abundantly pardon. ⁸For my thoughts *are* not your thoughts, neither *are* your ways my ways, saith the Lord. ⁹For *as* the heavens are higher than the earth, so are my ways higher than your ways, and my thoughts than your thoughts. ¹⁰For as the rain cometh down, and the snow from heaven, and returneth not thither, but watereth the earth, and maketh it bring forth and bud, that it may give seed to the sower, and bread to the eater: ¹¹So shall my word be that goeth forth out of my mouth: it shall not return unto me void, but it shall accomplish that which I please, and it shall prosper *in the thing* whereto I sent it. ¹²For ye shall go out with joy, and be led forth with peace: the mountains and the hills shall break forth before you into singing, and all the trees of the field shall clap *their* hands. ¹³Instead of the thorn shall come up the fir tree, and instead of the brier shall come up the myrtle tree: and it shall be to the Lord for a name, for an everlasting sign *that* shall not be cut off.

1. *Ho, all that are thirsty.* Here the prophet describes in lofty terms of commendation the goodness of God, which was to be poured down more copiously and abundantly than before under the reign of Christ, *in whose hand are hid all the treasures* (Col. 2:3) of the grace of God; for in him God fully explains his mind to us so that the saying of John is actually fulfilled, *We have all drawn from his fullness, and have received grace for grace* (John 1:16). The Fathers were, indeed, partakers of that divine goodness and spiritual kindness which is here mentioned. *How great,* says David, *is thy goodness, which hath been laid up for them that fear thee!* (Ps. 31:19). But he hath poured it out far more liberally and abundantly in Christ. Thus, it is a remarkable commendation of the grace of God, which is exhibited to us in the kingdom of Christ, for the prophet does not instruct us what has been done once, but also what is done every day, while the Lord invites us by his doctrine to the enjoyment of all blessings.

Come to the waters. Some view the word "waters" as referring to the doctrine of the Gospel, and others to the Holy Spirit, but neither of these expositions, in my opinion, is correct. They who think that it denotes the doctrine of the Gospel and who contrast it with the law (of which the Jewish writers think that the prophet speaks in this passage), include only one part of what the prophet meant. They who expound it as denoting the Holy Spirit have somewhat more plausibility and quote that passage of John's Gospel, *If thou knewest the gift of God, and who it is that saith to thee, Give me to drink, thou wouldest have asked of him, and he would have given thee living water* (John 4:10). And a little after, Christ appears to expound this passage when he says, *Everyone that drinketh of this water shall thirst again; but whosoever shall drink of the water which I shall give to him shall never thirst; but the water which I shall give to him shall become in him a fountain of water springing up to everlasting life* (John 4:13, 14).

But I have no doubt that under these words, "waters, milk, wine, bread," Isaiah includes all that is necessary for spiritual life, for the metaphors are borrowed from those kinds of food which are in daily use among us. As we are nourished by "bread, wine, milk, and water," so in like manner let us know that our souls are fed and supported by the doctrine of the Gospel, the Holy Spirit, and other gifts of Christ.

The prophet exclaims, as with a voice above the usual pitch, *He!* for so great is the sluggishness of men that it is very difficult to arouse them. They do not feel their wants, though they are hungry, nor do they desire food, which they greatly need; and therefore that indifference must be shaken off by loud and incessant cries. So much the more base and shameful is the indolence of those who are deaf to this exhortation, and who, even when they are so sharply urged forward, still indulge in their slothfulness. Besides, the invitation is general, for there is no man who is not in want of those "waters," and to whom Christ is not necessary, and therefore he invites all indiscriminately, without any respect of persons. But men are so miserable that although they know that they are in need of Christ, they contrive methods by which they may be deprived of this benefit, and rather believe the devil, who offers various obstructions than this kind invitation.

We must therefore inquire what is the true preparation for receiving this grace. The prophet describes it by the word "thirsty." Those who are puffed up with vain confidence and are satiated, or who, intoxicated by earthly appetites, do not feel thirst of soul, will not receive Christ because they have no relish for spiritual grace. They resemble those persons who are in want of nourishments, but who, because they are filled and swollen with wind, loathe food, or who, being carried away by their own vain imaginations, feed on their own stupidity, as if they were in want of nothing. The consequence is that they who are puffed up with pride or a false opinion of their own righteousness, or whom the allurements of the flesh have seized with lethargy, despise or reject the grace of God. It is therefore necessary that we have "thirst," that is, an ardent desire, in order that it may be possible for us to receive so great blessings.

Buy without money. He does not mean that there are any persons who have money in abundance, but the words ought to be explained thus. "Although they are poor, although they are sunk in the deepest poverty, yet the way is open for them to come to Christ, through whom these blessings are freely bestowed." "But how is it possible," it will be said, "to buy without a price?" I reply, "buying" denotes figuratively the method by which we procure anything, and שבר *(shavar)* is here put for "procure," and "price" for labor or industry, or any other method by which men obtain anything; he shows that we are poor and utterly destitute and that we have nothing by which we can become entitled to God's favor, but that he kindly invites us, in order that he may freely bestow everything without any recompense.

2. *Wherefore do ye spend money?* He complains of the ingratitude and madness of men, in rejecting or disdaining the kindness of God who offers all things freely, and yet harassing themselves greatly about various trifles which cannot yield them any advantage. Men are so enchanted by the devil that they choose rather to wander through deserts and to vex themselves in vain, than to rely on the grace which God offers to them. The experience of the present age abundantly shows that the prophet not only expostulated with his own nation, but exclaimed against all men, to whatever age they might belong, for all the posterity of Adam have been seized with such madness that, in seeking the road to a heavenly life, they altogether go astray and follow their own vain opinions rather than the voice of God.

The prophet does not complain of the slothfulness of those who, altogether forgetful of themselves and of God, take no concern about the spiritual life of the soul (there are many such persons), but of those who desire life and yet do not understand the method or way of obtaining it, and wander in uncertainty through deserts and untrodden paths. Here, therefore, are condemned all the methods which men contrive, in opposition to the Word of God, for obtaining salvation, and they are pronounced to be useless expenses, for by the word "money" he denotes all the industry, study, or labor which belongs to man. Not that God values a single farthing all our idle attempts to worship him, but because labors foolishly undertaken are reckoned valuable by the judgment of the flesh.

And your labor, not so as to be satisfied. We see that by the word *bread* is here meant the same as was formerly meant by "waters," and that he gives the name *labor* to that which he formerly called "money." As if he had said, "Men toil without any advantage, for when they follow their own inventions, however eagerly they may vex and weary themselves, they have no right to expect any reward." Thus he affirms that they who labor in an inconsiderate manner cannot *be satisfied*, for they who forsake God and attempt new methods of salvation can never "be satisfied." *They feed on wind,* as Hosea says (Hos. 12:1). They may, indeed, imagine that they are full when they are swelled with vain confidence, but are like persons who, in consequence of being swollen with wind, do not perceive their hunger. Yet it would be better for them to be sore-pressed by hunger and thirst, that it might lead them to call on the Lord with earnestness of heart, as it is said in the psalm, *My soul is as a thirsty land before thee* (Ps. 143:6). But bread alone, or water alone, would not be enough to "satisfy," and by neither of them could life be supported, and that is the reason why the prophet has made use of a variety of terms, in order to show that the Lord abundantly supplies everything that is necessary for life, that we may not think that we ought to seek aid from any other quarter.

Hear ye by hearing me. Because every person is led into error by his own counsel, and all who neglect God vanish away in wicked imaginations, the prophet here adds the remedy, which is that we must depend entirely on the mouth of God. Whoever shall submit to his word will have no reason to fear that he shall spend his strength on things of no value. Here we see the amazing goodness of God, who offers his grace to men, though they are unthankful and unworthy.

But he adds the condition, for there is no way by which we can enter into life but by "hearing" him, and as the cause of our destruction is that we are deaf to the voice of God, so the road to life is open, if we lend our ears to him. In order to make a deeper impression upon us, he repeats the same admonition and doubles the same word, "Hear ye by hearing"; and, in order to draw us more gently, he solemnly declares that it depends entirely on ourselves whether or not he will "delight" us even to fullness with all abundance of blessings.

3. *Incline your ear.* This assemblage of words makes still more evident what I slightly mentioned a little before, that God leaves nothing undone which is fitted to correct and arouse our tardiness. Yet there is an implied reproof, for they must be excessively stupid who, when they are so gently called, do not instantly obey. This is a remarkable passage, from which we see that our whole happiness lies in obeying the word of God. When God speaks in this manner,

the object which he has in view is to lead us to life, and therefore the blame lies wholly with ourselves, because we disregard this saving and life-giving word.

And come unto me. If God only commanded what we ought to do, he would indeed lay down the method of obtaining life, but without advantage; for the Law, which proceeded from the mouth of God, is the minister of death, but when he invites us "to himself," when he adopts us as children, when he promises pardon of sin and sanctification, the consequence is that they who hear obtain life from him. We ought, therefore, to take into view the kind of doctrine which contains life, in order that we may seek our salvation from it; and hence we infer that there is no hope of salvation if we do not obey God and his word. This reproves all mankind, so that they can plead no excuse for their ignorance, for he who refuses to hear can have no solid argument to defend his cause.

These repetitions describe the patience of God in calling us, for he does not merely invite us once, but when he sees that we are sluggish, he gives a second and even a third warning, in order to conquer our hard-heartedness. Thus he does not all at once reject those who despise him, but after having frequently invited them.

Besides, this is a description of the nature of faith, when he bids us "come to himself." We ought to hear the Lord in such a manner that faith shall follow, for they who by faith receive the word of God have laid aside their desires and despised the world, and may be said to have broken their chains, so that they readily and cheerfully "draw near to God." But faith cannot be formed without hearing (Rom. 10:17), that is, without understanding the word of God, and so he bids us "hear" before we "come to him." Thus, whenever faith is mentioned, let us remember that it must be joined to the word, in which it has its foundation.

And I will strike a covenant of eternity with you. It is asked, did not the Jews formerly enter into an everlasting covenant with God? For he appears to promise something that is new and uncommon. I reply, nothing new is here promised for which the Lord did not formerly enter into an engagement with his people, but it is a renewal and confirmation of the covenant, that the Jews might not think that the covenant of God was made void on account of the long continued banishment. For when they were banished from the country that had been promised to them, when they had no temple or sacrifices or any marks of the "covenant" except circumcision, who would not have concluded that it was all over with them? This mode of expression, therefore, Isaiah accommodated to the capacity of the people, that they might know that the covenant into which God entered with the Fathers was firm, sure, and eternal, and not changeable or temporary.

This is also what he means by *the mercies of David*, but by this phrase he declares that it was a covenant of free grace, for it was founded on nothing else than the absolute goodness of God. Whenever, therefore, the word "covenant" occurs in Scripture, we ought at the same time to call to remembrance the word "grace." By calling them *the faithful mercies of David*, he declares that he will be faithful in it and at the same time states indirectly that he is faithful and steadfast, and cannot be accused of falsehood, as if he had broken his covenant; that the Jews, on the other hand, are covenant breakers and traitors (for they have revolted from him), but that he cannot repent of his covenant or his promise.

He calls them *the mercies of David*, because this covenant, which has now been solemnly confirmed, was made in the land *of David*. The Lord indeed entered into a covenant with Abraham (Gen. 15:5; 17:7), afterward confirmed it by Moses (Ex. 2:24; 33:1), and finally ratified this very covenant in the land of David, that it might be eternal (2 Sam. 7:12). Whenever, therefore, the Jews thought of a Redeemer, that is, of their salvation, they ought to have remembered "David" as a mediator who represented Christ, for David must not here be regarded as a private individual, but as bearing this title and character. Yet some regard must be had to the time when this prophecy was uttered, for since the rank of the kingdom had been obliterated, and the name of the royal family had become mean and contemptible during the captivity in Babylon, it might seem as if, through the ruin of that family, the truth of God had fallen into decay, and therefore he bids them contemplate by faith the throne of David, which had been cast down.

4. *Behold, I have given him a witness to the peoples.* The prophet now explains more fully the reason why he mentioned "David." It was because into his hand had been committed the promise of a Redeemer that was to come, and this discourse might be expressed with a view to his public character, so far as he was the surety of the covenant, for he did not act for himself individually, but was

appointed to be a sort of mediator between God and the people. Yet it is beyond all doubt that the prophet leads them directly to Christ, to whom the transition from David was easy and natural, as if he had said, "That successor of David shall come forth, by whose hand perfect salvation and happiness hath been promised."

By calling him "a witness," he means that the covenant into which he entered shall be ratified and confirmed in Christ. There is a weighty meaning in the word "witness," for he clearly shows that this covenant shall be proved in Christ, by whom the truth of God shall be made manifest. He will testify that God is not false. But this testimony consists in doctrine, and if it were not added, we should receive little benefit from Christ's coming, as it is said, *I will publish the command* (Ps. 2:7). In this sense also Isaiah said in another passage that Christ will have a mouth like a sword or an arrow (Isa. 49:2).

A leader and instructor. This is added, in order to procure attention to his doctrine, for if we do not hear him when he speaks, and if we do not embrace by assured faith what he makes known to us concerning the Father's good pleasure, his power is set aside. In like manner, the name of Christ is pronounced loudly enough by the papists, but since they refuse to receive him as a teacher and instructor, and acknowledge him merely by name, their boasting is idle and ridiculous.

To the peoples. This was added for the purpose of amplification, because the Church could not be restored to her ancient dignity, or be enlarged, but by assembling the Gentiles, and therefore it was necessary that the voice of Christ should pierce even to the remotest countries, because he has been appointed a "witness, leader, and instructor" to the whole human race.

5. *Behold, thou shalt call a nation which thou knowest not.* Isaiah explains more largely what he formerly glanced at by a single word, for he declares that Christ shall be the "leader," not of a single people, but of all the peoples. "To call" here denotes possession, for there is a mutual relation between the words "call" and "answer." Christ therefore "calls" in the exercise of authority, as one who is invested with supreme power, and he "calls" the Gentiles that he may bring them into a state of obedience and may cause them to submit to his word.

He says that they shall be ready to obey, though hitherto they were unknown; not that the Son of God, by whom they were created, did not know them, but because he paid no regard to them until they began to be reckoned as belonging to the Church. God had in a peculiar manner called the Jews; the Gentiles appeared to be excluded as if they did not at all belong to him. But now, addressing Christ, he promises that Christ shall constrain the Gentiles to obey him, though formerly they were opposed to his authority. He expresses this still more plainly in what immediately follows.

A nation that knew not thee shall run to thee. By putting the verb ירוצו (yarutzu) *shall run*, in the plural number, he intends to explain more fully that the Church shall be collected out of various peoples, so that they who were formerly scattered shall be gathered into one body, for the word "run" relates to harmony of faith. When he now says that the Gentiles "did not know Christ," he employs the expression in a different sense from that in which he said, a little before, that they were unknown to Christ, for all heathens and unbelievers are declared, in a literal sense, to be in a state of ignorance, in consequence of their being destitute of the light of heavenly doctrine, without which they cannot have the knowledge of God. Although by nature the knowledge of God is engraven on the hearts of all men, yet it is so confused and dark, and entangled by many errors, that if the light of the word be not added to it, by knowing they know not God, but wander miserably in darkness.

Here we have a remarkable testimony of God as to the calling of the Gentiles, for whom, as well as for the Jews, Christ was appointed. Hence also we learn that God takes care of us, if we bow to his authority, and not only such care as he takes of all the creatures, but such care as a father takes of his children.

Yet the word "run" describes more fully the efficacy of this calling, for the object of it is that we shall obey God, that we shall readily and cheerfully place ourselves before him as teachable, and ready to comply with any expression of his will, in like manner, as Paul shows that obedience is the end of our calling (Rom. 1:5; 16:26). But as the Gentiles were at a great distance from God, it was necessary that they should labor earnestly to surmount every obstacle, that they might draw near to him.

For the sake of Jehovah thy God. He shows what is the source of this readiness and cheerfulness. It is because the Gentiles shall know that they have to do with God, for if we contemplate Christ merely as man, we shall not be powerfully affected by his doctrine, but when we behold God in him, an astonishing warmth of affection is kindled in our hearts. Now, Christ is here described as a minister appointed by God to perform his work, for he assumes the character of a servant along with our flesh, and in this respect there is no impropriety in his being subjected to the Father, as if he belonged to the rank of other men.

Yet we ought to keep in remembrance what we have frequently seen as to the union of the Head and the members, for what is now said concerning Christ relates to the whole body, and therefore the glorifying is common to the whole Church. Yet Christ always holds the highest rank, for, being raised on high, he is exalted above the whole world, that to him there may be a concourse of all nations. In a word, he shows that men obey Christ and submit to his doctrine, because God hath exalted him and hath determined to make his preeminence known to all men, for otherwise the preaching of the Gospel would be of little use, if God did not give power and efficacy to his doctrine by the Spirit.

6. *Seek ye Jehovah.* After having spoken of the good success of the Gospel among the Gentiles, who formerly were strangers to the kingdom of God, he urges the Jews to be ashamed of loitering while others run, for since they were the first who were called, it is shameful that they should be last. This exhortation, therefore, relates strictly to the Jews, to whom the example of the Gentiles is held out in order to excite their jealousy, in the same manner as the Lord hath foretold that *he would provoke the Jews to jealousy by a foolish nation* (Deut. 32:21).

While he is found. "The time of finding" is here used not exactly in the same sense as in Psalm 32:6, but as the time when God offers himself to us, as in other passages he has limited a fixed day for his good pleasure and our salvation (Isa. 49:8). Yet I readily admit that it likewise denotes the time when necessity prompts us to seek God's assistance; but we ought chiefly to remember that God is sought at a seasonable time, when of his own accord he advances to meet us, for in vain shall indolent and sluggish persons lament that they had been deprived of that grace which they rejected. The Lord sometimes endures our sluggishness and bears with us, but if ultimately he does not succeed, he will withdraw and will bestow his grace on others. For this reason Christ exhorts us to walk while it is day, for the night cometh when the means of pursuing our journey shall be taken from us (John 12:35). We ought to draw high consolation from being assured that it is not in vain for us to seek God. *Seek,* says Christ, *and ye shall find; knock, and it shall be opened; ask, and it shall be given to you* (Matt. 7:7).

Call upon him while he is near. The word "call" may here be taken in a general sense, but I think that it denotes one description of "seeking" God, which is of more importance than all the others, as if he commanded us to betake ourselves to him by prayers and supplications. He says that he is "near," when he opens the door and gently invites us to come to him, or when he comes forth publicly, so that we do not need to seek him through long windings. But we must attend to Paul's definition, who tells us that it denotes the preaching of the Gospel (Rom. 10:8). *The Lord is nigh* (Phil. 4:5) and exhibits himself to us when the voice of the Gospel cries aloud, and we do not need to seek far or to make long circuits as unbelievers do, for he exhibits himself to us in his word, that we, on our part, may draw near to him.

7. *Let the wicked man forsake his way.* He confirms the former statement; for having formerly called men to receive the grace of God, he now describes more largely the manner of receiving it. We know how hypocrites loudly call on God whenever they desire relief from their distresses and yet shut up their hearts by wicked obstinacy; and therefore, that the Jews may not be hypocritical in seeking God, he exhorts them to sincere piety. Hence we infer that the doctrine of repentance ought always to accompany the promise of salvation, for in no other way can men taste the goodness of God than by abhorring themselves on account of their sins and renouncing themselves and the world. And indeed no man will sincerely desire to be reconciled to God and to obtain pardon of sins till he is moved by a true and earnest repentance.

By three forms of expression he describes the nature of repentance, first, *Let the wicked man forsake his way;* second, *The unrighteous man his thoughts;* third, *Let him return to the Lord.* Under the word *way* he includes the whole course of life, and accordingly demands that they bring forth the fruits of righteousness as witnesses of their newness of life. By adding the word *thoughts* he intimates that we must not only correct outward actions, but must begin with the heart, for although in the opinion of men we appear to change our manner of life for the better, yet we shall have made little proficiency if the heart be not changed.

Thus repentance embraces a change of the whole man, for in man we view inclinations, purposes, and then works. The works of men are visible, but the root within is concealed. This must first be changed, that it may afterward yield fruitful works. We must first wash away from the mind all uncleanness and conquer wicked inclinations, that outward testimonies may afterward be added. And if any man boast that he has been changed, and yet live as he was wont to do, it will be vain-boasting, for both are requisite, conversion of the heart and change of life.

Besides, God does not command us to return to him before he has applied a remedy to revolt, for hypocrites will willingly endure that we praise what is good and right, provided that they be at liberty to crouch amid their filth. But we can have nothing to do with God if we do not withdraw from ourselves, especially when we have been alienated by wicked variance, and therefore self-denial goes before, that it may lead us to God.

And he will have mercy on him. We ought carefully to examine this context, for he shows that men cannot be led to repentance in any other way than by holding out assurance of pardon. Whoever, then, inculcates the doctrine of repentance without mentioning the mercy of God and reconciliation through free grace, labors to no purpose, just as the popish doctors imagine that they have discharged their duty well when they have dwelt largely on this point, and yet do but chatter and trifle about the doctrine of repentance. But although they taught the true method of repenting, yet it would be of little avail, seeing that they leave out the foundation of freely bestowed pardon by which alone consciences can be pacified. And indeed, as we have formerly said, a sinner will always shrink from the presence of God so long as he is dragged to his judgment seat to give an account of his life and will never be subdued to fear and obedience till his heart is brought into a state of peace.

For he aboundeth in pardoning. Now, because it is difficult to remove terror from trembling minds, Isaiah draws all argument from the nature of God, that he will be ready to pardon and to be reconciled. Thus the Holy Spirit dwells on this part of doctrine, because we always doubt whether or not God is willing to pardon us, for although we entertain some thoughts of his mercy, yet we do not venture fully to believe that it belongs to us. It is not without reason, therefore, that this clause is added, that we may not be hindered by uncertainty or doubt as to his infinite compassion toward us.

8. *For my thoughts are not your thoughts.* This passage is expounded in various ways. Some think that it condemns universally the life of men, that they may not be satisfied with it or flatter their vices, for we cannot approach to God but by taking away a false conviction of our own righteousness. And indeed none call for physicians but those who are driven by the violence of disease to seek both health and remedies. Accordingly, this passage is compared by them to that saying of our Lord, *What ranks high among men is abomination in the sight of God* (Luke 16:15).

But the prophet's meaning, I think, is different, and is more correctly explained, according to my judgment, by other commentators, who think that he draws a distinction between God's disposition and man's disposition. Men are wont to judge and measure God from themselves, for their hearts are moved by angry passions and are very difficult to be appeased, and therefore they think that they cannot be reconciled to God when they have once offended him. But the Lord shows that he is far from resembling men. As if he had said, "I am not a mortal man, that I should show myself to be harsh and irreconcilable to you. My thoughts are very different from yours. If you are implacable, and can with difficulty be brought back to a state of friendship with those from whom you have received an injury, I am not like you, that I should treat you so cruelly."

9. *For as the heavens are higher than the earth.* This agrees well with that passage in which David, describing the mercy of God, says (Ps. 103:11) that it is as much more excellent *as the heavens are higher than the earth*, for although the application is different, yet the meaning is the same. In short, God is infinitely compassionate and infinitely ready to forgive, so that it ought to be ascribed exclusively to our unbelief if we do not obtain pardon from him.

There is nothing that troubles our consciences more than when we think that God is like ourselves, for the consequence is that we do not venture to approach him, and flee from him as an enemy, and are never at rest. But they who measure God by themselves as a standard form a false idea and altogether contrary to his nature, and indeed they cannot do him a greater injury than this. Are men, who are corrupted and debased by sinful desires, not ashamed to compare God's lofty and uncorrupted nature with their own, and to confine what is infinite within those narrow limits by which they feel themselves to be wretchedly restrained? In what prison could any of us be more straightly shut up than in our own unbelief?

This appears to me to be the plain and simple meaning of the prophet. And yet I do not deny that he alludes, at the same time, to the life of men such as he formerly described it to be. In a word, he means that men must forget themselves when they wish to be converted to God, and that no obstacle can be greater or more destructive than when we think that God is irreconcilable. We must therefore root out of our minds this false imagination.

Moreover, we learn from it how widely they err who abuse the mercy of God, so as to draw from it greater encouragement to sin. The prophet reasons thus, "Repent, forsake your ways, for the mercy of God is infinite." When men despair or doubt as to obtaining pardon, they usually become more hardened and obstinate, but when they feel that God is merciful, this draws and converts them. It follows, therefore, that they who do not cease to live wickedly, and who are not changed in heart, have no share in this mercy.

10. *Surely, as the rain cometh down.* After having spoken of God's tender affection and inconceivable forbearance toward us, he again brings forward the promises, that, by relying on them, we may banish all doubt of being free from every danger. It would be of little avail to speak to us about the nature or the secret purpose of God, if we were not reminded of "the word," by which he reveals himself. Now, God speaks openly to us, so that it is unnecessary to make longer inquiry. We must therefore come to the word, in which his will is declared without obscurity, provided that all our senses are confined within those limits, for otherwise we remain in suspense and doubt what he has determined concerning us, even though the Lord declare a thousand times that he is altogether unlike men, for although men acknowledge this, yet they wish to be certain about themselves and their salvation. For

this reason we ought carefully to observe the order which is followed by the prophet. Thus also Moses recalled the people to the knowledge of God. *Say not thou, Who shall ascend to heaven? or, Who shall descend into the deep? The word is nigh, in thy mouth and in thy heart* (Deut. 30:12). *That is,* saith Paul, *the word of faith which we preach* (Rom. 10:8).

He employs a comparison drawn from daily experience and wonderfully appropriate, for if we see great efficacy in the rain, which waters and fertilizes the earth, much greater efficacy will God display in his word. The rain is transitory and liable to corruption; but the word is eternal, unchangeable, and incorruptible, and cannot, like the rain, vanish away.

That we may more fully understand the prophet's words, we must keep in view the end at which he aims. Men doubt if God will actually perform what he promises in his word, for we look upon the word as if it were suspended in the air and had no effect. How shocking this is he demonstrates from the very course of nature, for it is in the highest degree unreasonable to ascribe less to the word than to a dumb creature, and therefore he teaches us that his word never fails of its effect. Some understand this to mean that the preaching of the Gospel is never unprofitable, but always produces some fruit. This is true in itself, for the Lord worketh by his Spirit and *giveth increase* (1 Cor. 3:7) so that the labor of his servants is not unproductive. But the prophet's meaning was different; namely, that God does not speak in vain or scatter his promises into the air, but that we shall actually receive the fruit of them, provided that we do not prevent it by our unbelief.

But watereth the earth, and causeth it to bring forth. He mentions two effects produced by the watering of the rain, which fertilizes the earth; first, that men have abundance of food for their support; and second, that they have seed for procuring a crop in the following year. If therefore in things of a transitory nature the power of God is so great, what must we think of the word?

11. *So shall my word be.* The word goeth out of the mouth of God in such a manner that it likewise "goeth out of the mouth" of men, for God does not speak openly from heaven, but employs men as his instruments, that by their agency he may make known his will. But the authority of the promises is more fully confirmed when we are told that they proceed from the sacred mouth of

God. Although, therefore, he brings forward witnesses from the earth, he declares that all that they have promised shall be ratified and sure, and, in order to impress more deeply on the minds of men the power and efficacy of preaching, he declares that he does not cast that precious seed at random, but appoints it for a fixed purpose, and consequently that we ought to entertain no doubt as to the effect, for there is nothing to which mortals are more prone than to judge of God from themselves so as to withhold belief from his voice.

This doctrine must be frequently repeated and inculcated, that we may know that God will do what he hath once spoken. For this reason, when we hear the promises of God, we ought to consider what is his design in them, so that when he promises the free pardon of our sins, we may be fully assured that we are reconciled through Christ. But, as the word of God is efficacious for the salvation of believers, so it is abundantly efficacious for condemning the wicked, as Christ also teacheth, *The word which I have spoken, that shall judge him at the last day.*

12. *Therefore ye shall go out with joy.* The prophet concludes the subject of this chapter, for when he spoke of the mercy of God, his object was to convince the Jews that the Lord would deliver them. He now applies to his purpose what was contained in his discourse concerning the infinite goodness of God and shows that his thoughts are very unlike the thoughts of men. And the true way of teaching is this, that we should apply general statements for present use. Finally, he treats of the restoration of the people, which depended on the undeserved mercy of God.

The mountains and hills shall break out before you. By *the mountains and hills* he means that everything which they shall meet in the journey, though in other respects it be injurious, shall aid those who shall return to Jerusalem. They are metaphors, by which he shows that all the creatures bow to the will of God and rejoice and lend their aid to carry on his work. He alludes to the deliverance from Egypt (Ex. 14:22) as is customary with the prophets, for thus is it described by the psalmist, *The mountains leaped like rams, and the hills like lambs. What ailed thee, O sea, that thou fleddest, and Jordan* (Josh. 3:16) *that thou wast driven back?* (Ps. 114:4, 5). For the restoration of the Church may be regarded as a renovation of the whole world, and in consequence of this, heaven and earth are said to be changed, as if their order were reversed. But all this depended on former predictions, by which they had received a promise of their return.

13. *Instead of the bramble shall come up the fir tree.* He still extols the power of God, which would be visible in the restoration of the people, for he shows that the change will be such that they shall have an easy road to return. Some explain it allegorically and suppose that by "brambles" are meant men who wish to do injury and who inflict wounds on others, and that these shall be "fir trees," that is, trees that bear fruit and that are useful to their neighbors, but in expositions of that kind ingenuity is carried to excess. When they say that these things relate to the kingdom of Christ, and on that account ought to be understood in a spiritual sense, I agree with them, for the prophet begins with the departure from Babylon and includes the whole condition of the Church, till Christ was manifested to the world. But the propriety of that allegory must not therefore be admitted, for he speaks of the departure from Babylon, and, in order to open it up for his people, he says that he will remove every obstacle and will supply them with everything necessary, so that they shall suffer no inconvenience. In like manner, when Christ promises the benefit of redemption, he likewise takes away everything that would injure or retard and even turns those things to a different and totally opposite purpose, that from them also they may receive some benefit. All things (Rom. 8:28) tend to the advantage of believers, and those things which would otherwise be injurious and destructive are employed by God as remedies to purify them, that they may not be devoted to the world, but may become more ready and cheerful in the service of their Master.

And shall be to Jehovah for a name. When he says that it shall be to God "for a name," he shows what is the design of the restoration of the Church. It is that the name of God may be more illustrious among men, and that the remembrance of him may flourish and be maintained. On this account he adds that it shall be a perpetual sign, that is, a monument, and, as we commonly say, a memorial, and although amid these tempests the Church be tossed and agitated in various ways, yet, because the Lord wishes that the remembrance of his name may be everlasting, he will guard and defend her.

The New Testament

MATTHEW 5:1–12 / LUKE 6:20–26

The Beatitudes

<table>
<tr><td>MATTHEW 5:1–12</td><td>LUKE 6:20–26</td></tr>
</table>

MATTHEW 5:1–12

¹And when Jesus had seen the multitudes, he went up into a mountain, and when he had sat down, his disciples approached to him. ²And opening his mouth, he taught them, saying, ³Happy are the poor in spirit: for theirs is the kingdom of heaven. ⁴Happy are they who mourn: for they shall receive consolation. ⁵Happy are the meek: for they shall receive the earth by inheritance. ⁶Happy are they who hunger and thirst after righteousness: for they shall be satisfied. ⁷Happy are the merciful: for they shall obtain mercy. ⁸Happy are those who are of a pure heart: for they shall see God. ⁹Happy are the peacemakers: for they shall be called the children of God. ¹⁰Happy are those who suffer persecution on account of righteousness: for theirs is the kingdom of heaven. ¹¹Happy are you, when they shall throw reproaches on you, and shall persecute you, and lying, shall speak every evil word against you

LUKE 6:20–26

²⁰And he, lifting up his eyes on the disciples, said, Happy (are ye) poor: for yours is the kingdom of God. ²¹Happy are ye who hunger now: for ye shall be satisfied. Happy are ye who weep now: for ye shall laugh. ²²Happy shall ye be when men shall hate you, and shall separate you, and shall load you with reproaches, and shall cast out your name as evil, on account of the Son of Man. ²³Rejoice ye in that day, and leap for joy: for, lo, your reward is great in heaven: for according to these things their fathers did to the prophets. ²⁴But woe to you (who are) rich: for you have your consolation. ²⁵Woe to you who are filled: for you shall hunger. Woe to you who laugh now: for ye shall mourn and weep. ²⁶Woe to you, when all men shall applaud you: for according to these things their fathers did to the false prophets.

on my account. [12]Rejoice ye, and
leap for joy: for your reward is
great in heaven: for so did they
persecute the prophets who were
before you.

Matthew 5:1. *He went up into a mountain.* Those who think that
Christ's sermon, which is here related, is different from the sermon contained in the sixth chapter of Luke's Gospel rest their
opinion on a very light and frivolous argument. Matthew states
that Christ spoke to his disciples on a mountain, while Luke seems
to say that the discourse was delivered on a plain. But it is a mistake to read the words of Luke, *he went down with them, and stood
in the plain* (Luke 6:17) as immediately connected with the statement that, *lifting up his eyes on the disciples*, he spoke thus. For the
design of both evangelists was to collect into one place the leading
points of the doctrine of Christ which related to a devout and holy
life. Although Luke had previously mentioned a *plain*, he does not
observe the immediate succession of events in the history, but
passes from miracles to doctrine, without pointing out either time
or place, just as Matthew takes no notice of the time, but only
mentions the place. It is probable that this discourse was not delivered until Christ had chosen the twelve, but in attending to the
order of time, which I saw that the Spirit of God had disregarded,
I did not wish to be too precise. Pious and modest readers ought to
be satisfied with having a brief summary of the doctrine of Christ
placed before their eyes, collected out of his many and various discourses, the first of which was that in which he spoke to his disciples about true happiness.

2. *Opening his mouth.* This redundancy of expression
(πλεονασμος) partakes of the Hebrew idiom: for what would be
faulty in other languages is frequent among the Hebrews, to say,
He opened his mouth, instead of, *He began to speak.* Many look upon
it as an emphatic mode of expression, employed to draw attention
to anything important and remarkable, either in a good or bad
sense, which has been uttered, but as some passages of Scripture
countenance an opposite view, I prefer the former exposition. I
shall also dismiss the ingenious speculation of those who give an
allegorical turn to the fact of our Lord teaching his disciples on a

mountain, as if it had been intended to teach them to elevate their minds far above worldly cares and employments. In ascending the mountain, his design rather was to seek a retreat where he might obtain relaxation for himself and his disciples at a distance from the multitude.

Now let us see, in the first place, why Christ spoke to his disciples about *true happiness*. We know that not only the great body of the people, but even the learned themselves, hold this error, that he is the happy man who is free from annoyance, attains all his wishes, and leads a joyful and easy life. At least it is the general opinion that happiness ought to be estimated from the present state. Christ, therefore, in order to accustom his own people to bear the cross, exposes this mistaken opinion, that those are happy who lead an easy and prosperous life according to the flesh. For it is impossible that men should mildly bend the neck to bear calamities and reproaches, so long as they think that patience is at variance with a happy life. The only consolation which mitigates and even sweetens the bitterness of the cross and of all afflictions is the conviction that we are happy in the midst of miseries, for our patience is *blessed* by the Lord and will soon be followed by a happy result.

This doctrine, I do acknowledge, is widely removed from the common opinion, but the disciples of Christ must learn the philosophy of placing their happiness beyond the world and above the affections of the flesh. Though carnal reason will never admit what is here taught by Christ, yet he does not bring forward anything imaginary—as the Stoics were wont, in ancient times, to amuse themselves with their paradoxes—but demonstrates from the fact that those persons are truly happy, whose condition is supposed to be miserable. Let us therefore remember that the leading object of the discourse is to show that those are not unhappy who are oppressed by the reproaches of the wicked and subject to various calamities. And not only does Christ prove that they are in the wrong, who measure the happiness of man by the present state, because the distresses of the godly will soon be changed for the better, but he also exhorts his own people to patience, by holding out the hope of a reward.

3. *Happy are the poor in spirit.* **Luke 6:20.** *Happy (are ye) poor.* Luke gives nothing more than a simple metaphor, but as the

poverty of many is accursed and unhappy, Matthew expresses more clearly the intention of Christ. Many are pressed down by distresses and yet continue to swell inwardly with pride and cruelty. But Christ pronounces those to be happy who, chastened and subdued by afflictions, submit themselves wholly to God, and, with inward humility, betake themselves to him for protection. Others explain *the poor in spirit* to be those who claim nothing for themselves and are even so completely emptied of confidence in the flesh that they acknowledge their poverty. But as the words of Luke and those of Matthew must have the same meaning, there can be no doubt that the appellation *poor* is here given to those who are pressed and afflicted by adversity. The only difference is that Matthew, by adding an epithet, confines the happiness to those only who, under the discipline of the cross, have learned to be humble.

For theirs is the kingdom of heaven. We see that Christ does not swell the minds of his own people by any unfounded belief, or harden them by unfeeling obstinacy as the Stoics do, but leads them to entertain the hope of eternal life and animates them to patience by assuring them that in this way they will pass into the heavenly kingdom of God. It deserves our attention that he only who is reduced to nothing in himself and relies on the mercy of God is *poor in spirit*, for they who are broken or overwhelmed by despair murmur against God, and this proves them to be of a proud and haughty *spirit*.

4. *Happy are they that mourn.* This statement is closely connected with the preceding one, and is a sort of appendage or confirmation of it. The ordinary belief is that calamities render a man unhappy. This arises from the consideration that they constantly bring along with them *mourning* and grief. Now, nothing is supposed to be more inconsistent with happiness than *mourning*. But Christ does not merely affirm that *mourners* are not unhappy. He shows that their very *mourning* contributes to a *happy* life by preparing them to receive eternal joy and by furnishing them with excitements to seek true *comfort* in God alone. Accordingly, Paul says, *We glory in tribulations also knowing that tribulation produces patience, and patience experience, and experience hope: and hope maketh not ashamed* (Rom. 5:3-5).

5. *Happy are the meek.* By *the meek* he means persons of mild and

gentle dispositions who are not easily provoked by injuries, who are not ready to take offense, but are prepared to endure anything rather than do the like actions to wicked men. When Christ promises to such persons *the inheritance of the earth*, we might think it exceedingly foolish. Those who warmly repel any attacks, and whose hand is ever ready to revenge injuries, are rather the persons who claim for themselves the dominion of the earth. And experience certainly shows that the more mildly their wickedness is endured, the more bold and insolent does it become. Hence arises the diabolical proverb that "We must howl with the wolves, because the wolves will immediately devour everyone who makes himself a sheep." But Christ places his own protection, and that of the Father, in contrast with the fury and violence of wicked men, and declares, on good grounds, that *the meek* will be the lords and *heirs of the earth*. The children of this world never think themselves safe, but when they fiercely revenge the injuries that are done them and defend their life by the *weapons of war* (Ezek. 32:27). But as we must believe that Christ alone is the guardian of our life, all that remains for us is to *hide ourselves under the shadow of his wings* (Ps. 17:8). We must be sheep, if we wish to be reckoned a part of his flock.

It will perhaps be objected that what has been now said is contradicted by experience. I would first suggest that it be considered how greatly ferocious people are disturbed by their own restlessness. While they lead so stormy a life, though they were a hundred times lords of the earth, while they possess all, they certainly possess nothing. For the children of God, on the other hand, I answer, that though they may not plant their foot on what is their own, they enjoy a quiet residence on the earth. And this is no imaginary possession, for they know that the earth, which they inhabit, has been granted to them by God. Besides, the hand of God is interposed to protect them against the violence and fury of wicked men. Though exposed to every species of attack, subject to the malice of wicked men, surrounded by all kinds of danger, they are safe under the divine protection. They have already a foretaste, at least, of this grace of God, and that is enough for them, till they enter, at the last day, into the possession of the *inheritance* of the world.

6. *Happy are they who hunger.* To *hunger and thirst* is here, I

think, used as a figurative expression and means to suffer poverty, to want the necessaries of life, and even to be defrauded of one's right. Matthew says, *who thirst after righteousness*, and thus makes one class stand for all the rest. He represents more strongly the unworthy treatment which they have received when he says that, though they are anxious, though they groan, they desire nothing but what is proper. "Happy are they who, though their wishes are so moderate that they desire nothing to be granted to them but what is reasonable, are yet in a languishing condition, like persons who are famishing with hunger." Though their distressing anxiety exposes them to the ridicule of others, yet it is a certain preparation for *happiness*, for at length *they shall be satisfied*. God will one day listen to their groans and satisfy their just desires, for to him, as we learn from the song of the Virgin, it belongs to *fill the hungry with good things* (Luke 1:53).

7. *Happy are the merciful.* This paradox, too, contradicts the judgment of men. The world reckons those men to be *happy* who give themselves no concern about the distresses of others, but consult their own ease. Christ says that those are *happy* who are not only prepared to endure their own afflictions, but to take a share in the afflictions of others, who assist the wretched, who willingly take part with those who are in distress, who clothe themselves, as it were, with the same affections, that they may be more readily disposed to render them assistance. He adds, *for they shall obtain mercy*—not only with God, but also among men, whose minds God will dispose to the exercise of humanity. Though the whole world may sometimes be ungrateful, and may return the very worst reward to those who have done acts of kindness to them, it ought to be reckoned enough that grace is laid up with God for the merciful and humane, so that they, in their turn, will find him to be *gracious and merciful* (Ps. 103:8; 145:8).

8. *Happy are they who are of a pure heart.* We might be apt to think that what is here stated by Christ is in accordance with the judgment of all. *Purity of heart* is universally acknowledged to be the mother of all virtues. And yet there is hardly one person in a hundred who does not put craftiness in the place of the greatest virtue. Hence those persons are commonly accounted *happy* whose ingenuity is exercised in the successful practice of deceit, who gain dexterous advantages, by indirect means, over those with whom

they have intercourse. Christ does not at all agree with carnal reason when he pronounces those to be *happy* who take no delight in cunning, but converse sincerely with men and express nothing, by word or look, which they do not feel in their heart. Simple people are ridiculed for want of caution and for not looking sharply enough to themselves. But Christ directs them to higher views and bids them consider that, if they have not sagacity to deceive in this world, they will enjoy *the sight of God* in heaven.

9. *Happy are the peacemakers.* By *peacemakers* he means those who not only seek peace and avoid quarrels, as far as lies in their power, but who also labor to settle differences among others, who advise all men to live at peace, and take away every occasion of hatred and strife. There are good grounds for this statement. As it is a laborious and irksome employment to reconcile those who are at variance, persons of a mild disposition who study to promote peace are compelled to endure the indignity of hearing reproaches, complaints, and remonstrances on all sides. The reason is that everyone would desire to have advocates who would defend his cause. That we may not depend on the favor of men, Christ bids us look up to the judgment of his Father, who is *the God of peace* (Rom. 15:33) and who accounts us his children, while we cultivate peace, though our endeavors may not be acceptable to men, for *to be called* means *to be accounted the children of God.*

10. *Happy are they who suffer persecution.* The disciples of Christ have very great need of this instruction, and the more hard and disagreeable it is for the flesh to admit it, the more earnestly ought we to make it the subject of our meditation. We cannot be Christ's soldiers on any other condition, than to have the greater part of the world rising in hostility against us and pursuing us even to death. The state of the matter is this: Satan, the prince of the world, will never cease to fill his followers with rage, to carry on hostilities against the members of Christ. It is, no doubt, monstrous and unnatural that men who study to live a righteous life should be attacked and tormented in a way which they do not deserve. And so Peter says, *Who is he that will harm you, if ye be followers of that which is good?* (1 Pet. 3:13).

Yet, in consequence of the unbridled wickedness of the world, it too frequently happens that good men, through a zeal of righteousness, arouse against them the resentments of the ungodly.

Above all, it is, as we may say, the ordinary lot of Christians to be hated by the majority of men, for the flesh cannot endure the doctrine of the Gospel; none can endure to have their vices reproved.

Who suffer on account of righteousness. This is descriptive of those who inflame the hatred and provoke the rage of wicked men against them, because, through an earnest desire to do what is good and right, they oppose bad causes and defend good ones, as far as lies in their power. Now, in this respect, the truth of God justly holds the first rank. Accordingly, by this mark Christ distinguishes his own martyrs from criminals and malefactors.

I now return to what I said a little before, that as all that will live godly in Christ Jesus (Paul informs us) *shall suffer persecution* (2 Tim. 3:12), this admonition has a general reference to all the godly. But if, at any time, the Lord spares our weakness and does not permit the ungodly to torment us as they would desire, yet, during the season of repose and leisure, it is proper for us to meditate on this doctrine, that we may be ready, whenever it shall be necessary, to enter the field and may not engage in the contest till we have been well prepared. As the condition of the godly, during the whole course of this life, is very miserable, Christ properly calls them to the hope of the heavenly life. And here lies the main difference between Christ's paradox and the ravings of the Stoics, who ordered that every man should be satisfied in his own mind and should be the author of his own happiness: while Christ does not suspend our happiness on a vain imagination, but rests it on the hope of a future reward.

11. *When they shall cast reproaches on you.* **Luke 6:22.** *When men shall hate you, and separate you, and load you with reproaches, and cast out your name as evil.* By these words Christ intended to comfort those who believe in him, that they may not lose courage, even though they see themselves to be detestable in the eyes of the world. For this was no light temptation, to be thrown out of the Church as ungodly and profane. Christ knew that there is no class of men more envenomed than hypocrites, and foresaw with what furious madness the enemies of the Gospel would attack his small and despised flock. It was therefore his will to furnish them with a sure defense that they might not give way, though an immense mass of reproaches were ready to overwhelm them. And hence it appears how little reason there is to dread the

excommunication of the pope, when those tyrants banish us from their synagogues because we are unwilling to renounce Christ.

12. *Rejoice ye, and leap for joy.* The meaning is, a remedy is at hand, that we may not be overwhelmed by unjust reproaches, for as soon as we raise our minds to heaven, we there behold vast grounds of joy, which dispel sadness. The idle reasonings of the papists, about the word *reward*, which is here used, are easily refuted, for there is not (as they dream) a mutual relation between the reward and merit, but the promise of the *reward* is free. Besides, if we consider the imperfections and faults of any good works that are done by the very best of men, there will be no work which God can judge to be worthy of reward.

We must advert once more to the phrases, *on my account*, or, *on account of the Son of Man* (Luke 6:22), and *lying, shall speak every evil word against you*, that he who suffers persecution for his own fault (1 Pet. 2:20) may not forthwith boast that he is a martyr of Christ, as the Donatists, in ancient times, were delighted with themselves on this single ground, that the magistrates were against them. And in our own day the Anabaptists, while they disturb the Church by their ravings, and slander the Gospel, boast that they are carrying the banners of Christ, when they are justly condemned. But Christ pronounces those only to be happy who are employed in defending a righteous cause.

For so did they persecute. This was expressly added that the apostles might not expect to triumph without exertion and without a contest, and might not fail when they encountered persecutions. The restoration of all things under the reign of Christ being everywhere promised in Scripture, there was danger, lest they might not think of warfare, but indulge in vain and proud confidence. It is evident from other passages that they foolishly imagined the kingdom of Christ to be filled with wealth and luxuries. Christ had good reason for warning them that, as soon as they succeeded to the place of the prophets, they must sustain the same contests in which the prophets were formerly engaged. *The prophets who were before you.* This means not only that *the prophets were before them* with respect to the order of time, but that they were of the same class with themselves and ought therefore to be followed as their example. The notion commonly entertained, of making out nine distinct beatitudes, is too frivolous to need a long refutation.

Luke 6:24. *Woe to you that are rich.* As Luke has related not more than four kinds of *blessings*, so he now contrasts with them four *curses*, so that the clauses mutually correspond. This contrast not only tends to strike terror into the ungodly, but to arouse believers that they may not be lulled to sleep by the vain and deceitful allurements of the world. We know how prone men are to be intoxicated by prosperity or ensnared by flattery, and on this account the children of God often envy the reprobate when they see everything go on prosperously and smoothly with them.

He pronounces a curse on the *rich*—not on all the rich, but on those who *receive their consolation* in the world; that is, who are so completely occupied with their worldly possessions that they forget the life to come. The meaning is, riches are so far from making a man happy that they often become the means of his destruction. In any other point of view, the rich are not excluded from the kingdom of heaven, provided they do not become snares for themselves or fix their hope on the earth, so as to shut against them the kingdom of heaven. This is finely illustrated by Augustine, who, in order to show that riches are not in themselves a hindrance to the children of God, reminds his readers that poor Lazarus was received into the bosom of rich Abraham.

25. *Woe to you who are filled. Woe to you who laugh now.* In the same sense, he pronounces a curse on those who are *satiated and full*, because they are lifted up by confidence in the blessings of the present life and reject those blessings which are of a heavenly nature. A similar view must be taken of what he says about *laughter*, for by those who *laugh* he means those who have given themselves up to Epicurean mirth, who are plunged in carnal pleasures and spurn every kind of trouble which would be found necessary for maintaining the glory of God.

26. *Woe to you when all men shall applaud you.* The last woe is intended to correct ambition, for nothing is more common than to seek the applauses of men, or, at least, to be carried away by them; and, in order to guard his disciples against such a course, he points out to them that the favor of men would prove to be their ruin. This warning refers peculiarly to teachers, who have no plague

more to be dreaded than ambition, because it is impossible for them not to corrupt the pure doctrine of God when they *seek to please men* (Gal. 1:10). By the phrase *all men*, Christ must be understood to refer to the children of the world, whose applauses are wholly bestowed on deceivers and false prophets, for faithful and conscientious ministers of sound doctrine enjoy the applause and favor of good men. It is only the wicked favor of the flesh that is here condemned, for as Paul informs us (Gal. 1:10), no man who *seeks to please men* can be *the servant of Christ*.

"Judge not . . ."

MATTHEW 7:1–5	MARK 4:24	LUKE 6:37–42

¹Judge not, that you may not be judged. ²For with what judgment you judge you shall be judged, and with what measure you measure, it shall be measured to you again. ³And why seest thou the straw, which is in thy brother's eye, and perceivest not the beam which is in thine eye? ⁴Or how shall thou say to thy brother, Allow me to pull the straw out of thine eye, and, behold, a beam is in thine eye? ⁵Hypocrites, cast out first the beam out of thine eye, and then thou shall see clearly, that thou mayest pull out the straw from thy brother's eye.

²⁴With what measure you measure, the same shall be measured to you.

³⁷Judge not, and you shall not be judged: condemn not, and you shall not be condemned: forgive, and it shall be forgiven to you. ³⁸Give, and it shall be given to you. Good measure, and pressed down, and shaken together, and running over, shall they give into your bosom: for the same measure, with which you measure, shall be measured again to you. (Again.) ⁴¹And why seest thou a straw in thy brother's eye, and perceivest not a beam which is in thine own eye? ⁴²Or how will thou be able to say to thy brother, Brother, allow me to pull out the straw which is in thine eye, while thou seest not the beam which is in thine eye? Hypocrite, cast out first the beam out of thine eye, and then thou

> shalt see clearly, that
> thou mayest cast out the
> straw which is in thy
> brother's eye.

Matthew 7:1. *Judge not.* These words of Christ do not contain an absolute prohibition *from judging*, but are intended to cure a disease, which appears to be natural to us all. We see how all flatter themselves, and every man passes a severe censure on others. This vice is attended by some strange enjoyment, for there is hardly any person who is not tickled with the desire of inquiring into other people's faults. All acknowledge, indeed, that it is an intolerable evil that those who overlook their own vices are so inveterate against their brethren. The heathens, too, in ancient times, condemned it in many proverbs. Yet it has existed in all ages, and exists, too, in the present day. Nay, it is accompanied by another and a worse plague, for the greater part of men think that when they condemn others, they acquire a greater liberty of sinning.

This depraved eagerness for biting, censuring, and slandering is restrained by Christ when he says, *Judge not.* It is not necessary that believers should become blind and perceive nothing, but only that they should refrain from an undue eagerness to *judge*, for otherwise the proper bounds of rigor will be exceeded by every man who desires to pass sentence on his brethren. There is a similar expression in the Apostle James, *Be not many masters* (James 3:1), for he does not discourage or withdraw believers from discharging the office of teachers, but forbids them to desire the honor from motives of ambition. To *judge*, therefore, means here, to be influenced by curiosity in inquiring into the actions of others. This disease, in the first place, draws continually along with it the injustice of condemning any trivial fault, as if it had been a very heinous crime, and next breaks out into the insolent presumption of looking disdainfully at every action and passing an unfavorable judgment on it, even when it might be viewed in a good light.

We now see that the design of Christ was to guard us against indulging excessive eagerness, or peevishness, or malignity, or even curiosity, in *judging our* neighbors. He who *judges* according to the word and law of the Lord, and forms *his judgment* by the rule of charity, always begins with subjecting himself to examination and preserves a proper medium and order in his *judgments*. Hence it is evident that this passage is altogether misapplied by those persons who would desire to make that moderation, which Christ recommends, a pretense for setting aside all distinction between good and evil. We are not only permitted, but are even bound, to condemn all sins, unless we choose to rebel against God himself—nay, to repeal his laws, to reverse his decisions, and to overturn his judgment seat. It is his will that we should proclaim the sentence which he pronounces on the actions of men, only we must preserve such modesty toward each other as to make it manifest that he is the only *Lawgiver and Judge* (Isa. 33:22).

That you may not be judged. He denounces a punishment against those severe judges who take so much delight in sifting the faults of others. They will not be treated by others with greater kindness, but will experience, in their turn, the same severity which they had exercised toward others. As nothing is dearer or more valuable to us than our reputation, so nothing is more bitter than to be condemned or to be exposed to the reproaches and infamy of men. And yet it is by our own fault that we draw upon ourselves that very thing which our nature so strongly detests, for which of us is there who does not examine too severely the actions of others, who does not manifest undue rage against slight offenses, or who does not peevishly censure what was in itself indifferent? And what is this but deliberately to provoke God, as our avenger, to treat us in the same manner. Now, though it is a just judgment of God that those who have judged others should be punished in their turn, yet the Lord executes this punishment by the instrumentality of men. Chrysostom and others limit this statement to the present life, but that is a forced interpretation. Isaiah threatens (33:1) that *those who have spoiled others shall be spoiled.* In like manner, our Lord means that there will be no want of executioners to punish the injustice and slander of men with equal bitterness or severity. And if men shall fail to receive punishment in this world, those who have shown undue eagerness in condemning their brethren will not escape the judgment of God.

Luke 6:37, 38. *Forgive, and it shall be forgiven to you. Give, and it shall be given to you.* This promise, which is added by Luke, means that the Lord will cause him who is indulgent, kind, and just to his brethren to experience the same gentleness from others and to be treated by them in a generous and friendly manner. Yet it frequently happens that the children of God receive the very worst reward and are oppressed by many unjust slanders, and that to when they have injured no man's reputation and even spared the faults of brethren. But this is not inconsistent with what Christ says, for we know that the promises which relate to the present life do not always hold and are not without exceptions. Besides, though the Lord permits his people, when innocent, to be unjustly oppressed and almost overwhelmed, he fulfills what he says in another place, that *their uprightness shall break forth as the morning* (Isa. 58:8). In this way, his blessing always rises above all unjust slanders. He subjects believers to unjust reproaches that he may humble them, and that he may at length maintain the goodness of their cause. It ought also to be taken into the account that believers themselves, though they endeavor to act justly toward their brethren, are sometimes carried away by excessive severity against brethren who were either innocent or not so greatly to be blamed, and thus, by their own fault, provoke against themselves a similar judgment. If they do not receive *good measure, pressed down, shaken together, and running over*, though this is chargeable on the ingratitude of the world, yet they ought to acknowledge that it was partly deserved, for there is no man who is so kind and indulgent as he ought to be toward his brethren.

Matthew 7:3. *And why seest thou the straw?* He expressly touches upon a fault, which is usually found in hypocrites. While they are too quick-sighted in discerning the faults of others and employ not only severe, but intentionally exaggerated, language in describing them, they throw their own sins behind their back or are so ingenious in finding apologies for them that they wish to be held excusable even in very gross offenses. Christ therefore reproves both evils: the excessive sagacity, which arises from a defect of charity when we sift too closely the faults of brethren, and the indulgence by which we defend and cherish our own sins.

The Cure of the Centurion's Servant

MATTHEW 8:5-13	LUKE 7:1-10
5And when Jesus had entered into Capernaum, a centurion came to him, beseeching him, 6And saying, Lord, my servant is lying at home afflicted with palsy, and is grievously tormented. 7And Jesus saith to him, When I shall come, I will heal him. 8And the centurion answering him said, Lord, I do not deserve that thou shouldst come under my roof: but only say the word, and my servant will be healed. 9For I am a man subject to the power of another, and I have soldiers under me: and I say to this man, Go, and he goeth: and to another, Come, and he cometh: and to my servant, Do this, and he doeth it. 10And when Jesus had heard these things, he wondered, and said to those who followed, Verily I say to you, not even in Israel have I found so great faith. 11And I say to you, That many will come from the east and west, and will sit down with Abraham, Isaac, and Jacob, in the kingdom of heaven: 12But the children of the kingdom shall be cast into the darkness that is without: weeping and gnashing of	1Now, when he had finished all his words in the hearing of the people, he entered into Capernaum. 2And a servant of a certain centurion, who was very dear to him, was ill and near death. 3And when he had heard about Jesus, he sent to him elders of the Jews, to entreat him, that he would come and heal his servant. 4And when they had come to him, they entreated him earnestly, saying, He deserves that though shouldest do this for him: 5For he loveth our nation, and himself hath built a synagogue. 6And Jesus went with them. And when he was already not far from the house, the centurion sent friends to him, and they said to him, Lord, do not trouble thyself: for I do not deserve that thou shouldest enter under my roof. 7And for this reason I did not reckon myself worthy to come to thee: but say in a word, and my servant will be healed. 8For I am a man placed under authority, having soldiers under me: and I say to this man, Go, and he goeth; and to another, Come, and he cometh: and to my servant, Do

teeth will be there. [13]And Jesus said to the centurion, Go, and as thou believest, so may it be done to thee: and his servant was healed in that hour.

this, and he doeth it. [9]And having heard these things, Jesus wondered at him, and he turned and said to the crowd that followed him, I say to you, not even in Israel have I found so great faith. [10]And when those who had been sent returned to the house, they found the servant, who had been sick, in good health.

Matthew 8:5. *And when Jesus had entered.* Those who think that Matthew and Luke give different narratives are led into a mistake by a mere trifle. The only difference in the words is that Matthew says that *the centurion came to him*, while Luke says that he sent some of the Jews to plead in his name. But there is no impropriety in Matthew saying that the centurion did what was done in his name and at his request. There is such a perfect agreement between the two evangelists in all the circumstances, that it is absurd to make two miracles instead of one.

The band of soldiers, which the centurion had under his command, was stationed, I have no doubt, in the town of Capernaum, in the same manner as garrisons were usually appointed for the protection of the towns. Though he perceived the morals of the people to be very vicious and depraved (for we know that Capernaum, being on the seacoast, must have been more dissolute than other towns), yet this did not prevent him from condemning the superstitions of his country and acquiring a taste for true and sincere piety. He had not built a synagogue for the Jews without exposing himself to some hatred and to some risk, and the only reason why *he loved that nation* was that he had embraced the worship of one God. Before Christ healed his servant, he had been healed by the Lord.

This was itself a miracle. One who belonged to the military profession, and who had crossed the sea with a band of soldiers for the purpose of accustoming the Jews to endure the yoke of Roman tyranny, submits willingly and yields obedience to the God of Israel. Luke says that this *servant was very dear to him*; and thus anticipates a doubt which might have arisen in the mind of the reader, for we know that slaves were not held in such estimation as to make their masters so solicitous about their life, unless by extraordinary industry, or fidelity, or some other virtue, they had secured their favor. By this statement Luke means that this was not a low or ordinary slave, but a faithful servant, distinguished by many excellencies and very highly esteemed by his master, and that this was the reason why he was so anxious about his life and recommended him so earnestly. From both evangelists it is evident that it was a sudden palsy, which, from the first attack, took away all hope of life, for slow palsies are not attended by severe pain. Matthew says that he was *grievously tormented*, and Luke, that he was *near death*. Both descriptions—pain or agony and extreme danger—serve to enhance the glory of the miracle, and for this reason I am the more unwilling to hazard any absolute assertion as to the nature of the disease.

Luke 7:5. *For he loveth our nation.* This was, no doubt, a commendation given him by the Jews on account of his piety, for his *love of a nation* universally hated could proceed only from zeal for the Law and from reverence for God. By *building a synagogue*, he showed plainly that he favored the doctrine of the Law. The Jews had therefore good grounds for saying that, as a devout worshipper of God, he had claims on Christ for receiving such a favor. They discover, at the same time, a marvelous stupidity in admitting, by their own acknowledgment, that a Gentile possesses that grace of God which they despise and reject. If they consider Christ to be the minister and dispenser of the gifts of God, why do they not receive the grace offered to them before bringing foreigners to enjoy it? But hypocrites never fail to manifest such carelessness and presumption, as not to hesitate to look upon God as under some sort of obligation to them, and to dispose of his grace at their pleasure, as if it were in their own power; and then, when they are satisfied with it, or rather because they do not deign to taste it, they treat it as useless and leave it to others.

Matthew 8:8. *Lord, I do not deserve that thou shouldest come under my roof.* Matthew's narrative is more concise and represents the man as saying this, while Luke explains more fully that this was a message sent by his friends, but the meaning of both is the same. There are two leading points in this discourse. The centurion, sparing Christ by way of honoring him, requests that Christ will *not trouble himself*, because he reckons himself unworthy to receive a visit from him. The next point is that he ascribes to Christ such power as to believe that by the mere expression of his will and by a word, his servant may recover and live. There was astonishing humility in exalting so highly above himself a man who belonged to a conquered and enslaved nation. It is possible, too, that he had become accustomed to the haughty pretensions of the Jews, and, being a modest man, did not take it ill to be reckoned a heathen and therefore feared that he would dishonor a prophet of God if he pressed him to enter the house of a polluted Gentile. However that may be, it is certain that he speaks sincerely and entertains such reverence for Christ that he does not venture to invite him to his house, nay, as is afterward stated by Luke, he reckoned himself unworthy to converse with him.

But it may be asked, what moved him to speak of Christ in such lofty terms? The difficulty is even increased by what immediately follows, *only say the word, and my servant will be healed*, or, as Luke has it, *say in a word*, for if he had not acknowledged Christ to be the Son of God, to transfer the glory of God to a man would have been superstition. It is difficult to believe, on the other hand, that he was properly informed about Christ's divinity, of which almost all were at that time ignorant. Yet Christ finds no fault with his words, but declares that they proceeded from faith, and this reason has forced many expositors to conclude that the centurion bestows on Christ the title of the true and only God. I rather think that the good man, having been informed about the uncommon and truly divine works of Christ, simply acknowledged in him the power of God. Something, too, he had undoubtedly heard about the promised Redeemer. Though he does not distinctly understand that Christ is *God manifested in the flesh* (1 Tim. 3:16), yet he is convinced that the power of God is manifested in him, and that he has received a commission to display the presence of God by miracles. He is not therefore chargeable with superstition, as if he had ascribed to a man what is the prerogative of God, but looking at the commission which God had given to Christ, he believes that by a word alone he can heal his servant.

Is it objected that nothing belongs more peculiarly to God than to accomplish by a word whatever he pleases, and that this supreme authority cannot without sacrilege be yielded to a mortal man? The reply is again easy. Though the centurion did not enter into those nice distinctions, he ascribed this power to the word, not of a mortal man, but of God, whose minister he fully believed Christ to be; on that point he entertained no doubt. The grace of healing having been committed to Christ, he acknowledges that this is a heavenly power, and does not look upon it as inseparable from the bodily presence, but is satisfied with the word from which he believes such a power to proceed.

Matthew 8:9. *For I am a man subject to the power of another.* This comparison does not imply equality between the two cases, but is taken from the less to the greater. He forms a higher conception of the divine power, which is manifested in Christ, than of the authority which was possessed by himself over servants and soldiers.

10. *Jesus wondered.* Wonder cannot apply to God, for it arises out of what is new and unexpected, but it might exist in Christ, for he had clothed himself with our flesh and with human affections. *Not even in Israel have I found so great faith.* This is not spoken absolutely, but in a particular point of view. For if we consider all the properties of faith, we must conclude that the faith of Mary was greater, in believing that she would be with child by the Holy Ghost and would bring forth the only-begotten Son of God, and in acknowledging the Son whom she had borne to be her God, and the Creator of the whole world, and her only Redeemer.

But there were chiefly two reasons why Christ preferred the faith of a Gentile to the faith of all the Jews. One was that a slight and inconsiderable acquaintance with doctrine yielded so sudden and abundant fruit. It was no small matter to declare, in such lofty terms, the power of God, of which a few rays only were yet visible in Christ. Another reason was that while the Jews were excessively eager to obtain outward signs, this Gentile asks no visible sign, but openly declares that he wants nothing more than the bare word. Christ was going to him, not that it was necessary, but to try his faith; and he applauds his faith chiefly on the ground of his resting satisfied with the bare word. What would another have done, and he, too, one of the apostles? Come, Lord, see and touch. This man asks no bodily approach or touch, but believes the word to possess such efficacy as fully to expect from it that his servant will be cured.

Now, he ascribes this honor to the word, not of a man, but of God, for he is convinced that Christ is not an ordinary man, but a prophet sent by God. And hence may be drawn a general rule. Though it was the will of God that our salvation should be accomplished in the flesh of Christ, and though he seals it daily by the sacraments, yet the certainty of it must be obtained from the word. Unless we yield such authority to the word, as to believe that as soon as God has spoken by his ministers our sins are undoubtedly forgiven and we are restored to life, all confidence of salvation is overthrown.

11. *Many will come from the east and west.* In the person of the servant, Christ gave to the Gentiles a taste and a kind of firstfruits of his grace. He now shows that the master is an example of the future calling of the Gentiles and of the spread of faith throughout the whole world, for he says that *they will come*, not only from the neighboring countries, but from the farthest bounds of the world. Though this had been clearly foretold by many passages of the prophets, it appeared at first strange and incredible to the Jews, who imagined that God was confined to the family of Abraham. It was not without astonishment that they heard that those who were at that time strangers would be citizens and heirs of the kingdom of God; and not only so, but that the covenant of salvation would be immediately proclaimed, that the whole world might be united in one body of the Church. He declares that the Gentiles, who shall come to the faith, will be partakers of the same salvation *with Abraham, Isaac, and Jacob.* Hence we draw the certain conclusion that the same promise, which has been held out to us in Christ, was formerly given to the fathers; for we would not have had an inheritance in common with them, if the faith by which it is obtained had not been the same. The word ἀνακλιθήσονται, *shall recline*, contains an allusion to a banquet, but as we know that the heavenly life does not require meat and drink, this phrase has the same meaning as if he had said, *they shall enjoy the same life.*

12. *But the children of the kingdom.* Why does he call those persons *children of the kingdom,* who were nothing less than children of Abraham? For those who are aliens from the faith have no right to be considered a part of God's flock. I answer: Though they did not actually belong to the Church of God, yet as they occupied

a place in the Church, he allows them this designation. Besides, it ought to be observed that so long as the covenant of God remained in the family of Abraham, there was such force in it that the inheritance of the heavenly kingdom belonged peculiarly to them. With respect to God himself, at least, they were *holy branches from a holy root* (Rom. 11:16), and the rejection of them, which afterward followed, shows plainly enough that they belonged, at that time, to the family of God. Second, it ought to be observed that Christ does not now speak of individuals, but of the whole nation. This was still harder to endure than the calling of the Gentiles. That the Gentiles should be admitted, by a free adoption, into the same body with the posterity of Abraham, could scarcely be endured, but that the Jews themselves should be driven out to make way for their being succeeded by the Gentiles appeared to them altogether monstrous. Yet Christ declares that both will happen: that God will admit strangers into the bosom of Abraham and that he will exclude *the children*. There is an implied contrast in the phrase, *the darkness that is without*. It means that out of the kingdom of God, which is the kingdom of light, nothing but darkness reigns. By *darkness* Scripture points out that dreadful anguish, which can neither be expressed nor conceived in this life.

13. *Go away, and as thou believest, so may it be to thee.* Hence it is evident how graciously Christ pours out his grace when he finds the vessel of faith open. Though he addresses these words to the centurion, there can be no doubt that in his person, he invites us all to strong hope. Hence we are also taught the reason why God is, for the most part, so limited in his communications to us: it is because our unbelief does not permit him to be liberal. If we open up the entrance to him by faith, he will listen to our wishes and prayers.

The Woman Who Was a Sinner

36And one of the Pharisees requested him to take food with him; and he entered into the house of the Pharisee, and sat down at table. 37And, lo, a woman in the city, who was a sinner, when she knew that he sat at table in the house of the Pharisee, brought an alabaster box of ointment: 38And sitting at his feet behind him, and weeping, she began to wash his feet with tears, and wiped them with the hairs of her head, and kissed his feet, and anointed them with ointment. 39And the Pharisee, who had invited him, seeing it, said, speaking within himself, If this man were a prophet, he would certainly know who and what sort of woman this is that toucheth him; for she is a sinner. 40And Jesus answering, said to him, Simon, I have something to say to thee. And he said, Master, say on. 41A certain creditor had two debtors: one owed five hundred pence, and another fifty. 42And when they had nothing to pay, he forgave them both. Tell me then, which of them will love him more? 43Simon answering said, I suppose that it will be he to whom he forgave more. And he said to him, Thou hast decided aright. 44And turning to the woman, he said to Simon, Seest thou this woman? I entered into thy house, thou gavest not water for my feet; but she hath moistened my feet with tears, and wiped them with the hairs of her head. 45Thou gavest me not a kiss; but she, since the time that I entered, hath not ceased to kiss my feet. 46My head with oil thou didst not anoint: but this woman hath anointed my feet with ointment. 47For which reason I say to thee, Her many sins are forgiven, for she hath loved much; but he to whom less is forgiven loveth less. 48And he said to her, Thy sins are forgiven thee. 49And those who sat at table with him began to say within themselves, Who is this that even forgiveth sins? 50And he said to the woman, Thy faith hath saved thee; go in peace.

36. *And one of the Pharisees requested him.* This narrative shows the captious disposition, not only to take, but to seek out, offenses,

which was manifested by those who did not know the office of Christ. A *Pharisee* invites Christ, from which we infer that he was not one of those who furiously and violently opposed, nor of those who haughtily despised his doctrine. But whatever might be his mildness, he is presently offended when he sees Christ bestow a gracious reception on a woman who, in his opinion, ought not to have been permitted to approach or to converse with him, and, accordingly, disowns him as *a prophet* because he does not acknowledge him to be the Mediator, whose peculiar office it was to bring miserable sinners into a state of reconciliation with God. It was something, no doubt, to bestow on Christ the honor due to a prophet, but he ought also to have inquired for what purpose he was sent, what he brought, and what commission he had received from the Father. Overlooking the grace of reconciliation, which was the main feature to be looked for in Christ, the Pharisee concluded that he was *not a prophet*. And, certainly, had it not been that through the grace of Christ this woman had obtained the forgiveness of her sins, and a new righteousness, she ought to have been rejected.

Simon's mistake lies only in this: Not considering that Christ came to save what was lost, he rashly concludes that Christ does not distinguish between the worthy and the unworthy. That we may not share in this dislike, let us learn, first, that Christ was given as a Deliverer to miserable and lost men, and to restore them from death to life. Second, let every man examine himself and his life, and then we will not wonder that others are admitted along with us, for no one will dare to place himself above others. It is hypocrisy alone that leads men to be careless about themselves, and haughtily to despise others.

37. *A woman who was a sinner.* The words stand literally as I have translated them (ἥτις ἦν ἁμαζτωλός). Erasmus has chosen to take the pluperfect tense, *who Had Been a sinner*, lest anyone should suppose that at that time she still *was a sinner*. But by so doing, he departed from the natural meaning, for Luke intended to express the place which the woman held in society, and the opinion universally entertained respecting her. Though her sudden conversion had rendered her a different person in the sight of God from what she had previously been, yet among men the disgrace attaching to her former life had not yet been effaced. She

was, therefore, in the general estimation of men *a sinner*, that is, a woman of wicked and infamous life, and this led Simon to conclude, though erroneously, that Christ had not the Spirit of discernment, since he was unacquainted with that infamy which was generally known.

40. *And Jesus answering said.* By this reply Christ shows how egregiously Simon was mistaken. Exposing to public view his silent and concealed thought, he proves himself to possess something more excellent than what belonged to the *prophets*, for he does not reply to his words, but refutes the sentiment which he kept hidden within his breast. Nor was it only on Simon's account that this was done, but in order to assure every one of us that we have no reason to fear lest any sinner be rejected by him, who not only gives them kind and friendly invitations, but is prepared with equal liberality, and—as we might say—with outstretched arms, to receive them all.

41. *A certain creditor had two debtors.* The scope of this parable is to demonstrate that Simon is wrong in condemning the woman who is acquitted by the heavenly judge. He proves that she is righteous, not because she pleased God, but because *her sins were forgiven*, for otherwise her case would not correspond to the parable, in which Christ expressly states, that the creditor *freely forgave the debtors who were not able to pay.* We cannot avoid wondering, therefore, that the greater part of commentators have fallen into so gross a blunder as to imagine that this woman, by her *tears*, and her *anointing*, and her *kissing his feet*, deserved the pardon of her sins. The argument which Christ employs was taken, not from the cause, but from the effect, for until a favor has been received, it cannot awaken gratitude, and the cause of reciprocal love is here declared to be a free forgiveness. In a word, Christ argues, from the fruits or effects that follow it, that this woman has been reconciled to God.

44. *And turning to the woman.* The Lord appears to compare Simon with the woman, in such a manner as to make him chargeable with nothing more than light offenses. But this is spoken only in the way of concession. "Suppose now, Simon," he says, "that the guilt from which God discharges thee was light, and that this woman has been guilty of many and very heinous offenses. Yet

you see how she proves by the effect that she has obtained pardon. For what mean those profuse tears, those frequent kisses of the feet, that precious ointment? What mean they but to acknowledge that she had been weighed down by an enormous burden of condemnation? And now she regards the mercy of God with fervor of love proportioned to her conviction that her necessity had been great."

From the words of Christ, therefore, we are not at liberty to infer that Simon had been a debtor to a small amount or that he was absolved from guilt. It is more probable that, as he was a blind hypocrite, he was still plunged in the filth of his sins. But Christ insists on this single point, that however wicked the woman may have been, she gave undoubted proofs of her righteousness by leaving no kind of duty undone to testify her gratitude, and by acknowledging, in every possible way, her vast obligations to God. At the same time, Christ reminds Simon that he has no right to flatter himself, as if he were free from all blame, for that he too needed mercy; and that if even he does not obtain the favor of God without pardon, he ought to look upon this woman's gifts, whatever might have been her former sins, as evidences of repentance and gratitude.

We must attend to the points of contrast, in which the woman is preferred to Simon. She *moistened his feet with tears, and wiped them with the hairs of her head*, while *he* did not even order *water* to be given, according to custom. She *did not cease to kiss his feet*, while *he* did not deign to receive Christ with the kiss of hospitality. *She* poured precious *ointment on his feet*, while *he* did not even *anoint his head with oil*. But why did our Lord, who was a model of frugality and economy, permit the expense of the *ointment*? It was because, in this way, the wretched sinner testified that she owed all to him. He had no desire of such luxuries, was not gratified by the sweet odor, and did not approve of gaudy dress. But he looked only at her extraordinary zeal to testify her repentance, which is also held out to us by Luke as an example, for her sorrow, which is the commencement of repentance, was proved by her tears. By placing herself *at Christ's feet behind him*, and there lying on the ground, she discovered her modesty and humility. By the *ointment*, she declared that she offered, as a sac-

rifice to Christ, herself and all that she possessed. Every one of
these things it is our duty to imitate, but the pouring of the *ointment* was an extraordinary act, which it would be improper to
consider as a rule.

47. *Her many sins are forgiven.* Some interpret the verb differently, *may her many sins be forgiven*, and bring out the following
meaning: "As this woman evinces by remarkable actions that she
is full of ardent love to Christ, it would be improper for the
Church to act harshly and severely toward her, but, on the contrary, she ought to be treated with gentleness, whatever may have
been the aggravations of her offenses." But as αφεωνται is used,
in accordance with the Attic dialect, for αφείνται, we must dispense with that subtlety of exposition which is disapproved by the
context, for a little after, Christ uses the same words in his address
to the woman, where the imperative mood would not apply. Here,
too, is added a corresponding clause, that *he to whom less is forgiven
loveth less.*

The verb, which is in the present tense, must, no doubt, be
resolved into a preterit. From the eager desire which she had
manifested to discharge all the duties of piety, Christ infers that
although this woman might have been guilty of many sins, the
mercy of God was so abundant toward her that she ought no
longer to be regarded as a sinner. Again, *loving* is not here said to
be the cause of pardon, but a subsequent manifestation, as I have
formerly mentioned, for the meaning of the words is this: "They
who perceive the display of deep piety in the woman form an erroneous judgment, if they do not conclude that God is already reconciled to her"; so that the free pardon of sins comes first in order.
Christ does not inquire at what price men may purchase the favor
of God, but argues that God has already forgiven this wretched
sinner, and that, therefore, a mortal man ought not to treat her
with severity.

48. *Thy sins are forgiven.* It may be asked, why does Christ
now promise to her the pardon which she had obtained, and of
which she had been assured? Some reply that these words were
uttered, not so much on her own account, as for the sake of
others. For my own part, I have no doubt that it was chiefly on
her own account, and this appears more clearly from the words

that follow. Nor ought we to wonder that the voice of Christ again pronounces an absolution of the woman, who had already tasted his grace, and who was even convinced that he was her only refuge of salvation. Thus, at the present day, faith is previously necessary, when we pray that the Lord would forgive our sins, and yet this is not a useless or superfluous prayer, but the object of it is that the heavenly Judge may more and more seal his mercy on our hearts, and in this manner may give us peace. Though this woman had brought with her a confident reliance on that grace which she had obtained, yet this promise was not superfluous, but contributed greatly to the confirmation of her faith.

49. *And those who sat at table with him began to say within themselves.* Hence we again learn that ignorance of Christ's office constantly leads men to conceive new grounds of offense. The root of the evil is that no one examines his own wretched condition, which undoubtedly would arouse every man to seek a remedy. There is no reason to wonder that hypocrites who slumber amid their vices should murmur at it as a thing new and unexpected when Christ forgives sins.

50. *Thy faith hath saved thee.* To repress those murmurings, and, at the same time, to confirm the woman, Christ commends her faith. Let others grumble as they may, but do thou adhere steadfastly to that faith which has brought thee an undoubted salvation. At the same time, Christ claims for himself the authority which had been given to him by the Father, for as he possesses the power of healing, to him faith is properly directed. And this intimates that the woman was not led by rashness or mistake to come to him, but that, through the guidance of the Spirit, she had preserved the straight road of faith. Hence it follows that we cannot believe in any other than the Son of God without considering that person to have the disposal of life and death. If the true reason for believing in Christ be that God hath given him authority to forgive sins, whenever faith is rendered to another, that honor which is due to Christ must of necessity be taken from him. This saying refutes also the error of those who imagine that the forgiveness of sins is purchased by charity, for Christ lays down a quite different method, which is that we

embrace by faith the offered mercy. The last clause, *Go in peace,* denotes that inestimable fruit of faith which is so frequently commended in Scripture. It brings *peace* and joy to the consciences and prevents them from being driven hither and thither by uneasiness and alarm.

The Crucifixion

MATTHEW 27:45–56

45Now from the sixth hour there was darkness over the whole land till the ninth hour. 46And about the ninth hour Jesus cried with a loud voice, saying, Eli, Eli, lama sabachthani? that is, My God, my God, why hast thou forsaken me? 47And some of those who were standing by, when they heard it, said, He calleth Elijah. 48And immediately one of them ran, and took a sponge, and filled it with vinegar, and fastened it to a reed, and gave him to drink. 49But others said, Let him alone, let us see if Elijah will come to save him. 50And Jesus having again cried with a loud voice, gave up his spirit. 51And, lo, the veil of the temple was rent in two from the top to the bottom; and the earth

MARK 15:33–41

33But when the sixth hour was come, there was darkness over all the land till the ninth hour. 34And at the ninth hour Jesus cried with a loud voice, saying, Eloi, Eloi, lama sabachthani? which is, when interpreted, My God, my God, why hast thou forsaken me? 35And some of those who were standing by, when they heard it, said, Lo, he calleth for Elijah. 36And someone ran, and filled a sponge with vinegar, and fastened it to a reed, and held it out to him to drink, saying, Let him alone, let us see if Elijah will come to take him down. 37And Jesus, having uttered a loud voice, expired. 38And the veil of the temple was rent in two from the top to the bottom. 39And when the centurion,

LUKE 23:44–49

44Now it was about the sixth hour; and there was darkness over all the land till the ninth hour. 45And the sun was darkened, and the veil of the temple was rent in the midst. 46And Jesus having cried with a loud voice, said, Father into thy hands I commit my spirit. And having said this, he expired. 47And when the centurion saw what happened, he glorified God, saying, Certainly this was a righteous man. 48And all the multitudes who were present at that spectacle, when they saw what was done, returned, smiting their breasts. 49And all his acquaintances, and the women who had followed him from Galilee, stood at a distance, beholding these things.

trembled, and the rocks were split, 52And graves were opened, and many bodies of the saints who had slept arose, 53And came out of their graves, after his resurrection, and came into the holy city and appeared to many. 54Now the centurion, and they who were with him guarding Jesus, when they saw the earthquake, and those things which were done, were exceedingly terrified, saying, Truly this was the Son of God. 55And there were there many women looking on at a distance, who had followed Jesus from Galilee, ministering to him: 56Among whom were Mary Magdalene, and Mary, the mother of James and Joses, and the mother of Zebedee's sons.

who was standing opposite to him, saw that he thus expired after crying aloud, he said, Certainly this man was the Son of God. 40And there were also women looking on from a distance, among whom was Mary Magdalene, and Mary, the mother of James the less and of Joses, and of Salome; 41(Who also, when he was in Galilee, had followed him, and ministered to him), and many others, who had also gone up with him to Jerusalem.

Matthew 27:45. *Now from the sixth hour.* Although in the death of Christ the weakness of the flesh concealed for a short time the glory of the Godhead, and though the Son of God himself was disfigured by shame and contempt, and, as Paul says, *was emptied* (Phil. 2:7), yet the heavenly Father did not cease to distinguish him by some marks, and during his lowest humiliation prepared some indications of his future glory, in order to fortify the minds of the godly against the offense of the cross. Thus the majesty of Christ was attested by the *obscuration of the sun*, by the *earthquake*, by the *splitting* of the *rocks*, and the *rending* of *the veil*, as if heaven and earth were rendering the homage which they owed to their Creator.

But we inquire, in the first place, what was the design of the eclipse of *the sun?* For the fiction of the ancient poets in their tragedies, that the light of the sun is withdrawn from the earth whenever any shocking crime is perpetrated, was intended to express the alarming effects of the anger of God, and this invention unquestionably had its origin in the ordinary feelings of mankind. In accordance with this view, some commentators think that, at the death of Christ, God sent darkness as a mark of detestation, as if God, by bringing darkness over the sun, hid his face from beholding the blackest of all crimes. Others say that when the visible sun was extinguished, it pointed out the death of *the Sun of righteousness.* Others choose to refer it to the blinding of the nation, which followed shortly afterward. For the Jews, by rejecting Christ, as soon as he was removed from among them, were deprived of the light of heavenly doctrine, and nothing was left to them but the darkness of despair.

I rather think that as stupidity had shut the eyes of that people against the light, the *darkness* was intended to arouse them to consider the astonishing design of God in the death of Christ. For if they were not altogether *hardened*, an unusual change of the order of nature must have made a deep impression on their senses, so as to look forward to an approaching renewal of the world. Yet it was a terrific spectacle which was exhibited to them, that they might tremble at the judgment of God. And, indeed, it was an astonishing display of the wrath of God that he did not spare even his only-begotten Son, and was not appeased in any other way than by that price of expiation.

As to the scribes and priests, and a great part of the nation, who paid no attention to the eclipse of the sun, but passed it by with closed eyes, their amazing madness ought to strike us with horror, for they must have been more stupid than brute beasts, who when plainly warned of the severity of the judgment of heaven by such a miracle did not cease to indulge in mockery. But this is the spirit of stupidity and of giddiness with which God intoxicates the reprobate, after having long contended with their malice. Meanwhile, let us learn that when they were bewitched by the enchantments of Satan, the glory of God, however manifest, was afterward hidden from them, or, at least, that their minds were darkened, so that, *seeing they did not see* (Matt. 13:14). But as it was a general admonition, it ought also to be of advantage to us, by informing us that the sacrifice by which we are redeemed was of as much importance as if the sun had fallen from heaven, or if the whole fabric of the world had fallen to pieces, for this will excite in us deeper horror at our sins.

As to the opinion entertained by some who make this eclipse of the sun extend to every quarter of the world, I do not consider it to be probable. For though it was related by one or two authors, still the history of those times attracted so much attention that it was impossible for so remarkable a miracle to be passed over in silence by many other authors who have described minutely events which were not so worthy of being recorded. Besides, if the eclipse had been universal throughout the world, it would have been regarded as natural and would more easily have escaped the notice of men. But when the sun was shining elsewhere, it was a more striking miracle that Judea was covered with *darkness*.

46. *And about the ninth hour Jesus cried.* Though in the *cry* which Christ uttered a power more than human was manifested, yet it was unquestionably drawn from him by intensity of sorrow. And certainly this was his chief conflict, and harder than all the other tortures, that in his anguish he was so far from being soothed by the assistance or favor of his Father, that he felt himself to be in some measure estranged from him. For not only did he offer his body as the price of our reconciliation with God, but in his soul also he endured the punishments due to us, and thus he became, as Isaiah speaks, *a man of sorrows* (53:3). Those interpreters are widely mistaken who, laying aside this part of redemption, attended solely to the outward punishment of the flesh, for in order that Christ might satisfy for us, it was necessary that he should be placed as a guilty person at the judgment seat of God. Now nothing is more dreadful than to feel that God, whose wrath is worse than all deaths, is the Judge. When this temptation was presented to Christ, as if having God opposed to him, he were already devoted to destruction, he was seized with horror, which would have been sufficient to swallow up a hundred times all the

men in the world, but by the amazing power of the Spirit, he achieved the victory. Nor is it by hypocrisy, or by assuming a character, that he complains of having been *forsaken by the Father*. Some allege that he employed this language in compliance with the opinion of the people, but this is an absurd mode of evading the difficulty, for the inward sadness of his soul was so powerful and violent that it forced him to break out into a *cry*. Nor did the redemption which he accomplished consist solely in what was exhibited to the eye (as I stated a little ago), but having undertaken to be our surety, he resolved actually to undergo in our room the judgment of God.

But it appears absurd to say that an expression of despair escaped Christ. The reply is easy. Though the perception of the flesh would have led him to dread destruction, still in his heart faith remained firm, by which he beheld the presence of God, of whose absence he complains. We have explained elsewhere how the divine nature gave way to the weakness of the flesh, so far as was necessary for our salvation, that Christ might accomplish all that was required of the Redeemer. We have likewise pointed out the distinction between the sentiment of nature and the knowledge of faith, and, therefore, the perception of God's estrangement from him, which Christ had, as suggested by natural feeling, did not hinder him from continuing to be assured by faith that God was reconciled to him. This is sufficiently evident from the two clauses of the complaint, for before stating the temptation, he begins by saying that he betakes himself to God as *his God*, and thus by the shield of faith he courageously expels that appearance of *forsaking* which presented itself on the other side. In short, during this fearful torture his faith remained uninjured, so that, while he complained of being forsaken, he still relied on the aid of God as at hand.

That this expression eminently deserves our attention is evident from the circumstance that the Holy Spirit, in order to engrave it more deeply on the memory of men, has chosen to relate it in the Syriac language, for this has the same effect as if he made us hear Christ himself repeating the very words which then proceeded from his mouth. So much the more detestable is the indifference of those who lightly pass by, as a matter of jesting, the deep sadness and fearful trembling which Christ endured. No one who considers that Christ undertook the office of Mediator on the condition of suffering our condemnation, both in his body and in his soul, will think it strange that he maintained a struggle with the sorrows of death, as if an offended God had thrown him into a whirlpool of afflictions.

47. *He calleth Elijah.* Those who consider this as spoken by the soldiers, ignorant and unskilled in the Syriac language, and unacquainted with the Jewish religion, and who imagine that the soldiers blundered through a resemblance of the words, are, in my opinion, mistaken. I do not think it at all probable that they erred through ignorance, but rather that they deliberately intended to mock Christ and to turn his prayer into an occasion of slander. For Satan has no method more effectual for ruining the salvation of the godly than by dissuading them from calling on God. For this reason, he employs his agents to drive off from us, as far as he can, the desire to pray. Thus he impelled the wicked enemies of Christ basely to turn his prayer into derision, intending by this stratagem to strip him of his chief armor. And certainly it is a very grievous temptation, when prayer appears to be so far from yielding any advantage to us, that God exposes his name to reproaches instead of lending a gracious ear to our prayers. This ironical language, therefore—or rather this barking of dogs—amounts to saying that Christ has no access to God, because, by imploring *Elijah*, he seeks relief in another quarter. Thus we see that he was tortured on every hand, in order that, overwhelmed with despair, he might abstain from calling on God, which was, to abandon salvation. But if they hired brawlers of Antichrist, as well as wicked men existing in the Church, are now found to pervert basely by their calumnies what has been properly said by us, let us not wonder that the same thing should happen to our Head. Yet though they may change *God* into *Elijah*, when they have ridiculed us to their heart's content, God will at length listen to our groanings, and will show that he vindicates his glory and punishes base falsehood.

48. *And immediately one ran.* As Christ had once refused to drink, it may be conjectured with probability that it was repeatedly offered to him for the sake of annoyance, though it is also not improbable that *the vinegar* was held out to him in a cup before he

was raised aloft, and that *a sponge* was afterward applied to his mouth while he was hanging on the cross.

Mark 15:36. *Saying, Let him alone, let us see if Elijah will come to save him.* Mark relates these words as having been spoken by the soldier, while holding out the vinegar, but Matthew tells us that others used the same language. There is no inconsistency here, however, for it is probable that the jeering was begun by one person, but was eagerly seized by others and loudly uttered by the multitude. The phrase, *let him alone*, appears to have implied not restraint, but ridicule; accordingly, the person who first mocked Christ, ironically addressing his companions, says, *Let us see if Elijah will come.* Others quickly followed, and everyone sung the same song to his next neighbor, as usually happens with men who are agreed about any course. Nor is it of any importance to inquire if it was in the singular or plural number, for in either case the meaning is the same, the word being used in place of an interjection, as if they had said, *Hush! Hush!*

Matthew 27:50. *Jesus having again cried with a loud voice.* Luke, who makes no mention of the former complaint, repeats the words of this second *cry*, which Matthew and Mark leave out. He says that Jesus cried, *Father, into thy hands I commit my spirit,* by which he declared that though he was fiercely attacked by violent temptations, still his faith was unshaken and always kept its ground unvanquished. For there could not have been a more splendid triumph than when Christ boldly expresses his assurance that God is the faithful guardian of his soul, which all imagined to be lost. But instead of speaking to the deaf, he betook himself directly to God and committed to his bosom the assurance of his confidence. He wished, indeed, that men should hear what he said, but though it might be of no avail to men, he was satisfied with having God alone as his witness. And certainly there is not a stronger or more decided testimony of faith than when a pious man—perceiving himself attacked on every hand so that he finds no consolation on the part of men—despises the madness of the whole world, discharges his sorrows and cares into the bosom of God, and rests in the hope of his promises.

Though this form of prayer appears to be borrowed from Psalm 31:5, yet I have no doubt that he applied it to his immediate object, according to present circumstances, as if he had said, "I see, indeed, O Father, that by the universal voice I am destined to destruction, and that *my soul* is, so to speak, hurried to and fro; but though, according to the flesh, I perceive no assistance in thee, yet this will not hinder me from committing my spirit into thy hands and calmly relying on the hidden safeguard of thy goodness." Yet it ought to be observed that David, in the passage which I have quoted, not only prayed that his soul, received by the hand of God, might continue to be safe and happy after death, but committed his life to the Lord, that, guarded by his protection, he might prosper both in life and in death. He saw himself continually besieged by many deaths; nothing, therefore, remained but to commit himself to the invincible protection of God. Having made God the guardian of his soul, he rejoices that it is safe from all danger, and, at the same time, prepares to meet death with confidence, whenever it shall please God, because the Lord guards the souls of his people even in death. Now as the former was taken away from Christ, to commit his soul to be protected by the Father during the frail condition of the earthly life, he hastens cheerfully to death and desires to be preserved beyond the world, for the chief reason why God receives our souls into his keeping is that our faith may rise beyond this transitory life.

Let us now remember that it was not in reference to himself alone that Christ committed his soul to the Father, but that he included, as it were, in one bundle all the souls of those who believe in him, that they may be preserved along with his own, and not only so, but by this prayer he obtained authority to save all souls, so that not only does the heavenly Father, for his sake, deign to take them into his custody, but, giving up the authority into his hands, commits them to him to be protected. And therefore Stephen also, when dying, resigns his soul into his hands, saying, *Lord Jesus, receive my spirit* (Acts 7:59). Everyone who, when he comes to die, following this example, shall believe in Christ, will not breathe his soul at random into the air, but will resort to a faithful guardian, who keeps in safety whatever has been delivered to him by the Father.

The *cry* shows also the intensity of the feeling, for there can be no doubt that Christ, out of the sharpness of the temptations by which he was beset, not without a painful and strenuous effort, broke out into this *cry*. And yet he likewise intended, by this loud and piercing exclamation, to assure us that his soul would be safe and uninjured by death, in order that we, supported by the same confidence, may cheerfully depart from the frail hovel of our flesh.

51. *And, lo, the veil of the temple was rent.* When Luke blends *the rending of the veil* with the eclipse of the sun, he inverts the order, for the evangelists, as we have frequently seen, are not careful to mark every hour with exactness. Nor was it proper that the *veil* should be *rent* until the sacrifice of expiation had been completed, for then Christ, the true and everlasting Priest, having abolished the figures of the law, opened up for us by his blood the way to the heavenly sanctuary that we may no longer stand at a distance within the porch, but may freely advance into the presence of God. For so long as the shadowy worship lasted, a *veil* was hung up before the earthly sanctuary, in order to keep the people not only from entering but from seeing it (Exod. 26:33; 2 Chron. 3:14). Now Christ, by *blotting out the handwriting which was opposed to us* (Col. 2:14), removed every obstruction, that, relying on him as Mediator, we may all be *a royal priesthood* (1 Pet. 2:9). Thus the *rending* of the *veil* was not only an abrogation of the ceremonies which existed under the law, but *was*, in some respects, an opening of heaven, that God may now invite the members of his Son to approach him with familiarity.

Meanwhile, the *Jews* were informed that the period of abolishing outward sacrifices had arrived, and that the ancient priesthood would be of no further use; that though the building of the temple was left standing, it would not be necessary to worship God there after the ancient custom; but that since the substance and truth of the shadows had been fulfilled, the figures of the law were changed into spirit. For though Christ offered a visible sacrifice, yet, as the apostle tells us (Heb. 9:14), it must be viewed spiritually, that we may enjoy its value and its fruit. But it was of no advantage to those wretched men that the outward sanctuary was laid bare by *the rending of the veil*, because the inward *veil* of unbelief, which was in their hearts, hindered them from beholding the saving light.

And the earth trembled, and the rocks were split. What Matthew adds about the earthquake and the *splitting of the rocks*, I think it probable, took place at the same time. In this way not only did the earth bear the testimony to its Creator, but it was even called as a witness against the hard-heartedness of a perverse nation, for it showed how monstrous that obstinacy must have been on which neither the *earthquake* nor *the splitting of the rocks* made any impression.

52. *And graves were opened.* This was also a striking miracle, by which God declared that his Son entered into the prison of death, not to continue to be shut up there, but to bring out all who were held captive. For at the very time when the despicable weakness of the flesh was beheld in the person of Christ, the magnificent and divine energy of his death penetrated even to hell. This is the reason why, when he was about to be shut up in a sepulchre, other sepulchres *were opened* by him. Yet it is doubtful if this *opening of the graves* took place before his resurrection, for, in my opinion, *the resurrection of the saints*, which is mentioned immediately afterward, was subsequent to the resurrection of Christ. There is no probability in the conjecture of some commentators that, after having received life and breath, they remained three days concealed in their graves. I think it more probable that, when Christ died, the *graves* were immediately *opened*, and that when he rose, some of the godly, having received life, *went out of their graves, and were seen* in the city. For Christ is called *the firstborn from the dead* (Col. 1:18), and *the firstfruits of those who rise* (1 Cor. 15:20), because by his death he commenced, and by his resurrection he completed, a new life; not that when he died the dead were immediately raised, but because his death was the source and commencement of life. This reason, therefore, is fully applicable, since the opening of the graves was the presage of a new life, that the fruit or result appeared three days afterward, because Christ, in rising from the dead, brought others along with him out of their graves as his companions. Now by this sign it was made evident, that he neither died nor rose again in a private capacity, but in order to shed the odor of life on all believers.

But here a question arises. Why did God determine that only some should arise, since a participation in the resurrection of Christ belongs equally to all believers? I reply: As the time was not fully come when the whole body of the Church should be gathered to its Head, he exhibited in a few persons an instance of the new life which all ought to expect. For we know that Christ was received into heaven on the condition that the *life* of his members should still *be hid* (Col. 3:3), until it should be manifested by his coming. But in order that the minds of believers might be more quickly raised to hope, it was advantageous that the resurrection, which was to be common to all of them, should be tasted by a few.

Another and more difficult question is, what became of those saints afterward? For it would appear to be absurd to suppose that after having been once admitted by Christ to the participation of a new life, they again returned to dust. But as this question cannot be easily or quickly answered, so it is not necessary to give ourselves much uneasiness about a matter which is not necessary to be known. That they continued long to converse with men is not probable, for it was only necessary that they should be *seen* for a short time, that in them, as in a mirror or resemblance, the power of Christ might plainly appear. As God intended, by their persons, to confirm the hope of the heavenly life among those who were then alive, there would be no absurdity in saying that, after having performed this office, they again rested in their graves. But it is more probable that the life which they received was not afterward taken from them, for if it had been a mortal life, it would not have been a proof of a perfect resurrection. Now, though the whole world will rise again, and though Christ will raise up the wicked to judgment, as well as believers to salvation, yet as it was especially for the benefit of his Church that he rose again, so it was proper that he should bestow on none but *saints* the distinguished honor of rising along with him.

53. *And went into the holy city.* When Matthew bestows on Jerusalem the honorable designation of *the holy city*, he does not intend to applaud the character of its inhabitants, for we know that it was at that time full of all pollution and wickedness, so that it was rather *a den of robbers* (Jer. 7:11). But as it had been chosen by God, its *holiness*, which was founded on God's adoption, could not be effaced by any corruptions of men, till its rejection was openly declared. Or, to express it more briefly, on the part of man it was profane, and on the part of God it was *holy*, till the destruction or pollution of the temple, which happened not long after the crucifixion of Christ.

54. *Now the centurion.* As Luke mentions the *lamentation* of the people, *the centurion* and his soldiers were not the only persons

who acknowledged Christ to be *the Son of God*, but the evangelists mention this circumstance respecting him for the purpose of
heightening their description, for it is wonderful that an irreligious man, who had not been instructed in the Law and was ignorant of true religion, should form so correct a judgment from the
signs which he beheld. This comparison tends powerfully to condemn the stupidity of the city, for it was an evidence of shocking
madness that when the fabric of the world *shook and trembled*,
none of the Jews were affected by it except the despised rab-
ble. And yet, amid such gross blindness, God did not permit the
testimonies which he gave respecting his Son to be buried in
silence. Not only, therefore, did true religion open the eyes of
devout worshippers of God to perceive that from heaven God was
magnifying the glory of Christ, but natural understanding compelled foreigners, and even soldiers, to confess what they had not
learned either from the law or from any instructor.

When Mark says that *the centurion* spoke thus, because Christ,
when he had uttered a loud voice, expired, some commentators think
that he intends to point out the unwonted strength which remained
unimpaired till death; and certainly, as the body of Christ was
almost exhausted of blood, it could not happen, in the ordinary
course of things, that the sides and the lungs should retain sufficient rigor for uttering so loud a cry. Yet I rather think that
the centurion intended to applaud the unshaken perseverance of
Christ in calling on the name of God. Nor was it merely the cry
of Christ that led the centurion to think so highly of him, but this
confession was extorted from him by perceiving that his extraordinary strength harmonized with heavenly miracles.

The words, *he feared God*, must not be so explained as if he had
fully repented. It was only a sudden and transitory impulse, as it
frequently happens, that men who are thoughtless and devoted to
the world are struck with the fear of God, when he makes an
alarming display of his power, but as they have no living root,
indifference quickly follows and puts an end to that feeling. The
centurion had not undergone such a change as to dedicate himself
to God for the remainder of his life, but was only for a moment the
herald of the divinity of Christ.

When Luke represents him as saying no more than *certainly this
was a righteous man*, the meaning is the same as if he had plainly

said that he was *the Son of God*, as it is expressed by the other two evangelists. For it had been universally reported that Christ was put to death, because he declared himself to be the Son of God. Now when the centurion bestows on him the praise of *righteousness*, and pronounces him to be innocent, he likewise acknowledges him to be *the Son of God*; not that he understood distinctly how Christ was begotten by God the Father, but because he entertains no doubt that there is some divinity in him, and, convinced by proofs, holds it to be certain that Christ was not an ordinary man, but had been raised up by God.

As to *the multitudes*, by *striking their breasts*, they expressed the dread of punishment for a public crime, because they felt that public guilt had been contracted by an unjust and shocking murder. But as they went no further, their lamentation was of no avail, unless, perhaps, in some persons it was the commencement or preparation of true repentance. And since nothing more is described to us than the lamentation which God drew from them to the glory of his Son, let us learn by this example that it is of little importance, or of no importance at all, if a man is struck with terror when he sees before his eyes the power of God, until, after the astonishment has been abated, the fear of God remains calmly in his heart.

55. *And there were also many women there.* I consider this to have been added in order to inform us that while the disciples had fled and were scattered in every direction, still some of their company were retained by the Lord as witnesses. Now though the Apostle John did not depart from the cross, yet no mention is made of him, but praise is bestowed on *the women* alone, who accompanied Christ till death, because their extraordinary attachment to their Master was the more strikingly displayed when the men fled trembling. For they must have been endued with extraordinary strength of attachment, since, though they could render him no service, they did not cease to treat him with reverence, even when exposed to the lowest disgrace. And yet we learn from Luke that all the men had not fled, for he says that *all his acquaintances stood at a distance.* But not without reason do the evangelists bestow the chief praise on the women, for they deserved the preference above the men. In my opinion, the implied contrast suggests a severe reproof of the apostles. I speak of the great body of them, for since

only one remained, the three evangelists, as I mentioned a little ago, take no notice of him. It was in the highest degree disgraceful to chosen witnesses to withdraw from that spectacle on which depended the salvation of the world. Accordingly, when they afterward proclaimed the Gospel, they must have borrowed from *women* the chief portion of the history. But if a remedy had not been miraculously prepared by Providence against a great evil, they would have deprived themselves, and us along with them, of the knowledge of redemption.

At first sight, we might think that the testimony of the women does not possess equal authority, but if we duly consider by what power of the Spirit they were supported against that temptation, we shall find that there is no reason why our faith should waver, since it rests on God, who is the real Author of their testimony. Yet let us observe that it proceeded from the inconceivable goodness of God, that even to us should come that Gospel which speaks of the expiation by which God has been reconciled to us. For during the general desertion of those who ought to have run before others, God encouraged some, out of the midst of the flock, who, recovering from the alarm, should be witnesses to us of that history, without the belief of which we cannot be saved. Of the women themselves, we shall presently have another opportunity of saying something. At present, it may be sufficient to take a passing notice of one point, that their eagerness for instruction led them to withdraw from their country and constantly to learn from the lips of Christ, and that they spared neither toil nor money, provided that they might enjoy his saving doctrine.

The Women at the Tomb of Jesus

MATTHEW 28:1-7	MARK 16:1-7	LUKE 24:1-8

¹Now in the evening of the Sabbaths, which began to dawn toward the first of the Sabbaths, came Mary Magdalene, and the other Mary, to see the sepulchre. ²And lo, there was a great earthquake; for the angel of the Lord came down from heaven, and approached, and rolled away the stone from the door, and sat upon it. ³And his countenance was like lightning, and his raiment was white as snow. ⁴And through fear of him the guards trembled, and became as dead men. ⁵But the angel answering, said to the women, Fear not; for I know that you seek Jesus, who was crucified. ⁶He is not here; for he is risen, as he said. Come, see the place where the Lord lay: ⁷And go

¹And when the Sabbath was past, Mary Magdalene, and Mary, the wife of James, and Salome, bought spices to come and anoint him. ²And very early in the morning of the first day of the Sabbaths, They came to the tomb at the rising of the sun. ³And they said among themselves, Who shall roll away the stone for us from the door of the tomb? ⁴And having looked, they saw that the stone was rolled away; for it was very great. ⁵And entering the tomb, they saw a young man sitting on the right side, clothed in a white robe; and they were afraid. ⁶But he saith to them, Be not terrified: you seek Jesus of Nazareth, who was crucified; he is risen, he is not here: lo, the

¹And on the first day of the Sabbaths, very early in the morning, they came to the tomb, carrying the spices which they had prepared, and some women with them. ²And they found the stone rolled away from the tomb. ³And having entered, they found not the body of the Lord Jesus. ⁴And it happened, while they were in consternation on this account, lo, two men stood near them in shining garments. ⁵And when the women were terrified, and bowed their face to the earth, they said to them, Why do you seek the living among the dead? ⁶He is not here, but is risen: remember how he told you, while he was still in Galilee, ⁷Saying, that the

quickly, and tell his disciples that he is risen from the dead; and, lo, he goeth before you into Galilee; there shall you see him: lo, I have told you. ⁷But go away, tell his disciples and Peter, that he goeth before you into Galilee; there shall you see him, as he said to you. Son of man must be delivered into the hands of the wicked men, and be crucified and rise again on the third day. ⁸And they remembered his words.

We now come to the closing scene of our redemption. For the lively assurance of our reconciliation with God arises from Christ having come from hell as the conqueror of death, in order to show that he had the power of a new life at his disposal. Justly, therefore, does Paul say that there will be no Gospel, and that the hope of salvation will be vain and fruitless, unless we believe that *Christ is risen from the dead* (1 Cor. 15:14). For then did Christ obtain righteousness for us, and open up our entrance into heaven; and, in short, then was our adoption ratified, when Christ, by rising from the dead, exerted the power of his Spirit and proved himself to be the Son of God. Nor though he manifested his resurrection in a different manner from what the sense of our flesh would have desired, still the method of which he approved ought to be regarded by us also as the best. He went out of the grave without a witness, that the emptiness of the place might be the earliest indication; next, he chose to have it announced to the women by the angels that he was alive; and shortly afterward he appeared to the women; and, finally, to the apostles, and on various occasions.

Thus he gradually brought his followers, according to their capacity, to a larger measure of knowledge. He began with *the women*, and not only presented himself to be seen by them, but even gave them a commission to announce the Gospel to the apostles, so as to become their instructors. This was intended, first, to chastise the indifference of the apostles, who were like persons half-dead with fear, while the women ran with alacrity to the sepulchre, and likewise obtained no ordinary reward. For though their design to anoint Christ, as if he were still dead, was not free from blame, still he forgave their weakness and bestowed on them distinguished honor by taking away from men the apostolic office and committing it to them for a short time. In this manner also he exhibited an instance of what Paul tells us, that he *chooses those things which are foolish and weak in the world* to abase the loftiness of the flesh. And never shall we be duly prepared to learn this article of our faith in any other manner than by laying aside all pride and submitting to receive the testimony of the women. Not that our faith ought to be confined within such narrow limits, but because the Lord, in order to make trial of our faith, determines that we shall become fools before he admits us to a more ample knowledge of his mysteries.

So far as regards the narrative, Matthew says only that *the two Marys came to see the sepulchre*; Mark adds a third, Salome, and says that they *bought spices to anoint the body*; and from Luke we infer that not two or three only, but many women came. But we know that it is customary with the sacred writers, when speaking of a great number, to name but a few of them. It may also be conjectured with probability that Mary Magdalene, with another companion—whether she was sent before or ran forward of her own accord—arrived at the grave before the rest of the women. And this appears to be conveyed by the words of Matthew, that those two women *came for the purpose of seeing*, for without *seeing* Christ, they had no means of anointing him. He says nothing, in the meantime, about the purpose which they had formed of doing honor to him, for the principal object which he had in view was to testify of the resurrection.

But it may be asked, how could this zeal of the women, which was mixed with superstition, be acceptable to God? I have no doubt that the custom of anointing the dead, which they had borrowed from the Fathers, was applied by them to its proper object, which was to draw consolation amid the mourning of death, from the hope of the life to come. I readily acknowledge that they sinned in not immediately raising their minds to that prediction which they had heard from the lips of their Master, when he foretold that he would rise again on the third day. But as they retain the general principle of the final resurrection, that defect is forgiven, which would justly have vitiated, as the phrase is, the whole of the action. Thus God frequently accepts, with fatherly kindness, the works of the saints, which, without pardon, not only would not have pleased him, but would even have been justly rejected with shame and punishment. It is, there-

fore, an astonishing display of the goodness of Christ that he
kindly and generously presents himself alive to the women, who
did him wrong in seeking him among the dead. Now if he did not
permit them to come in vain to his grave, we may conclude with
certainty that those who now aspire to him by faith will not be disappointed, for the distance of places does not prevent believers
from enjoying him who fills heaven and earth by the power of his
Spirit.

Mark 16:1. *And when the Sabbath was past.* The meaning is the
same as in Matthew, *In the evening, which began to dawn toward the
first day of the Sabbaths,* and in Luke, on *the first day of the Sabbaths.*
For while we know that the Jews began to reckon their day from
the commencement of the preceding night, everybody understands that when the Sabbath was past, the women resolved
among themselves to visit the sepulchre, so as to come there before
the dawn of day. The two evangelists give the name of *the first
day of the Sabbaths* to that which came first in order between
two Sabbaths. Some of the Latin translators have rendered it *one*
and many have been led into this blunder through ignorance
of the Hebrew language, for though (אחד) sometimes means
one, and sometimes *first*, the evangelists, as in many other passages, have followed the Hebrew idiom and used the word μίαν,
one. But that no one may be led astray by the ambiguity, I have
stated their meaning more clearly. As to *the purchase of the spices*,
Luke's narrative differs, in some respects, from the words of
Mark, for Luke says that they *returned* into the city, and *procured
spices, and then rested* one day, *according to the commandment of the
law* before pursuing their journey. But Mark, in introducing into
the same part of the narrative two different events, attends less
accurately than Luke to the distinction of dates, for he blends
with their setting out on the journey what had been previously
done. In the substance of the fact they perfectly agree that the
women, after having observed the holy rest, left home during the
darkness of the night that they might reach the sepulchre about
the break of day.

We ought also to recollect what I have formerly suggested, that
the custom of anointing the dead, though it was common among
many heathen nations, was applied to a lawful use by the Jews

alone, to whom it had been handed down by the Fathers, to confirm them in the faith of the resurrection. For without having this object in view, to embalm a dead body, which has no feeling, would be an idle and empty solace, as we know that the Egyptians bestowed great labor and anxiety on this point, without looking for any advantage. But by this sacred symbol, God represented to the Jews the image of life in death, to lead them to expect that out of putrefaction and dust they would one day acquire new vigor. Now as the resurrection of Christ, by its quickening vigor, penetrated every sepulchre, so as to breathe life into the dead, so it abolished those outward ceremonies. For himself, he needed not those aids, but they were owing to the ignorance of the women, who were not yet fully aware that he was free from corruption.

3. *And they said among themselves.* Mark alone expresses this doubt, but as the other evangelists relate that *the stone was rolled away by the angel*, it may easily be inferred that they remained in perplexity and doubt as to what they should do, until the entrance was opened up by the hand of God. But let us learn from this that in consequence of having been carried away by their zeal, they came there without due consideration. They had seen *a stone* placed before the sepulchre, to hinder anyone from entering. Why did not this occur to them, when they were at home and at leisure, but because they were seized with such fear and astonishment, that thought and recollection failed them? But as it is a holy zeal that blinds them, God does not charge them with this fault.

Matthew 28:2. *And, lo, a great earthquake.* By many signs the Lord showed the presence of his glory, that he might more fully prepare the hearts of the holy women to reverence the mystery. For since it was not a matter of little consequence to know that the Son of God had obtained a victory over death (on which the principal point of our salvation is founded), it was necessary to remove all doubts, that the divine majesty might be openly and manifestly presented to the eyes of the women. Matthew says, therefore, that *there was an earthquake*, by which the divine power which I have mentioned might be perceived. And by this prodigy, it was proper that the women should be allowed to expect nothing human or earthly, but to raise their minds to a work of God which was new and surpassed the expectations of men.

The *raiment* and *the countenance* of the angel, too, might be said to be rays by which the splendor of Godhead was diffused, so as to enable them to perceive that it was not a mortal man that stood near them, having the face of a man. For though *dazzling light* or *the whiteness of snow* is nothing in comparison to the boundless glory of God, but rather, if we wish to know him aright, we ought not to imagine to ourselves any color; yet when he makes known by outward signs that he is present, he invites us to him, as far as our weakness can endure. Still we ought to know that the visible signs of his presence are exhibited to us that our minds may conceive of him as invisible, and that, under bodily forms, we obtain a taste of his spiritual essence, that we may seek him spiritually. Yet it cannot be doubted that, together with outward signs, there was an inward power, which engraved on the hearts of the women an impression of Deity. For though at first they were struck with amazement, yet it will appear, from what follows, that they gathered courage and were gradually instructed in such a manner that they perceived the hand of God to be present.

Our three evangelists, from a desire of brevity, leave out what is more fully related by John (20:1–12), which, we know, is not unusual with them. There is also this difference, that Matthew and Mark mention but *one angel*, while John and Luke speak of *two.* But this apparent contradiction also is easily removed, for we know how frequently in Scripture instances occur of that figure of speech by which a part is taken for the whole. There were *two angels*, therefore, who appeared first to Mary and afterward to her other companions, but as the attention of the women was chiefly directed to the angel who spoke, Matthew and Mark have satisfied themselves with relating his message. Besides, when Matthew says that *the angel sat on a stone*, there is in his words (νστερον προτερον), *an inversion of the order of events*, or at least that order was disregarded by him, for *the angel* did not immediately appear, but while the women were held in suspense and anxiety by an event so strange and astonishing.

4. *Through fear the guards trembled.* The Lord struck *the guards* with *terror*, as if he had engraved their consciences with a hot iron,

so as to constrain them reluctantly to feel his divine power. The *terror* had, at least, the effect of hindering them from treating with careless mockery the report of the resurrection which was to be spread abroad shortly afterward. For though they were not ashamed of prostituting their tongues for him, still they were compelled, whether they would or not, to acknowledge inwardly what they wickedly denied before men. Nor can it be doubted that when they were at liberty to talk freely among their acquaintances, they frankly admitted what they dare not openly avow, in consequence of having been gained over by money.

We must attend to the distinction between the two kinds of *terror*, between which Matthew draws a comparison. The soldiers, who were accustomed to tumults, were terrified, and were so completely overwhelmed by alarm, that they fell down like men who were almost dead, but no power was exerted to raise them from that condition. A similar terror seized the women, but their minds, which had nearly given way, were restored by the consolation which immediately followed, so as to begin, at least, to entertain some better hope. And, certainly, it is proper that the majesty of God should strike both terror and fear indiscriminately into the godly, as well as the reprobate, that all flesh may be silent before his face. But when the Lord has humbled and subdued his elect, he immediately mitigates their dread, that they may not sink under its oppressive influence, and not only so, but by the sweetness of his grace heals the wound which he had inflicted. The reprobate, on the other hand, he either overwhelms by sudden dread or suffers to languish in slow torments. As to the soldiers themselves, they were, no doubt, *like dead* men, but without any serious impression. Like men in a state of insensibility, they tremble, indeed, for a moment, but presently forget that they were afraid; not that the remembrance of their terror was wholly obliterated, but because that lively and powerful apprehension of the power of God, to which they were compelled to yield, soon passed away from them. But we ought chiefly to attend to this point, that though they, as well as the women, were afraid, no medicine was applied to soothe their terror, for to the women only did the angel say, *Fear not.* He held out to them a ground of joy and assurance in the resurrection of Christ. Luke adds a reproof,

Why do you seek the living among the dead? as if the angel pulled their ear that they might no longer remain in sluggishness and despair.

7. *And go quickly, and tell his disciples.* Here God, by the angel, confers extraordinary honor on the women by enjoining them to proclaim to the apostles themselves the chief point of our salvation. In Mark's account of it, they are expressly enjoined to carry this message to Peter, not because he was at that time higher in rank than the others, but because his crime, which was so disgraceful, needed peculiar consolation to assure him that Christ had not cast him off, though he had basely and wickedly fallen. He had already entered into the sepulchre, and beheld the traces of the resurrection of Christ, but God denied him the honor, which he shortly afterward conferred on the women, of hearing from the lips of the angel that Christ *was risen.* And, indeed, the great insensibility under which he still labored is evident from the fact that he again fled trembling to conceal himself, as if he had seen nothing, while Mary sat down to weep at the grave. It cannot be doubted, therefore, that she and her companions, in beholding the angel, obtained the reward of their patience.

And, lo, he goeth before you into Galilee. When the angel sent the disciples *into Galilee*, he did so, I think, in order that Christ might make himself known to a great number of persons, for we know that he had lived a long time in Galilee. He intended also to give his followers greater liberty, that by the very circumstance of their retirement, they might gradually acquire courage. Besides, by being accustomed to the places, they were aided in recognizing their Master with greater certainty, for it was proper to adopt every method of confirming them, that nothing might be wanting to complete the certainty of their faith.

Lo, I have told you. By this manner of speaking the angel earnestly assures them that what is said is true. He states this, not as from himself, as if he had been the first to suggest it, but gives his signature to the promise of Christ, and, therefore, in Mark's account of it, he merely recalls to their remembrance the very words of Christ. Luke carries out the address still further by saying that the disciples were informed by Christ *that he must be crucified, and rise again on the third day.* But the meaning is the same, for along with his resurrection he had foretold his death. He then adds—

Luke 24:8. *And they remembered his words,* by which we are taught that, though they had made little proficiency in the doctrine of Christ, still it was not lost, but was choked up, until in due time it yielded fruit.

"If you love me, keep my commandments."

¹⁵If you love me, keep my commandments. ¹⁶And I will pray to the Father, and he will give you another Comforter, that he may abide with you forever; ¹⁷The Spirit of truth, whom the world cannot receive, because it seeth him not, and knoweth him not; but you know him; for he dwelleth with you, and shall be in you. ¹⁸I will not leave you orphans; I come to you.

15. *If you love me.* The *love* with which the disciples *loved* Christ was true and sincere, and yet there was some superstition mixed with it, as is frequently the case with ourselves, for it was very foolish in them to wish to keep him in the world. To correct this fault, he bids them direct their love to another end, and that is, to employ themselves in *keeping the commandments* which he had given them. This is undoubtedly a useful doctrine, for of those who think that they *love* Christ, there are very few who honor him as they ought to do, but, on the contrary, after having performed small and trivial services, they give themselves no further concern. The true *love* of Christ, on the other hand, is regulated by the observation of his doctrine as the only rule. But we are likewise reminded how sinful our affections are, since even the love which we bear to Christ is not without fault, if it be not directed to a pure obedience.

16. *And I will pray to the Father.* This was given as a remedy for soothing the grief which they might feel on account of Christ's absence, but at the same time, Christ promises that he will give them strength *to keep his commandments*, for otherwise the exhortation would have had little effect. He therefore loses no time in informing them that though he be absent from them in body, yet he will never allow them to remain destitute of assistance, for he will be present with them by his Spirit.

Here he calls the Spirit the gift of *the Father*, but a gift which he will obtain by his prayers; in another passage he promises that he will give the Spirit. *If I depart,* says he, *I will send Him to you*

(John 16:7). Both statements are true and correct, for insofar as Christ is our Mediator and Intercessor, he obtains from *the Father* the grace of the Spirit, but insofar as he is God, he bestows that grace from himself. The meaning of this passage therefore is: "I was given to you by *the Father* to be *a Comforter*, but only for a time; now, having discharged my office, I will pray to him to give another *Comforter*, who will not be for a short time, but will remain always with you."

And he will give you another Comforter. The word *Comforter* is here applied both to Christ and to the Spirit, and justly, for it is an office which belongs equally to both of them, to *comfort* and exhort us, and to guard us by their protection. Christ was the Protector of his disciples, so long as he dwelt in the world, and afterward he committed them to the protection and guardianship of the Spirit. It may be asked, are we not still under the protection of Christ? The answer is easy. Christ is a continual Protector, but not in a visible way. So long as he dwelt in the world, he openly manifested himself as their Protector, but now he guards us by his Spirit.

He calls the Spirit another *Comforter*, on account of the difference between the blessings which we obtain from both. The peculiar office of Christ was to appease the wrath of God by atoning for the sins of the world, to redeem men from death, to procure righteousness and life; and the peculiar office of the Spirit is to make us partakers not only of Christ himself, but of all his blessings. And yet there would be no impropriety in inferring from this passage a distinction of Persons, for there must be some peculiarity in which the Spirit differs from the Son so as to be *another* than the Son.

17. *The Spirit of truth.* Christ bestows on the Spirit another title, namely, that he is the Master or Teacher of truth. Hence it follows that until we have been inwardly instructed by him, the understandings of all of us are seized with vanity and falsehood.

Whom the world cannot receive. This contrast shows the peculiar excellence of that grace which God bestows on none but his elect, for he means that it is no ordinary gift of which the world is deprived. In this sense, too, Isaiah says, *For, the darkness shall cover the earth, and thick darkness the people, but the Lord shall arise on thee, O Jerusalem!* For the mercy of God toward the Church deserves so much the higher praise, when he exalts the Church, by a distinguished privilege, above the whole world. And yet Christ exhorts the disciples that they must not be puffed up, as the world is wont to be, by carnal views, and thus drive away from themselves the grace of the Spirit. All that Scripture tells us about the Holy Spirit is regarded by earthly men as a dream, because trusting to their own reason, they despise heavenly illumination. Now, though this pride abounds everywhere, which extinguishes, so far as lies in our power, the light of the Holy Spirit, yet, conscious of our own poverty, we ought to know that whatever belongs to sound understanding proceeds from no other source. Yet Christ's words show that nothing which relates to the Holy Spirit can be learned by human reason, but that he is known only by the experience of faith.

The world, he says, *cannot receive the Spirit, because it knoweth him not; but you know him, because he dwelleth with you.* It is the Spirit alone therefore, who, by *dwelling in us,* makes himself to be known by us, for otherwise he is unknown and incomprehensible.

18. *I will not leave you orphans.* This passage shows what men are, and what they can do, when they have been deprived of the protection of the Spirit. They are *orphans,* exposed to every kind of fraud and injustice, incapable of governing themselves, and, in short, unable of themselves to do anything. The only remedy for so great a defect is if Christ govern us by his Spirit, which he promises that he will do. First then, the disciples are reminded of their weakness, that, distrusting themselves, they may rely on nothing else than the protection of Christ, and, second, having promised a remedy, he gives them good encouragement, for he declares that he will *never leave them.* When he says, *I will come to you,* he shows in what manner he dwells in his people, and in what manner he fills all things. It is by the power of his Spirit, and hence it is evident that the grace of the Spirit is a striking proof of his Divinity.

God's Righteousness

[16]For I am not ashamed of the gospel of Christ: for it is the power of God unto salvation to every one that believeth; to the Jew first, and also to the Greek. [17]For therein is the righteousness of God revealed from faith to faith: as it is written, The just shall live by faith.*

16. *I am not indeed ashamed*, et cetera. This is an anticipation of an objection, for he declares beforehand that he cared not for the taunts of the ungodly; and he thus provides a way for himself, by which he proceeds to pronounce a eulogy on the value of the Gospel, that it might not appear contemptible to the Romans. He indeed intimates that it was contemptible in the eyes of the world, and he does this by saying that he was not ashamed of it. And thus he prepares them for bearing the reproach of the cross of Christ, lest they should esteem the Gospel of less value by finding it exposed to the scoffs and reproaches of the ungodly; and, on the other hand, he shows how valuable it was to the faithful. If, in the first place, the power of God ought to be extolled by us, that power shines forth in the Gospel; if, again, the goodness of God deserves to be sought and loved by us, the Gospel is a display of his goodness. It ought then to be reverenced and honored, since veneration is due to God's power, and as it avails to our salvation, it ought to be loved by us.

But observe how much Paul ascribes to the ministry of the word, when he testifies that God thereby puts forth his power to save, for he speaks not here of any secret revelation, but of vocal preaching. It hence follows that those, as it were, willfully despise

---

* This is the Bible verse made central to the Reformation by Martin Luther, who as a monk had struggled with his inability to attain to righteousness by his own efforts. When he finally "solved" this verse—the famous "Tower experience"—he said, "This phrase of Paul was for me the very gate of paradise."

the power of God and drive away from them his delivering hand, who withdraw themselves from the hearing of the word.

At the same time, as he works not effectually in all, but only where the Spirit, the inward Teacher, illuminates the heart, he subjoins, *To every one who believeth.* The Gospel is indeed offered to all for their salvation, but the power of it appears not everywhere: and that it is the savor of death to the ungodly does not proceed from what it is, but from their own wickedness. By setting forth but one Salvation, he cuts off every other trust. When men withdraw themselves from this one salvation, they find in the Gospel a sure proof of their own ruin. Since then the Gospel invites all to partake of salvation without any difference, it is rightly called the doctrine of salvation: for Christ is there offered, whose peculiar office is to save that which was lost; and those who refuse to be saved by him, shall find him a Judge. But everywhere in Scripture the word salvation is simply set in opposition to the word destruction; and hence we must observe, when it is mentioned, what the subject of the discourse is. Since then the Gospel delivers from ruin and the curse of endless death, its salvation is eternal life.

First to the Jew and then to the Greek. Under the word *Greek*, he includes all the Gentiles, as it is evident from the comparison that is made, for the two clauses comprehend all mankind. And it is probable that he chose especially this nation to designate other nations, because, in the first place, it was admitted, next to the Jews, into a participation of the Gospel covenant; and, second, because the Greeks, on account of their vicinity, and the celebrity of their language, were more known to the Jews. It is then a mode of speaking, a part being taken for the whole, by which he connects the Gentiles universally with the Jews, as participators of the Gospel; nor does he thrust the Jews from their own eminence and dignity, since they were the first partakers of God's promise and calling. He then reserves for them their prerogative; but he immediately joins the Gentiles, though in the second place, as being partakers with them.

17. *For the righteousness of God*, and so on. This is an explanation and a confirmation of the preceding clause—that the Gospel is the power of God unto salvation. For if we seek salvation, that is, life with God, righteousness must be first sought, by which being rec-

onciled to him, we may, through him being propitious to us, obtain that life which consists only in his favor; for, in order to be loved by God, we must first become righteous, since he regards unrighteousness with hatred. He therefore intimates that we cannot obtain salvation otherwise than from the Gospel, since nowhere else does God reveal to us his righteousness, which alone delivers us from perdition. Now this righteousness, which is the groundwork of our salvation, is revealed in the Gospel; hence the Gospel is said to be the power of God unto salvation. Thus he reasons from the cause to the effect.

Notice further how extraordinary and valuable a treasure does God bestow on us through the Gospel, even the communication of his own righteousness. I take the righteousness of God to mean that which is approved before his tribunal; as that, on the contrary, is usually called the righteousness of men, which is by men counted and supposed to be righteousness, though it be only vapor. Paul, however, I doubt not, alludes to the many prophecies in which the Spirit makes known everywhere the righteousness of God in the future kingdom of Christ.

Some explain it as the righteousness which is freely given us by God, and I indeed confess that the words will bear this sense; for God justifies us by the Gospel, and thus saves us: yet the former view seems to me more suitable, though it is not what I make much of. Of greater moment is what some think, that this righteousness does not only consist in the free remission of sins, but also, in part, includes the grace of regeneration. But I consider that we are restored to life because God freely reconciles us to himself, as we shall hereafter show in its proper place.

But instead of the expression he used before, *to everyone who believeth*, he says now, *from faith*; for righteousness is offered by the Gospel and is received by faith. And he adds, *to faith*: for as our faith makes progress, and as it advances in knowledge, so the righteousness of God increases in us at the same time, and the possession of it is in a manner confirmed. When at first we taste the Gospel, we indeed see God's smiling countenance turned toward us, but at a distance; the more the knowledge of true religion grows in us, by coming as it were nearer, we behold God's favor more clearly and more familiarly. What some think, that there is here an implied comparison between the Old and New Testament, is more refined than well founded, for Paul does not here compare the Fathers who lived under the law with us, but points out the daily progress that is made by every one of the faithful.

As it is written, et cetera. By the authority of the Prophet Habakkuk he proves the righteousness of faith; for he, predicting the overthrow of the proud, adds this—that the life of the righteous consists in faith. Now we live not before God, except through righteousness; it then follows that our righteousness is obtained by faith, and the verb, being future, designates the real perpetuity of that life of which he speaks, as though he had said that it would not be momentary, but continue forever. For even the ungodly swell with the false notion of having life, but when they say, "Peace and safety," a sudden destruction comes upon them (1 Thess. 5:3). It is therefore a shadow, which endures only for a moment. Faith alone is that which secures the perpetuity of life, and whence is this, except that it leads us to God and makes our life to depend on him? For Paul would not have aptly quoted this testimony had not the meaning of the prophet been that we then only stand, when by faith we repose upon God; and he has not certainly ascribed life to the faith of the godly, but in as far as they, having renounced the arrogance of the world, resign themselves to the protection of God alone.

He does not indeed professedly handle this subject, and hence he makes no mention of gratuitous justification, but it is sufficiently evident from the nature of faith that this testimony is rightly applied to the present subject. Besides, we necessarily gather from his reasoning that there is a mutual connection between faith and the Gospel; for as the just is said to live by faith, he concludes that this life is received by the Gospel.

We have now the principal point or the main hinge of the first part of this Epistle—that we are justified by faith through the mercy of God alone. We have not this, indeed as yet distinctly expressed by Paul, but from his own words it will hereafter be made very clear—that the righteousness, which is grounded on faith, depends entirely on the mercy of God.

Faith and Good Works

¹⁴What *doth it* profit, my brethren, though a man say he hath faith, and have not works? can faith save him? ¹⁵If a brother or sister be naked, and destitute of daily food, ¹⁶And one of you say unto them, Depart in peace, be *ye* warmed and filled; notwithstanding ye give them not those things which are needful to the body; what *doth it* profit? ¹⁷Even so faith, if it hath not works, is dead, being alone. ¹⁸Yea, a man may say, Thou hast faith, and I have works: show me thy faith without thy works, and I will show thee my faith by my works. ¹⁹Thou believest that there is one God; thou doest well: the devils also believe, and tremble. ²⁰But wilt thou know, O vain man, that faith without works is dead? ²¹Was not Abraham our father justified by works, when he had offered Isaac his son upon the altar? ²²Seest thou how faith wrought with his works, and by works was faith made perfect? ²³And the scripture was fulfilled which saith, Abraham believed God, and it was imputed unto him for righteousness: and he was called the Friend of God. ²⁴Ye see then how that by works a man is justified, and not by faith only. ²⁵Likewise also was not Rahab the harlot justified by works, when she had received the messengers, and had sent *them* out another way? ²⁶For as the body without the spirit is dead, so faith without works is dead also.

14. *What doth it profit.* He proceeds to commend mercy. And as he had threatened that God would be a severe Judge to us, and at the same time very dreadful, except we be kind and merciful toward our neighbors, and as on the other hand hypocrites objected and said that faith is sufficient to us, in which the salvation of men consists, he now condemns this vain boasting. The sum, then, of what is said is that faith without love avails nothing, and that it is therefore wholly dead.

But here a question arises: Can faith be separated from love? It is indeed true that the exposition of this passage has produced that common distinction of the Sophists, between unformed and formed faith, but of such a thing James knew nothing, for it appears from the first words that he speaks of false profession of faith, for he does not begin thus, "If anyone has faith," but, "If any says that he has faith," by which he certainly intimates that hypocrites boast of the empty name of faith, which really does not belong to them.

That he calls it then *faith* is a concession, as the rhetoricians say, for when we discuss a point, it does no harm, nay, it is sometimes expedient, to concede to an adversary what he demands, for as soon as the thing itself is known, what is conceded may be easily taken away from him. James then, as he was satisfied that it was a false pretext by which hypocrites covered themselves, was not disposed to raise a dispute about a word or an expression. Let us, however, remember that he does not speak according to the impression of his own mind when he mentions faith, but that on the contrary he disputes against those who made a false pretense as to faith, of which they were wholly destitute.

Can faith save him? This is the same as though he had said that we do not attain salvation by a frigid and bare knowledge of God, which all confess to be most true, for salvation comes to us by faith for this reason, because it joins us to God. And this comes not in any other way than by being united to the body of Christ, so that, living through his Spirit, we are also governed by him. There is no such thing as this in the dead image of faith. There is then no wonder that James denies that salvation is connected with it.

15. *If a brother*, or, *For if a brother*. He takes an example from what was connected with his subject, for he had been exhorting them to exercise the duties of love. If anyone, on the contrary, boasted that he was satisfied with faith without works, he compares this shadowy faith to the saying of one who bids a famished man to be filled without supplying him with the food of which he is destitute. As, then, he who sends away a poor man with words, and offers him no help, treats him with mockery, so they who devise for themselves faith without works and without any of the duties of religion, trifle with God.

17. *Is dead, being alone*. He says that faith is dead, being by itself, that is, when destitute of good works. We hence conclude that it is indeed no faith, for when dead, it does not properly retain the

name. The Sophists plead this expression and say that some sort of faith is found by itself, but this frivolous caviling is easily refuted, for it is sufficiently evident that the apostle reasons from what is impossible, as Paul calls an angel anathema, if he attempted to subvert the Gospel (Gal. 1:8).

18. *Yea, a man may say.* Erasmus introduces here two persons as speakers, one of whom boasts of faith without works and the other of works without faith, and he thinks that both are at length confuted by the apostle. But this view seems to me too forced. He thinks it strange that this should be said by James, *Thou hast faith,* who acknowledges no faith without works. But in this he is much mistaken, that he does not acknowledge an irony in these words. Then αλλα I take for "nay rather" and τις for "anyone," for the design of James was to expose the foolish boasting of those who imagined that they had faith when by their life they showed that they were unbelievers; for he intimates that it would be easy for all the godly who led a holy life to strip hypocrites of that boasting with which they were inflated.

Show me. Though the more received reading is, "by works," yet the old Latin is more suitable, and the reading is also found in some Greek copies. I therefore hesitated not to adopt it. Then he bids to show faith without works and thus reasons from what is impossible to prove what does not exist. So he speaks ironically. But if anyone prefers the other reading, it comes to the same thing, "Show me by works thy faith," for since it is not an idle thing, it must necessarily be proved by works. The meaning then is, "Unless thy faith brings forth fruits, I deny that thou hast any faith."*

---

* This verse is a key to the meaning of James: faith is to be *proved* by works; then faith properly justifies and saves, and works prove its genuineness. When he says that a man is justified by works, the meaning according to this verse is that a man is proved by his works to be justified, his faith thereby being shown to be a living and not a dead faith. We may well be surprised, as Doddridge was, should ever think that any, taking a view of this whole passage, should ever think that there is any contrariety in what is here said to be the teaching of Paul. The doctrine of Paul, that man is justified by faith and not by works, that is, by a living faith, which works by love, is perfectly consistent with what James says, that is, that a man is not justified by a dead faith but by that faith which proves its living power by producing good works, or by rendering obedience to God. The sum of what James says is that a dead faith cannot save, but a living faith, and that a living faith is a working faith—a doctrine taught by Paul as well as by James.

But it may be asked whether the outward uprightness of life is a sure evidence of faith? For James says, *I will show thee my faith by my works*. To this I reply that the unbelieving sometimes excel in specious virtues and lead an honorable life free from every crime, and hence works apparently excellent may exist apart from faith. Nor indeed does James maintain that everyone who seems good possesses faith. This only he means, that faith, without the evidence of good works, is vainly pretended, because fruit ever comes from the living root of a good tree.

19. *Thou believest that there is one God*. From this one sentence it appears evident that the whole dispute is not about faith, but of the common knowledge of God, which can no more connect man with God than the sight of the sun carry him up to heaven, but it is certain that by faith we come nigh to God. Besides, it would be ridiculous were anyone to say that the devils have faith, and James prefers them in this respect to hypocrites. The devil *trembles*, he says, at the mention of God's name, because when he acknowledges his own judge, he is filled with the fear of him. He then who despises an acknowledged God is much worse.

Thou doest well, is put down for the purpose of extenuating, as though he had said, "It is, forsooth! a great thing to sink down below the devils."

20. *But wilt thou know*. We must understand the state of the question, for the dispute here is not respecting the cause of justification, but only what avails a profession of faith without works, and what opinion we are to form of it. Absurdly then do they act who strive to prove by this passage that man is justified by works, because James meant no such thing, for the proofs which he subjoins refer to this declaration, that no faith, or only a dead faith, is without works. No one will ever understand what is said, nor judge wisely of words, except he who keeps in view the design of the writer.

21. *Was not Abraham*. The Sophists lay hold on the word *justified*, and then they cry out as being victorious, that justification is partly by works. But we ought to seek out a right interpretation according to the general drift of the whole passage. We have already said that James does not speak here of the cause of justification, or of the manner how men obtain righteousness, and this is plain to everyone, but that his object was only to show that good

works are always connected with faith; and, therefore, since he declares that Abraham was *justified by works*, he is speaking of the proof he gave of his justification.

When, therefore, the Sophists set up James against Paul, they go astray through the ambiguous meaning of a term. When Paul says that we are justified by faith, he means no other thing than that by faith we are counted righteous before God. But James has quite another thing in view, even to show that he who professes that he has faith, must prove the reality of his faith by his works. Doubtless James did not mean to teach us here the ground on which our hope of salvation ought to rest; and it is this alone that Paul dwells upon.

That we may not then fall into that false reasoning which has deceived the Sophists, we must take notice of the twofold meaning of the word *justified*. Paul means by it the gratuitous imputation of righteousness before the tribunal of God; and James, the manifestation of righteousness by the conduct, and that before men, as we may gather from the preceding words, *Show to me thy faith*, et cetera. In this sense we fully allow that man is justified by works, as when anyone says that a man is enriched by the purchase of a large and valuable chest, because his riches, before hid, shut up in a chest, were thus made known.

22. *By works was faith made perfect.* By this he again shows that the question here is not respecting the cause of our salvation, but whether works necessarily accompany faith, for in this sense it is said to have been perfected by works, because it was not idle. It is said to have been perfected by works, not because it received thence its own perfection, but because it was thus proved to be true. For the futile distinction which the Sophists draw from these words, between formed and unformed faith, needs no labored refutation, for the faith of Abram was formed and therefore perfected before he sacrificed his son. And this work was not as it were the finishing or last work. Formerly things afterward followed by which Abraham proved the increase of his faith. Hence this was not the perfection of his faith, nor did it then for the first time put on its form. James then understood no other thing, than that the integrity of his faith then appeared, because it brought forth that remarkable fruit of obedience.

23. *And the Scripture was fulfilled.* They who seek to prove from

this passage of James that the works of Abraham were imputed for righteousness must necessarily confess that Scripture is perverted by him, for however they may turn and twist, they can never make the effect to be its own cause. The passage is quoted from Moses (Gen. 15:6). The imputation of righteousness which Moses mentions preceded more than thirty years the work by which they would have Abraham to have been justified. Since faith was imputed to Abraham fifteen years before the birth of Isaac, this could not surely have been done through the work of sacrificing him. I consider that all those are bound fast by an indissoluble knot, who imagine that righteousness was imputed to Abraham before God, because he sacrificed his son Isaac, who was not yet born when the Holy Spirit declared that Abraham was justified. It hence necessarily follows that something posterior is pointed out here.

Why then does James say that it was fulfilled? Even because he intended to show what sort of faith that was which justified Abraham; that is, that it was not idle or evanescent, but rendered him obedient to God, as also we find in Hebrews 11:8. The conclusion, which is immediately added, as it depends on this, has no other meaning. Man is not justified by faith alone, that is, by a bare and empty knowledge of God; he is justified by works, that is, his righteousness is known and proved by its fruits.

25. *Likewise also was not Rahab.* It seems strange that he connected together those who were so unlike. Why did he not rather choose someone from so large a number of illustrious Fathers and join him to Abraham? Why did he prefer a harlot to all others? He designedly put together two persons so different in their character in order more clearly to show that no one, whatever may have been his or her condition, nation, or class in society, has ever been counted righteous without good works. He had named the patriarch, by far the most eminent of all; he now includes under the person of a harlot all those who, being aliens, were joined to the Church. Whosoever, then, seeks to be counted righteous, though he may even be among the lowest, must yet show that he is such by good works.

James, according to his manner of speaking, declares that Rahab was justified by works, and the Sophists hence conclude that we obtain righteousness by the merits of works. But we deny that the dispute here is concerning the mode of obtaining righteousness. We, indeed, allow that good works are required for righteousness; we only take away from them the power of conferring righteousness, because they cannot stand before the tribunal of God.

Selected
Prayers and Sermons

PRAYERS*

May the Lord grant that we may engage in contemplating the mysteries of his heavenly wisdom with really increasing devotion, to his glory and to our edification. Amen.
>   —The prayer John Calvin was wont to use at the
>   beginning of his lectures

*   *   *

Grant, Almighty God, that since to a perverse, and in every way a rebellious people, thou didst formerly show so much grace, as to exhort them continually to repentance, and to stretch forth thy hand to them by thy prophets—O grant that the same word may sound in our ears; and when we do not immediately profit by thy teaching, O cast us not away, but, by thy Spirit, so subdue all our thoughts and affections, that we, being humbled, may give glory to thy majesty, such as is due to thee, and that, being allured by thy paternal favor, we may submit ourselves to thee, and at the same time embrace that mercy which thou offerest and presentest to us in Christ, that we may not doubt but thou wilt be a Father to us, until we shall at length enjoy that eternal inheritance, which has been obtained for us by the blood of thine only-begotten Son. Amen.

*   *   *

Grant, Almighty God, that as thou hast made known thy Law, and hast also added thy Gospel, in which thou callest us to thy service, and also invitest us with all kindness to partake of thy grace—O grant that we may not be deaf, either to thy command or to the promises of thy mercy, but render ourselves in both

* The following prayers have been selected from Calvin's commentaries on the Minor Prophets. This selection is only a representative, not a complete, one. In their original setting, these prayers accompanied each lecture of Calvin's running commentary, or *lectio continua*, on the books of the Bible.

instances submissive to thee, and so learn to devote all our faculties to thee, that we may in truth avow that the rule of a holy and religious life has been delivered to us in thy law, and that we may also firmly adhere to thy promises, lest through any of the allurements of the world, or through the flatteries and crafts of Satan, thou shouldst suffer our minds to be drawn away from that love which thou hast once for all manifested to us in thine only-begotten Son, and in which thou daily confirmest us by the teaching of the Gospel, until we at length shall come to the full enjoyment of this love in that celestial inheritance, which has been purchased for us by the blood of thine only Son. Amen.

*   *   *

Grant, Almighty God, that, being warned by so many examples, the record of which thou hast designed to continue to the end of the world, that we may learn how dreadful a judge thou art to the perverse—O grant that we may not, at this day, be deaf to thy teaching, which is conveyed to us by the mouth of thy prophet, but that we may strive to be so reconciled to thee, that, passing by all men, we may present ourselves unreservedly to thee, so that, relying on thy mercy alone which thou hast promised to us in Christ, we may not doubt but thou wilt be propitious to us, and be so touched with the spirit of true penitence, that, if we have been to others a bad example and an offense, we may lead others to the right way of salvation, and each of us may so endeavor to assist our neighbors in a holy life that we may together attain that blessed and celestial life, which thine only-begotten Son has procured for us by his own blood. Amen.

*   *   *

Grant, Almighty God, that as we now carry about us this mortal body, yea, and nourish through sin a thousand deaths within us; O grant that we may ever by faith direct our eyes toward heaven, and to that incomprehensible power, which is to be manifested at the last day by Jesus Christ our Lord, so that in the midst of death we may hope that thou wilt be our Redeemer, and enjoy that redemption which he completed when he rose from the dead, and not doubt that the fruit which he then brought forth by his Spirit will come also to us when Christ himself shall come to judge the world; and may we thus walk in the fear of thy name, that we may be really gathered among his members, to be made partakers of that glory which by his death he has procured for us. Amen.

* * *

Grant, Almighty God, that as thou not only invitest us continually by the voice of thy Gospel to seek thee, but also offerest to us thy Son as our mediator, through whom an access to thee is open, that we may find thee a propitious Father; O grant that relying on thy kind invitation, we may through life exercise ourselves in prayer, and as so many evils disturb us on all sides and so many wants distress and oppress us, may we be led more earnestly to call on thee, and in the meanwhile be never wearied in this exercise of prayer; until having been heard by thee throughout life, we may at length be gathered to thine eternal kingdom where we shall enjoy that salvation which thou hast promised to us, and of which also thou daily testifiest to us by thy Gospel, and be forever united to thine only-begotten Son of whom we are now members; that we may be partakers of all the blessings which he has obtained for us by his death. Amen.

* * *

Grant, Almighty God, that as thou shinest on us by thy word, we may not be blind at midnight, nor willfully seek darkness, and thus lull our minds asleep, but may we be roused daily by thy words, and may we stir up ourselves more and more to fear thy name and thus present ourselves and all our pursuits as a sacrifice to thee, that thou mayest peaceably rule, and perpetually dwell in us, until thou gatherest us to thy celestial habitation, where there is reserved for us eternal rest and glory through Jesus Christ our Lord. Amen.

* * *

Grant, Almighty God, that since under the guidance of thy Son we have been united together in the body of thy Church, which has been so often scattered and torn asunder, O grant that we may continue in the unity of faith and perseveringly fight against all the temptations of this world, and never deviate from the right course, whatever new troubles may daily arise; and though we are exposed to many deaths, let us not be seized with fear, such as may extinguish in our hearts every hope; but may we, on the contrary, learn to raise up our eyes and minds and all our thoughts to thy great power, by which thou quickenest the dead, and raisest from nothing things which are not, so that, though we be daily exposed to ruin, our souls may ever aspire to eternal salvation, until thou at length really showest thyself to be the fountain of life, when we shall enjoy that endless felicity which has been obtained for us by the blood of thine only-begotten Son our Lord. Amen.

Examples of prayers from Calvin's commentary on the prophet Hosea

Grant, Almighty God, that as we were from our beginning lost, when thou wert pleased to extend to us thy hand, and to restore us to salvation for the sake of thy Son; and that as we continue even daily to run headlong to our own ruin—O grant that we may not, by sinning so often, so provoke at length thy displeasure as to cause thee to take away from us the mercy which thou hast hitherto exercised toward us, and through which thou hast adopted us, but by thy Spirit destroy the wickedness of our heart and restore us to a sound mind, that we may ever cleave to thee with a true and sincere heart, that being fortified by thy defense, we may continue safe even amid all kinds of danger, until at length thou gatherest us into that blessed rest, which has been prepared for us in heaven by our Lord Jesus Christ. Amen.

*   *   *

Grant, Almighty God, that as we set up against thee so many obstacles through the depravity of our flesh and natural disposition that we seem as it were to be designedly striving to close up the door against thy goodness and paternal favor, O grant that our hearts may be so softened by thy Spirit, and the hardness which has hitherto prevailed may be so corrected, that we may submit ourselves to thee with genuine docility, especially as thou dost so kindly and tenderly invite us to thyself, that being allured by thy sweet invitation, we may run, and so run as not to be weary in our course, until Christ shall at length bring us together to thee, and, at the same time, lead us to thee for that eternal life, which he has obtained for us by his own blood. Amen.

* * *

Grant, Almighty God, that since thou hast at this time deigned in thy mercy to gather us to thy Church, and to enclose us within the boundaries of thy word, by which thou preserves us in the true and right worship of thy majesty—O grant that we may continue contented in this obedience to thee: and though Satan may, in many ways, attempt to draw us here and there, and we be also ourselves, by nature, inclined to evil, O grant that being confirmed in faith, and united to thee by that sacred bond, we may yet constantly abide under the guidance of thy word, and thus cleave to Christ, thy only-begotten Son, who has joined us forever to himself, that we may never by any means turn aside from thee, but be, on the contrary, confirmed in the faith of his Gospel, until at length he will receive us all into his kingdom. Amen.

* * *

Grant, Almighty God, that as we are prone to every kind of wickedness, and are so easily led away to imitate it, when there is any excuse for going astray and any opportunity is offered— O grant that being strengthened by the help of thy Spirit, we may continue in purity of faith, and that what we have learned concerning thee, that thou art a Spirit, may so profit us, that we may worship thee in spirit and with a sincere heart and never turn aside after the corruptions of the world, nor think that we can deceive thee; but may we so devote our souls and bodies to thee that our life may in every part of it testify that we are a pure and holy sacrifice to thee in Christ Jesus our Lord. Amen.

* * *

Grant, Almighty God, that since thou hast once shone upon us by thy Gospel—O grant that we may always be guided by this light, and so guided, that all our lusts may be restrained; and may the power of thy Spirit extinguish in us every sinful fervor, that we may not grow hot with our own perverse desires, but that all these being subdued, we may gather new fervor daily, that we may breathe after thee more and more, nor let the coldness of our flesh ever take possession of us, but may we continually advance in the way of piety, until at length we come to that blessed rest, to which thou invite us, and which has been obtained for us by the blood of thy only-begotten Son, our Lord Jesus Christ. Amen.

*   *   *

Grant, Almighty God, that inasmuch as thou drawest us at this time to thyself by so many chastisements, while we are yet insensible, through the slothfulness and the indolence of our flesh—O grant that Satan may not thus perpetually harden and fascinate us, but that we, being at length awakened, may feel our evils and be not merely affected by outward punishments, but rouse ourselves and feel how grievously we have in various ways offended thee, so that we may return to thee with real sorrow, and so abhor ourselves that we may seek in thee every delight, until we at length offer to thee a pleasing and acceptable sacrifice, by dedicating ourselves and all we have to thee, in sincerity and truth, through Jesus Christ our Lord. Amen.

*   *   *

Grant, Almighty God, that as thou shinest on us by thy word, we may not be blind at midday, nor willfully seek darkness, and thus lull our minds asleep, but that exercising ourselves in thy word, we may stir up ourselves more and more to fear thy name, and thus present ourselves and all our pursuits, as a sacrifice to thee, that thou mayest peaceably rule and perpetually dwell in us, until thou gatherest us to thy celestial habitation, where there is reserved for us eternal rest and glory, through Jesus Christ our Lord. Amen.

SERMON ON THE FOURTH COMMANDMENT

(FRIDAY, JUNE 21, 1555)

Deuteronomy 5:13–15

¹³Six days thou shalt labor, and do all thy work: ¹⁴But the seventh day is the sabbath of the Lord thy God: in it thou shalt not do any work, thou, nor thy son, nor thy daughter, nor thy manservant, nor thy maidservant, nor thine ox, nor thine ass, nor any of thy cattle, nor thy stranger that is within thy gates; that thy manservant and thy maidservant may rest as well as thou. ¹⁵And remember that thou wast a servant in the land of Egypt, and that the Lord thy God brought thee out thence through a mighty hand and by a stretched out arm: therefore the Lord thy God commanded thee to keep the sabbath day.

Yesterday we discussed how and why the commandment to keep the sabbath day was given to the Jews: (in brief) it was said that it stood as a symbol for spiritual rest which the faithful had to observe in order to worship God. Now insofar as our Lord Jesus Christ has brought us the fulfillment of that, we are no longer obligated to be limited by this shadow of the law, rather let us be satisfied that our old man has been crucified in virtue of the passion and death of our Lord Jesus Christ in order that we might be renewed for the purpose of fully serving our God. But nevertheless we [still] have need of some order and guidance in our midst. Thus it is fitting that we should have a particular day for our assemblage in order that we might be confirmed in the doctrine of God and benefit from it every day, that is to say, for the rest of our life; that we might also be well trained to call upon his name [and] to make a confession of our faith. And in the meantime the remainder of the day should be spent in considering the favors which we receive all the time from God's hand in order that he might be glorified in them that much more.

But now we need to note what is said in Moses' text. *Thou shalt work six days*, says the Lord. This must not be interpreted to mean that God commands us to work. Truly we are [already] born to that [end]. Moreover we know that God does not intend for us to be lazy living in this world for he has given men hands and feet; he has given them industry. And even before the fall, it is said that Adam was placed in a garden in order to tend it. But the work in which men are now engaged is a punishment for sin. For it is pointed out to them: "You will eat your bread by the sweat of your brow; it is a curse which has been placed on all human beings." For we are unworthy of hearing of this condition which [supposedly] belonged to our father, that he could live a life of ease without harming himself. But still before sin had come into the world and we have been condemned by God to painful and forced work, men were already required to engage in some [type of] labor. And why? Because it is contrary to our nature to be like a block of useless wood. Therefore it is certain that we must apply ourselves to some [form of] labor all the days of our life. But the text does not simply command [us] to work six days. For in fact, under the law there were other solemn occasions whose purpose was not rest; there were feasts which certainly came in the middle of the week. But because their number was small, four days out of the year, God did not mention them here; he simply speaks of rest.

And when he says, "Thou shalt work six days," our Lord shows that we must not begrudge giving and dedicating one specific day to him, seeing he has given us six for one. It's as if he were saying: "Is it asking too much of you to choose one day which can be fully reserved for my service in order that you might do nothing else in it but read and practice my law, or at least hear the doctrine which can be preached to you, or come to the church in order that you might be confirmed there by the sacrifices which are offered in it, or to call upon my name and confess that you belong to the company of my people? Is it not fitting that you should do that, seeing that you have six entire free days for taking care of your needs and business affairs? Therefore, when I act with such humanity toward you, asking not for seven but only one day, does it not amount to unacceptable ingratitude when you invest that time as if it were badly employed, or behave parsimoniously toward me over the seventh part of time? I give you all your life; the sun never shines on you but that you ought to be able to recognize my goodness and that I am a generous father toward you. For I cause my sun to shine in order to give you light for your path, in order for each of you to pursue your needs. Therefore why shouldn't I have one day out of seven [in which] each person withdraws from his affairs in order that you might not be enveloped by such worldly solicitude so as to be unable to think of me?" Thus we now see that this statement about working six days was not given as a commandment, but it is rather a permission which God gives in order to reproach men for their ingratitude, unless, as he has indicated, they observe the sabbath day and keep it holy.

Now from this we need to glean a good and useful admonition, that when we are slow to obey God, it is helpful to remember his gracious favors. For what could better stimulate our zeal for following what God commands than the thought that he does not treat us harshly nor excessively crowd us? For God could use a stern check if he pleased. He could restrain us by things so difficult that it would be impossible for us to break free of them. But he prefers to guide us as a father does his children. Seeing then that he so upholds us, shouldn't we be that much more motivated to do what he commands us? Therefore whenever the commandments of God are difficult for us, or seem to be so, let us realize that if he pressed us as much as he could, they would be exceedingly more [difficult]. For if our Lord wanted to exercise his authority to the fullest, we would be harrassed far more. Therefore let us understand that he upholds us and utilizes an infinitely paternal goodness [toward us].

In truth the law of God is impossible for us [to fulfill], let alone keep with perfection, but when a person relying on his own strength wants to acquit himself before God, he cannot lift a finger nor have one single good idea as to how it should be done. In fact, we are so far from being ready to obey God and to do what his law contains, that all our thoughts and affections are at enmity with God. If men were able on their own strength to fulfill the law, he would have said to them: "Work!" But on the contrary he said: "Rest in order that God might work." Thus from our perspective the law may well be impossible to do, but it is possible for God to engrave it upon our hearts and to govern us by his Holy Spirit, indeed, so much so that it will seem like a gentle and light burden to us, involving no hardship which we cannot bear. Thus once men have carefully considered it, they will be convinced that God upholds them like a father who is merciful toward his children. Still let us learn not to be ungrateful and to be exceedingly more motivated to worship our God, [especially] in view of the fact that he does not command us [to do] things which might seem too galling to us, or too painful, but he remembers our frame. That is what we need to note in this passage where our Lord reveals that he permits men [to enjoy] their comfort.

It is true, as was touched on yesterday, that we ought to be so spiritual as to gather every day to call upon the name of God and aim at a celestial life, forgetting all [our] earthly concerns. But what actually happens? God sees that we are surrounded by our flesh, that we creep upon the earth, that our weaknesses so dominate us that we are unable to lead an angelic life. Thus God, seeing such ignorance and debility in us, [and] having mercy because we cannot fully justify ourselves because of our current condition, releases us and does not at all display his utmost rigor. He even says that he will be satisfied if we will dedicate one day to him; especially will he be content if this day helps us throughout the rest of the week. And why? For (as I have said) he has not gone to the extremity, for he knew that we were too weak. Therefore seeing that he upholds us in this way and that he permits us to enjoy our comforts, so much the more are we cowardly, and shameless, and inexcusable, if we are not inspired to surrender ourselves to him.

Now at the same time it is said, *that neither shall* [your] *manservant, nor chambermaid, nor cattle, nor ass, nor beasts work on the sabbath day, nor the stranger who is within your gates.* As for the beasts, we might find it strange that God included them under the commandment to rest, seeing that it is a high and holy mystery as was discussed yesterday. But does it apply to cattle and asses? God says: "I gave you the sabbath day as a sign that I sanctify you, [and] that I am your God who reigns in your midst; that is something which is not common to all mortal men." For God does not extend that grace and privilege to pagans and unbelievers; he does not sanctify them. He speaks only to the people whom he has chosen as a heritage and whom he has adopted. Therefore insofar as the sabbath day is a sign that God has separated the faithful of his Church from all the rest of the world, why is that extended to [cover] cattle and asses?

Now let us note that this [action] was not taken for the sake of dumb animals, but in order that men might have a reminder before their eyes in order to be that much more moved. Therefore this sacrament was not addressed to beasts which possess neither intelligence nor reason, but it is addressed to men who must keep it for their [own] benefit. We see that the sacrifices were made of dumb beasts; we know that they engaged in elaborate preparations; that they possessed vessels of gold and silver and similar things. And when all of that was sanctified, are we to suppose that God had put his Spirit into corruptible metals, into materials which had no conscience? No! But all of that existed for men, as all creatures are made for our usage and benefit. [For] God is not the only one who benefits from them in this present and transient life; rather in the course of it, he provides us with the marks of his grace in order that we might possess that many more means and aids for drawing us up to heaven. Thus when God willed for cattle and asses to be rested on the seventh day, it wasn't because he had made them participants in that spiritual rest which we discussed earlier, but it was in order that the Jews, seeing their stables closed, might understand. And what were they to understand? [That] God sets in our midst before our eyes even dumb animals as a sign and visible sacrament. And their purpose is that, for our part, we might be that much more retained for God's service, knowing that we would be violating the entire law if we did not think of that which forms the principal point of all our life, which is, that we learn to denounce ourselves and no longer follow our [own] appetites, or reason, or wisdom. For our God should govern us. And we should become like dead creatures in order that he might live in us and we no longer pursue our own course which is so utterly corrupt. Accordingly, that is how God meant for the Jews to regard dumb brutes: as a visible sign which he had given them to the end that they might be that much more restrained and thereby admonished to keep the sabbath day in complete reverence.

We also see how God has always treated men according to their hardness and has provided them with remedies which were appropriate to them, seeing that they are not very inclined to come to him, before whom they might be so attracted. And that is [true] not only of the Jews, but equally of us. Therefore let us perceive the goodness of our God when we see that he neither forgets nor neglects anything at all that can heal our vices. And at the same time let us also understand the perversity which dominates us in order that we [might] neither flatter nor ease up on the reins of our affections, seeing that we need to be constrained and that God gives us so many coaxing nudges, as to stubborn horses. Therefore seeing that God goads us in this way, let us understand that it is not without cause that he does, but it is due to the fact that we are perverse and still rebellious. Therefore let us be displeased with all our affections and learn to become enslaved by nothing which might impede our following the course which God commands us. And furthermore, lest our nature resist this, let us be so captivated [by what God commands] that we may press on without ceasing until we are fully subdued by our God. That is what we must emphasize in this passage beyond what will soon be said next with regard to slaves and servants.

Now concerning the latter, God reminds the Jews *that they had been slaves in the land of Egypt* and that now they must humanely treat those who are under their powers. He says: *Your servant and your maidservant shall rest.* And for what reason? Because you were once in bondage. Certainly you would have liked for them to have given you some rest and relief; therefore it is imperative that now you show such a humanity toward those who are in your hand.

Now it certainly appears here that God may have ordered the sabbath day as [a form of] civil order, [and] not as a spiritual one, as we earlier discussed, it being done for [the sake of] charity. For he says: "When you were in bondage, didn't you want someone to give you some reprieve? Did you want to be harried all the time? Certainly not! Therefore it is crucial for you to be considerate of others." [Now that would mean that] this command isn't given for the service of God, but rather serves as a common charity which [we] ought to exercise toward our neighbors, no matter to what degree they might be inferior to us. But [on the contrary] insofar as this commandment is contained in the first table of the law, certainly this argument is only accessory.

I say the first table. For it is not without reason that God divided his law in this way, that is that he wrote it on two stones. Had he willed, could he not have simply written it on one stone? Why then did he do it in two parts? It wasn't without reason. For there are two principal articles in the law of God: the one concerns what we owe him; the other what we owe our neighbors with whom we live. Everything that concerns our life is grounded here. In the first place, knowing that we have a God to whom we belong, we ought to walk in his obedience. Then [knowing] that we owe our life to him, we ought to do homage to him; [and] insofar as he has created us to a better hope and adopted us as his children, we ought to glorify him for such a goodness. Seeing [then] that he has purchased us through the blood of his Son that we might be totally his and has taken the trouble to retrieve us from the pollutions of the world in order that we might be his true sacrifices, let us call upon his name and put our refuge in him alone. Let us praise him for all his benefits. That is the first point of our life, that is the honor which we must render to our God. And second, seeing that he wishes to test our obedience, there is also [the fact] that, when we live with men in complete integrity, we should not abandon ourselves to our own particular interests, but we should undertake to help each other. Indeed, there should be a mutual honesty [between us], not simply for the purpose of abstaining from fraud, violence, and cruelty, but in order that our life might be sober and modest, and that we might not become profligate, shameless, and brutal. That is the second point of our life.

Now insofar as this is the case, that the commandment concerning the sabbath day is contained in the first table, it follows that it belongs to the spiritual service of God and that it is pointedly not a question about the charity which we owe our neighbors. Why then is it mentioned here? It's as much as if our Lord were saying: "This superabundant day of rest will serve you in order that your servants and maidservants may have respite with you." Not that this was the goal toward which God was tending, [for] it was not his principal aim for there to be one day a week in which people ceased to work in order to catch their breath and be spared total exhaustion. This was not the reason why God was motivated to ordain the sabbath day. It was in order that the faithful might understand that it is truly necessary to live in a holy way, that they must rest from all their affections and desires, and that God must entirely work in them. Besides, as the saying goes, there is something here of an unexpected nature. "Listen" (our Lord says), "remember that when you have this testimony in your midst, I am at work sanctifying you, and [when] you are trying to surrender yourself to me, consider that there is still one thing that will benefit you and that exists for your profit: that your family will not have to exhaust itself forever, for it is appropriate that your servants and maidservants and your beasts enjoy some respite. Therefore you shall have that as [a kind of] superabundance."

Now we see why it is purposely mentioned here that the Jews were slaves in Egypt and that it is incumbent upon them to have respect for those who were held as captives under their hand. For Moses, [when] speaking of servants and chambermaids, does not mean the same as is meant among us today. For, lo, servants were slaves whom one worked like cattle and asses; there existed such a harsh and inhumane condition that it was pitiful. Thus God shows that the Jewish people, [by] observing the sabbath day, will even gain profit and comfort for their family. "So far from" (he says) "being grieved over the fact that I have reserved one day out of every seven for myself, if you are not too cruel, and if you do not exercise tyranny against those who are in your power, that day" (he says) "is still to your benefit. If you should have no other consideration than this order, that is, that on the sabbath day your servants enjoy rest, the commandment would serve you well. But always be aware that I have not simply ordered the commandment for your family, but in order that you might be advised concerning what I have shown you, that, when you are separated from unbelievers, you might be a royal sacrifice to me, asking for nothing but to serve me with full integrity and pure conscience. When you hold that view, then you understand that this day can still provide you with some earthly gain; nevertheless, that is not what you ought to seek." In sum, our Lord shows us here what Jesus Christ also proclaimed: that if we seek the kingdom of God, the rest will be added to us. For it appears to us that if we aspire to a heavenly life, we shall die of hunger, that such will deprive us of all our pleasures; in brief, when it comes to serving God, the devil always surfaces to solicit our disgust under the shadow and ruse that if we want to engage ourselves in God's service, we shall surely die of hunger, it will be a pity for us, [and] we shall have to take leave of the whole world.

Now it is true that we cannot serve God, that we may not be

able to empty ourselves of our affections, and that we may not reject those earthly cares that press on us from every side, but nevertheless it is still necessary for us to lean on this benediction which we are promised, that is, that when we seek the kingdom of God, we shall be blessed in transient things, that our Lord will have mercy on us and will give us all that he knows we need for this present life; only let us look to him for those things which we cannot acquire by our [own] industry. Thus you see what we are shown in this passage

Now this counsel must always serve us as a goad to induce us to follow what God commands us. For the primary thing which prevents us from regulating and submitting our life in obedience to God is the conviction that being slaves to ourselves is more to our advantage. Plus we always want to provide for our own comforts, no matter what, and [enjoy] whatever belongs to the world. That is why men cannot follow God, but rather wander farther from him and pull in the opposite direction of his law, because it seems to them that in serving God they will not be able to do so to their advantage.

Now this is such a wretched, ungrateful response that it [only] aggravates their rebellion a hundred times more. What then must be done? Let us carefully note that we shall never be able to serve God with a free and easy heart, for we do not have that [kind of] resolve [that believes] that God foresees our entire life and forgets none of it, as he explained to Joshua. For the apostle in the Letter to the Hebrews applies this doctrine to all the faithful, especially to spare them too much anxiety. He says: "Your God will never abandon you; he will never forget you." Now if we could only be persuaded just once that God watches over us and that he foresees all our necessities, certainly we would not be so mired in our earthly concerns, we would not be led astray from serving him, we would not be prevented from meditating on the spiritual life, so much that we would pass through this world and make use of created things as if not to use them at all, because we would know that it is forever necessary to hold to more than this. Therefore, in brief, you see what we have to retain in this doctrine which our Lord points out. [For] although what he has commanded with respect to keeping the sabbath day is spiritual, nevertheless men will not fail to be conscious of their benefit, knowing that God will bless them when they rightly remember him and do not look everywhere for what they know serves their earthly comfort.

Now nevertheless we are admonished that if there are some who rule over others, they must not scorn their neighbors no matter how inferior they may be to them. And this [provision] extends even further. For we must not only take into account servants and chambermaids, but [also] the poor, and all who are not in authority or esteemed, all subjects who are not deemed worthy in the eyes of the world to be compared to us. For we know how proud men are, for although we may have no occasion to be swelled, we are each covetous for some preeminence. Seeing then that such arrogance indwells us, that we each want to be elevated over our neighbors—in spite of any basis for it—what happens when we are elevated? Look at those who are in the seat of justice. It almost appears to them that the world might be their creation, except for the fact that God restrains them by his Holy Spirit and shows them that they must walk in all forbearance and must not oppress those who are under their charge. Rather they must fulfill a fatherly function on their behalf, regarding their neighbors as their children, and still further, seeing that God honors them, they must walk in the greatest humility. [As for] those who proclaim the Word of God and have charge of leading others, how unfortunate they are if they think that they ought to be exempt from the common ranks and [may] despise others. For it would be better if they broke their necks while mounting the pulpit than to be unwilling to be the first to walk after God and to live peaceably with their neighbors, demonstrating that they are the sheep of our Lord Jesus Christ's flock.

Now nonetheless it is true that the rich can certainly help the poor. When a man has servants and chambermaids working for him, he does not set his servant above himself at table, nor does he permit him to sleep in his bed. But in spite of any [right of] superiority which might exist, it is essential that we always arrive at this point: that we are united together in one flesh as we are all made in the image of God. If we believe those who are descended of Adam's race are our flesh and our bone, ought that not make us subject to humanity, though we behave like savage beasts toward each other? When the Prophet Isaiah wants to persuade men of their inhumanity, he says: "You shall not despise your flesh." That is how I must behold myself in a mirror, in light of how many human beings there are in the world. That is one point.

But there is still more: that is that the image of God is engraved in all men. Therefore not only do I despise my [own] flesh whenever I oppress anyone, but to my fullest capacity I violate the image of God. Therefore let us carefully note that God willed in this passage to point out to those who are in authority and who receive esteem, who are richer than others and who enjoy some degree of honor, that they must not abuse those who are under their hand; they must not torment them beyond measure. They must always reflect the fact that we are all descended from Adam's race, that we possess a common nature, and that even the image of God is engraved on us. That is what we have to note. Moreover, our Lord Jesus Christ has descended to earth for the purpose of being entirely destroyed in order to condemn all pride and to show that there is no other means of serving God except in humility. That being the case, he has made us all members of his body, including slaves and those who are masters and superiors, without any distinction.

When we come to our Lord Jesus Christ and behold him, it is essential that we follow [his example]. Seeing that both the great and the small are members of his body and that he is our master, that is reason enough for each [of us] to be conformed to his neighbors. And in addition, seeing that God has declared himself our father in more familiar terms than he did to those who lived under the law, may that inspire us to maintain fraternity among us. That again is what we have to glean from this text.

Now there is still one point with regard to what God institutes [as] a reminder to the Jews: *that they were like poor slaves in the land of Egypt.* Now we know that they were badly treated there with cruelty. But insofar as they sighed and groaned to God, and were heard, and behold wanted someone to help them, God declares that indeed they must also do the same. Now this contains a good lesson, which is that when we think of ourselves, we will always be caught up in the need to perform our duty. And on the contratry, when we are cruel toward our neighbors, it's as much as if we are intoxicated with our comforts and do not think about our poverty and miseries. Whoever has been hungry and thirsty, [and] especially wanted someone to relieve his need, and sees a poor man, and thinks: "Now I have been in that condition and certainly wanted to be helped; indeed it seemed to me that people ought to have pitied me in order to help me." Whoever (I say) entertains thoughts like that upon seeing a poor man in need, must he not have a soft heart? But what [is the usual case]? When we are comfortable, it is not a matter of our remembering our human poverty, rather we imagine that we are exempt from that and that we are no longer part of the common class. And that is the reason why we forget, and no longer have any compassion for our neighbors, or for all that they endure. Therefore, seeing that we are blindly in love with ourselves, and are content to be plunged in our [own] delights, and hardly think of those who are suffering and in want, so much the more do we need to hear this passage that our Lord may point out: "And who are you? Have you not been in need yourself?" And even if you should happen to get angry with them, does it ever occur to you that they are creatures made in the image of God? And if we insult them, why should God have mercy on us?

Therefore let us practice this doctrine all our life. And as often as we see people racked with misery, may this [thought] come to mind: "Lo, have I not been in need as well as they?" And if right now we were to be in such a state, would we not want to be helped? Therefore insofar as this is true, is it right for us to be exempt from such a condition? The least we can do is to do unto others as we would have them do unto us (Matt. 7:12). Our [own] nature teaches us that. We don't have to go to school to learn that. Thus we need no other trial to condemn us than what our Lord already teaches us by experience. When we are guided by that thought, certainly we will be touched by humanity to aid those who are indigent and in need. We will be moved to compassion, seeing them suffer, so much so that if we have the means and capacity to help and assist them, we will use it. Therefore you see what we have to note in this passage when it is said that you were strangers in the land of Egypt, therefore it is now proper for you to consider how to alleviate those who are in your hand, for when you were a slave, you certainly wanted someone to help you.

Now we come to those who were not [members] of the Jewish people, but solely did business among them. Indeed, God also

wills for them to keep the sabbath day, even if God has not sanctified them and even though this sign could not belong to them, as
we have already said. Thus it seems that God profanes the sacrament when he makes it apply to unbelievers and to those who
were not circumcised as a sign of the covenant, to those who possessed neither the law nor the promises. But we have to observe
that what God says here about strangers always applies to the people whom he chose and adopted. For we know that if we permit
conditions [to exist] which are contrary to the service of God, even
though some might say: "These people are not [members] of our
group," we may [still] be misled by their bad examples. [For] if one
had permitted foreigners to work among the Jewish people, what
would it have led to? The Jews would have traded with them and
would have been profaned; there would have been no discretion
on that day. For when opportunity presents itself, we are easily led
toward evil. And though it may not be a great occasion, our nature
is so inclined toward evil that we are immediately led astray.
Therefore what [good] does it serve if everyone is corrupted?
Thus if one had given foreigners the liberty to work in the
midst of the Jewish people, they might have been induced to corruption; each would have exempted himself and given himself the
license to violate the sabbath day and not keep it. Therefore, in the
same way that God willed for animals to rest, he ordered the same
for foreigners in order that such an evil occasion might be avoided
and this day be kept with the greatest reverence.

Now this [commandment] must serve us today. For its purpose
is to show us that vices must not be permitted in a people who
make a Christian confession, so much so that they have to be punished even among those who are only passing through.* Why is
that? When blasphemies are condemned among ourselves, if we
were to hear a passerby blaspheme, or make fun of God, and such
should be endured and kept secret, would it not be a kind of pro-

---

*Possibly a reference to Michael Servetus who was "only passing through"
Geneva when detected and arrested. The immediate context seems to suggest
this. See Roland Bainton, *Hunted Heretic: The Life and Death of Michael Servetus,
1511–1553* (Boston: Beacon Press, 1953), pp. 209–10. Concerning the latter's attitude of Servetus's trial and fate, Bainton comments: "Nowhere does Calvin
more clearly disclose himself as one of the last great figures of the Middle Ages,"
pp. 209ff.

fanation that would infect everything else if such blasphemies were upheld, or considered in vogue, and nothing were done to repress them? Yet it exists. [For] the truth is that blasphemies are far from being punished as they should be in those who are not of our religion, in those who mix with us and make the Christian confession; [indeed] we see how they are tolerated much to our own confusion.

But in any event, if we permit papists and others just anything (for today the world is crammed full of despisers of God), if we permit them (I say) to slander the doctrine of the Gospel and to blaspheme the Name of God, it creates a corruption that lives on in such a way that it becomes increasingly difficult to cure. If we allow the debauched and ruffians to influence us with their corrupt ways and bring into our midst more evil than we have, if we permit the profligate and corrupt to come here to practice their lewdness, will we not of necessity become debauched and totally corrupt with them?

Therefore let us carefully note that our Lord wills to train his people in complete purity to the extent that those who profess to be Christian may not only abstain from evil, but insofar as possible, may equally refuse to tolerate it at all. For we must understand that the earth is profaned when the worship of God is contaminated here and his holy name is dishonored. The ground on which he wants us to live is polluted and cursed and nothing will make him come to us. In any event, when God gave this privilege to his children in order that they might remove idolatry from the country in which they [were to] live, it is certain that if they failed they would provoke his anger and vengeance against themselves. [In the same way] today if we were to ask for the abominations of the papacy to be combined here with the pure worship of God and out of privilege were to grant a mass to the obstinate papists who would like to live here, thus providing them some corner in which they could perform their idolatries and superstitions, it would be like inviting God's anger against us and lighting the very fire of his vengeance. And why? Because since God has given those who hold the sword of justice in hand, who control the government in this life, the power to root out idolatries and these papal infections, then certainly if they were to maintain them, it would be like running God out in order to end his presence and reign in their midst.

Therefore let us carefully note that it is not without cause that our Lord willed for the foreigners who were living in the midst of the people—though they were of a different faith and religion—to be forced to keep the seventh day. He willed it not on their behalf, nor for their instruction—for they were incapable of that—but in order to curtail any scandal that might corrupt the people and violate the worship of God that the land which he had given his servant Abraham as a heritage might be totally dedicated to him.

Now hereby we are not only admonished to be sanctified by the Word of God, but not to tolerate in our midst any commission of scandals and corruptions. For all of that must be put away from us. Besides, when our Lord wills for us to have such a zeal for maintaining his service that even those who have not professed to belong to his Church are constrained to affiliate with and conform themselves to us when they are talking in our company, I beg of you, what excuse will we have if on our part we are not totally yielded to him and are not like mirrors for drawing and winning poor unbelievers to our God? For if we hope to recover them when they have fallen and nevertheless they perceive in us similar and even worse vices, will they not be justified in mocking all our remonstrances? Therefore seeing that foreigners have been prohibited from doing anything that is contrary to the worship of God, let us understand that we have been doubly commanded to walk in all solicitude and in such humility and sobriety that foreigners may be convinced that it is in good conscience and without hypocrisy that we want God to be honored and that we cannot allow anyone to bring opprobrium to his majesty and glory.

Consequently that is what we have to emphasize in this text if today we want to keep what was commanded to the Jews, as by right in truth and substance it belongs to us. Thus in the same way that our Lord of old delivered his people from Egypt, so today he has delivered us from the pit of hell, and reclaimed us from eternal death and the abyss of flames into which we have plunged in order to gather us into his heavenly kingdom, for he has purchased us through the blood of his beloved Son, our Lord Jesus Christ.

SERMON ON THE FIFTH COMMANDMENT

(WEDNESDAY, JUNE 26, 1555)

Deuteronomy 5:16

¹⁶Honor thy father and thy mother, as the Lord thy God hath commanded thee; that thy days may be prolonged, and that it may go well with thee, in the land which the Lord thy God giveth thee.

We have come to the second table of the law in which God shows us how we have to live here together in harmony. For as it has been discussed earlier, there are two principal things in our life: that we should worship God in purity, and second, that we should deal with men in complete integrity and honesty, rendering to each what is properly his. Now inasmuch as the honor of God is more excellent than all that concerns men, it was appropriate that in the first and highest stage the rule was given for God to be honored as [indeed] we ought. That was dispensed with in the first table. Now God begins to explain for us here how our life ought to be governed if we wish to serve him with respect to men.

Now we have already explained that God does not require any honor from us for any need he may have, or would such benefit him, [rather] it is for our good that he does it. Thus in this way he wills to test our obedience and the love which we bring him when he commands us to walk with our neighbors in all honesty and equity, and [commands] that we should live together in such communion and concord that we not live solely for ourselves, but work together, and, according as each has the means and power to work effectively, compel and employ ourselves [to that end]. That is one test (I say) that God has taken in order to know whether we worship him with our heart. For we could put on a good show and [participate in] ceremonies, but God would not be content with that. For this same reason our Lord Jesus Christ (see Matt. 23:23) says that the principal meaning of the law is justice, judgment, integrity, and faith; for such is the meaning of the word *faith.* Therefore when we live among men without pretense, when we are not given over to craftiness or malice, [and show] that we want to be of service to everyone and to uphold the good, then that is the essence of the law. However [the essence is] not that the worship of God might be forgotten because it is of less importance, but because it is impossible for men to act as they should toward their neighbors unless they are led by the fear of God.

Now let us discuss this commandment which was [just] read: that of *honoring* [our] *father and mother.* Now although particular mention is made here of the father and the mother, there can be no doubt about God's wanting to provide a general doctrine with respect to honoring all [forms of] authority. That such is the case, we know that the law is a perfect norm in which there are no faults. Now if the law said nothing about other authorities, such as princes and magistrates and those who wield the sword of justice, if it said nothing about masters, it would contain errors. Thus we are forced to conclude in this text that God has commanded that all [persons] who enjoy any superior status are to be honored and obeyed. The advantage then is that all preeminence comes from God and forms an order which he has established, without which even the world cannot subsist. For what would it be like if God had not taken this into consideration when he gave us a definite, holy form for upright living? Nor must we find it strange that all of this is contained under one heading. For we have already discussed the fact that such can be observed in the law, whose advantage we shall yet see. Nor was it due to the fact that God could not speak more fully, rather the better it serves to our benefit and instruction. For in spite of the fact that men crave to be seen as sharp and subtle, we know that they do not neglect to cover themselves with a shield of ignorance; [for] when we see that the law of God is about to crowd us, then we want an excuse to exempt ourselves from being under its subjection.

Now if the law of God was not suitable for teaching the most ignorant and stupid, many could cite that they are not scholars and have not been to school; thus it would appear that the law of God was not binding on them. But when we see that God has humbled himself to our ignorance and has spoken in the rough language of our capacity, that removed every excuse from us and every pretext, [so much so] that it is imperative for each [of us] to constrain ourself and confess that nothing [shall] hinder us [from doing God's will]: unless, of course, we are rebellious against God and do not want to bear his yoke.

That is why God included everything under one heading, in order to lead us like little children who are not capable of being taught in true perfection. In any event this is the true and natural sense of the passage, as we shall soon see. For in this way God gave all the ten laws which he lists; he also added exposition so that nothing would be obscure and we would not have to question or dispute what had been heard. Thus we see that God fully explained and pointed out that he not only wished for us to obey fathers and mothers, but all [our] superiors without exception.

In addition let us note that God spoke here about *honoring the father and mother* because he wanted to draw us [to himself] by the most suitable and proper means [according] to our nature. We know that men are so proud that they will not willingly bend their neck for anyone, [as] each thinks [himself] capable of being master. But the fact remains that it is difficult for men to humble themselves and to descend to the point that God might easily subdue them, [that is] simply to obey those who have any authority over them. Therefore, God, seeing that subjection is such a contrary thing to our nature, set before us here [the figures of] father and mother, in order to attract us in a most amiable way.

Now it is quite a detestable thing, as well as contrary to nature, for a child not to acknowledge those through whom he came into the world, those who have fed and clothed him. Therefore when a child disowns his father and his mother, he is a monster. Everyone will look upon him with disgust. And why? [Because] without God speaking a word, without our having any holy Scripture, or anyone preaching to us, nature already shows us that a child's duty toward his father and mother is one which cannot be broken.

Thus we see our God's intention, for in putting before us [the figures of] father and mother, he willed to win us to himself in order that we might not be so cantankerous and might peaceably come to receive the yoke he lays on us. And insofar as all authority which men possess comes from him, he speaks according to the legitimate civil order, [which means] that if we are careful to render him the homage which he is due, if each in his own place obeys those who are in authority over him, [if] each takes into account his own estate and condition, if children honor their fathers and mothers, if everyone honors those who sit in the seat of justice, and servants do the same toward their masters, in brief, there will be a beautiful harmony among us for our peace, according to the order which our Lord has established, which is to be held inviolable by us.

Moreover, when honor is spoken of here, it doesn't simply mean that children ought to make a display of affection for their father[s] and mother[s], to tip their hat and make a bow, for God does not care to be entertained in such a way. Honor means much more. It means for children to follow the advice of their fathers and mothers, for them to let themselves be guided by them, to take the trouble to fulfill their duty to them: in brief, a child ought to understand that he is not at liberty with respect to his father and mother. In summation, that's what God meant by this word "Honor." This being the case, we cannot have a better or more faithful expositor of the law than the Holy Spirit who spoke by the mouth of Moses, by all the prophets, and especially by Saint Paul. For we shall see hereafter that God made known the summary of this view, that is, that it is insufficient for children to nod their head toward or simply bow in front of their father[s] and mother[s], rather they must be subject to them and serve them to their fullest capacity. And [certainly] Paul (see Eph. 6:1; Col. 3:20) does not cite this point in order to exhort us to undertake some [kind of] formality; rather he says that children ought to be subject to their fathers and mothers. And he especially uses this word "subjection." Thus we see what is involved, as well as the natural sense of this passage.

Now let us return to what we have briefly discussed in order to benefit from it and reap [some] doctrine that might be useful to us. In the first place, seeing that God has given children their fathers and mothers, let them understand that such is reason enough for them to obey them, or otherwise they reveal that they are contemptuous of God. And this rebellion which they flaunt toward their superiors is not directed against men or animals, but is as much as if the majesty and glory of God were being trampled underfoot. Properly speaking, it is said that we only have one Father in heaven. And that is not only meant with regard to souls, but also with regard to bodies. Therefore this honor of being called Father properly belongs to God alone and can only apply to men when it pleases him to confer it on them. Seeing then that this title of Father is like a mark which God has engraved on men, we see that if children do not take their father and mother into consideration, they insult God. The same is true of those who disobey their princes and magistrates. And of servants who would like to confuse all orders and lord it about without them. And that is also why the pagans associated the word *piety* with the honor we render father[s] and mother[s] and all who are in authority over us. *Piety*, properly speaking, is that reverence we owe God, but the pagans, although they were terribly blind, understood that God not only wants to be worshipped in his majesty, but when we are obedient to those who rule over us, in brief, he tests our obedience by this means. Therefore, insofar as fathers and mothers, magistrates and all who exercise authority, are lieutenants of God and represent him, certainly if we despise and reject them, it's as much as if we should declare that we don't want to obey God. Of course, one can argue the opposite; nevertheless it is true. If poor unbelievers understood that, and God permitted (see Eph. 3:15) such an attitude among them, what excuse can we offer if we do not grasp it still better? When we hear that all parenthood comes from God, as Saint Paul states it, and that we are restored to it through union with Jesus Christ, isn't that a far more express declaration [than theirs]? Must the pagans still be our teachers? But when those who call themselves Christians make [themselves] blind on this point, or cut off their ears in order not to understand what God has explained through the pagan mind, how unfortunate they are and how much more horrible [their] condemnation! Therefore, in summary, let us carefully note that we cannot live together here unless this order which God has established is holily kept, that is, unless we esteem and honor and obey all those who possess authority. Without that, there would be one horrible confusion.

Therefore those who cannot submit themselves to the magistrates, who rebel against their fathers and mothers, who cannot bear the yoke of masters or mistresses, sufficiently show that they cannot join up with anyone who doesn't reverse the complete order of nature and jumble heaven and earth, as people say. For that is the sole means by which God has willed to preserve the human race. In fact we see that he says that when he sends magistrates and princes, he not only causes men to fear them but

even animals. That is how he puts it in Daniel (see Dan. 2:38;
1 Pet. 2:13–14). And from that fact we are able to learn that those
who oppose the civil order which God has instituted, who strive to
trouble everyone and reduce everything to confusion, are worse
than brute beasts and deserve to be sent to their school. For our
Lord, in order to shame men who are rational creatures, says that
the fear of princes and magistrates ought to be extended to include
dumb animals. Therefore, as we have already explained, [can] we
not see that the devil possesses everyone who cannot submit in all
modesty to the subjection which God has established and without
which everything would perish and result in confusion in this
world?

Nevertheless, if we are aware of any haughtiness in ourselves,
and if it makes us ill to be subjects, let us fight against such pride
and let the authority of God suffice to check us. For no matter how
wild we might be, this [commandment] ought still enchain us (in a
manner of speaking), hearing that God explains that he is not honored by us unless we render him homage through those whom he
has established in his place and in whom he has engraved his
image.

In brief, we see that charity begins by this end: that we should
be humble and modest, and that no one should elevate himself
in arrogance and presumption, and overrate himself, rather we
should be ready to humble ourselves in order to submit to whatever pleases God. And that is also why Saint Paul (Rom. 13:7)
directs us toward charity when he expounds this commandment
concerning the obedience of magistrates. For he shows that if we
do not possess this gentleness in ourselves, to bend our neck when
our Lord lays a yoke upon it, then we have no charity for our
neighbors. If we crave for confusion and disorder, and if superiors
no longer receive respect, then everything may as well be up for
plunder. It would be much better if each one [of us] lived apart
and without company than to see the confusion that would arise if
we were not to keep the civil order which God has instituted.

Therefore, let us hold on to the fact that in order to live with
our neighbors, we each have to correct this [tendency toward]
arrogance and presumption and not retain it in our hearts, but we
must learn to be humble and modest; we must realize that it is
[even] our responsibility to be subject to the least, as Saint Paul

(Rom. 13:7) explains it. And in order to do that we must take account of our own worth. For that is what we abuse, for we would each like to enjoy a greater preeminence than God gives us. For we become blind in order not to see things in ourselves. And beyond that, we do not understand our [own] poverty and vices. Thus we each attempt to be marvelous, or we are nothing. And then we are so inclined not to take account of our neighbors that we even despise all the virtues that God has put in them. And as a result so much malice and ingratitude ensue that we are incited toward pride, so much so that we each attribute to ourself more than is ours. And that is why we cannot submit ourselves as we should.

But instead of that, let us learn to do homage to God when we see that he has commanded us to be obedient to our supervisors; and then, let us understand that such as they are, they represent his will. When a child has his father and mother, it is highly inappropriate for him to say: "O there is my father. He is not at all what he should be. I find fault with him." For he is still your father. [And] it is imperative for the word to satisfy you, unless you want to annihilate everything; unless you want to abolish the order of nature. Either the order which God has instituted has no value or effect, or you must honor your father such as he is. And why [is that]? [Because] the one who has commanded you to honor your father and mother has given you such a father as you have. The same holds true for masters, princes, and superiors, for as Saint Paul (see Rom. 13:1; 1 Tim. 2:2; also 1 Pet. 2:14) and all the Scripture repeatedly demonstrates, they are not the products of chance; it is God who sends them. Above all we are also led to understand the Providence of God through experience, as well as the paternal care in which he holds us when he institutes magistrates. Therefore let us learn to behold the goodness of God in all who have authority over us in order to submit ourselves to their obedience. That is what we want to retain.

Now insofar as God has given us in one phrase and in one brief summary the rule to obey all [our] superiors, let us mark that in so doing he does not resign his right; he does not relinquish anything that is properly his. Therefore it is essential that God always retain the sovereign position. And in fact, inasmuch as all parentage comes from him (as we have already cited in the passage in Paul), let us note that when we obey father[s] and mother[s], princes and magistrates, it's as if we were obeying officers of God. Therefore it is fitting that God should be honored over and above all, indeed, to such an extent that the honor we render to mortal men should not impede the service we must render to God nor the homage we owe him, for we each ought to strive to justify ourselves primarily before him. Indeed it would be something for a man to obey an officer and then spit in the face of the judge or the prince. Where would that lead? The same is true when we want to denude God of his preeminence and yet want to obey men, for in the process we are not taking account of him who is above all. For that is contrary to nature, as the authority that belongs to men should in no way obscure God's glory. Therefore let us carefully mark that when we are commanded to be obedient to our superiors, the exception remains that nonetheless this [commandment] must not detract from any of those prerogatives which belong to God, which have already been treated in the first table. For we know that the service by [means of] which God is worshipped must precede everything else. And that is also why Saint Paul, (see Eph. 6:1) desirous to give us an exposition of this test, notably adds that it is "in the Lord" that children must obey their fathers and mothers. Besides, we have said that this is the foundation upon which we must build in order to be obedient, humble, and subject to our superiors, which is, to understand that God is represented in them. Now once we have removed the foundation, isn't it obvious that the entire edifice will slip and come crashing down? Now in the same way, those who have no consideration for God remove the foundation of this doctrine; consequently, the procedure is too tricky and perverse.

Now this ought to warn those who are in authority, as much as it does their subjects. Thus if men and women have any children, they must understand that they should not unduly subject them, insofar as God rules over all. What must be done then? Let a father carefully instruct his children in the fear of the Lord and begin to show the way. Let the mother do the same. Let God receive his homage above the great and the small, the old and the young. Let magistrates labor to the end that God may be served and honored. Let them maintain that goal in all that they do and with all their strength. Let them demonstrate that they are truly his officers seeing that he pays them the honor of being worthy to sit on the seat which is dedicated to his majesty [and] to carry the sword which is sacred to him. And insofar as he has elevated them to such dignity, of which they were unworthy, let them at least demonstrate that it is in his name that they have authority and that they are accountable to him. That is how princes must account for their duty.

Each must do the same in his home and in his family. Let those on whom God has bestowed the fortune of having servants and chambermaids clearly remember that there is a master over [us] all, and that he truly must be obeyed, and that his right must be preserved in its entirety. That is the instruction (I say), that must apply to all superiors, whatever their station, for they too are commanded to obey God. In addition, when fathers and mothers and magistrates want to elevate themselves against God, and elevate themselves in such tyranny that they usurp what properly belongs to God alone, and when they want to divert us from his obedience, that constitutes an exception which must not be obeyed. Thus it is necessary for God to lead the procession and, afterward, as the phrase goes, for creatures to follow in descending order. And, in fact, that is the reason why modesty and humility are so often ill kept in the world, why children rise up against fathers and mothers and behave like wild beasts, why people are full of malice and rebellion, why servants are also full of disloyalty, and why you can never come to the end of that sort of thing. It is a fitting punishment of God on all who have abused the dignity which he has given them. For we often see that princes do not rule in order to magnify the name of God or strive that he might be honored as he deserves, but on the contrary they prefer to set up idols and almost wrest God out of his throne in order to replace him with themselves.

We see [plenty of] that. Or at least we see princes ruling without restraint. Thus it is right for God to avenge himself. For what zeal and affection do fathers and mothers have for instructing their children in the fear of God? It's all the same to them, provided they advance according to the world. It even seems that they want to rear them in complete impiety and in disrespect for God and his Word. Where fathers have been [like] wolves, they want to have wolfish [children]; where they have been old foxes, they want to have little sly devils; where they have been serpents, they want to have posterity after their kind. We know that. Therefore God is amply justified in avenging himself when creatures consequently forget who they are, and above all when men do not acknowledge that God has taken their hand in order to lift them up and bestow upon them a portion of his honor, albeit it is a lesser degree. We must always hold fast to that.

Nevertheless, isn't it the height of ingratitude when a man in a position of authority and justice does not understand: "Who am I? I am [only] a poor earthworm and [yet] God wants me to carry his name for his sake, to exercise it with respect to the authority which he has given me." When a man doesn't understand that, isn't that the height of ingratitude? In the next place, when fathers fail to consider: "Behold, God is the unique father of the whole human race and yet he has attributed that highly honorable title to me. Isn't that a sufficient reason for me to be advised to render an account to him?" When masters and mistresses do not perceive: "We are no better than others and [yet] God has willed to honor us, not only by creating us in his image, but in addition by giving us a position which is above those who are subject to us." (I say) when people cannot grasp all of that, isn't it fitting to say that they have become entirely stupid?

Let us clearly note then that rebellions often proceed from such [thinking] as that, that those who are in authority have not understood their office which is that first of all they must procure homage for God and that people serve him and become subject to him. Certainly children, the people, and servants will not be excused if the magistrates fail. We can see that God's vengeance is still just. But even more, we need to be motivated to follow what we have been shown, whether in this passage or throughout the holy Scripture, concerning what this commandment enjoins. Therefore, in brief, we are clearly warned that each shall have to account for himself in his own vocation and life. And those on whom God has bestowed the honor of bearing the sword of justice and sitting in his seat, let them be carefully advised to rule in the name of God and see that he is worshipped and honored by all. And let them be like mirrors in order to set a good example. Let them hold their subjects in reasonable check and in such order that the Name of God is blessed and the mouth of every slanderer closed. That is one point. [Further] let fathers and mothers take care to instruct their children well; let them teach them to recognize God as their only father. And with regard to their servants and chambermaids, let them teach them to serve in such a way that God is always the principal [end of their service]. May they not keep performing in the customary way. For it is all the same to men, provided their benefit and contentment are enhanced, though God is forgotten. Rather, may masters realize that it is essential for God to rule over them as well as over those who are their subjects. That is what is involved here with respect to those in authority.

Now for our part, let us be carefully warned that when we are rebellious against magistrates, and when we dare to elevate ourselves in opposition to the civil order, and when we attempt to ruin the order which God has established, we do not commit an outrage against creatures [alone], but it is God whom we assail. And what can we gain by making war against him? Are we able to emerge the stronger? No! Rather he will avenge himself with the greatest of ease, and people will be completely stupefied that he actually maintains what he has ordained by his mouth, indeed, with an admirable strength. So much then for this first point.

Next, let children be warned not to be presumptuous or fickle, or given to their desires, but let them peaceably submit to their fathers and mothers, knowing that they are fighting against God when they cannot submit to the yoke that our Lord places on them. Let servants and chambermaids realize that when they refuse to be subject to those whom they serve that God is offended by their action and that of necessity in the end they are guilty of not being willing to be governed by his hand.

Now therefore let us note that it is necessary for God to be honored first [and] for the people genuinely to obey their princes and magistrates, as the latter in no way detracts from any of God's prerogatives which he reserves for himself and of which he is worthy. For if princes want to lead us into evildoing and should try to overturn the pure doctrine of God, may God forbid their success in this endeavor. For too frequently we observe that this madness prevails in many who would like [to see] religion twisted to serve their gain, or who treat it like a wax figure and bend it to suit their will. Who are they anyway? They have lost all authority in revolting against him who possesses the highest sovereignty. Devils are required to bend their knee before God and our Lord Jesus Christ, yet here are mortal men who would like to usurp such power to the extent that the honor of God is overthrown and all his religion cast out. Therefore let us so learn to obey princes and fathers and mothers that God might retain his right in all integrity and that we might not be hindered from rendering him the homage which belongs to him, but insofar as we can without offending our conscience, it is important for us to obey them peaceably. And although those in authority over us may not fulfill their duty, nevertheless children should still not misbehave, [even] when their fathers and mothers are too strict and exercise too much control over them. It is true that fathers are forbidden to use cruelty against their children or even discourage them, nevertheless, although fathers may not have been properly counseled to rule their children gently, it still follows that children [should] bear that patiently. In brief, it is essential for us to endure all who have authority over us. That is what God intended to mean in this passage.

Now he also adds this promise: *In order that your days* (he says) *might be prolonged and that you might prosper in the land which the Lord your God gives you* (Deut. 5:16). Seeing that it is difficult for us to be humble, God has provided us a nudge with his spurs saying, *Your God commands you to do it.* (Deut. 5:16). And its purpose is to confirm the doctrine which we have already discussed, that is, that it is a frivolous and vain subterfuge to dispute whether those who enjoy a degree of honor above us deserve to be there, whether they take a sufficient account of their privilege, now that they have attained it. All of that must be cast aside. And why? For we ought to be content with what God has enjoined and completely acquiesce in his good pleasure. That is why, in particular, Moses adds here: *According as the Lord your God has commanded you.* It's as if he were saying: "It is true that men always resist as much as they can. If people want to subjugate them, it will not be done willingly. And then there is their arrogance which is always soliciting them to want to be excessively elevated." Consequently there is no voluntary subjection such as God wants, rather you choose to be God's rebels (he says) when you engage in such disputes as: "Why should that person rule over me and why should I obey him, seeing that he is not better than I am?" If you harbor envy that way toward men, you only confront God who wants to know whether you will serve him or not. And if you do not receive his lieutenants when he sends them to you, that is a definite sign that you equally reject his yoke, and as a result his justice is violated and he feels insulted by you. And that such is the case, recognize [the fact] (says Moses) that children who rebel against their fathers and mothers readily cite first one thing and then another; that people who stir up trouble against their superiors have plenty of excuses. But it serves to no avail. The reason? Because God who has established positions of authority in this world also intends for them to be kept. He has declared his will which cannot be retracted. Once God has made his decree, it is no longer fitting to entertain the question as to what must be done, rather we ought to acquiesce and keep our mouths closed.

Now, nevertheless, in this commandment our Lord still acts out of his goodness, in order the better to win and hold us, to the end that we might obey our superiors. Such is the force of this promise. For as Saint Paul (see Eph. 6:2) says, this is the first commandment of the law which contains a special promise. True, we have already seen earlier that God is merciful to a thousand generations of those who love him, [a note] that was added to the commandment in which God showed us that he wanted his service to be kept in all purity and that we should not fall back into idolatry or superstition. But that promise applies to the whole law, as we have seen. This promise here only applies to the commandment to obey [our] fathers and mothers. When we see that this is a sacrifice pleasing to God, that those who are in subjection should maintain that condition and not attempt to rebel or be wild, but should bend their neck in order to submit themselves and should demonstrate that they truly want to obey God—[and] especially not refuse to be subject to those mortal men whom he has sent and established in his name—then there you have the purpose for which this promise was given. For God, seeing that we are hard to motivate, willed to mollify our hearts and willed to win us by gentleness and kindness, in order that he might not hurt us or make it difficult for us to be obedient to our superiors. Now because the main point cannot be totally resolved here, in summary we retain [the argument] that in order to serve God well, we have to subdue all pride and presumption in ourselves. [For] although by nature we possess this wretched tendency to want to elevate ourselves—for ambition dominates the great and the small—nevertheless, in order for us to prepare to worship God, it is essential that such ambition be overcome. And why? Because the point at which we must begin true obedience is humility. For with respect to men, let us carefully mark that we cannot live in peace and concord unless those whom God has installed in office and dignity are obeyed, unless we receive them in God's Name, and unless we subjugate ourselves to them. Otherwise, everything is subverted and we are worse [off] than wild beasts in the heart of the forest. Thus all who rebel against legitimate authority are both God and nature's enemies, as well as the enemies of the whole human race; they are monsters, whom we ought to detest.

Now once we have demonstrated our obedience, being subject to those whom God has installed over us, let us equally realize that we have an ample reason for humbling ourselves under him, and in such a way that he may be worshipped by us. [And] may we render him the homage which he is due, not in a ceremonial way only, but in true and pure conscience. And above all, may his honor be highly regarded by us. May all the civil constitutions of the world point us there, that God's throne may be elevated above the highest heavens. And although children may obey their fathers and mothers, and people obey their magistrates, and in each home we find the order which God approves, along with its various [social] grades, may this motivate us [still] higher, to the end that we grasp that God, who possesses the world's highest sovereignty, must preside over every creature and in brief over our entire life. Thus in this way we see that all obedience that is rendered to mortal creatures ought to tend toward this goal, that God is purely worshipped.

And so much the more we see why the wretched papacy must be detested by us. For there you confront an arrogance that has swelled itself in the world; but to what end, unless it is that of chasing God from both his throne and his honor, which are his? For the pope readily attests that it is necessary to be subject to one's superiors. But what [does he do]? Does he abide by either God's order or nature's? No! But on the contrary, he has purposely despised everything contained in the holy Scripture, reversing the entire order and civil government that God has commanded us.

He is called the Vicar of Jesus Christ, and yet we see that he has deprived Christ of his seat, [and] that he is no longer the head of his Church.

Therefore let us hold in revulsion whatever the devil has instituted in the world. And although we often see that things do not turn out as they ought, and that authorities abuse their power, let us understand that, with respect to kingdoms, and empires, and the covenant of righteousness, they cannot thwart what God has ordained. Of necessity, all that will prevail. For it has its foundation in God. It isn't like this hellish papacy which has no foundation. But on the contrary we know that God wills for there to be kings and princes and people of justice. Consequently they must be heeded. And when they cease to be responsible for their power, and Fathers behave with tyranny toward their children, let us bend our knees, knowing that such is the result of our sins. And when God permits the order which he has established to go unobserved and for everything to be overwhelmed, let us realize how much more urgently we need to flee back to him and pray for him to remove the current conditions that we might perceive that we should ask for nothing but to be governed by him. For it is by this means that he procures our salvation.

THE LORD ANSWERS JOB

Job 38:1-4

[1]The Lord, answering Job from a whirlwind, said, [2]"Who is this who obscures counsel by words without knowledge? [3]Gird thy loins like a valiant man, and show me that which I shall ask thee. [4]Where wast thou when I founded the earth? Declare it, if thou hast understanding."

We have seen previously that Elihu, wishing to rebuke Job, protested that he, Elihu, was also a mortal man, in order that Job might not complain of being treated by too high a power. He showed then, that God wished him to proceed by reason, and with sweetness, as he also uses it toward us, for he spares us, causing his Word to be preached to us by men like us, so that we can come with greater familiarity to what he proposes to us; the doctrine is chewed for us. We see, then, that God has pitied us, when he ordains men who are ministers of his Word and who teach us in his Name and by his authority, for he knows what we can bear, and that since we are feeble, we would soon be swallowed up by his majesty; we would be cast down by his glory. And that is why he condescends to our littleness, when he instructs us by means of men. However, it is also needful that we be touched, in order to bear toward him the reverence which he deserves, for without this we would abuse his goodness, and when he draws near to us, finally we would as it were make companionship with him. This is what is now narrated to us: that God, seeing that Job was not sufficiently subdued by the propositions and reasons which Elihu had brought forward, causes him to experience his grandeur *from a whirlwind*, in order that, being thus frightened, he might reform by recognizing his fault, and that he might obey entirely what is set before him. Thus we see how God in every way accommodates himself to us, in order to win us. For on the one hand he abases himself. And why? Seeing that we are too crude and gross to ascend to him. However, because there is too great a pride in our brains, we must experience him as he is, in order that we may

learn to fear him, and to hear his Word in all humility and solicitude. This is a point that we have to observe well, for by this we see
the love which he has for our salvation. For he surely must be concerned about us when he is thus transfigured, so to speak, that he
is not satisfied to speak on equal terms, but when he sees that it is
good and proper for us, he begs with us; and then, seeing that this
goodness cannot turn us from scorn, he rises and magnifies himself as is proper to him, in order that we might know our condition so as to subject ourselves entirely to him. And all the more
ought we to desire to be taught by his Word, seeing that it is conformed to the measure of our understanding, and that God has
forgotten nothing of that which was required and useful for our
salvation. Seeing then, that our God was so willing to come down
to our level, and that, however, he ascends to reform us to obey
him, may we take all the more courage to listen to him when he
speaks. And let us not use the frivolous excuse that the Word of
God is too high and obscure for us; or perhaps that it is too terrifying, or perhaps that it is too simple. For when we shall have taken
account of and reduced everything, it is certain that our Lord proposes to us a majesty in his Word, which is to make all creatures
tremble; there is also a simplicity, in order to make it be received
by the most ignorant and foolish; there is such a great clearness
that we can eat away at it without having been to school, if we are
teachable, for it is not without cause that he is called "Master" by
the humble and little ones.

This is what we have to note in the first place from this passage:
namely, that when God speaks to us through the mouth of men, it
is in order that we may draw near to him more freely, that we may
receive what he proposes to us on his part with greater leisure, and
that we may not be astonished beyond measure; but since we are
hardened beyond hope, and we do not bear toward him the honor
which he deserves, he makes us to experience him as he is, and he
rises in his majesty, in order that it may induce us to do him
homage.

Now it is specially said that *the Lord spoke to Job from a whirlwind*; that it was not enough that he gave him some sign of his
presence, but that he was there like a storm. We shall find very
often in the Scripture that God moved thus by claps of thunder
when he wished to speak to his believers; but especially here we

have to weigh the circumstance of the place, that inasmuch as Job was not yet completely checkmated, God had to show him a terrible force. For this cause, then, he thundered and moved this whirlwind in order that Job might know with what master he had to do. In general it is well said that God dwells as it were in an obscure cloud, or perhaps that he is surrounded by clearness; and yet we cannot comprehend this, that if we wish to contemplate God our senses are dazzled, that there is a very special obscurity. It is, then, thus well said of the glory of God in general, in order that we may not presume to inquire too much into his incomprehensible counsel, but that we may thereby relish, what it pleases him to reveal to us, and meanwhile that we know that all our senses are worthless, unless it pleases him to draw near to us, or perhaps to raise us to himself; but for still another consideration: namely, because of our rebellion God must show himself in terror. It is true that he may ask only to draw us to himself in sweetness, and we see that he uses a loving manner, when men are well disposed to submit to him, that he invites us with as much humaneness as possible; but when he perceives some hardness of heart, he must cast us down at the beginning. For otherwise what will it profit that he speaks to us? His Word will be despised by us, or perhaps it will not enter into our hearts at all. And that is why in publishing his law he moved the thunderbolts, that the trumpets might sound in the air, that everyone might tremble in such a way that the people might be frightened by it, so as to say, "Let the Lord not speak to us, or we are all dead, we are then cast down." Why is it that God thus moved all the earth, and that his voice rang out with such a fright? Did he wish to chase the people so far away that he would not be heard at all? On the contrary, it is said, "He did not give his law in vain"; but he wished to give a certain instruction to the people, namely, the way of life.

So, then, it was not to frighten when he moved the thunderbolts and the tempests in the air; that was not, I say, his intention, but this served as a preparation in order to bring down the haughtiness of the people, who never would have obeyed God or his Word, who never would have known even the authority of him who spoke, without these marks which were added to it. So let us note well that it is not a superfluous thing that God thus spoke to Job from a whirlwind. And if such a holy man who had applied all his study to honoring God needed to be thus checked, what about us? Let us compare ourselves with Job. Here is a mirror of angelic holiness. We have seen the protestations that he made here below, and although he was afflicted to the limit, though he murmured, and although there escaped from him extravagant statements, yet he always retained the principle of worshipping God and of humbling himself under his majesty; he kept this in general, although he fell down in part. Now we are as carnal as could be, and our vanities so carry us away that we are as it were drunk; we hardly judge that there is a God in heaven, and when his Word is proposed to us, we are even more crude than asses. Is there not need, then, that our Lord shall cause us to experience his majesty, and that we should be consciously affected by it? Now it is true that God will not stir up tempests and whirlwinds in order that we may know that it is he who speaks; but he must by other means dispose us to come to him, as we also see that he does. When, then, one will have some scruples and some troubles in his conscience, another will be afflicted by illnesses, another will have other adversities, let us know that it is God who calls us to himself, seeing that we do not come to these things of our own free will, seeing that we do not draw near to hear his word; he checks such hardness of heart, as is required in order that our spirits may be beaten down into right obedience. Does God, then, see such a rebellion in us, he must use these manners and means that I have already spoken of to draw us and win us to himself; in order that we may hear it, he must speak to us as it were from a whirlwind, not that it should be in all; for we see some who kick against the spur, and they act like restless horses, and although God cares for them, they gain nothing by it. How many are seen of these ill-starred fellows whom God will have chastised in so many ways, whom he will have struck on the head with great blows of the hammer, so that no matter how hard they are they should have softened? However, they never cease to gnash their teeth. It is seen that they cannot move without showing that they are full of pride and rebellion against God, and they despise him as much as is possible.

So then, it is very necessary that those whom God chastises should be disposed to come to him, for such is his intention. So let us be advised not to frustrate our God; always and whenever he sends us some adversity, let us learn to run to him, as if he spoke with thunder, and as if it had to happen to us in order to make us hear. Let us know this, and let us know it in such a way that our spirits may be truly checked under him, and that we may seek nothing but to humble ourselves fully in his obedience. That is what we have to remember in this passage. Besides, let us note that, although today God does not thunder from heaven, yet all the signs which have been given in ancient times to prove his Word ought to serve us today. When the law of God is preached to us, we must join to it what is narrated in the nineteenth chapter of Exodus, that is, that the law has been duly ratified, and that our Lord has given it full authority, when he sent thunderbolts and flashes of lightning from heaven, which he did to call to mind the appearance of trumpets; that all this was in order that his law might be received until the end of the world in all reverence. So is it in this passage. For when it is said that *God appeared from a whirlwind*, we must know that he wished to ratify what is contained in this book, and not only that, but we must extend this authority through all his Word. There is still this consideration, that if God began by an amiable manner to call us to himself and he showed himself rough and bitter in the end, we should not find that at all strange, but rather let us examine our lives to know if we have obeyed him, and in that let us know his goodness is all of one piece; and then we know that it is very necessary that he should use this second means to win us, when he sees that he has profited nothing by his grace which he had shown us. Example: God may be kind toward us sometimes when he wishes to have us for his own and of his band; without sending us any affliction, he will propose his Word. Or perhaps we see that it is his will, and we acquiesce in it. However, we do not profit by it, by being made sure as we should of his goodness, by renouncing our wicked desires, by forgetting the world, and by giving ourselves entirely to him. He supports us for a time; but in the end when he sees that we are so indifferent, he begins to strike. By this we surely ought to experience that not without cause he speaks as from a whirlwind, because we have not heard him when he wished to teach us graciously and in a humane and fatherly manner. It is needful, then, that God speaks to us with such a vehemence, since he sees that we would never draw near to him until he had thus prepared us. It is true that he will win some by the simple Word, but when he sees that others are peevish, he sends them some trouble, some affliction. In fact, there are many who might never have come to the Gospel, who might never have been rightly touched in their hearts to obey God, unless he had released to them some sign that he wished to chastise them. Upon that, when they have experienced by afflictions that there are only miseries in this world, they have been constrained to be displeased with themselves, and to curtail their delicacies, in which they were previously plunged.

That, then, is how God in various ways draws men to himself. But let us always profit by the means he uses with us. Besides, when he does not speak in a whirlwind, let us on our part become familiar with him, and let us allow ourselves to be governed by him like sheep and lambs, for if he sees some hardness in us, he must check us perhaps with a curse, and if for a time he lets us run like escaped horses, yet in the end we shall experience his terrible majesty to be frightened by it; indeed, if it pleases him to give us grace, for it is a special benefit that God gives us, when he thus awakens us, and he thunders with his voice, in order that it may enter into our hearts, and that we may be deeply grieved by it. That, I say, is a privilege which he does not give to everyone. Besides, when he thunders against unbelievers it is too late, for there is no longer any hope that they may return to him. He summons them to hear the condemnation. Furthermore, we ought to receive peaceably this help which God gives us, when to check all the rebellions of our flesh he stirs up some whirlwind; that is to say, he causes us to experience his majesty. This, in summary, is what we have to remember from this passage.

Now we come to the saying, *Who is this who obscures counsel by words without knowledge? Gird thy loins like a valiant man, and answer all my questions.* God here, in the first place, mocks Job, inasmuch as he was rebellious, and it seemed to him that by arguments he could win his case. That is why he says, *And who art thou?* Now when the Scripture shows us who we are, it is to empty us of all pride. It is true that men will prize themselves too much, making themselves believe that there is some great dignity in them. Now they can well prize themselves; however, God knows in them only odor and stink, he rejects them; indeed, he holds them to be detestable. And so, although we may be so foolish, and though we may be so presumptuous as to glorify ourselves in our own imaginations to have power and wisdom in ourselves, yet God to empty us and render us confounded uses only the word, "And who are you? Thou man." When this is pronounced, it is as it were to completely despoil us of all occasion to glory. For we know that there is not a single drop of good in us; and then we no longer have any occasion whatever to commend ourselves.

And that is why God also adds, *Gird thy loins like a valiant man,* that is to say, "Dress thyself as thou pleasest, make thyself believe that thou art as it were a giant, mayest thou be well equipped, mayest thou be armed from head to foot. Very well, what wilt thou gain thereby in the end? When I shall oppose thee, poor creature, wilt thou think of a way to subsist? What hast thou?" Here, then, we see the intention of God. For (as I have already said) this folly of prizing ourselves and of presuming that we are worth something is so deeply rooted in us that it is very difficult to lead us to a right knowledge of our poverty, so that we may be void of all pride and presumption. Furthermore, then, we must note well the passages of the Scripture, in which it shows us that there is in us no worth whatever. And let us weigh that well, for it is spoken of not only part of the world, but of mankind in general.

May great and small, then, learn to be ashamed of themselves, since God includes everything as it were in a sheaf, when he says that the wisdom of man is only foolishness and vanity, that instead of power there is only weakness, that instead of righteousness there is only filthiness and dirt. For when God speaks in these terms, it is not for two or three people, but for everyone in general. Let us learn, then, from the greatest to the least, to humble ourselves, knowing that all our glories are only confusion and shame before God. May we think thus on the word, *Who is he?* Let us not take it as referring only to the person of Job, but let us take it as referring to all mortal creatures; as if our Lord said, "Why? Is there, then, such an audacity in a man who is only a fragile earthen pot? in a man who is only a vessel full of all filth and villainy, and in a man who is less than nothing? that there should be the audacity to dispute against me, and to wish to inquire so far? and where is this to stop? Who art thou, man?" As we see also that Saint Paul rebukes us by this word (Rom. 9:20), *And man, who art thou who repliest to God, and who pleadest against him?* When he has set down the objections which men suppose to have some plausibility for disputing against God by saying, "And why will God lose those whom he has created? And without having reason, that he may come to discern one from another, that one may be called to salvation, and that he may reject another; why is this done?" When, then, Saint Paul has said this, although men please themselves with such objections, he says, *O man, who art thou, that thou addressest thyself thus to God?* This is what we have to note from the word, *Who is he?* May each one, then, always and whenever he will be tempted with pride, think to himself, "Alas! who art thou?" It is not here a matter of entering into combat against our fellow-creatures, and against those who are like us, but if we wish to be so bold as to inquire into the secrets of God, if we release the bridle to our fancies and to our tongues to imagine useless things, or to speak against God and his honor, we must think, "Alas ! and who am I?" When each one will have looked inside himself, that he will have regarded his weakness, when he will have known in summary that he is nothing at all, we shall be sufficiently rebuked, all these cacklings will be put down, that we may have conceived previously; even all our fancies will be bridled and held captive, as will afterward be yet more fully declared.

Now it is especially said, *Gird thy loins like a valiant man* to signify that when all the world will have amassed its forces, and will have displayed them, it is nothing at all. That, then, is why God here defies Job by saying, "Let him be equipped, and let him come armored and armed as a giant, or as the most agile man that could be found." By this he expresses still better what we have said: namely, that if men are comdemned in the Scripture, this is not intended simply for the vulgar, for those who are contemptible, who have neither credit nor dignity, but it is extended to the greatest, to those who suppose they touch the clouds. And so, then, although men think they have in themselves some appearance of being honored, may they know that this is nothing with respect to God. As for example: Those who are excellent when they compare themselves with their neighbors, it is true that they will conceive some opinion of their own persons, and they will be content with themselves; when a man will be reputed wise, of good mind, of good grace—well, he will be prized in the eyes of those who have not the same qualities; a man will be rich, man will be endowed with great and praiseworthy virtues—as men go. That, then,

could well enable us to feel very bighearted (as they say) to commend ourselves, when we shall thus have special virtues, but when
we shall draw near to God, all must be emptied. There is then
none so gallant nor so robust that he may have a single drop of
strength; there is here no longer any holiness; there is no longer
any wisdom; there is nothing whatever. So, then, may all the
world know that its equipment will profit nothing before God;
but we must be completely emptied, God must void us, that he
may not leave a single drop of virtue in us, unless that which we
shall take from him, as though borrowing, knowing that all proceeds from his pure goodness. We see, now, what the word *valiant
man* implies; it is to signify that though we may have some special
virtues, it ought not to give us occasion to pride ourselves before
God.

Besides it is also said that *Job wrapped counsel* [or obscured it] *in
propositions without knowledge.* By that God declares that, having
treated his secrets, we surely ought to think of ourselves, in order
to proceed here soberly and in all fear; for under the word "counsel" God wished to signify the high things of which Job had spoken. We can well dispute about much minor rubbish, and dispute
it willingly—well, our propositions will be vain and frivolous—
but yet there will not be blasphemies, and the Name of God will
not be at all profaned. But when we enter into the doctrine of salvation, that we enter into the works of God, and that we dispute
about his Providence and about his will, then it is not proper to
come thus heedlessly; for we wrap or entangle counsel in propositions without knowledge. We see, then, for what it is that God
rebukes Job: namely, in that he had too hastily spoken of that
which was beyond his grasp, for although he had excellent gifts,
yet he ought always to have humbled himself, knowing his infirmity; and he ought also to hold himself in check when he was as it
were at the end of his senses, that he had only to think of the judgments of God; and finding himself thus confounded, he ought to
have regarded the feebleness of his spirit; and knowing himself as
a mortal man he ought to have said, "Alas! there is only ignorance
and silliness in me." Meanwhile he ought also to have regarded the
inestimable majesty of God and his incomprehensible counsel;
that ought to have rendered him humble. He did neither the one
nor the other. So, then, although he was not led astray from the

right road but he always aspired to the true end, yet we see that he is here rebuked by the mouth of God.

Now this passage ought to warn us of the reverence which God wishes us to bear toward his high mysteries, and to that which concerns his heavenly kingdom. If we dispute about our affairs—very well—we need not proceed with such extreme caution, for these are things which pass; but always and whenever it is a matter of speaking of God, of his works, of his truth, of that which is contained in his Word, may we come to it with fear and solicitude; may we not have our mouths open, to cough up everything which will come to us in fancy; may we not even have our minds too open to inquire into what does not pertain to us, and is not lawful for us; but let us hold back our minds, let us bridle our tongues. And why? For it is the counsel of God, that is to say, these things are too obscure for us and too high; we must not, then, presume to come to them, unless God will wish to instruct us in them through his pure goodness. And may it please God that these things might be well practiced, and that we did not have the combats which are throughout all the world. But why are they? It is seen that very few are affected by the majesty of God; when one discusses his Word, and the doctrine of our salvation, and of all the Holy Scripture, each one will go his own way; if anyone chats about it under the shadow of a lamp, each one will beg his leave of it. These are things that surpass all human understanding; however it is seen that we shall be more bold to discuss such high mysteries of God—which ought to carry us away in astonishment, and which we ought to adore with all solicitude—we shall be, I say, more bold to babble of them than if one discussed a transaction involving five cents, and I do not know what. And what is the cause of this, unless that men have not considered that God hides from us and obscures his counsel and that in the Scripture he has displayed to us his will to which we must be subject? We see on the one hand the papists who blaspheme against God, and who turn upside down, falsify, deprave, and corrupt all the Holy Scripture, so that it costs them nothing to mock God and all his Word. And why? For they have never tasted the meaning of the word *counsel*. Among us are seen drunkards, who also would subject God to their fancy. When they will be the most agile in the world, most experienced in the Holy Scripture, still they must come to this:

The counsel of God is above us. But they are stupid and entirely brutish; there is neither sense nor reason; wine rules them like pigs, and they will wish nevertheless to be theologians and to upset things in such a way that we believed them today, we would have to build and forge an entirely new Gospel. Yet let us remember what is here shown us: When we speak of God, we must not take license to chat and babble what seems good to us; but let us know that he has revealed his counsel in the Holy Scripture, that both great and small may submit to adore it. And this is what is said about *propositions without knowledge*. Now then, God here shows that always and whenever we speak of him and of his works, it is a doctrine of counsel, a high doctrine. And on the contrary, that which we shall be able to put forward, and which we shall be able to conceive in our minds, what is it? Propositions without knowledge. Let men put themselves in the balance, and they will be found to be lighter than vanity as it is said in the psalm [Ps. 62:9]. Furthermore, then, we must well note this doctrine, that there will be in us no knowledge, there will be no grace to know how to discuss the works of God, unless he will have instructed us. That is how we shall be wise, being governed by the Spirit of God and by his Word. However, when we shall not find in the Word of God what we wish to know, let us know that we must remain ignorant, and then, after that we must keep our mouths closed, for as soon as we may wish to say a word, there will be no knowledge; there will be only deception in us. This, then, is the accusation which God here makes against Job.

Upon that he says, *Answer all my questions; indeed, if thou hast understanding, mayest thou also give me to understand that which I wish to know of thee.* Here God persists in mocking the foolish presumption of men, when they think they have so much subtlety in them that they can dispute and plead against him. He says then, "Very well, it is true that you are very ingenious, it seems to you, when you speak, and that I release the rein from you; but I must have my turn, and I must speak a little to you, and you must reply to me, and you will surely see your default." What is the cause, then, that men are so rash as to advance themselves so foolishly against God? It is because they give themselves license to speak, and they occupy the place, and it seems to them that God has no reply. Now here is the remedy that God gives us to put down the

foolish temerity that is in us: it is that we think of that which he
will be able to ask of us. If God begins to interrogate us, what shall
we answer? If this came, into our memory, oh! it is certain that we
would be entirely held back; and although we had very frisky
minds, and though it seemed that we could move all the world, we
would be, as it were, put in our place by following in simplicity
that which our Lord shows us, provided, I say, that we could
think, "Alas! and if we come before God, has he not his mouth
open, and has he not the authority and mastery to interrogate us?
And what shall we answer him?" This, then, is where we must
come. It is what we have to remember from this passage, to have
right instruction from it. Then, may we not be too hasty to speak,
that is to say, that we have the vice by nature of meddling in more
than what pertains to us; let us learn to keep our mouths shut. For
why is it that we immediately open our mouths to vomit up what
is unknown to us? It is that we do not think that it is our office
rather to respond to God than to advance ourselves to speak. For is
it not to pervert the order of nature that mortal man who is nothing anticipates his Creator and makes him give audience, and that
God meanwhile keeps silence? How far does this go? It is, nevertheless, what we do, always and whenever we shall murmur
against God when we shall tear his Word in pieces, as we frame
propositions at will, saying, "This is how it seems to me." What is
the cause of this, unless we wish that God keep silence before us,
and that we be heard above him? Is this not a pure rage? So then,
to correct this arrogance that is in us, let us learn not to presume to
answer our God, knowing that when we shall come before him,
he will have the authority to examine us; indeed, according to his
will and not according to our appetite for it; and at our station; and
that when he will have closed our mouth, and he will have commenced to speak, we shall be more than confounded. Let us learn
to humble ourselves, so that we may be taught by him; and when
we shall have been taught, may he make us contemplate his
brightness in the midst of the shadows of the world. Meanwhile,
let us also learn to serve him and to adore him in everything and
by everything. For this is also how we shall have well profited in
the school of God; it will be when we shall have learned to magnify him, and to attribute to him such a glory that we may find
good, everything that proceeds from him. Meanwhile, may we

also be advised to be displeased with ourselves, in order to run to him to find there the good that is lacking in us. And beyond that may it please him to so govern us by his Holy Spirit that, being filled with his glory, we may have wherewith to glorify ourselves, not in us, but in him alone.

Now we shall bow in humble reverence before the face of our God.

WHEN CURSE BECOMES BLESSING

Galatians 3:13–18

¹³Christ hath redeemed us from the curse of the law, being made a curse for us: for it is written, Cursed is every one that hangeth on a tree: ¹⁴That the blessing of Abraham might come on the Gentiles through Jesus Christ; that we might receive the promise of the Spirit through faith. ¹⁵Brethren, I speak after the manner of men; Though it be but a man's covenant, yet if it be confirmed, no man disannulleth, or addeth thereto. ¹⁶Now to Abraham and his seed were the promises made. He saith not, And to seeds, as of many; but as of one, And to thy seed, which is Christ. ¹⁷And this I say, that the covenant, that was confirmed before of God in Christ, the law, which was four hundred and thirty years after, cannot disannul, that it should make the promise of none effect. ¹⁸For if the inheritance be of the law, it is no more of promise: but God gave it to Abraham by promise.

As we have seen, if our only hope of salvation rested upon the condition that we fulfill our duty, we would all be condemned, for we have all fallen short in many different ways and are, therefore, guilty in the eyes of God. Indeed, even the holiest among us can never claim to have reached a state of perfection, never again to fall, and free from all infirmity! We are, therefore, led to conclude that we will all be lost and condemned when God calls us to account. This is man's true condition, despite the high regard he may have for himself! Therefore, we need some means of escape from the curse we are under. Otherwise, what good will it do us to have our ears daily assailed by the Word of God? It will only push us closer toward eternal death. Thus, in order that the Word of God should profit and assist us to find salvation, we have to find a way of escape from the sentence of judgment pronounced upon the human race. Paul points out the way of escape to us here: *Christ hath redeemed us from the curse of the law, being made a curse for us.* He shows us that it was not in vain that our Lord Jesus

Christ hung on the tree, for he suffered to bear the curse of all those he would call to salvation.

As we have said, we are all under this curse, which means it was necessary for our Lord to take our burden of sin upon himself. In the law of Moses, it is written: *Cursed is everyone that hangeth on a tree* (Deut. 21:23). Our Lord commanded that the bodies of the dead should be removed from sight, because it was a disgrace to see a human body thus defiled and therefore he desired it to be taken away. Yet, when God pronounced this curse upon all who hung upon a tree, he knew only too well what was going to happen to his only Son. For the Lord Jesus Christ did not suffer such a death by accident, nor according to the whim of man. While it is true that he was crucified by unbelievers, it had been ordained by the will of God (Acts 2:23; 4:28). As it is written, God so loved the world that he did not even spare his only Son, but delivered him up to death for us. Indeed, if his death had been determined by Judas alone, who had him wickedly and forcibly led away, this could not be the foundation for our salvation at all! We must remember that God had appointed it thus, as Peter expounds in greater depth in Acts 2:23, where he states that the wicked hands that crucified our Lord Jesus did no more than God had previously determined in his will. Thus, when we read that our Lord Jesus Christ was crucified, we must remember that it was all for our salvation, because by this means God was seeking to reconcile us to himself. Therefore, when God said, *Cursed is everyone that hangeth on a tree,* he was not ignorant of what was going to occur, for all had been settled and predetermined.

These two facts must be carefully held together—that God has said that whoever hangs upon a tree is cursed, but that it was his will for his own Son to suffer thus. Why was this? He took our burden upon himself, as our substitute, and made himself, as it were, the chief of sinners on our behalf. Jesus Christ became a curse in order to deliver us from the curse of the law. It may seem harsh and strange at first sight that the Lord of Glory, he who has all sovereign authority, and before whom all the angels of heaven tremble and prostrate themselves, should be subject to a curse. But we must call to mind what Paul wrote in the first letter to the Corinthians, that is to say, that Gospel teaching is foolishness to the human race, who regard themselves as wise (1 Cor. 1:18, 23). Indeed, in this way, God humbles us for our folly. For there is enough wise and good instruction, if we care to heed it, in the heaven and earth around us, yet we are blind and shut our eyes to God's wisdom displayed in nature. This is why he has opened up a new way to draw us to himself—through something which we deem foolish! Thus, we must not judge what we read here, concerning the curse to which the Son of God was subject, by our own human reasoning. Instead, we should delight in such a mystery and give glory to God that he loved our souls so much that he redeemed them at such inestimable cost to himself. Far from detracting from the majesty of our Lord Jesus Christ, or obscuring the glory which the Holy Scriptures attribute to him, this teaching provides occasion to glorify him even more. Indeed, may we all do so, for here is our Lord Jesus Christ refusing to consider it robbery (as Paul expresses it) to reveal himself in his infinite glory (Phil. 2:6). He willingly emptied himself; he not only took upon himself a human nature and became a man, but he also submitted to a most shameful death in the sight of both God and man. How precious to him we must have been for him to allow himself to experience such extreme suffering for our redemption! If we could but taste something of what this implies, we would forever magnify the unspeakable grace which surpasses all human understanding. However, although we cannot comprehend it fully, and can only fathom the hundredth part of it, it delights us to know that we can grasp something of its meaning, however small!

Yet, how this exposes the malice and perversity that is in man! For when Paul declares that our Lord Jesus Christ became a curse for us, it washes over us. There are even those who are so depraved that they will see this as an occasion to behave scandalously, abandoning the Gospel altogether when they hear of the way in which Christ has redeemed us. Such people say, "What! Can it be that the Son of God, the fountain of all that is good, and the one who sanctifies us, has been cursed?" To their way of thinking, God has acted in an unreasonable and disorderly fashion! But (as I have been saying), God had to stoop to this "folly" because we did not respond to his wisdom, though the way was clearly evident; thus he exposes our own ignorance! We can only wonder at the mysteries of God, for their significance may be obscure to us and seem strange; for in the face of such wonders, our intellect fails and our powers of reasoning are confounded!

The fact that the Son of God became a curse for us demands a fuller examination of our sinful state. Indeed, we begin to realize that we are detestable in the eyes of God, that is, until our sins and iniquities have been cleansed in the blood of the Lord Jesus Christ. For even if all the angels of heaven were to be made answerable for us, the price they would pay would be insufficient. The only one able to make satisfaction for our sins is the Lord Jesus Christ. But, when he came to this world, it was not by a display of divine and heavenly power that he paid our debt of eternal death. How, then, did he come? In weakness; indeed, not only so, but he was accursed. If this had not been the case, our burdens would have crushed us and all would have perished in the abyss. When we understand that the Son of God, the Lamb without blemish, the mirror and fountain of all righteousness, that this One was cursed for us, should we not be horrified at the thought of all our sins and engulfed in despair until God rescues us in his grace and infinite mercy? Therefore, let us be aware that when God says he has redeemed us from the curse of the law, it is to bring us to a state of complete humility. We can never be humble unless we are first stripped of self-confidence and become ashamed at what lies within us. Then we are frightened and lost, knowing that the wrath of God hangs over us until the remedy is applied to us through our Lord Jesus Christ. Thus, our whole life is detestable in God's sight and there is no means of reconciliation with him apart from the Lord Jesus Christ, who takes away the curse which is upon us and bears it himself. Now, each time that we read this passage, we should arise and present ourselves before the judgment seat of God, aware that there is a pit waiting to swallow us up if we remain as we are. Let us feel our lost condition and be ashamed before God. Furthermore, let us magnify the grace bought for us by the Son of God, and be careful not to detract from his worth in any way whatsoever, even though he became a curse. This ought, rather, to stir us to render all the praise that he deserves, for he has proved our salvation to be so precious to him.

Moreover, let us properly appreciate such a pledge of our salva-

tion and display of the love God has for us, and let us not doubt
that we are acceptable in God's sight when we approach him.
For he has redeemed us at such a cost, as Peter shows in his First
Epistle—not with silver or corruptible things but with the Lord
Jesus Christ who became a ransom for us (1 Pet. 1:18). Therefore,
we must trust that whenever we come in his name to ask for
mercy, it will be bestowed upon us. But if we come believing that
we have a scrap of merit, what good is it? We know how much the
Father loves the Son, and how precious his death was in his sight.
For this reason, we can have full confidence that God will forgive
us and be favorable and kind to us if we cleave to what Paul shows
us here: namely, that our Lord Jesus Christ spared nothing for us,
even to the point of bearing our curse.

However, let us turn our attention to what Paul continues to
say: *That the blessing of Abraham might come on the Gentiles through
Jesus Christ; that we might receive the promise of the Spirit through
faith.* By mentioning Abraham, he reveals that the promise
belonged first to those who descended from him. For the gift of
salvation was for the Jews until God opened the doors to everyone
else and spread his Gospel abroad, that all might share in the
redemption purchased by the Lord Jesus Christ. For although this
promise originally belonged to the Jews and was peculiar to them,
it was made applicable to the whole world. How is this possible?
Because the promise originated in the Spirit and was not dependent upon observing the ceremonies. By referring us to the Spirit,
Paul blots out all the false doctrines taught by seducers who sought
to mix the law and the Gospel together. He is revealing that now
all these things are superfluous, that is to say, sacrifices, circumcision, and suchlike. This is not to argue that we cannot profit by
reading what is contained in the law: no, but the practice of it has
been abolished. This is why we can say that the promise is a spiritual one for us today, because we no longer need the types and
shadows of days gone by. Now we are simply called and invited to
commune with our God. Now we are able to cry to him with complete confidence, because, having been adopted by him, we lean
entirely upon the Lord Jesus Christ, who is the only foundation
the Gospel allows; we find all we need in him. This is, in effect,
what Paul intends us to learn from this passage.

To reinforce the message, he adds another point which proves that the Gospel is the perfect revelation of the way of salvation, and that we need no other teaching but the simple doctrine of justification through the free grace of our God. He tells us that the law was given four hundred and thirty years after the free promise of salvation. Now we know that a covenant made between men, if it is to be authentic, must stand, no matter what happens. It follows, therefore, that the law was not given to cancel what God had promised to Abraham and his descendants (and consequently to the rest of us). We may at first question this argument of Paul's, thinking that a second contract must annul the first. As soon as men have entered an agreement, they are liable to have second thoughts and change their minds, making the first contract null and void. The same applies to laws and statutes, for a first law can easily be broken and invalidated by a second. But Paul presupposes something which needs to be considered, which is that if a man has promised and solemnly obligated himself to do something, he cannot retrace his steps—the agreement must remain firm. Yet, if two parties were to agree together to change their previous resolutions by mutual consent, this is a different case. Indeed, such an example is almost irrelevant here if we bear in mind that men change their ideas so lightly at the slightest whim. Paul, however, presupposes that the "person" in question has made a covenant which will endure, and which will not be disputed or contravened afterward in any way whatsoever. If one of the parties were to break that original covenant, it would be counted terrible treachery, which all men alike would judge intolerable, since the agreement was so solemnly and formally recorded that it must be upheld and maintained without the slightest contradiction. Now, is it possible that there could be less constancy in God than in a man, who is mere vanity by comparison? Therefore, I conclude that the Gospel promise holds firm because the free promise was made before the arrival of the law.

All this could mystify us if it were not explained in greater detail. We have already dealt with the contrast Paul makes between the law and the Gospel in previous studies. When God promised salvation, it was upon condition that we served him, completely fulfilling our duty to him. This, however, is not possible; thus, we are excluded from all hope of salvation by the law. It is not that God is unfaithful on his part: it is we who do not meet his requirements! It is like a man who says, "I am willing to sell goods to you on condition that you have the money." Thus, whoever does not have a penny cannot buy any of the goods, for this is the condition that was set down in the first place. Similarly, God promises that we will inherit salvation if we serve him, but this does not benefit us because we cannot fulfill what he demands. Indeed, we are so full of iniquity, so polluted and infected in his sight, that he quite justly regards us with detestation. Therefore, we all stand condemned under the law. However, God freely and graciously accepts us through the Lord Jesus Christ, who offers us the remission of our sins. In fact, he greatly desires us to accept the grace that we are offered and to lean completely on the Lord Jesus Christ, not upon ourselves.

Now Paul asks, *Which is more ancient—the free promise of salvation or the law?* We are aware of the difference between them. Now, if the law were the more ancient, it must hold firm, because God never changes and is not subject to variation. However, if the free promise came first and was made before the law was decreed, then we must conclude that God has not changed his mind, nor withdrawn his original promise. He would not have desired the abolition of this covenant, for such would have been a withdrawal of his kindness and mercy. If, at one time, he bound himself out of his free bounty to give salvation to men on a basis other than merit, subsequently changing his mind as if he desired us to enrich him by our good works, it would be absurd! Paul tells us that the free promise was given before the law. It therefore follows that the law does not change anything about the promise; its nature and its force remain intact. While it is true that the Lord Jesus Christ had not yet been born on earth when the promise was made to our father Abraham, he had already been chosen as our Mediator, because through him we would be reconciled to God.

Now, in case we think that the law must have been unnecessary, or that there must have been a change of mind on the part of God, Paul next addresses this matter. We must not become confused; though it is not possible to explain everything in an hour, nor indeed in a day, it is enough for the moment for us to have this one fact clearly understood: that the promise to ordain us to be his children was made by God before the law. Indeed, it was not made with reference to our merit or personal worthiness; God did this out of his own goodness and mercy and expected nothing from us because he knew we were full of nothing but wretched sin. This promise had its foundation in the Lord Jesus Christ, whose office was already that of Mediator, granting access to God the Father. Having said this, we conclude that this promise will endure to the end of the world. The main reason this must be said is because the Jews tended to boast in their heritage. Paul seeks to tell them that their father Abraham did not have the law and yet was content, although he did, of course, offer sacrifices and the like. But, even though he was eventually circumcised, at the time he received the promise no written code as yet existed and not even any circumcision. For although Abraham was not circumcised when he received the promise, he was, nevertheless, justified apart from circumcision by faith alone. Therefore, Paul demonstrates to the Jews that it is very foolish indeed to count themselves in a category apart from the rest of humanity, and to base their hopes upon the types and shadows of the law, seeing that their father Abraham, the chief patriarch of the Church, was justified in the same way as people today. In other words, he was justified by the mercy of God alone, having recognized that he was a poor sinner, lost and condemned in Adam, and that the only blessing he could hope for was to be included in the promise made in the name of the Lord Jesus Christ. This is what we are to remember.

Next, we must carefully consider the promise addressed directly to Abraham, which revealed to him that all nations on earth would be blessed through his seed (Gen. 12:3). Now, there are two main points made here. One is that the blessing is not only promised to the earthly descendants of Abraham (as we have seen), but to the whole world in general. Thus, we who descend from Gentile stock (that is, from those who are unclean and who were originally banished from the heavenly kingdom) can also share in this promise. Although we do not belong to that holy lineage that God chose at the beginning, yet now salvation extends even to us. How is this? Because it was promised that all the nations on earth would be blessed. This being the case, dare we

speak as if God has withdrawn his liberal hand, and only seeks
the descendants of Abraham, when he had already declared that
he would reveal himself as the Savior and Father of mankind
when the time was right? Thus, the most important point here is
this: though this promise was made to Abraham, it did not apply
to his physical descendants alone, but to all men, even though this
was not apparent at first because the fullness of time had not come,
as we shall see in the following chapter.

The second point is that the blessing promised to Abraham was
for his seed. Paul says that he does not refer to "seeds" in the
plural, but to one seed; we must, therefore, conclude that he is
referring to Jesus Christ. We might perhaps have felt that Paul is
making much of something which has little relevance; after all,
the term "seed" refers simply to descendants, not specifically to
one man, nor to ten, nor to forty! Surely, it speaks of a whole race
of people, the seed of Abraham being the race that descends from
him. Indeed, this comprised such a great multitude that it was said
to be like twelve peoples (Gen. 17:6); for when we refer to a people,
we speak of about a hundred thousand men, and there were more
than this in the tribe of Judah alone! Thus, it would seem that
Paul had not properly considered what God intended by this word
"seed," when he says that it refers to just one man. But we must
weigh up Paul's conclusions in order to realize that they are correct and firmly established; indeed, we shall see that his argument
is utterly infallible.

Abraham did not have just one son; after Ishmael, he had Isaac.
And what happened to his oldest son? He was cast out of his
house, as we shall see when we come to consider the next chapter. Thus, here is Ishmael, who has all the privileges of being the
firstborn of Abraham's household, being cast out like a stranger,
just as it is written, *Cast out this bondwoman and her son: for
the son of this bondwoman shall not be heir with my son, even
with Isaac* (Gen. 21:10). After this, other children were born to
him (Gen. 25:1ff.). He gave each one their allotted portion
and then sent them away. Only Isaac remained with Abraham.
In time Isaac had two children, twins born of the same womb.
(Gen. 25:22–23). The firstborn, Esau, who ought to have had the
authority, was rejected and not counted as a descendant of Abra-

ham; thus, he had no share in the promised blessings. That left only Jacob, for his father ignorantly and mistakenly blessed him, then declared that he could not withdraw that blessing, nor alter what he had said since he had been the instrument of the Holy Spirit (Gen. 27:37). If we take the term "seed" to apply to those who descend from Abraham, then surely this will include such people as the Ishmaelites and Hagarenes (as they are called) and the like. If this were so, the Idumaeans, their servants, might also be counted as part of his household. But the inheritance was taken away from these people. Therefore, the phrase *the seed of Abraham* must be understood in a rather different way.

Let us think through the issue for a moment. Without faith, what would unite the Church? There would be no sure means of discerning the spiritual seed of Abraham. How would we distinguish them from the rest of mankind? The only way is by coming to the Head, in other words, to the Lord Jesus Christ. The unity of the body depends on its Head, on its Redeemer. This is why Paul says that the promise does not refer to seed in the plural, but to one man, to whom we must come if we are to discover his spiritual people. In other words, if we desire to locate the Church of God, we must start with the Lord Jesus Christ, because his own will be gathered round him. All who belong to his body and cleave to him by faith are the children of God, and are his servants. These are truly the seed of Abraham. This is discussed more fully in the Epistle to the Romans, chapter 9, verse 6, where it says, *They are not all Israel who are of Israel.* How is this? Well, there was really only one child of promise: Isaac. Therefore, we must come to the Lord Jesus Christ, for in him all the promises of God are "yes and amen," being absolutely firm and sure (2 Cor. 1:20). Without him, we would all be lost. This is why it is written in the first chapter of Colossians, verse 20, that the office of the Lord Jesus Christ was to gather together all that had been scattered in heaven and on earth; without him, we would all be confounded.

Now we can see much more clearly the line of Paul's argument. Before the law was imparted to the world, that is, before we were informed of our duty to obey all that is written therein, God had already revealed his good pleasure. Seeing the human race lost and condemned, he desired to bring his elect to himself in order to bestow mercy on them. This was not only for one race but for "all nations," as the Scripture asserts. And the source of that mercy is the Lord Jesus Christ. Indeed, when Abraham was alive, our Lord Jesus Christ had already been appointed Mediator, that through him the wrath of God against us might be appeased. Thus, when we come in his name asking for grace, it will be supplied to us and our expectations will not be disappointed. This had already been established and, happily, nothing has changed; we can be sure that God accepts us today if we are fully rooted and grounded in the Lord Jesus Christ. For the covenant made in his name shall not change—it is permanent and will always be in force. Thus, we may freely come before God and call upon him as our Father since he has adopted us as his children; not because there was anything worthy in us, but only because of his mercy are we united by faith to the Lord Jesus Christ.

However, in order to receive the grace of God and have assurance of salvation, we need to renounce all opinions we might have of our own worth. We must give heed to what is declared in this passage concerning faith, for it is only through faith that we are enabled to enjoy such blessing. Faith (as we have explained) means that we embrace the mercy of God. But we cannot have faith until we have been touched with a sense of our own poverty, for the Lord Jesus Christ, by becoming a curse for us, presents us with a picture of our cursed state. Faith, therefore, cannot exist without repentance, for it is not possible for us to come to God seeking salvation and asking him to pity our miserable condition, unless we have been convicted in our souls and led to deplore ourselves. Hypocrites who mock at God by wallowing, intoxicated, in their sins, must not expect Jesus Christ to receive them as his own; for such people may not even so much as approach him. Indeed, his invitation is intended for those who labor and are heavy laden (Matt. 11:28), who can bear no more and who stagger under the burden of their sins. This is how we must approach the Lord Jesus Christ, not with any merit of our own; for all the ceremonial law and all the sacrifices we could offer cannot contribute to our salvation. Rather, before God shows us mercy, we must come in a state of humility, fully aware of our miserable condition. We are first brought low in order that we might perceive the curse that we are under, before we can rejoice that we have been purchased at such inestimable cost. This has been our theme throughout our study.

Thus, it is by faith that we receive the promise of the Spirit and become united to the Lord Jesus Christ. We become part of the spiritual seed of Abraham. Although we do not physically descend from his family, it is enough that we are united together with him by faith. Indeed, we have been regenerated by incorruptible seed, as Peter says, in other words by the Word of God, the Scriptures (1 Pet. 1:23). Having been transformed, we understand that God accepts us as part of the body of his only Son. Though of Gentile descent, we can still be joined to his Church, since faith is all that is required. Here, all pride in human virtues and merits must cease, and men must recognize that they shall be utterly confounded unless they seek God in the way that he has appointed. Having said this, let us learn not to be blown here and there, like unstable men, who will not be content with what God has declared but must always add something to it of their devising. We need to guard against such an unholy mixture. I intend to expand upon this after lunch in the will of God. Let Jesus Christ be our sufficiency, since our salvation depends entirely upon him; we will lack nothing if we have an interest in him. This is the point to which Paul frequently returns in this book. Furthermore, he desires that we hold fast to God's truth, knowing that it does not allow for any additions. Were we to add to it, we would corrupt, pervert, and falsify the covenant upon which our salvation depends. Having embraced our Lord Jesus Christ, we are expected to remain fully in him, because this one man has sufficient grace for us all. In him, we can call upon God boldly, knowing that, although we descend from the accursed race of Adam, we, nevertheless, receive blessing in Jesus Christ. He now accepts us as his children and freely adopts us. He desires that this message should be heard throughout the world—there is now an open door and free access by which we may draw near to him.

Now let us fall before the majesty of our great God, acknowledging our sins and asking that he would make us increasingly conscious of them, that we may detest them. May we spend our lives seeking and striving to honor and serve him in strict obedience. And since we cannot free ourselves owing to our great infirmity, may he bear us up until he has freed us from all the defilements of the flesh, and clothed us in his righteousness. Indeed, he has begun this work in us now and affords us solid ground of assurance that what he has begun, he will complete. Thus, we all say, Almighty God and our heavenly Father, et cetera.

SERMON ON
THE DOCTRINE OF ELECTION

2 Timothy 1:9, 10

9Who hath saved us, and called us with an holy calling, not according to our works, but according to his own purpose and grace, which was given us in Christ Jesus before the world began; 10but is now made manifest by the appearing of our Savior Jesus Christ, who hath abolished death, and hath brought life and immortality to light through the gospel.

We have shown this morning, according to the text of Saint Paul, that if we will know the free mercy of our God in saving us, we must come to his everlasting counsel: whereby he chose us before the world began. For there we see, he had no regard to our persons, neither to our worthiness, nor to any deserts that we could possibly bring. Before we were born, we were enrolled in his register; he had already adopted us for his children. Therefore let us yield the whole to his mercy, knowing that we cannot boast of ourselves, unless we rob him of the honor which belongs to him.

Men have endeavored to invent cavils, to darken the grace of God. For they have said, although God chose men before the world began, yet it was according as he foresaw that one would be diverse from another. The Scripture shows plainly that God did not wait to see whether men were worthy or not when he chose them: but the Sophists thought they might darken the grace of God by saying, though he regarded not the deserts that were passed, he had an eye to those that were to come. For, say they, though Jacob and his brother Esau had done neither good nor evil, and God chose one and refused the other, yet notwithstanding he foresaw (as all things are present with him), that Esau would be a vicious man, and that Jacob would be as he afterward showed himself.

But these are foolish speculations: for they plainly make Saint Paul a liar who says, God rendered no reward to our works when he chose us, because he did it before the world began. But though the authority of Saint Paul were abolished, yet the matter is very plain and open, not only in the Holy Scripture, but in reason; insomuch that those who would make an escape after this sort show themselves to be men void of all skill. For if we search ourselves to the bottom, what good can we find? Are not all mankind cursed? What do we bring from our mother's womb, except sin?

Therefore we differ not one whit, one from another; but it pleases God to take those to himself whom he would. And for this cause, Saint Paul uses these words in another place, when he says men have not whereof to rejoice, for no man finds himself better than his fellows unless it is because God discerns him. So then, if we confess that God chose us before the world began, it necessarily follows that God prepared us to receive his grace; that he bestowed upon us that goodness, which was not in us before; that he not only chose us to be heirs of the kingdom of heaven, but he likewise justifies us and governs us by his Holy Spirit. The Christian ought to be so well resolved in this doctrine that he is beyond doubt.

There are some men at this day that would be glad if the truth of God were destroyed. Such men fight against the Holy Ghost like mad beasts and endeavor to abolish the Holy Scripture. There is more honesty in the papists than in these men: for the doctrine of the papists is a great deal better, more holy, and more agreeable to the sacred Scripture than the doctrine of those vile and wicked men who cast down God's holy election; these dogs that bark at it, and swine that root it up.

However, let us hold fast that which is here taught us: God having chosen us before the world had its course, we must attribute the cause of our salvation to his free goodness; we must confess that he did not take us to be his children, for any deserts of our own, for we had nothing to recommend ourselves into his favor. Therefore, we must put the cause and fountain of our salvation in him only, and ground ourselves upon it: otherwise, whatsoever and howsoever we build, it will come to nought.

We must here notice what Saint Paul joins together; to wit, the grace of Jesus Christ, with the everlasting counsel of God the Father: and then he brings us to our calling, that we may be assured of God's goodness and of his will, that would have remained hid from us unless we had a witness of it. Saint Paul says in the first place, that the grace which hangs upon the purpose of God and is comprehended in it is given in our Lord Jesus Christ. As if he said, seeing we deserve to be cast away and hated as God's mortal enemies, it was needful for us to be grafted, as it were, into Jesus Christ, that God might acknowledge and allow us for his children. Otherwise, God could not look upon us, only to hate us, because there is nothing but wretchedness in us; we are full of sin and stuffed up, as it were, with all kinds of iniquity.

God, who is justice itself, can have no agreement with us, while he considers our sinful nature. Therefore, when he would adopt us before the world began, it was requisite that Jesus Christ should stand between us and him, that we should be chosen in his person, for he is the well-beloved Son: when God joins us to him, he makes us such as pleases him. Let us learn to come directly to Jesus Christ, if we will not doubt God's election, for he is the true looking glass, wherein we must behold our adoption.

If Jesus Christ is taken from us, then is God a judge of sinners; so that we cannot hope for any goodness or favor at his hands, but look rather for vengeance, for without Jesus Christ, his majesty will always be terrible and fearful to us. If we hear mention made of his everlasting purpose, we cannot but be afraid, as though he were already armed to plunge us into misery. But when we know that all grace rests in Jesus Christ, then we may be assured that God loved us, although we were unworthy.

In the second place, we must notice that Saint Paul speaks not simply of God's election, for that would not put us beyond doubt, but we should rather remain in perplexity and anguish, but he adds, *the calling*, whereby God has opened his counsel, which before was unknown to us, and which we could not reach. How shall we know then that God has chosen us, that we may rejoice in him and boast of the goodness that he has bestowed upon us? They that speak against God's election, leave the Gospel alone; they leave all that God lays before us, to bring us to him; all the means that he has appointed for us and knows to be fit and proper for our use. We must not go on so, but according to Saint Paul's rule, we must join the calling with God's everlasting election.

It is said, we are called; and thus we have this second word, *calling*. Therefore God calls us: and how? Surely, when it pleases him to certify us of our election, which we could by no other means attain unto. For who can enter into God's counsel? as says the Prophet Isaiah, and also the Apostle Paul. But when it pleases God to communicate himself to us familiarly, then we receive that which surmounts the knowledge of all men: for we have a good and faithful witness, which is the Holy Ghost, that raises us above the world and brings us even into the wonderful secrets of God.

We must not speak rashly of God's election and say we are predestinate, but if we will be thoroughly assured of our salvation, we must not speak lightly of it, whether God has taken us to be his children or not. What then? Let us look at what is set forth in the Gospel. There God shows us that he is our Father, and that he will bring us to the inheritance of life, having marked us with the seal of the Holy Ghost in our hearts, which is an undoubted witness of our salvation, if we receive it by faith.

The Gospel is preached to a great number, which notwithstanding, are reprobate; yea, and God discovers and shows that he has cursed them, that they have no part or portion in his kingdom because they resist the Gospel and cast away the grace that is offered them. But when we receive the doctrine of God with obedience and faith, and rest ourselves upon his promises, and accept this offer that he makes us, to take us for his children, this, I say, is a certainty of our election. But we must here remark that when we have knowledge of our salvation, when God has called us and enlightened us in the faith of his Gospel, it is not to bring to nought the everlasting predestination that went before.

There are a great many in these days that will say, who are they whom God has chosen, but only the faithful? I grant it; but they make an evil consequence of it, and say faith is the cause, yea, and the first cause of our salvation. If they called it a middle cause, it would indeed be true, for the Scripture says, *By grace are ye saved through faith* (Eph. 2:8). But we must go up higher; for if they attribute faith to men's free will, they blaspheme wickedly against God and commit sacrilege. We must come to that which the Scripture shows; to wit, when God gives us faith, we must know that we are not capable of receiving the Gospel, only as he has framed us by the Holy Ghost.

It is not enough for us to hear the voice of man, unless God work within and speak to us in a secret manner by the Holy

Ghost; and from hence comes faith. But what is the cause of it? Why is faith given to one and not to another? Saint Luke shows us, saying *As many as were ordained to eternal life believed* (Acts 13:48). There were a great number of hearers, and yet but few of them received the promise of salvation. And what few were they? Those that were appointed to salvation. Again, Saint Paul speaks so largely upon this subject in his Epistle to the Ephesians that it cannot be but the enemies of God's predestination are stupid and ignorant, and that the devil has plucked out their eyes, and that they have become void of all reason, if they cannot see a thing so plain and evident.

Saint Paul says, God has called us and made us partakers of his treasures and infinite riches, which were given us through our Lord Jesus Christ, according as he had chosen us before the world began. When we say that we are called to salvation because God has given us faith, it is not because there is no higher cause; and whosoever cannot come to the everlasting election of God takes somewhat from him and lessens his honor. This is found in almost every part of the Holy Scripture.

That we may make a short conclusion of this matter, let us see in what manner we ought to keep ourselves. When we inquire about our salvation, we must not begin to say, "Are we chosen?" No, we can never climb so high; we shall be confounded a thousand times and have our eyes dazzled before we can come to God's counsel. What then shall we do? Let us hear what is said in the Gospel: when God has been so gracious as to make us receive the promise offered, know we not that it is as much as if he had opened his whole heart to us and had registered our election in our consciences!

We must be certified that God has taken us for his children, and that the kingdom of heaven is ours because we are called in Jesus Christ. How may we know this? How shall we stay ourselves upon the doctrine that God has set before us? We must magnify the grace of God and know that we can bring nothing to recommend ourselves to his favor; we must become nothing in our own eyes, that we may not claim any praise, but know that God has called us to the Gospel, having chosen us before the world began. This election of God is, as it were, a sealed letter, because it consists in itself and in its own nature; but we may read it, for God gave a witness of it when he called us to himself by the Gospel and by faith.

For even as the original or first copy takes nothing from the letter or writing that is read, even so must we be out of doubt of our salvation. When God certifies us by the Gospel that he takes us for his children, this testimony carries peace with it, being signed by the blood of our Lord Jesus Christ and sealed by the Holy Ghost. When we have this witness, have we not enough to content our minds? Therefore, God's election is so far from being against this that it confirms the witness which we have in the Gospel. We must not doubt but what God has registered our names before the world was made, among his chosen children, but the knowledge thereof he reserved to himself.

We must always come to our Lord Jesus Christ when we talk of our election, for without him (as we have already shown), we cannot come nigh to God. When we talk of his decree, well may we be astonished, as men worthy of death. But if Jesus Christ be our guide, we may with cheerfulness depend upon him, knowing that he has worthiness enough in him to make all his members beloved of God the Father, it being sufficient for us that we are grafted into his body and made one with him. Thus we must muse upon this doctrine, if we will profit by it aright, as it is set forth by Saint Paul when he says this grace of salvation was given us *before the world began.* We must go beyond the order of nature if we will know how we are saved, and by what cause, and from whence our salvation comes.

God would not leave us in doubt, neither would he hide his counsel, that we might not know how our salvation was secured; but has called us to him by his Gospel and has sealed the witness of his goodness and fatherly love in our hearts. So then, having such a certainty, let us glorify God, that he has called us of his free mercy. Let us rest ourselves upon our Lord Jesus Christ, knowing that he has not deceived us when he caused it to be preached that he gave himself for us and witnessed it by the Holy Ghost. For faith is an undoubted token that God takes us for his children, and thereby we are led to the everlasting election, according as he had chosen us before.

He says not that God has chosen us because we have heard the

Gospel, but on the other hand, he attributes the faith that is given us to the highest cause; to wit, because God has foreordained that he would save us, seeing we were lost and cast away in Adam. There are certain dolts, who, to blind the eyes of the simple and such as are like themselves, say the grace of salvation was given us because God ordained that his Son should redeem mankind, and therefore this is common to all.

But Saint Paul spoke after another sort; and men cannot by such childish arguments mar the doctrine of the Gospel, for it is said plainly that God has saved us. Does this refer to all without exception? No; he speaks only of the faithful. Again, does Saint Paul include all the world? Some were called by preaching, and yet they made themselves unworthy of the salvation which was offered them; therefore they were reprobate. God left others in their unbelief, who never heard the Gospel preached.

Therefore Saint Paul directed himself plainly and precisely to those whom God had chosen and reserved to himself. God's goodness will never be viewed in its true light, nor honored as it deserves unless we know that he would not have us remain in the general destruction of mankind wherein he has left those that were like unto us, from whom we do not differ; for we are no better than they, but so it pleased God. Therefore all mouths must be stopped; men must presume to take nothing upon themselves, except to praise God, confessing themselves debtors to him for all their salvation.

We shall now make some remarks upon the other words used by Saint Paul in this place. It is true that God's election could never be profitable to us, neither could it come to us, unless we knew it by means of the Gospel; for this cause it pleased God to reveal that which he had kept secret before all ages. But to declare his meaning more plainly, he adds that this grace is revealed to us now. And how? "By the appearing of our Savior Jesus Christ." When he says that this grace is revealed to us by the appearing of Jesus Christ, he shows that we should be too unthankful if we could not content and rest ourselves upon the grace of the Son of God. What can we look for more? If we could climb up beyond the clouds and search out the secrets of God, what would be the result of it? Would it not be to ascertain that we are his children and heirs?

Now we know these things, for they are clearly set forth in Jesus Christ. For it is said that all who believe in him shall enjoy the privilege of being God's children. Therefore we must not swerve from these things one jot, if we will be certified of our election. Saint Paul has already shown us that God never loved us, nor chose us, only in the person of his beloved Son. When Jesus Christ appeared he revealed life to us, otherwise we should never have been the partakers of it. He has made us acquainted with the everlasting counsel of God. But it is presumption for men to attempt to know more than God would have them know.

If we walk soberly and reverently in obedience to God, hearing and receiving what he says in the Holy Scripture, the way will be made plain before us. Saint Paul says, when the Son of God appeared in the world, he opened our eyes that we might know that he was gracious to us before the world was made. We were received as his children and accounted just, so that we need not doubt but that the kingdom of heaven is prepared for us. Not that we have it by our deserts, but because it belongs to Jesus Christ, who makes us partakers with himself.

When Saint Paul speaks of the appearing of Jesus Christ, he says, *He hath brought life and immortality to light through the gospel.* It is not only said that Jesus Christ is our Savior, but that he is sent to be a mediator, to reconcile us by the sacrifice of his death; he is sent to us as a lamb without blemish, to purge us and make satisfaction for all our trespasses; he is our pledge, to deliver us from the condemnation of death; he is our righteousness; he is our advocate, who makes intercession with God that he would hear our prayers.

We must allow all these qualities to belong to Jesus Christ if we will know aright how he appeared. We must look at the substance contained in the Gospel. We must know that Jesus Christ appeared as our Savior, and that he suffered for our salvation; and that we were reconciled to God the Father through his means; that we have been cleansed from all our blemishes and freed from everlasting death. If we know not that he is our advocate, that he hears us when we pray to God, to the end that our prayers may be answered, what will become of us; what confidence can we have to call upon God's name, who is the fountain of our salvation? But Saint Paul says, Jesus Christ has fulfilled all things that were requisite for the redemption of mankind.

If the Gospel were taken away, of what advantage would it be to us that the Son of God had suffered death and risen again the third day for our justification? All this would be unprofitable to us. So then, the Gospel puts us in possession of the benefits that Jesus Christ has purchased for us. And therefore, though he is absent from us in body and is not conversant with us here on earth, it is not that he has withdrawn himself, as though we could not find him; for the sun that shines does no more enlighten the world than Jesus Christ shows himself openly to those that have the eyes of faith to look upon him when the Gospel is preached. Therefore Saint Paul says, Jesus Christ has brought *life to light*, yea, everlasting life.

He says, the Son of God has abolished death. And how did he abolish it? If he had not offered an everlasting sacrifice to appease the wrath of God; if he had not entered even to the bottomless pit to draw us from thence; if he had not taken our curse upon himself; if he had not taken away the burden wherewith we were crushed down, where should we have been? Would death have been destroyed? Nay, sin would reign in us, and death likewise. And indeed, let everyone examine himself, and we shall find that we are slaves to Satan, who is the prince of death. So that we are shut not in this miserable slavery unless God destroy the devil, sin, and death. And this is done, but how? He has taken away our sins by the blood of our Lord Jesus Christ.

Therefore, though we are poor sinners, and in danger of God's judgment, yet sin cannot hurt us; the sting, which is venomous, is so blunted that it cannot wound us, because Jesus Christ has gained the victory over it. He suffered not the shedding of his blood in vain, but it was a washing wherewith we were washed through the Holy Ghost, as is shown by Saint Peter. And thus we see plainly that when Saint Paul speaks of the Gospel, wherein Jesus Christ appeared, and appears daily to us, he forgets not his death and passion, nor the things that pertain to the salvation of mankind.

We may be certified that in the person of our Lord Jesus Christ we have all that we can desire; we have full and perfect trust in the goodness of God and the love he bears us. But we see that our sins separate us from God and cause a warfare in our members, yet we have an atonement through our Lord Jesus Christ. And why so?

Because he has shed his blood to wash away our sins; he has offered a sacrifice whereby God has become reconciled to us; to be short, he has taken away the curse, that we may be blessed of God. Moreover, he has conquered death and triumphed over it, that he might deliver us from the tyranny thereof, which otherwise would entirely overwhelm us.

Thus we see that all things that belong to our salvation are accomplished in our Lord Jesus Christ. And that we may enter into full possession of all these benefits we most know that he appears to us daily by his Gospel. Although he dwells in his heavenly glory, if we open the eyes of our faith we shall behold him. We must learn not to separate that which the Holy Ghost has joined together. Let us observe what Saint Paul meant by a comparison to amplify the grace that God showed to the world after the coming of our Lord Jesus Christ; as if he said, the old Fathers had not this advantage, to have Jesus Christ appear to them as he appeared to us.

It is true they had the self-same faith, and the inheritance of heaven is theirs, as well as ours, God having revealed his grace to them as well as us; but not in like measure, for they saw Jesus Christ afar off, under the figures of the law, as Saint Paul says to the Corinthians. The veil of the temple was as yet stretched out, that the Jews could not come near the sanctuary, that is, the material sanctuary. But now, the veil of the temple being removed, we draw nigh to the majesty of our God; we come most familiarly to him, in whom dwells all perfection and glory. In short, we have the body, whereas they had but the shadow (Col. 2:17).

The ancient Fathers submitted themselves wholly to bear the affliction of Jesus Christ, as it is said in the eleventh chapter of the Hebrews; for it is not said Moses bore the shame of Abraham, but of Jesus Christ. Thus the ancient Fathers, though they lived under the law, offered themselves to God in sacrifices, to bear most patiently the afflictions of Christ. And now, Jesus Christ having risen from the dead, has brought *life to light*. If we are so delicate that we cannot bear the afflictions of the Gospel, are we not worthy to be blotted from the book of God and cast off? Therefore, we must be constant in the faith and ready to suffer for the name of Jesus Christ, whatsoever God will, because life is set before us, and we have a more familiar knowledge of it than the ancient Fathers had.

We know how the ancient Fathers were tormented by tyrants and enemies of the truth, and how they suffered constantly. The condition of the Church is not more grievous in these days than it was then. For now has Jesus Christ brought life and immortality to light through the Gospel. As often as the grace of God is preached to us, it is as much as if the kingdom of heaven were opened to us; as if God reached out his hand and certified us that life was nigh, and that he will make us partakers of his heavenly inheritance. But when we look to this life, which was purchased for us by our Lord Jesus Christ, we should not hesitate to forsake all that we have in this world, to come to the treasure above, which is in heaven.

Therefore, let us not be willingly blind, seeing Jesus Christ lays daily before us the life and immortality here spoken of. When Saint Paul speaks of life, and adds immortality, it is as much as if he said we already enter into the kingdom of heaven by faith. Though we are as strangers here below, the life and grace of which we are made partakers through our Lord Jesus Christ shall bring its fruit in convenient time; to wit, when he shall be sent of God the Father to show us the effect of things that are daily preached, which were fulfilled in his person when he was clad in humanity.

The Death of
John Calvin

(taken from *The Life of John Calvin,*

by Théodore de Bèze, first published in 1565)

The year 1564 was to him the commencement of perpetual felicity, and to us of the greatest and best-founded grief. On the 6th of February, the asthma impeding his utterance, he delivered his last sermon, and from that time, with the exception of his being sometimes carried to the meeting of the congregation, where he delivered a few sentences (the last occasion was on the last day of March), he entirely desisted from his office of preaching. His diseases, the effect of incredible exertions of body and mind, were various and complicated, as he himself states in a letter which he addressed to the physicians of Montpelier. Besides being naturally of a feeble and spare body, inclining to consumption, he slept almost waking, and spent a great part of the year in preaching, lecturing, and dictating. For at least ten years he never dined, taking no food at all till supper, so that it is wonderful he could have so long escaped consumption. Being subject to *hemicrania*, for which starvation was the only cure, he, in consequence, sometimes abstained from food for thirty-six hours in succession. Partly also from overstraining his voice, and partly from the immoderate use of aloes, a circumstance not attended to till it was too late, he became afflicted with ulcerated hemorrhoids, and occasionally, for about five years before his death, discharged considerable quantities of blood. When the quartan fever left him, his right limb was seized with gout; every now and then he had attacks of colic; and, last of all, he was afflicted with the stone, though he had never been aware of its existence till a few months before his death. The physicians used what remedies they could; and there was no man who attended more carefully to the prescriptions of his physicians, except that in regard to mental exertions, he was most careless of his health, not even his headaches preventing him from taking his turn in preaching. While oppressed with so many diseases, no man ever heard him utter a word unbecoming a man of firmness, far less unbecoming a Christian. Only raising his eyes toward heaven, he would say, "O Lord, how long"; for even when he was in health this was an expression which he often used in reference to the calamities of his brethren, which night and day affected him much more than his own sufferings. We advising and entreating him that while sick he should desist from all fatigue of dictating, or at least of writing—"What," he would say, "would you have the Lord to find me idle?"

On the 10th of March, having gone to him in a body, as we were wont to do, we found him dressed and sitting at his little table where he usually wrote or meditated. On seeing us, after he had remained silent for some time, with his forehead leaning on one hand as was his custom in studying, he at length, with a voice now and then interrupted, but with a bland and smiling countenance, says, "My dearest brethren, I feel much obliged to you for your great anxiety on my account, and hope that in fifteen days (it was the stated day for censure of manners) I will be present for the last time at your meeting; for I think that by that time the Lord will manifest what he has determined to do with me, and that the result will be that he is to take me to himself."

Accordingly, on the 24th of same month, he was present at the censures, as he had been wont to be; and these having been quietly performed, he said that he felt that the Lord had given him a short respite, and taking a French New Testament into his hands, he read some passages from the notes which are appended to it and asked the opinion of the brethren respecting them, because he had undertaken to get them corrected. The next day he felt worse, as if fatigued by the previous day's labor; but on the 27th, being conveyed to the door of the senate-house, he went up, leaning on two attendants, into the hall, and there having introduced a new rector of the school, uncovered his head and returned thanks for the kindness he had received, and especially for the attention which the Senate had shown him during this his last illness; "for I feel," says he, "that I am now in this place for the last time." Having thus spoken, with faltering voice, he took his leave, amid sobs and tears. On the second day of April, which was Easter day, although much exhausted, he was carried to the church in a chair, and was present during the whole service. He received the Lord's Supper from my hand, and sung the hymn along with the others, though with tremulous voice, yet with a look in which joy was not obscurely indicated on his dying countenance.

On the 25th of April, he made his will in the following terms:

THE TESTAMENT OF JOHN CALVIN

In the name of God, Amen. On the 25th day of April, in the year of our Lord 1564, I, Peter Chenalat, citizen and notary of Geneva, witness and declare that I was called upon by that admirable man, John Calvin, minister of the Word of God in this church at Geneva, and a citizen of the same State, who, being sick in body, but of sound mind, told me that it was his intention to execute his testament and explain the nature of his last will, and begged me to receive it and to write it down as he should rehearse and dictate it with his tongue. This I declare that I immediately did, writing down word for word as he was pleased to dictate and rehearse; and that I have in no respect added to or subtracted from his words, but have followed the form dictated by himself.

"In the name of the Lord, Amen. I, John Calvin, minister of the Word of God in this church of Geneva, being afflicted and oppressed with various diseases, which easily induce me to believe that the Lord God has determined shortly to call me away out of this world, have resolved make my testament and commit my last will to writing in the manner following: First of all, I give thanks to God, that taking mercy on me, whom he had created and placed in this world, he not only delivered me out of the deep darkness of idolatry in which I was plunged, that he might bring me into the light of his Gospel, and make me a partaker in the doctrine of salvation, of which I was most unworthy; and not only, with the same mercy and benignity, kindly and graciously bore with my faults and my sins, for which, however, I deserved to be rejected by him and exterminated, but also vouchsafed me such clemency and kindness that he has designed to use my assistance in preaching and promulgating the truth of his Gospel. And I testify and declare that it is my intention to spend what yet remains of my life in the same faith and religion which he has delivered to me by his Gospel, and that I have no other defense or refuge for salvation than his gratuitous adoption, on which alone my salvation depends. With my whole soul I embrace the mercy which he has exercised toward me through Jesus Christ, atoning for my sins with the merits of his death and passion, that in this way he might satisfy for all my crimes and faults, and blot them from his remembrance. I testify also and declare that I suppliantly beg of him that he may be pleased so to

wash and purify me in the blood which my Sovereign Redeemer has shed for the sins of the human race, that under his shadow I may be able to stand at the judgment seat. I likewise declare that, according to the measure of grace and goodness which the Lord hath employed toward me, I have endeavored, both in my sermons and also in my writings and commentaries, to preach his Word purely and chastely, and faithfully to interpret his sacred Scriptures. I also testify and declare that in all the contentions and disputations in which I have been engaged with the enemies of the Gospel, I have used no impostures, no wicked and sophistical devices, but have acted candidly and sincerely in defending the truth. But, woe is me! My ardor and zeal (if indeed worthy of the name) have been so careless and languid, that I confess I have failed innumerable times to execute my office properly, and had not he, of his boundless goodness, assisted me, all that zeal had been fleeting and vain. Nay, I even acknowledge that if the same goodness had not assisted me, those mental endowments which the Lord bestowed upon me would, at his judgment seat, prove me more and more guilty of sin and sloth. For all these reasons, I testify and declare that I trust to no other security for my salvation than this, and this only, namely, that as God is the Father of mercy, he will show himself such a Father to me, who acknowledge myself to be a miserable sinner. As to what remains, I wish that, after my departure out of this life, my body be committed to the earth (after the form and manner which is used in this church and city), till the day of a happy resurrection arrive. As to the slender patrimony which God has bestowed upon me, and of which I have determined to dispose in this will and testament, I appoint Anthony Calvin, my very dear brother, my heir, but in the way of honor only, giving to him for his own the silver cup which I received as a present from Varanius, and with which I desire he will be contented. Everything else belonging to my succession I give him in trust, begging he will at his death leave it to his children. To the Boys' School I bequeath out of my succession ten gold pieces; as many to poor strangers; and as many to Joanna, the daughter of Charles Constans and myself by affinity. To Samuel and John, the sons of my brother, I bequeath, to be paid by him at his death, each 400 gold pieces; and to Anna, and Susanna, and Dorothy, his daughters, each 300 gold pieces; to David, their brother, in reprehension of his juvenile levity and petulance, I leave only 25 gold pieces. This is the amount of the whole patrimony and goods which the Lord has bestowed on me, as far as I can estimate, setting a value both on my library and movables, and all my domestic utensils, and, generally, my whole means and effects; but should they produce a larger sum, I wish the surplus to be divided proportionally among all the sons and daughters of my brother, not excluding David, if, through the goodness of God, he shall have returned to good behavior. But should the whole exceed the above-mentioned sum, I believe it will be no great matter, especially after my debts are paid, the doing of which I have carefully committed to my said brother, having confidence in his faith and goodwill; for which reason I will and appoint him executor of this my testament, and along with him my distinguished friend, Lawrence Normand, giving power to them to make out an inventory of my effects, without being obliged to comply with the strict forms of law. I empower them also to sell my movables, that they may turn them into money, and execute my will above written, and explained and dictated by me, John Calvin, on this 25th day of April, in the year 1564."

After I, the foresaid notary, had written the above testament, the aforesaid John Calvin immediately confirmed it with his usual subscription and handwriting. On the following day, which was the 26th day of April of same year, the same distinguished man, Calvin, ordered me to be sent for, and along with me, Théodore de Bèze, Raymund Chauvet, Michael Cop, Lewis Enoch, Nicholas Colladon, and James Bordese, ministers and preachers of the Word of God in this church of Geneva, and likewise the distinguished, Henry Scrimger, professor of arts, all citizens of Geneva, and in presence of them all testified and declared that he had dictated to me this his testament in the form above written; and, at the same time, he ordered me to read it in their hearing, as having been called for that purpose. This I declare I did articulately, and with clear voice. And after it was so read, he testified and declared that it was his last will, which he desired to be ratified. In testimony and confirmation whereof, he requested them all to subscribe said testament with their own hands. This was immediately done by them, month and year above written, at Geneva, in the street commonly called Canon Street, and at the dwelling-place of said testator. In faith and testimony of which I have written the foresaid testament, and subscribed it with my own hand, and sealed it with the common seal of our supreme magistracy.

Peter Chenalat

. . . His utterance, indeed, was much impeded, but his eyes, which to the very last were clear and sparkling, he raised toward heaven with an expression of countenance on which the ardor of the suppliant was fully displayed. In his sufferings he often groaned like David, "I was silent, O Lord, because thou didst it"; and sometimes in the words from Isaiah, "I did mourn like a dove." I have also heard him say, "Thou, O Lord, bruisest me; but it is enough for me that it is thy hand." His door must have remained open night and day, had all who wished to show their duty to him been admitted. When he saw that owing to his impeded utterance, which we have mentioned, he could not address them, he asked each one rather to pray for him than take any trouble about visiting him. He also often hinted to me, though I was aware that my presence was never disagreeable to him, that I ought not to allow my regard for him to interfere in the least with my avocations, so sparing was he of the time which required to be devoted to the Church, and so exceedingly careful not to be at all burdensome to his friends.

In this way, resigned in himself, and consoling his friends, he lived till the 19th of May, on which day we ministers were wont to have our privy censures, and to dine together as a mark of our friendship; Pentecost and the dispensation of the Lord's Supper being to follow two days after. On that day, therefore, when he had allowed us to have a common supper prepared beside himself, and having, as it were, collected his strength, had been conveyed from his bed to the adjoining room, he says, "I come to you, brethren, for the last time. I am never again to sit at table." This was a very sad commencement to our supper. He, however, offered up a prayer and took a little food, conversing cheerfully as might be when we were at table. Before supper was completely finished, he called to be removed into the adjoining chamber, and addressing us with a smiling countenance, says, "The intervening wall, though it make me absent in body, will not prevent me from being present with you in spirit."

The event was as he had predicted. From that day he never rose from his bed. There was very little change on his countenance, but his whole body was so emaciated that nothing seemed left but the spirit. On the day of his departure, namely, the 27th of May, he seemed to be stronger and to speak with less difficulty. But it was nature's last effort, for in the evening, about eight o'clock, symptoms of approaching death suddenly appeared. I had just left him a little before, and on receiving intimation from the servants, immediately hastened to him with one of the brethren. We found he had already died, and so very calmly, without any convulsion of his feet or hands, that he did not even fetch a deeper sigh. He had remained perfectly sensible and was not entirely deprived of utterance to his very last breath. Indeed, he looked much more like one sleeping than dead. On that day, then, at the same time with the setting sun, this splendid luminary was withdrawn from us. ...

He lived 54 years, 10 months, 17 days, the half which he spent in the ministry. He was of moderate stature, of a pale and dark complexion, with eyes that sparkled to the moment of his death, and bespoke his great intellect. In dress he was neither overcareful nor mean, but such as became his singular modesty. In diet he was temperate, being equally averse to sordidness and luxury. He was most sparing in the quantities of his food, and for many years took only one meal a day, on account of the weakness of his stomach. He took little sleep, and had such an astonishing memory, that any person whom he had once seen he instantly recognized at the distance of years, and when, in the course of dictating, he happened to be interrupted for several hours, as often happened, as soon as he returned he commenced at once to dictate where he had left off. Whatever he required to know for the performance of his duty, though involved in a multiplicity of other affairs, he never forgot. On whatever subject he was consulted, his judgment was so clear and correct, that he often seemed almost to prophesy; nor do I recollect of any person having been led into error in consequence of following his advice. He despised mere eloquence, and was sparing in the use of words, but he was by no means a careless writer. No theologian of this period (I do not speak invidiously) wrote more purely, weightily, and judiciously, though he wrote more than any individual either in our recollection or that of our fathers. For, by the hard studies of his youth, and a certain acuteness of judgment, confirmed by practice in dictating, he was never at a loss for an appropriate and weighty expression, and wrote very much as he spoke. In the doctrine which he delivered at the first, he persisted steadily to the last, scarcely making any change.

Of few theologians within our recollection can the same thing be affirmed. With regard to his manners, although nature had formed him for gravity, yet, in the common intercourse of life, there was no man who was more pleasant. In bearing with infirmities he was remarkably prudent; never either putting weak brethren to the blush or terrifying them by unseasonable rebuke; yet never conniving at or flattering their faults. Of adulation, dissimulation, and dishonesty, especially where religion was concerned, he was as determined and severe an enemy as he was a lover of truth, simplicity, and candor. He was naturally of a keen temper, and this had been increased by the very laborious life which he had led. But the Spirit of the Lord had so taught him to command his anger that no word was heard to proceed from him unbecoming a good man. Still less did he ever allow his passion to proceed to extremes. Nor was he easily moved, unless when religion was at stake, though he had to do with men of a petulant and obstinate temper.

That one endowed with so great and so many virtues should have had numerous enemies, both at home and abroad, will astonish no one who has read even the account which profane history gives of men who were distinguished by their love of virtue. Little ground is there for wondering that one who was both a most powerful defender of sound doctrine, and an example of purity of life, should have been bitterly assailed. The thing to be wondered at rather is, that a single man, as if he had been a kind of Christian Hercules, should have been able to subdue so many monsters, and this by that mightiest of all clubs, the Word of God. Wherefore, as many adversaries as Satan stirred up against him (for his enemies were always those who had declared war against piety and honesty), so many trophies did the Lord bestow upon his servant. Some of those enemies give out that Calvin was a heretic, as if this were not the very name under which Christ was condemned, and that, too, by priests. He was expelled from Geneva! True; but he was also recalled. What, I ask, happened to the apostles, what to Athanasius, what to Chrysostom? Other charges are brought against him, but of what kind? He was ambitious, forsooth, nay, he even aspired to a new popedom—he who, above all things, preferred this mode of life, this republic, in fine, this Church, which I may with truth describe as the abode of poverty. But he was a hoarder of wealth!—he, whose whole effects, including the proceeds of his library which was well sold, scarcely amounted to three hundred gold pieces. Hence, when refuting this impudent calumny, he observed, not less shrewdly than truly, "If some will not be persuaded while I am alive, my death, at all events, will show that I have not been a moneymaking man." The Senate can testify that though his stipend was very small, yet he firmly refused any increase. Others make it a charge against him, that his brother, Anthony Calvin, divorced his first wife for adultery. What would they say if he had continued to keep the adulteress? But if such misconduct is to be turned against him, what will become of the family of Jacob, and David, and the Son of God himself, who declared that one of his twelve was a devil? As to indulgence in delicacies and luxury, let his labors bear witness. But then some are not ashamed to say and to write, that he reigned at Geneva, both in church and state, so as to supplant the ordinary tribunals. Others also give out that he procured a living man, and, in presence of the whole people, called him up as if he had been bringing a dead body to life—a lie just as vile as if they had said he was the pope at Rome. And yet Claudius Sponse, that rhapsodist of Sorbonne, has dared to repeat it in his most slanderous book. For what would these people be ashamed to say? No refutation is required by those who knew this great man when he was alive, nor by posterity, who will judge him by his works.

Having been a spectator of his conduct for sixteen years, I have given a faithful account both of his life and of his death, and I can now declare that in him all men may see a most beautiful example of the Christian character, an example which it is as easy to slander as it is difficult to imitate.

*The strength of that heretic (John Calvin)
consisted in this, that money never had the
slightest charm for him. If I had such
servants, my dominion would extend from
sea to sea.*

— POPE PIUS IV (1559–65)

SUGGESTIONS
FOR FURTHER READING

WORKS OF JOHN CALVIN

Institutes of the Christian Religion. Edited by John T. McNeill. Translated by Ford Lewis Battles. In 2 vols. The Library of Christian Classics, vol 20. Philadelphia: Westminster Press, 1960.

John Calvin: Selections from His Writings. Edited and with an introduction by John Dillenberger. New York: Anchor Press, 1971; reprinted by Scholars Press, 1975.

SECONDARY WORKS

Benedict, Philip. *Christ's Churches Purely Reformed: A Social History of Calvinism.* New Haven: Yale University Press, 2002.

de Bèze, Théodore. *The Life of John Calvin.* Translated by Henry Beveridge. Philadelphia: Westminster Press, 1909.

Cottret, Bernard. *Calvin: A Biography.* Translated by M. Wallace McDonald. Grand Rapids, Mich.: William B. Eerdmans, 2000; orig. pub. in French as *Calvin: Biographie,* 1995.

McGrath, Alister E. *A Life of John Calvin: A Study in the Shaping of Western Culture.* Oxford: Blackwell Publishers, 1990.

McKim, Donald K., ed. *The Cambridge Companion to John Calvin.* New York and Cambridge: Cambridge University Press, 2004.

McNeill, John T. *The History and Character of Calvinism.* New York: Oxford University Press, 1954; rev. pb. ed., 1967.

Raitt, Jill, ed. *Christian Spirituality: High Middle Ages and Reformation.* Vol. 17 of World Spirituality: An Encyclopedic History of the Religious Quest Series. New York: Crossroad, 1987. See especially chapter 14, "The Spirituality of John Calvin," by William J. Bouwsma.

Robinson, Marilynne. *The Death of Adam: Essays on Modern Thought.* Boston: Houghton Mifflin, 1998; Mariner pb. ed., 2000.

Walker, Williston. *John Calvin: The Organizer of Reformed Protestantism, 1509-1564.* New York: Schocken Books, 1969, repr. edn.; first published New York: G. P. Putnam, 1906.

Wallace, Ronald. *Calvin, Geneva and the Reformation: A Study of Calvin as Social Reformer, Churchman, Pastor and Theologian.* Edinburgh: Scottish Academic Press, 1988.

Wendel, François. *Calvin: The Origins and Development of His Religious Thought.* Grand Rapids, Mich.: Baker, 1997.

SELECTED WEB SITES

http://www.reformed.org/calvinism/index.html
    Web site of the Center for Reformed Theology and Apologetics.
http://ccel.org/index/author-C.html
    Christian Classics Ethereal Library. A comprehensive selection of the works of John Calvin translated into English. Includes:

Commentaries on the Catholic Epistles
Commentary on Acts—Volume 1
Commentary on Acts—Volume 2
Commentary on Corinthians—Volume 1
Commentary on Corinthians—Volume 2
Commentary on Daniel—Volume 1
Commentary on Daniel—Volume 2
Commentary on Ezekiel—Volume 1
Commentary on Ezekiel—Volume 2
Commentary on Galatians and Ephesians
Commentary on Genesis—Volume 1
Commentary on Genesis—Volume 2
Commentary on Habakkuk, Zephaniah, Haggai
Commentary on Hebrews
Commentary on Hosea
Commentary on Isaiah—Volume 1
Commentary on Isaiah—Volume 2
Commentary on Isaiah—Volume 3
Commentary on Isaiah—Volume 4
Commentary on Jeremiah and Lamentations—Volume 1
Commentary on Jeremiah and Lamentations—Volume 2
Commentary on Jeremiah and Lamentations—Volume 3
Commentary on Jeremiah and Lamentations—Volume 4
Commentary on Jeremiah and Lamentations—Volume 5
Commentary on Joel, Amos, Obadiah
Commentary on John—Volume 1
Commentary on John—Volume 2
Commentary on Jonah, Micah, Nahum
Commentary on Joshua

Commentary on Matthew, Mark, Luke—Volume 1
Commentary on Matthew, Mark, Luke—Volume 2
Commentary on Matthew, Mark, Luke—Volume 3
Commentary on Philippians, Colossians, and Thessalonians
Commentary on Psalms—Volume 1
Commentary on Psalms—Volume 2
Commentary on Psalms—Volume 3
Commentary on Psalms—Volume 4
Commentary on Psalms—Volume 5
Commentary on Romans
Commentary on Timothy, Titus, Philemon
Commentary on Zechariah, Malachi
Harmony of the Law—Volume 1
Harmony of the Law—Volume 2
Harmony of the Law—Volume 3
Harmony of the Law—Volume 4
Institutes of the Christian Religion

http://www.calvin.edu/library/database/card/
Calvinism Resources Database. Access to articles, essays, and lectures dealing with John Calvin and Calvinism from the 16th century to the present.

http://www.calvin.edu/library/
The Hekman Collection of Calvin College, Grand Rapids, Michigan. More than 1,800 books on John Calvin.

MARILYNNE ROBINSON is the author of two highly acclaimed novels: *Housekeeping* (1981), which was included in *The New York Times Books of the Century* and listed as one of the hundred greatest novels of all time by the UK *Guardian Observer;* and *Gilead* (winner of the National Book Critics Circle Award in 2004 and the Pulitzer Prize for Fiction in 2005); and two nonfiction books, *The Death of Adam* (1998) and *Mother Country* (1989). She teaches at the Iowa Writers' Workshop of the University of Iowa in Iowa City, Iowa. In 1997 she received a Mildred and Harold Strauss Living Award from the American Academy of Arts and Letters.

JOHN F. THORNTON is a literary agent, former publishing executive, and the coeditor, with Katharine Washburn, of *Dumbing Down* (1996) and *Tongues of Angels, Tongues of Men: A Book of Sermons* (1999). He lives in New York City.

SUSAN B. VARENNE is a New York City teacher with a strong avocational interest in and wide experience of spiritual literature. She holds an M.A. from the University of Chicago Divinity School and a Ph.D. from Columbia University.

Printed in the United States
by Baker & Taylor Publisher Services